Famine and
Human De

Famine and Human Development

THE DUTCH HUNGER WINTER OF 1944-1945

Zena Stein
> Professor of Public Health (Epidemiology), Columbia University, and Director of Psychiatric Research, New York State Department of Mental Hygiene

Mervyn Susser
> Professor of Epidemiology, Columbia University

Gerhart Saenger
> Senior Research Associate (Epidemiology), Columbia University, and Principal Research Scientist, New York State Department of Mental Hygiene

Francis Marolla
> Assistant Professor of Public Health (Epidemiology), Columbia University, and Senior Research Scientist, New York State Department of Mental Hygiene

New York   OXFORD UNIVERSITY PRESS
London 1975 Toronto

Copyright © 1975 by Oxford University Press, Inc.
Library of Congress Catalogue Card Number: 74-83991
Printed in the United States of America

Preface

The writing of a book is like a journey into unmapped country. Only at the end does one know what road was traveled, and the Preface, which the reader meets first, is written last. For it then becomes possible to say what has been done rather than what is to be attempted. Required to look back, the writer has earned a small indulgence. He may tarry over what the book signifies to him, and even explain intimacies of its growth and development.

This book had its scientific origins in the study of mental retardation. Although stigma once relegated mental retardation to the backwaters of medical care and medical research, the condition is of increasing social significance; the burden of care placed on society grows as prevalence rises. At the same time, scientists have come to appreciate the opportunities for generalization to be found in this field. For mental retardation is a consequence of disordered human development, and development begins with the conjunction of two sets of genes in the fertilized ovum, and continues through the whole process of intrauterine and extrauterine growth.

Our own studies in the field began in the late 1950's. They have focused on the environmental causes of the polarities in the social distribution of mild degrees of mental retardation. In the mid-1960's in New York City our interest in the field was rekindled. There social polarities seemed far to exceed those of the more prosaic English cities that were the sites of our previous studies. At this point we turned in a new diretion. Within the past decade, animal experiments have shown that nutritional deprivation during phases of rapid brain growth can cause a deficiency of brain cells. By extrapolation, the hypothesis that in humans prenatal nutrition affected the development of the brain and subsequent mental competence quickly gained currency. The hypothesis did not lend itself easily to rigorous test. There are two difficulties: the means are lacking to measure individual nutrient intake in free-living populations with the precision needed to make comparisons of different levels of nutrition, and there is a long and daunting interval between prenatal experience and ultimate mental competence.

Our first approach was through an intervention study. Specified levels of food supplements were assigned at random to pregnant women drawn from a population with a high frequency of low birthweight and reasonably presumed to be less well nourished than average. This experimental design, yet to be completed, circumvents the difficulty of measuring food intake by adding known amounts to the diet. The design does not dispose of the problem of the long wait before the ultimate effects of prenatal nutrition can be measured. The prospect of years of follow-up into adulthood, with the anticipated erosion of an initial study population and the dilution of the controlled intervention experience over the years, is likely to deter the most persevering researcher.

To cope with this problem, our thoughts turned to observational studies. These are the staple of epidemiology. The epidemiologist devotes himself to studies of humans, which alone can provide the ultimate test of hypotheses about human development and human health. The advantage of experimental studies in matters of control of extraneous factors and in the quality of their measures is offset by the advantage of observational studies in matters of representativeness of populations and of natural setting, and above all in feasibility in the pursuit of determinants. To pursue such studies, the epidemiologist seeks out "experiments of opportunity," situations in which a given hypothesis can be tested by judicious comparison.

As we pondered the problem of the ultimate consequences of prenatal nutrition, we recalled a situation that had long ago fascinated us. In 1952 we came upon Clement Smith's demonstration that the Dutch famine of 1944-45 had slowed fetal growth. At that time two of us (Z.S. and M.S.) worked in Johannesburg, as members of what might now be described as a medical collective, in a black ghetto afflicted by malnutrition and heavy infant mortality. Although our health center was always crowded with patients, the collective was able to send one of us (Z.S.) on combined study and maternity leave to Durban to explore problems of child development and nutrition under the guidance of Sidney Kark, then director of the only *training* health center in the country (perhaps in the world). Smith's paper on the Dutch famine was a lasting treasure found on that early sally into the continent of our ignorance.

As we reflected on our problem in 1967, we realized that the subjects of Smith's study, who had been exposed to the famine *in utero,* were then 22 years old. The possibility existed, therefore, of observing their health and mental state in adulthood. It remained to conceive of a viable study design and to execute it. This task, it turned out, was to absorb a good part of our energies in the succeeding seven years.

PREFACE

We had written a preliminary research proposal by the spring of 1968 and had made a first visit to the Netherlands in the summer of that year. One of us (G.S.), who has the good fortune to have married a Dutch woman, had recently spent a year in that country, and through friends and colleagues he arranged meetings with key people. Within the course of a short visit, we had explored the feasibility of a study design, obtained future access to our major data sources in the Central Bureau of Statistics and the Ministry of Defense, secured most of the membership of a steering committee, and tentatively arranged for the execution of field work. This extraordinary facility in planning must be credited to the people of the Netherlands. True, the problem under investigation was of intense interest to them, for the hunger winter had left a profound scar. Yet nowhere else can we imagine that government and military administrations would cooperate so readily and freely with foreign scientists not officially sponsored.

These preparations made, we obtained a research grant from the National Institutes of Health in the summer of 1969 and proceeded with our studies. Less than two years later we were able to report results of the rest of the central hypothesis.* These results appeared in print at the end of 1972 after much working and reworking of the data.**

The hiatus of more than three years between our first reports and the publication of this book has not passed in procrastination nor merely in the unfolding of the publication process. The result we had obtained was a negative one: no association could be demonstrated between prenatal nutrition and all the measures of mental competence available to us. An hypothesis of major biological and social significance was thereby discounted. It seemed to us that we had a responsibility to secure our result by eliminating the alternative explanations that were accessible to testing. This negative process of elimination is the basic scientific procedures that leads to positive inferences. As Francis Bacon wrote, "The induction which is to be available for the discovery and demonstration of sciences and arts, must analyze nature by proper rejections and exclusions; and then after a sufficient number of negatives, come to a conclusion on the affirmative instances."

To pursue proper rejections and exclusions, we traced the experience of the study cohorts through developmental stages. In anticipation of the need, as well as for intrinsic scientific interest, we had from the outset undertaken to collect data on births, maternities, deaths, and migration. We were thus in a position to examine those events accessible to us through the 20 years of the life cycle between conception and military induction. These additional analyses enriched our study. Drawn from unique bodies of data, they have yielded findings that we

---

*At the meeting of the Society for Epidemiological Research in Atlanta, April 1971; at the International Congress of Applied Psychology, Liege, July 1971; at the meeting of the International Epidemiological Association in Primošten, Yugoslavia, in August 1971; and at the Society for Social Medicine in Dublin in September 1971.

**Stein, Susser, Saenger, and Marolla, 1972a, 1972b.

believe are biologically and socially significant. Some of these findings, described in Chapters 10 and 11 of this book, appear in print elsewhere.*

Much labor was involved in collecting, coding, and processing data on maternities from as many as 12 hospitals, and on births and deaths from the more than 300 local population registers across the country.** No less intensive a labor was devoted to the task of analysis. The linking of disparate data from many sources, often not relating to individuals identifiable across these sources, presented problems both in techniques of analysis and in logical inference that we found difficult indeed. As we began, we knew of no helpful precedent for a retrospective cohort study that went beyond the linking of hypothetical cause to final outcome and melded in data relating to the intervening time gap. In the course of the work, we applied techniques and evolved procedures of inference new to us, we combined several techniques together, and we constantly tested one method against another. To follow the manipulations of so many relationships among so many bodies of data may ask much of the reader who thoroughly scours our work. It should also reward him with some assurance that our inferences are tested and our conclusions tried.

We are not under the illusion that fallacies and inferential jumps have been removed from this report. In testing alternatives to our negative result, we took deliberate risks. The material was unique and the hypotheses under test important; we acted on the belief that we should stretch the data as far as they would go. We have tried to specify the weaknesses in our arguments and procedures to the degree that we judged readers could bear. This has been done, if not always in the main text, then in the notes appended to each chapter. Almost all of the analyses from which we state conclusions can be replicated or expanded from the data provided in the book. At the end of each chapter we provide tables relevant to that chapter. In the Appendix at the end of the book, we provide the raw data on births, maternities, deaths, and adult health state for each month of the three-year study period. In several instances where a curious or dubious reader can derive results for himself from these data, we have commented on but not presented our own analyses. This was done when there was a choice between presenting raw or sophisticated data. We preferred to make available the raw data, in part to satisfy sceptics but mainly for the use of future researchers.

The book is organized into four broad sections: (1) the scientific questions, (2) the context and design of the study, (3) birth, development and death, and (4) the outcome in young adults. Nearly all chapters that report results end with summaries; some longer chapters have summaries interspersed at the end of each section. The book ends with a chapter that summarizes our conclusions.

*Stein, Z. A., and M. W. Susser, 1975.

**The data collection from the population registers was carried out by Dr. F. Sturmans and his team from the Institute of Social Medicine of Nijmegen University. With respect to the maternity hospitals, we finally used data from only five.

PREFACE

Through this work we sought to add to knowledge about health. Medical science thrives on individual woe. Its one defense is that the knowledge garnered may relieve future suffering. In our study we have exploited the collective woe of a whole people, and, impelled by scientific obligations, have done so to the extent of our capacities. To add to knowledge rather than obscure it such work must be disinterested. It need not be without passion, care, and concern for the people whose suffering was the object of our studies.

M.S.

New York
March 1974

Acknowledgments

A large scale study such as ours perforce drew on many official and unofficial sources. In a country to which we were strangers, only the extraordinary courtesy and generosity of many Dutch people and agencies made possible the execution of the study. Because the number of people who came to our aid over the several years of the study was large, we mention by name only those whose contributions were exceptional. We are not less grateful to the many people who helped us and whom we have not named.

Our advisory committee under the chairmanship of Professor J. Bastiaans, of Leiden University (who became our friend as well as our adviser) opened the doors that made the study possible. Professor J. Godefroy of Tilburg University was Co-chairman; members were Dr. P. Baan, Chief Medical Officer for Mental Health of the Ministry of Public Health and Environmental Hygiene; Dr. M.J.W. de Groot, Central Bureau of Statistics; Professor C. Den Hartog, School of Agriculture, Wageningen; Colonel J.M. Lagendijk, Chief, Armed Forces Selective Service, Ministry of Defense (now retired); Professors H.H. van Gelderen, J.J. Groen and N. Speijer, all of Leiden University; and Mr. A. Straatsma, Central Bureau of Statistics.

Official agencies provided access to data with truly remarkable openness, while preserving all the safeguards for confidentiality. The Ministry of Defense cooperated in every possible way; for this we owe a particular debt to Colonel J.M. Lagendijk. The Central Bureau of Statistics was equally helpful: Dr. M.J.W. de Groot, formerly Chief of the Department of Health Statistics, and his successor, Dr. H.M.H. van den Berg, and Mr. A. Straatsma gave personal attention to many queries. From Dr. P. Baan and his staff we obtained data from national registers of mental disorder in institutions, and from Dr. A. Vermeulen,

Institute for Social Research, Tilburg University, data from a special survey of institutions for mental retardation.

For data on maternities we are indebted to Dr. J.J. Huisjes of Groningen, Professor A. Sikkel of Leiden University, Professor G. J. Kloosterman of the University of Amsterdam, Dr. R.J.J. Omers of the St. Elizabeth Clinic in Heerlen, and Dr. R. van Wering of the Midwives Hospital in Rotterdam. Dr. W. op den Velde, Ms. B.L. Huidekoper and Ms. H.v.d. Made were also instrumental in gathering obstetric data. Dr. L. de Jong, Netherlands State Institute for War Documentation, led us to historical sources on the Netherlands under occupation. Professors J.J. Groen, J.H.P. Jonxis, and A.T.C. Schmidt, Doctors J.P. van Loon and Th.F.S.M. van Schaik, and a great many others recounted for us their experiences of the famine and helped in a variety of other ways.

For unstinting help and canny advice we give special thanks to Dr. F. Sorel, now Director of the Mental Health Commission of Limburg. Dr. F. Sturmans of the Institute of Social Medicine (Director: Prof. Dr. A. Ph. L.M. Mertens) of Nijmegen University and Ms. G. Verkade Gemeert carried out a major part of the field work in the Netherlands with great diligence and organizational talent.

Dr. D.J. Treiman coached us in the development of the path analysis. Doctors L. Belmont, D. Rush, and J. Wittes read the whole book; Doctors S. Richardson, E. Widdowson, F. Warburton, and Dr. M. Winick read the introductory chapters; Dr. J. Fleiss and Professor A.M. Thomson read the chapters on indices of reproduction. Their comments and discussion have clarified many points and we are grateful to them. Ms. J. Hand, Ms. P. Townsend, and Ms. P. Zybert spent many hours on the production of the diagrams, proofreading, and other tasks; Ms. M. Cohen, Ms. U. Collins, Ms. N. Foster, and Ms. S. Starkman patiently typed and retyped the manuscript.

This work was supported by grants from the National Institutes of Health (HD-04454, HD-06751, and HD-00322). The Association for the Aid of Crippled Children provided an initial grant for visiting the Netherlands. A John Simon Guggenheim Fellowship was awarded to one of us (M.S.) to enable the analysis and the writing of this book to be completed.

Contents

I The Scientific Questions

1 Introduction 3
   Environment, Development, and Mental Competence 3
2 Social Environment and Mental Competence 8
3 Nutrition, the Brain, and Behavior 15
   Phase of Development and Brain Growth 19
4 Prenatal Nutrition and Mental Competence 22
   Nutrition, Fetal Growth, and Mental Development 23
5 Postnatal Nutrition and Mental Competence 28
6 Specifying Nutrient Deficiencies 33

II The Context and Design of the Study

7 Famine in a Highly Developed Society 39
   The Dutch People During World War II 39
   The Netherlands During World War II 42
8 The Design of the Study 54
   Military Induction 59
   Validation Study 60
   Developmental Process 61
   Food Rations 64
   Notes 67

III Birth, Development, and Death

9 Fertility 71
  Fertility and Famine 73
  Fecundity and Famine 76
  Interpretations 83

10 Indices of the Reproductive Process 87
  Methods 88
  Birthweight 92
  Placental Weight 96
  Infant Length at Birth 99
  Head Size at Birth 101
  Duration of Gestation 104
  Maternal Weight 106
  Summary and Conclusions 108
  Notes on Method 109
  Tables 112

11 Interrelations Among Indices of the Reproductive Process 119
  Graphic Presentation 120
  Foundations for a Model of Interrelations 123
  Caloric Intake, Maternal Weight, and Birthweight 124
  Path Models 135
  Interpretations 138
  Summary 139
  Notes and Tables 141
  Three Variable Sequences 143

12 Deaths From Infancy to Adulthood 149
  Forms of Analysis 149
  Stillbirths 151
  First-Week Deaths 153
  Deaths at 7 to 29 Days 155
  Deaths at 30 to 89 Days 158
  Deaths at 90 to 364 Days 161
  Deaths at 1 to 18 Years 163
  Notes and Tables 165
  Periodic Death Rates 167

13 Death Rates Refined and Specified 179
  Assigned Causes of Death 179
  Specification by Social Class 183
  Conclusions About Mortality 184

IV Outcome in Young Adults

14 Mental Performance After Prenatal Exposure to Famine 197
  Measures of Mental Performance 198
  Raven Progressive Matrices 202

CONTENTS

Other Standardized Tests of Mental Performance 204
Mild Mental Retardation 205
Severe Mental Retardation 205
Selective Survival and Mortality 207

15 Prenatal Famine Effects on Body Size 215
Height 215
Weight 220

16 Prenatal Famine Effects on Health Status 223
ICD Categories 223
ABOHZIS 225
Fitness Categories 230

17 Conclusions 231

Appendix 237

References 259

Author Index 275

Subject Index 279

Figures

Chapter 3	3.1	Brain growth spurt in relation to conception and birth, compared in rat, pig, and man 16
Chapter 4	4.1	Some confounding variables that may affect birthweight and intellect 25
	4.2	Diagram of three among many possible causal paths between maternal undernutrition, low birthweight, and intellectual deficit 25
Chapter 7	7.1	Average quarterly distribution of food rations, 1941 through 1945 48
	7.2	Deaths in three famine cities, January to June 1944 and 1945 52
Chapter 8	8.1	Design of study. Cohorts by month of conception and month of birth 57
	8.2	The Netherlands 58
Chapter 9	9.1	Fertility and caloric ration 74
	9.2	Fertility and social class 80
Chapter 10	10.1	Birthweight 93
	10.2	Placental weight at birth 97
	10.3	Length at birth 100
	10.4	Head circumference at birth 103
	10.5	Length of gestation 105
	10.6	Postpartum maternal weight 107
Chapter 11	11.1	Birthweight, maternal weight, and placental weight 121

	11.2	Birthweight and placental weight 132
	11.3	Birthweight, placental weight, and caloric ration 133
	11.4	Birthweight, placental weight and length at birth 135
	11.5	Path diagram of reproductive process: Model A 136
	11.6	Path diagram of reproductive process: Model B 137
Chapter 12	12.1	Stillbirths 152
	12.2	First-week deaths 153
	12.3	Deaths at 7 to 29 days 155
	12.4	Deaths at 30 to 89 days 158
	12.5	Deaths at 90 to 364 days 161
	12.6	Deaths at 1 to 18 years 163
	12.7	Cohort and periodic death rate at 30 to 89 days 169
	12.8	Cohort and periodic death rate at 90 to 364 days 171
	12.9	Cohort death rates by area 173
	12.10	Periodic death rates by area 174
Chapter 13	13.1	Cohort deaths by cause and area 180
Chapter 14	14.1	Raven scores 203
	14.2	Raven scores by social class 203
	14.3	Mild mental retardation by social class 206
	14.4	Severe mental retardation 207
	14.5	Raven scores and mortality 210
	14.6	Mild mental retardation and mortality 211
	14.7	Severe mental retardation and mortality 213
Chapter 15	15.1	Height by area and class 217
	15.2	Height and mortality 218
	15.3	Quételet's index 221
Chapter 16	16.1	Medical diagnoses (ICD) at military induction examination 227
Chapter 17	17.1	Causal model of the effects of prenatal exposure to famine 237

Tables

Chapter 7	7.1	Ration of Calories in three month averages for the period June 1944 through August 1946 49
	7.2	Calorie intake by sources of supply in Amsterdam 49
	7.3	Adequacy of official Calorie and protein ration expressed as percentage of Oxford nutrition survey standard allowances, September 1944, February 1945, and April 1945 51
	7.4	Reported deaths during selected weeks in The Hague 53
Chapter 9	9.1	Hospital maternities by parity and age of mother 85
	9.2	Birth order and family size among Netherlands men examined for military service 86
Chapter 10	10.1.1	Calories and birthweight under the famine condition 113
	10.1.2	Calories and birthweight under the non-famine condition 114
	10.2	Differences by area in Calories and outcome variables 114
	10.3.1	Calories and placental weight under the famine condition 115
	10.3.2	Calories and placental weight under the non-famine condition 115
	10.4.1	Calories and length at birth under the famine condition 116
	10.4.2	Calories and length at birth under the non-famine condition 116
	10.5	Calories and head circumference: Rotterdam only 117

	10.6.1	Calories and length of gestation under the famine condition 117
	10.6.2	Calories and length of gestation under the non-famine condition 118
	10.7	Calories and maternal weight 118
	11.1	Calories, maternal weight, and birthweight 144
Chapter 11	11.2	Fetal age, birthweight, and placental weight 145
	11.3	Calories, birthweight, and placental weight 146
	11.4	Length, birthweight, and placental weight 147
	11.5	Descriptive statistics and correlations for path models 148
Chapter 12	12.1	Food rations and mortality 176
	12.2	Fetal growth and mortality 177
	12.3	Intrauterine growth and mortality 178
Chapter 13	13.1	Causes of infant death rates 188
	13.2	Cause of death at older ages 192
	13.3	Mortality by social class 193
Chapter 14	14.1	Food rations, social variables, mental performance, and height 214
Chapter 15	15.1	Correlations of height and body size with food rations 222
APPENDIX	1	Births and deaths 238
	2	Food rations by trimester of gestation 241
	3	Indices of the reproductive process 244
	4	19-year-old men at induction 248
	5	Raven Progressive Matrices 249
	6	Global psychometric score 252
	7	Mental retardation 253
	8	Medical diagnosis (ICD) at military induction 254
	9	Stature 256
	10	Quételet's index 258

The Scientific Questions

1 Introduction

Environment, Development, and Mental Competence

The course of development in children, including mental development, is intimately related to environment. Marked variations are found among social strata: at birth in the size and the motor behavior of infants; during childhood in various measures of physical health and in the level of intelligence test scores; and at pubescence in the frequency of mental retardation, in emotional states, and in behavior. Some of these variations are certainly a product of the environment.

A main focus of the studies of physical and mental health reported in this book is on the development of mental competence. To show that social environment has an effect on mental characteristics would be to show that these characteristics are malleable and subject to improvement. It would not be to distinguish from one another the particular contributions of the many elements of the social environment. Wealth and poverty, food habits and nutrition, education and the cultural milieu, and types of occupation almost always vary concomitantly with social class. These and many other components of the social environment, including the distribution of measured intelligence itself, have a potential influence on mental competence. The broad research task is to unravel the complex of components that contributes to the observed variation in mental competence among social strata.

A strong and plausible hypothesis is that prenatal nutrition affects brain development, which in turn affects mental competence. Some of the large disparities in mental performance among social groups may thus be caused by disparities in prenatal nutrition. This hypothesis has proved difficult to test in humans. One difficulty lies in the seemingly simple technical problem of measuring the nutrient intake of free-living human beings. An adequate test of the hypothesis requires an adequate measure of nutrient intake for sufficient numbers over a sufficient period of time. No means of making valid measurements of nutrient intake in such numbers are ordinarily available. The difficulty can be circumvented, although partially at best, by experimental intervention. We have reported elsewhere on an ongoing attempt to carry out such an experiment by giving measured food supplements to pregnant women living in poor circumstances and presumed to have poor diets (Rush, Stein, and Susser, 1973; Rush, Stein, Christakis, and Susser, 1974). There is no direct means of assuring that food supplements do not serve as substitutes for regular diet, so long as there is no good measure of regular diet. Resort must be made to such indirect means as monitoring maternal weight.

Experimental studies do not overcome a second difficulty in testing the hypothesis, which is the long interval that must elapse between exposure to prenatal nutrition and the end result in adult mental competence. Even when completed we do not expect to have followed the subjects of our experimental study beyond childhood. The circumstances of the Dutch famine have enabled us to cope with the difficulty both of measuring nutrient intake and of follow-up into adulthood.

In the winter of 1944-45, in an unhappy cadenza to the Nazi occupation of the Netherlands during World War II, this hard-pressed and once-prosperous small country was overwhelmed by famine. War-time disaster created a unique situation. The situation holds the promise that the contribution of nutritional deprivation to health and mental competence can be isolated from other social factors. The form and degree of the nutritional deprivation can be specified with a precision unknown for any other sizable human population before or since. The deprivation can be specified in terms of food constituents, of the people and places affected, of duration and severity, and of phase of individual development at the time of impact.

A combination of circumstances made the study a tragic experiment of opportunity. Famine has seldom struck where extensive, reliable, and valid data can be gathered that enable its effects to be separated from other intertwined effects of the social environment (compare Blix, Hofvander, and Vahlquist 1971). The famine was circumscribed in time and place with a remarkable clarity of definition. Equally important, the Netherlands has one of the best vital statistics and population registration systems in the world. Thus the progress of the famine can be documented by the local food ration before, during, and after the famine. The ready access we were given to excellent central and local sources of records, especially military records, has made it possible to identify those exposed to the famine during gestation and early infancy, and to compare their state of health in young adulthood with the health of those who escaped exposure.

INTRODUCTION

Adult mental competence is a main endpoint in this study, and one object of the research design is to relate measures of adult mental competence to prenatal experience. We have not been content, however, to relate the endpoint in adulthood only to an initial prenatal insult. Instead, we chose to examine as best we could, within the limits of the available data, the intervening experience of those affected. Mental competence is only an ultimate outcome of ontogeny, the process of development. The outcome of this process in the adult rests on the physical development of the brain from conception onward, and on the acquisition and elaboration of the functions of the nervous system as a whole. For several reasons, thorough appreciation of mental abilities in an adult population requires understanding of the development of that population.

An adult population at any point in time comprises an array of cohorts defined by their time of birth. At birth the members of cohorts are distributed across the strata of society according to the fertility of those strata year by year; as they age and develop, they flow into social positions governed by the dynamics of mobility within the social system. Each cohort in its life cycle is exposed to a unique complex of experience defined by its own particular piece of history. Thus the constitution of each cohort at conception follows from the pattern of fertility at the time, and interacts with the succeeding pattern of prenatal and postnatal experience. The surviving adult population carries the imprint of these favorable and unfavorable experiences during development; morbidity has marked them, and mortality has thinned their ranks, in a way specific to each cohort.

What the imprint of known morbidity and mortality during development might be on the adult state of any cohort has been open to speculation. One hypothesis that has been strongly advanced since the 1950's is that adverse prenatal experience causes a continuum of reproductive casualty, and that the severity and number of insults determine the severity of the injury inflicted (Pasamanick and Lilienfeld, 1955; Lilienfeld and Pasamanick, 1956; McMahon and Sowa, 1961; Knobloch and Pasamanick, 1962; Pasamanick and Knobloch, 1966). Postulated insults include nutritional deficiency, toxemia of pregnancy, and antepartum hemorrhage. The hierarchy of postulated injuries ranges from fetal death through such severe disorders of the brain as cerebral palsy and mental retardation, to the milder disorders of reading, speech, and behavior.

A contrary hypothesis was fashionable in the preceding decades. The developing fetus was thought to be well-protected from adverse environment by the mother. She interposed, between the fetus and the outside world, a buffer exemplified by the placental barrier to the passage of certain bacteria, and by the seemingly adequate nutrition of the fetus in the face of certain specific nutritional deficiencies in the mother.

Other hypotheses might be advanced. An insult to the fetus might tend toward an all-or-none effect: that is, a damaged fetus would be unlikely to survive. For instance, 100% risk of fetal loss attends conceptions with certain developmental anomalies. In such an event, the adult survivors of a cohort would fail to represent individuals exposed to the factor under investigation.

Alternatively, impairment of the fetus induced by prenatal insult might be overshadowed or compensated by postnatal experience. If the prenatal insult is overshadowed, longitudinal observation at suitable intervals might reveal that the prenatal contribution to the manifestation under study diminished with age until eventually it disappeared. If the prenatal insult is compensated, one might expect interaction between the prenatal insult and the quality of postnatal experience.

Finally, the same experience might influence some manifestations, and not others, even within an integrated system. The developing organism, its nervous system, and its function and behavior must be conceived as an integrated whole. Yet each of these elements may be differently affected by experience. For instance, with intrauterine growth retardation, the same experiences affect some fetal dimensions and organs more than others. Usually, weight is affected more than length, and among several organs measured, the brain seems most likely to be spared. Where the brain is not spared, it may be that the reserve of brain tissue is so large that its depletion might not affect function or behavior.

A salient elaboration of all these hypotheses takes into account the timing of an insult to the organism, as well as its nature, severity, and duration. The critical period hypothesis states that developing organ systems are most vulnerable at the period of maximum growth: interruption of development at such a critical period is likely to be irreversible or, at the least, subsequent development is likely to be retarded (Stockard, 1921).

Where so many possible pathways can be postulated by which a cohort may reach a given adult state, analysis of the adult state of the population alone is insufficient to reach firm conclusions about the biological significance of its association or lack of association with a given early experience. It is essential to try to fill in the process of development through the life cycle, including the losses from death and migration, and the scars of morbidity.

Regardless of which hypotheses are given support or negated, the results of such an exploration will be significant. A firm conclusion will have equivalent importance for biological theory whether prenatal nutritional deprivation of the mother causes impairment in the fetus that persists into adult life; whether the mother affords the fetus complete protection from nutritional deprivation; whether prenatal nutritional deprivation does not permit the fetus to survive and exhibit impairment in adult life; whether prenatal nutritional deprivation is overshadowed or compensated for by postnatal experience so that no impairment is apparent in adult life; or whether organic impairment is not translated into detectable dysfunction. To reach conclusions on these matters, the interaction of the developing populations with the environment, as they traverse the life arc, must be taken into account.

Within the limits of a historical approach, this study of the effects of the

INTRODUCTION 7

Dutch famine aims to provide such a longitudinal perspective of development in the context of environment. As with any study, however, its contribution must be weighed in the light of existing knowledge. In Chapters 2 to 6 we review the scientific questions that provoked us to undertake the study. We begin with the relation of social disadvantage to mental competence, and go on to consider the part that nutrition could play in that relationship.

2 Social Environment and Mental Competence

Poor mental performance,* social deprivation, and nutritional deprivation are commonly found in the same strata of society. Their conjunction is of central interest in the search for links between mental performance and environment. We shall consider the relations of mental performance with social deprivation in this chapter and with nutritional deprivation in succeeding chapters.

The link between mental competence and the social environment is most clearly seen in the varied levels of mental performance among social classes. According to educational, psychological, and clinical assessments, poor mental performance clusters among the lower social classes. Early in this century, Binet in Paris and Burt in London described the concentration of children backward in school in the slums (Binet, 1911; Burt, 1912, 1943). All subsequent studies have confirmed these findings on the social class gradient of backwardness (Peterson, 1925; Scottish Council for Research in Education, 1953; Stein and Susser, 1963; Birch, Richardson, Baird, Horobin, and Illsley, 1970; Rutter, Tizard, and Whitmore, 1970).

The use of more precise psychological measures has refined but not altered the findings. In local and national studies of many countries, the distribution of mean intelligence quotients shows a regular gradient that declines with social class. In the highest social classes, IQ scores below the threshold of normality **

---

*The measurement of mental performance, although a matter of controversy, is here taken for granted. The difficulties of measurement are discussed with the results of the study in Chapter 14.

**"Normality" is used interchangeably in three different senses. In the statistical sense implied here, "normality" delimits the modal area of variation on a measure; the limits of this mode are derived from the distribution of the measure in a population, particularly the are rare. A national survey in Scotland in 1947 classified 10-year-old children into high and low scorers. Of the professional classes, 52% of 143 children were high scorers and none were low scorers. Of the children of unskilled manual workers, 12% of 1141 were high scorers, and 26% were low scorers (Scottish Council for Research in Education, 1949). Data from the United States show similar social class distributions of intelligence test scores (Eells, Davis, Havighurst, Herrick, and Tyler, 1951).

Social environments defined in other ways also vary in measures of mental competence. Ethnic divisions demarcate cultural, racial, and national affiliations and also have distinctive patterns of performance on a range of mental tests. In New York City, Chinese, Jewish, Negro, and Puerto Rican children were given tests of four mental abilities: verbal ability, reasoning, number facility, and space conceptualization. The effects of social class remained pervasive; within each ethnic group, children from higher social classes performed better on these tests than did those from lower classes. However, each ethnic group had a pattern of strengths and weaknesses that crossed social class and that distinguished the performances of children in one ethnic group from those of the others (Lesser, Fifer, and Clarke, 1965).

Where the groups are defined by skin color, as between black and white children in the United States, distinctive patterns of mental performance have also been found (Jensen, 1969; Roberts, 1971; Schaie and Roberts, 1971). Where groups are defined by place of residence, city children generally score higher on tests of mental performance than rural children. Where groups are defined by occupation, several occupations that engender characteristic styles of life also engender characteristic levels of mental performance. Farm workers, coal miners, fishermen, tinkers, canal-boat workers, and migrant laborers all tend to score poorly (Gordon, 1923; Scottish Council for Research in Education, 1953; Fairweather and Illsley, 1960).

Although they cannot be regarded as independent, clinical indices reinforce the results of psychometric indices. Clinical judgments of abnormally poor mental competence are designated by the diagnosis of mental retardation in various grades of severity. The pioneering epidemiologic surveys of E. O. Lewis in England in the late 1920's established the first reliable distributions of mental retardation in communities (Lewis, 1929). He found a much higher rate of mental retardation in three rural areas he studied than in three urban areas, but in all areas there was a consistent and sharp social class gradient in the distribution of the condition.

---

average values and the standard deviation, which is the dispersal of individual values around the average. In a clinical sense, "normality" distinguishes all that is unimpaired, functioning, and well from all that is impaired, malfunctioning, and ill. In a social sense, "normality" is derived from the norms generated by social values: "ideal norms" of what should be, "norms of expectation" that modify ideals in the face of real social situations, and "norms of behavior" that describe what is done in actuality.

Mental retardation is a heterogeneous diagnostic rubric that encompasses many types of manifestation and many causes. In a classic paper of 1933, Lewis made a fundamental distinction between two types of mental retardation. He distinguished between a pathological type and a subcultural type. The pathological type could be ascribed to some form of organic impairment that affected the constituent elements of intelligence. This type comprised a minority of the mentally retarded population, and was evenly distributed across the social classes.

The subcultural type could not be ascribed to detectable organic impairment. Only a functional disability was detectable among these cases, and Lewis ascribed this type to an extreme but non-pathological deviation from the norm of intelligence in the population. The deviation was in magnitude or degree of intelligence, not in other constituent elements of normal mental function. "The subcultural type," Lewis noted, "is concentrated to a large extent in that section of the community with which is associated various chronic social evils—pauperism, slumdom and their concomitants."

Over the last two decades, studies have given substance to these generalizations and refined them. Children with diagnosed mild mental retardation, it was confirmed, differed from those with severe retardation in particular social attributes: their fathers were in lower class occupations, their families large, and their home circumstances poor (Roberts, 1952). Successive studies have shown that the condition, now described as "cultural-familial" retardation, is almost entirely to be found in the lowest social strata (Stein and Susser, 1963; Birch, Richardson, Baird, Horobin, and Illsley, 1970; Rutter, Tizard, and Whitmore, 1970).

In Salford, England, the rate of mild mental retardation without clinically detectable handicaps to learning in the publicly supported schools of low social standing was fifteen times as high as the rate in the schools of high social standing. Related studies showed that this syndrome was virtually specific to families of particular cultural types (Stein and Susser, 1960 a, b, c). It was found only among demotic families, that is, families of the lowest social classes whose members showed no signs of upward mobility in terms of occupation or education over at least three generations. No cases of the syndrome were discovered among aspirant families, which did show signs of upward mobility. A similar result was obtained in Aberdeen (Birch, Richardson, Baird, Horobin, and Illsley, 1970).*

---

*Anthropologists and sociologists imply by the term "subculture" a definable segment or subgroup of society that shares a distinctive culture within the general culture. E. O. Lewis implied by this term a stratification of culture, as of a class of individuals who could not share in the general culture of society because they functioned at a level below acceptable social norms and had been precipitated out from it. This subcultural type suffered from mild retardation and comprised the large majority of the mentally retarded

The discovery of social distributions of a condition lends plausibility to the existence of environmental determinants of the condition. Such explanations are hypothetical, and throughout this century alternative genetic explanations of the social distribution of mental performance have flourished (Pearson, 1909; Burt, 1912; Burt and Howard, 1956, 1957; Conway, 1958; Jensen, 1969). There is no need here to enter into controversy on heredity in intelligence. Some genetic models emphasize that the relative contribution of heritable and environmental factors in populations is by no means fixed and may change with changed environmental conditions (Falconer, 1967; Edwards, 1969). The heritable components of a characteristic that has a continuous distribution, like IQ, are assumed to be polygenic and to result from a number of genes at several loci on the chromosome. Each gene may be polymorphic, in that each gene may express itself in different forms and each form in different degrees. These multifarious forms of expression allow for a subtle and complex interaction of heredity with environment.

The interaction produces change and diversity in the characteristics and health disorders of populations. Even where the heritable component of a particular manifestation appears to be large, polygenic models are compatible with dramatic changes in the frequency of the manifestation produced by changing environment. Tuberculosis and rheumatic fever, diseases for which a genetic element has seemed established, have dwindled to a small fraction of the rates of a half-century ago. The heritable component of height has been estimated to be larger than that of IQ, yet this century has seen substantial increases in the height of the populations of industrial societies.

In the case of measured intelligence too, explanatory models must accommodate changes over time. In industrial societies, the adverse impact of most of the environmental elements suspected of depressing mental performance has diminished as economic production has increased. A prediction based on a hypothesis of environmental determinants of intelligence, therefore, must be that the mean level should have improved with time. Two national surveys in Scotland that used identical IQ tests on all 11-year-old schoolchildren in 1932 and in 1947 support the prediction (Scottish Council for Research in Education, 1949). Less complete data from England, from Sweden, and from Appalachia also support the results (Wheeler, 1942; Cattell, 1950; Emmett, 1950; Rayner, 1964; Stein and Susser, 1970). Although the changes are not large and the evidence needs to be tried and strengthened, the trends reveal at least a rising average ability to use native wit in responding to intelligence tests.

These are broad studies that depend on ecological relations among groups.

---

population. Although E. O. Lewis' use of the term "subcultural" did not conform to the current use of the term by social anthropologists, he yet seemed to have in mind an idea similar to the concept of the culture of poverty described thirty years later by Oscar Lewis (1966). On the assumption that these family types belong to distinct subcultures within the working class, the syndrome can be described in the current sociological sense after all.

More direct studies at the individual level demonstrate the effect of environment on mental performance. The chief of these are observational studies of identical twins and intervention studies aimed at producing IQ change.

Identical twins show a high degree of concordance for many characteristics including IQ (Erlenmeyer-Kimling and Jarvik, 1963). Shared genes and shared environment both contribute to this concordance. When identical twins are reared apart, the concordance between them could be sufficient to account for from 60 to 75% of the variance in their IQ depending on the tests used (Newman, Freeman and Holzinger, 1937; Shields, 1962; Burt, 1966).* The maximum leaves 25% of the variance in IQ unaccounted for. Cultural differences between the homes of rearing of separated monozygotic twins could explain from 7 to 18% of the variance in their IQ, and material differences from 3% to 4% (Burt, 1966). Measures of the difference in the environment of separated twins are necessarily cruder than the measure of genetic concordance, which is much more precisely known. The environmental measures therefore introduce substantially more error into correlations and thereby reduce their explanatory power. Despite this low level of explanatory power the measurable effect of environmental factors in the mental competence of separated twins could be great enough to account for the disparity in average IQ between social classes (about 5% of the variance in IQ in the Dutch population in our study is accounted for by social class, when social class is assigned by father's occupation).

That environmental factors do contribute to the disparities is made plausible by the known environmental differences between social classes. These are precisely the differences measured in Burt's study cited above, and found to be associated with differences in the mental performance of separated identical twins. Recently an effort has been made to estimate the size of the contributions of environment and heredity to mental performance among ethnic groups and social classes from a large-scale study of pairs of separated twins and controls in Philadelphia (Scarr-Salapatek, 1971a, b). The problems of design and statistical evaluation in such a study are considerable (Jinks and Fulker, 1970), and the question cannot be said to have been answered (Eaves and Jinks, 1972). Yet this is the sole twin study of which we are aware that avoids the ecological fallacy in estimating genetic and environmental components of mental performance among groups. All others that purport to do so make fallacious extrapolations from data on individuals or pairs to inferences about groups (Robinson, 1950; Blalock, 1964).

*Burt found a correlation among monozygotic twins reared apart of 0.77 on group intelligence tests, and 0.86 on individual tests, which would account respectively for 60% and 75% of the variance in scores. Since we could find no indication in this, the major study, that IQ tests and environmental assessments were made without foreknowledge of the twins examined on the part of the assessors, we incline to accept the group scores as less likely to be biased.

We conclude from twin studies that the genetic component in mental competence probably explains a large proportion of variation in IQ among *individuals*. No means have yet succeeded, however, in measuring the genetic component in mental competence among social or ethnic *groups*. All the evidence taken together suggests that genetic make-up is capable of explaining a much smaller proportion of the variation among groups than among individuals. Disparities in IQ and in mild mental retardation between the social classes of the same ethnic groups are large; demonstrable genetic differences between them are little evident. Thus some of the variation among groups can very likely be explained by environment, while some of the variation among individuals can certainly be so explained.

Strong evidence of environmental effects in individuals comes from studies that have produced IQ changes in children by planned intervention on an experimental model. In at least two instances the intervention achieved dramatic results. In one study, homeless infants retarded in development were removed from an Iowa orphanage to the personal care of mentally subnormal girls in another institution (Skodak and Skeels, 1945; Skeels, 1966). After making some recovery, the children were adopted into families. The adopted children, followed through 30 years, achieved intelligence test scores, and social and mental adjustment, that was far superior to a comparison group of orphanage children who had not been removed from the orphanage in early childhood. In its first stages, the study faced powerful criticism because of the imperfections of its design (McNemar, 1940) but the long-term follow-up reinforced the initial findings and has yielded a cogent result.

A recent study devised an experimental program of social and sensory stimulation (Heber, Garber, Harrington, Hoffman, and Falender, 1972). The program began with the identification of pregnant ghetto mothers with below normal scores on IQ tests and continued through the first five years of life of their children. From an early age the children spent their days in a setting where the adult-child ratio was as high as 1 to 2; the daily activity was concentrated on verbal skills and problem solving. Although the series is small, by the age of school entry the reported difference in mean IQ scores between the 20 stimulated children and the 18 controls was remarkable, and the stimulated children were much advanced in verbal and numerical ability.

Changes with age in measured intelligence, and in the frequency of mild mental retardation, cohere with the postulated effects of environment. A number of studies, although not all, show that in the poorest social circumstances the intelligence test scores of children at school entry are higher than at pubescence; and all studies show a greater disadvantage in educational attainment at pubescence than at school entry and an increase in the frequency of mild mental retardation (Stein and Susser, 1970). Among those with the cultural-familial syndrome of mild mental retardation at puberty, follow-up into young adulthood shows a rise in IQ (Clarke, Clarke, and Reiman, 1958; Stein and Susser,

1960a,b,c); at the same ages there is also a steep decline in the frequency of mild mental retardation.

These changes with age in the cultural-familial syndrome can be interpreted in terms of maturation: a delay in maturation, environmentally induced during childhood, manifests as mental and social retardation; maturation continuing into young adulthood manifests as recovery from retardation. The cultural-familial syndrome presumably occurs in individuals endowed with relatively low innate intelligence, or high sensitivity to the environment; adverse environment depresses their performance below the threshold for normality in the society at large. The syndrome, as mentioned above, is absent from the higher social classes and concentrated in the lowest. In those studies that provide data, social mobility between the generations through marriage, education, or occupation do not seem to us to have the force to separate the intellectual heritage of the social classes to the degree required to explain the observed distribution of the syndrome solely in genetic terms (Susser, 1968; Birch, Richardson, Baird, Horobin, and Illsley, 1970).

The recognition that a social component influences mental competence has great significance in the context of the demands of contemporary societies. An immediate necessity is to discover the origins of this social influence. Are mental abilities trained with the spread of education, or are they elicited by values, pursuits, and economic pressures arising from the wider socio-cultural environment? Is superior mental performance owed to organic development favored by high living standards, good health, and improved nutrition, or to organic constitution changed by interactions between such environmental factors and a multiplicity of polymorphic genes?

We cannot answer these imposing and difficult questions, and to raise them in this report of a study may seem imprudent. We anticipate that the study will clarify some issues germane to these questions, however, because it is built around a sharp and measurable change in the social environment. The social component in mental competence, we have noted, points to an area in which the sequence of links in the chain between cause and manifestation can be sought. The factor associated with social environment which the present study is most particularly designed to explore is nutrition. In the following chapters we shall review what is known about the effect of nutrition on mental competence.

3 Nutrition, the Brain, and Behavior

Speculation about the effect of nutrition on human intelligence is plentiful and knowledge scant. Little evidence bears directly on the relationship. In humans, the evidence is drawn from observational studies of the association of early nutritional deprivation either with retarded brain growth at autopsy, or with retarded mental development in later childhood. Other evidence is drawn, by analogy, from animal experiments. These experiments likewise test the effects of early nutritional deprivation either on brain growth or on subsequent mental development. Neither in human nor in animal studies has the sequence of nutritional deprivation, retarded brain growth, and subsequent mental development been conclusively demonstrated in longitudinal cohort studies.

Phase of Development and Brain Growth

Certain conditions are thought to moderate the effects of nutrition on brain development and mental competence. One condition of particular interest for this study is the phase of development of the organism at the time of nutritional deprivation. The period of most active growth of the brain is supposedly its critical period, the time of its greatest vulnerability to insult and irreversible damage. A number of experiments on rats, dogs, and pigs support the critical period postulate. In rats, nutritional deprivation at the time of maximum brain growth reduced the estimated number of brain cells, and the number remained deficient thereafter (Winick and Noble, 1966; Zamenhof, van Marthens, and Margolis, 1968). Myelin deposition also was found to be restricted and to remain deficient in studies of dogs and pigs (Dobbing, 1964; Platt and Stewart, 1969).

Some of the apparent inconsistencies in critical period experiments can be accounted for by the fact that species vary in the phase of life at which the maximum rate for brain growth takes place (Figure 3.1). In pigs, for instance, the peak growth rate is prenatal, while in rats it is postnatal. If birth is seen as an event that supervenes earlier or later in embryonic development among different species, we can explain the vulnerability of the brain of the rat (born at an early stage of development) to experimental nutritional deficiency in the immediate postnatal phase, and of the brain of the pig (born at a later stage of development) in the prenatal phase.

The critical period hypothesis is not supported in every respect by experiments on growth. In some experiments, no effects from starvation during the maximum growth period could be demonstrated; the investigators found a raised ratio of brain weight to body weight which they believed indicated a relative sparing of the brain (Platt and Stewart, 1971). McCance and Widdowson (1974),

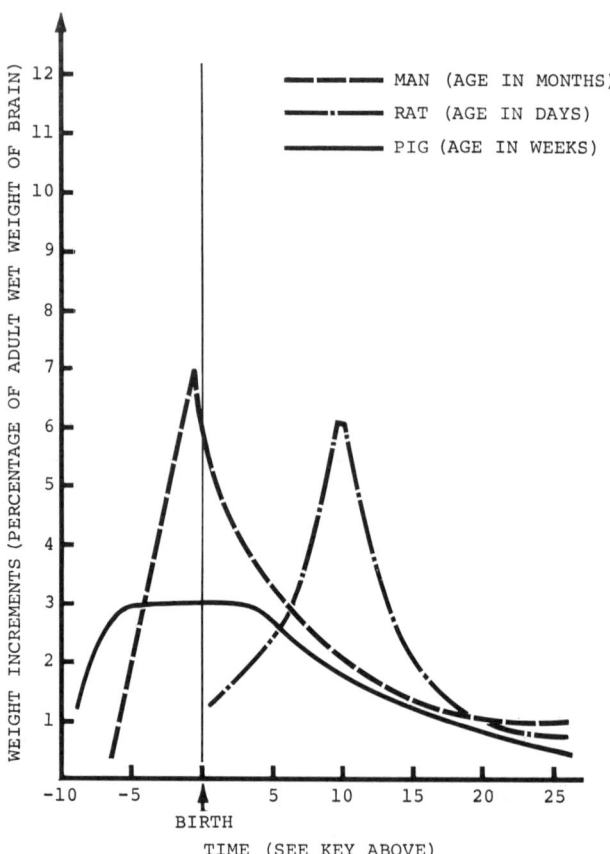

Figure 3.1. Brain growth spurt in relation to conception and birth, compared in rat, pig, and man. (Adapted from A. N. Davison and J. Dobbing. 1966. Myelinization as a vulnerable period in brain development, *Brit. Med. Bull.* 22:40-44)

comparing growth rates in different species undernourished at various ages, considered that a critical period of development might occur when, early in life, "the regulating centres of the hypothalamus are being co-ordinated with ... rate of growth." The runt in a pig litter, born underweight, is presumed to be deprived of nutrients in utero by deficient blood supply. If the runt is well-fed after birth, it grows at the normal rate for its size and age, stops growing at the same age as its littermates, becomes a normally formed adult, but remains small. Thus, although the pattern of growth is normal, the gap induced by the presumed prenatal disturbance of the hypothalamus is never made up. Prenatal determination of growth pattern lends support to the notion of a critical period.

On the other hand, McCance and Widdowson did not fully reconcile their findings with the notion of a single critical period determined by the brain growth spurt. They produced malformed organs in pigs by postnatal and not by prenatal protein malnutrition. In pigs of normal birthweight, severe malnutrition after birth greatly slowed growth. When rehabilitated, such pigs showed rapid "catch-up" growth, and also continued to grow beyond the age when littermates had ceased growing. The investigators believe that postnatal malnutrition temporarily disturbed a growth pattern that was set in prenatal life. With rehabilitation, the prenatally determined pattern re-asserted itself, and adjustments in the rate and duration of growth brought the pigs close to their predetermined size. Unlike the runts, however, certain organs were malformed, presumably because of deficient diet at the growing period combined with selective access of the organs to the limited nutrient supply.

A theory that postulates a critical period of brain growth must take account of at least two recognized growth processes. One process, hyperplasia, refers to an increase in cell number; the other process, hypertrophy, refers to an increase in cell size. Hyperplasia and hypertrophy of brain cells take place at separate phases of development. To complicate matters further, different anatomical structures and cell types of the brain have different time tables. Thus in the rat, the growth of cortex, hindbrain and cerebellum proceeds each according to its own schedule (Fish and Winick, 1969).

Hyperplasia and hypertrophy of two cell types, neurones (the functional cells of the nervous system) and glia (the connective tissue cells of the nervous system) contribute asynchronously to rapid brain growth. In humans hyperplasia of neurones seems mainly to occur in the second trimester of pregnancy (Dobbing, 1974). Maximum velocity of growth in total brain weight has been placed at a later phase, in the months just before and after birth. Both neurones and glia are thought to contribute to the rapid growth of these months. In this phase, the growth of neurones occurs in the form of hypertrophy, and the growth of glia in the form of hyperplasia. The hypertrophy of neurones continues with their arborization into dendrites and synapses. The recent work of Dobbing and Sands (1973) shows this phase of rapid growth extending through the second year of life.

Nutritional deprivation in humans can seldom be pinpointed in time with the precision required by a test of the critical period hypothesis. No evidence bears on the effects of malnutrition during the postulated period of hyperplasia of neurones in the second trimester of gestation. Although some evidence bears on the effects of malnutrition during the postulated period of combined hyperplasia and hypertrophy of brain cells in late prenatal and infant life, the chains of inference are long. Thus the timing implied by observations from autopsy studies of brains of a few infants who died of acute malnutrition is compatible with a critical period effect produced by nutritional insult. Those who died during the first year of life had a marked deficiency of cell number in the brain, while those who died in the second year of life had no such deficiency. The finding suggests that malnutrition during gestation or in early infancy but not later had affected brain cell proliferation (Winick, Brasel, and Rosso, 1972). The deficiency of cell number was more marked in infants of low birthweight. Prenatal malnutrition is a plausible cause of such low birthweight (Bergner and Susser, 1970), and hence of retarded brain growth in these infants.

Some recent interpretations have clouded the specificity of the critical period hypothesis. One question relates to the timing of the maximum growth of the two cell types, and another to the duration of the maximum growth period. Both questions influence predictions about the effects of injury or deprivation sustained at different phases of growth.

The problem of timing arises from the asynchrony between the early phase of hyperplasia of neurones during the second trimester, and the later phase of hypertrophy of neurones and hyperplasia of glia during the third trimester and after. The appeal of the critical period hypothesis rests in part on the fact that neurones, unlike connective tissue cells, are irreplaceable (although their extensions may regenerate) and that the integrity of neurones underlies the integrity of brain function. On this basis the second trimester of pregnancy, when neurones multiply, seems more likely to be a critical period in which irreversible damage might occur than does the third trimester, when glia multiply and neurones grow larger and extend their dendrites. Thus while the third trimester is the prenatal phase of maximum brain growth, and also the period when fetal growth in general is most sensitive to nutritional deprivation, it may not be the period when the most critical brain development occurs. Moreover, during neuronal hyperplasia in the second trimester, the nutritional needs of the fetus may be small enough for the mother to sustain under any conditions that support her own life. Hence the fetus may be protected from irreversible damage to neurones.

The problem of the duration of maximum brain growth may also detract from the importance of prenatal growth in the third trimester for subsequent development. The longer is the period of rapid growth, the longer is the duration of the period of deprivation required to produce irreversible brain impairment likely to be. Short periods of deprivation covering a small fraction of the critical period might be recoverable or undetectable. Since the most recent research indicates that rapid brain growth may persist into the second year of life or longer, prenatal deprivation alone might not be decisive if rapid brain growth continues for a long time postnatally. In fact, the later postnatal period might be critical for arborization of dendrites and establishing the connections between synapses (Dobbing, 1974).

Phase of Development and Mental Competence

The animal and human evidence discussed above relates only to the first two sequences of the following postulated causal chain: Critical period nutritional deficiency → retarded brain growth → permanent organic impairment of brain → persisting mental effects. The assumption that impaired brain growth caused by nutritional deficiency is expressed in functional deficits in mental competence is not secure. In animals, some relevant studies discussed above have demonstrated organic impairment, and others have demonstrated learning deficits or behavior change. The crucial experiments will need to demonstrate that all these effects occur together and in sequence under the same experimental conditions. In humans, some autopsy studies suggest, as indicated above, that prenatal malnutrition retards brain growth. Other studies suggest also that early childhood malnutrition retards later mental performance—although some do not. So far none provide the knowledge that brain impairment is an intervening factor in the causal chain leading from nutrition to mental competence. Autopsy at death cannot prove the irreversibility of the brain cell depletion reported in fatal cases of early malnutrition, nor indeed can we know from such studies whether the depletion is compatible with life and ever to be found in survivors.

We must therefore turn to evidence that indirectly supports the postulated causal sequence. The additional evidence bears on the effects of nutritional deprivation on mental competence and behavior. We shall first review relevant animal experiments and then, in succeeding chapters, the relevant human observational studies.

Animal experiment to test effects of nutritional deprivation is a rapidly growing field. The use of a variety of animals, a variety of methods of depriving them of nutrients, and a variety of outcome measures leads one to anticipate a variety of results. Most of the experiments have been on rats. Since the main part of the rat brain growth spurt occurs during suckling, postnatal deprivation provides a reasonable test of critical period hypotheses. The nutritional deprivation is achieved either through the mothers' diets or through the milk supplied to the young in lactation. According to design, mothers are fed scanty balanced diets or diets unbalanced in some constituents (usually protein) before, during, or after pregnancy. Milk supply is reduced by curtailing suckling time, or by manipulating litter size through random allocation of varying numbers of offspring to lactating mothers.

All these manipulations are likely to alter the environment of the suckling test animals as well as their nutrient supply. Undernourished mothers do not treat their offspring in the same manner as well-nourished mothers, and their nurturing seems to be less effective (Frankova, 1971; Bell, 1973). In addition, the social milieu of large and small litters is not the same; for instance, competition for the dam's nipples or for her attention is bound to be more intense in large than in small litters. Hence observed behavioral change in offspring can be the result of mother-child interaction altered by maternal nutrition or social milieu rather than of the deficient nutrition of the offspring.

The effects studied in nutritional experiments have been grouped by Dobbing and Smart (1973) under the five headings of (1) developmental delays, (2) activity level, (3) responses to food, (4) responses to stressors, and (5) learning ability. Recent studies have paid special attention to the modification of such effects by the social situation (Levitsky and Barnes, 1970; Zimmermann, Strobel, Steere, and Geist, 1973).

Nutritional experiments with rats have induced delay in the development of reflexes and of simple behavior patterns including exploratory behavior and motor ability (Cowley and Griesel, 1959; Frankova and Barnes, 1968; Simonson, Sherwin, Anilane, Yu, and Chow, 1969; Smart and Dobbing, 1971 a, b; Altman, Sudarshan, Das, McCormick, and Barnes, 1971). Such effects may be transient, and the consequences in adulthood of lags in early development cannot be predicted.

In adult rats poorly nourished in early life, exploratory activity in novel surroundings seems to be reduced on initial exposure, but it increases on continued exposure over long periods (Dobbing and Smart, 1973). This increased exploratory activity is found with food incentives (Barnes, Moore, Reid, and Pond, 1968) but other forms of activity sustained over long periods, like that on "running wheels," are also increased (Guthrie and Brown, 1968).

Responses made by hungry rats to stimuli and situations involving food (Barnes, Moore, Reid, and Pond, 1968; Smart and Dobbing, 1971 a, b), however, suggest that they have an altered level of motivation about food, which may flow from either psychological or metabolic changes. Exaggerated responses to food are also found in rhesus monkeys. When spurred by rewards of food, starved monkeys learn more quickly than controls (Zimmermann, Strobel, Steere, and Geist, 1973). These changes in "hunger drive" complicate the interpretation of learning experiments.

Overreaction to stressors other than food also occurs in animals exposed to early malnutrition. In undernourished rats, loud bangs reduced movement in an "open field" as compared with controls; electric shocks inhibited behavior or induced avoidance more than they did in controls (Levitsky and Barnes, 1970; Smart and Dobbing, 1971a, b). Malnourished nesting mothers emit a higher rate of ultrasonic sounds when their offspring are interfered with (Bell, 1973). The behavior of pigs and rhesus monkeys can be similarly interpreted as overreactive (Barnes, Moore, and Pond, 1970; Zimmermann, Strobel, Steere, and Geist, 1973). In rats, such exaggerated responses are coherent with the finding of raised corticosterone levels in the blood (Adlard and Smart, 1971).

Studies of the effects of nutrition on learning ability must clearly be approached with caution because of possible confounding by nutritional effects on other behavior. Strength of hunger drive and level of initial deprivation might confound experiments where the stimulus is food, and overreaction to stressors might confound experiments where the stimulus is aversive. Moreover, the measures of learning themselves are problematic as valid indicators of general mental competence. In addition to the difficulties of analogy with human tests, correlations between separate tests are likely to be poor (Searle, 1949).

On the whole, as Dobbing and Smart (1973) conclude in their review of the subject, the balance among the inconsistent results is in favor of an adverse effect of early malnutrition on learning (Barnes, Moore, Reid, and Pond, 1968; Howard and Granoff, 1968; Simonson and Chow, 1970). Many tests of associative learning, including reversals, reveal no disadvantage for the malnourished. More complex tests, however, are more suggestive of adverse effects of early malnutrition. Thus Turkewitz (1973), working with Stewart's strain of rats malnourished over several generations, found increasing disparities between experimental and control rats as the complexity of the learning task increased. Zimmermann, Strobel, Steere, and Geist (1973), who worked with rhesus monkeys, could detect no disparity in a wide range of learning tasks, but did detect a disparity in "discrimination reversal" learning, in which they suggested a deficit in attention might be involved. Disparities in learning ability related to early nutrition, however, have proved sensitive to social situation. Thus among rats, nutritional effects found in small litters have not emerged in larger litters, and in rhesus monkeys effects found in those reared in isolation have not emerged among those reared in groups (Levitsky, 1973; Zimmermann, Strobel, Steere, and Geist, 1973).

To summarize the results of animal studies, it is probable that nutritional deficiency of sufficient duration during critical growth periods retards brain growth, and that such growth retardation may be irrecoverable. It is less certain that this organic impairment is expressed in functional deficits, either in learning ability or in other behavior. Behavior other than learning has more often been influenced by nutritional deprivation than has learning itself; rhesus monkeys with induced kwashiorkor-like syndromes show striking changes in response to food, and unadaptive reactions to unpleasant and to novel stimuli. In experiments that expose pregnant or suckling mothers of other species to undernutrition, some of the changed behavior in the offspring could arise from changed behavior in the mothers, induced by the conditions of the experiment, rather than from a direct effect of nutrition on the developing organism. In addition, learning and behavioral manifestations following early nutritional deprivation have proved sensitive to social milieu. These results could point to interaction between the effects of nutritional deprivation and social situation, or to interaction between the socialization process of the young and social situation. They are not conclusive.

4 Prenatal Nutrition and Mental Competence

There are several indicators of mental competence. These indicators are likely to reflect the influence of nutrition to differing degrees. In any individual the manifestations of mental competence belong to at least three distinct levels of organization: organic integrity, psychological function, and social roles. Organic integrity of the brain can be inferred from the degree of structural impairment observed, from biochemical and histopathological measures of brain growth, or from clinical neurological state. The functional component of mental competence can be inferred in humans from psychometric indices and educational tests, and in animals from tests of associative learning. The social component of mental competence can be inferred from role performance, which is sustained behavior in social situations; in human groups the diagnosis of mental retardation is an index of failure to sustain normal social roles.

Manifestations at each organizational level are of course closely related. The integrity of the brain is necessary to psychological function, and capacity for psychological function is necessary to the performance of social roles. The assumption cannot be made, however, that integrity or impairment at one level implies an equivalent state at another level. Normal psychological function may be sustained in the presence of brain impairment, and conversely dysfunction may occur without impairment. Normal role performance may be sustained in the presence of psychological dysfunction, and conversely failure may occur in the absence of dysfunction. The fact that effects at one level of organization cannot be taken as a direct index of effects at another needs to be kept in mind in the following discussion, which ranges across animal and human studies; the effects obtained in any one study generally refer to only one level.

If early malnutrition or undernutrition detracts from later mental competence, the effect is likely to be seen at both the functional and social levels, but not in the form of detectable lesions at the organic level. In the populations of industrial societies, low mean IQ, the cultural-familial syndrome, and food deficiencies not due to mental or bodily disorders occur almost exclusively among the poor. By contrast, forms of mental retardation that are severe or evince neurological impairment show at most a slight predilection for the poor. In societies like the United States, Great Britain, and Sweden, therefore, it would be safe to predict that any effects induced by malnutrition would be seen in the cultural-familial syndrome and would be reflected in indicators of psychological function and social role rather than of neurological impairment.

In the peasant and tribal societies of India, Africa and South America, little is known of the distribution of measured intelligence and of different forms of mental retardation. It is known that in these harsher environments there is widespread malnutrition in infancy, and the likelihood of malnutrition-induced cases of mental retardation must be greater than in industrial societies. Conceivably such retardation could be of the severe form with neurological impairment, but there is nothing to suggest it. In peasant societies making the transition to urbanism or industrialism various studies suggest rather that the distributions of poverty, nutritional deprivation and depressed IQ are similar to those in industrial societies (Stoch and Smythe, 1963; Monckeberg, 1968).

It remains now to consider the causal link between nutritional deficiency and mental development in humans. The discussion can conveniently be divided into prenatal and postnatal deficiencies. Although this division cuts across the postulated period of rapid brain growth in humans, the profound physiological and social transition at birth demarcates an appropriate framework for the discussion of environmental factors.

Nutrition, Fetal Growth, and Mental Development

The human brain develops considerably during gestation. We have noted the marked growth in brain mass in the late fetal period, and the inference from autopsy studies that this growth can be retarded by prenatal nutritional deficiency. Evidence that poor nutrition during pregnancy has a sequel in depressed mental performance in the offspring, however, is confusing. In human beings it is rarely possible to separate entirely experiences of malnutrition in the prenatal period from those of the postnatal period. One reason is that children of mothers malnourished while pregnant seldom have optimum diets in postnatal life.* They cannot be fostered at random, in favorable and unfavorable nutritional conditions, as experimental animals have been.

The view that prenatal nutrition affects development of the central nervous

---

*Infants on the breast alone do not sustain good growth beyond six months of age.

system is consistent with some studies of congenital anomalies. In West Germany, the frequency of malformations of the central nervous system rose during the food shortages after World War II and fell when conditions improved (Eichmann and Gesenius, 1952). In the United States, too, a rise and fall in the incidence of anencephaly has run parallel to the level of living conditions (Naggan, 1969) and among salient changes in living conditions, prenatal nutrition is one that must be considered. But it is one among many factors that changed concomitantly with the incidence of the anomaly.

Twin studies point indirectly to effects of intrauterine nutrition on intelligence. In most studies of twins of unequal birthweight, the heavier twin has most often, if not always, been found superior on intelligence test scores (Churchill, 1965; Kaelber and Pugh, 1969). Since duration of gestation (as well as genetic predisposition, in the case of uniovular twins) is held constant in twin comparisons, the differences in birthweight between pairs have been attributed to differences in intrauterine nutrition mediated by the arrangement of the blood supply to the twin fetuses. Other types of studies also suggest that the internal disposition of nutrients by the vascular supply through the placenta is a cause of retarded fetal growth (Gibson and McKeown, 1950, 1951; McKeown and Gibson, 1951; McLaren and Michie, 1963; Payne and Wheeler, 1967a, b). Low birthweight in twins may thus be part of a sequence in which deficiency in nutrients reaching the fetus leads to depressed intelligence in childhood.

There is reason to believe also that fetal nutrition and growth are more directly affected by maternal nutrition (Bergner and Susser, 1970). C. A. Smith's study of the Dutch famine (which was a starting point for our own study), as well as Antonov's report on the Leningrad famine, and McCance and Widdowson's studies of Wuppertal during World War II, provided strong evidence that maternal starvation reduced average birthweight (Smith, 1947; Antonov, 1947; McCance, Widdowson, Dean, and Thrussell, 1951). Support for the idea that maternal nutrition affects birthweight in more mundane circumstances comes from the strong association of birthweight both with maternal weight before pregnancy and with maternal weight gain during pregnancy. Maternal weight and weight gain account for virtually the whole of the well-known associations of birthweight with maternal age, height, and parity (Weiss and Jackson, 1969; Rush, Davis, and Susser, 1972). Nutrition may be a factor too in the social class disparity in birthweight in Britain, the United States, and elsewhere. Few pregnant mothers living in poverty in these countries may actually go hungry, but many take a diet deficient in certain nutrients, especially protein.

Many studies suggest that low birthweight is an antecedent of reduced mental competence (Benton, 1940; Drillien, 1970); the lower the birthweight, the greater the mental handicap tends to be (Wiener, 1970). All these observations taken together show that poor nutrition, low birthweight, and mental retardation are associated under certain conditions. The simplest assumption is that poor maternal nutrition causes low birthweight, and that low birthweight leads

PRENATAL NUTRITION AND MENTAL HEALTH

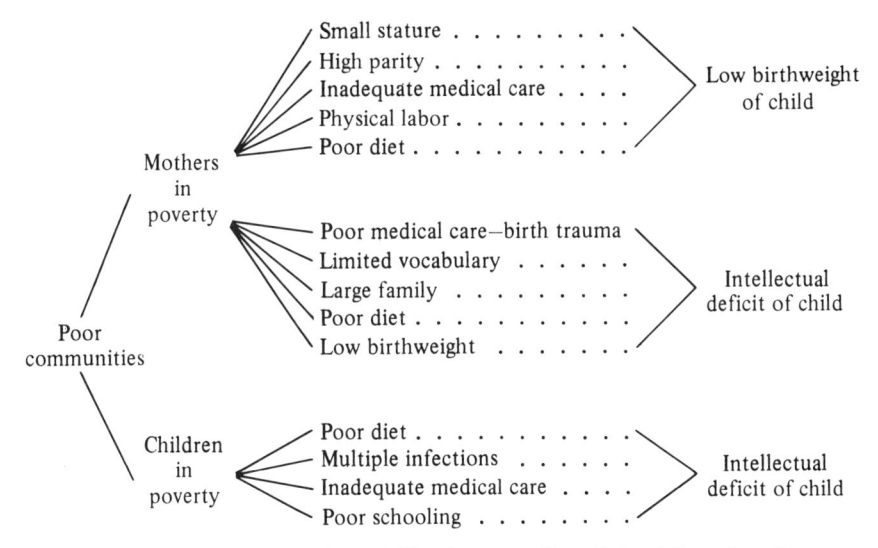

```
                    ┌ Small stature .........┐
                   ╱┌ High parity ...........│
                  ╱╱┌ Inadequate medical care│──► Low birthweight
                 ╱╱╱┌ Physical labor .........│     of child
          Mothers ╱── Poor diet ..............┘
            in
         ╱ poverty
        ╱          ┌── Poor medical care–birth trauma ┐
       ╱          ╱┌── Limited vocabulary .............│
      ╱          ╱╱┌── Large family ...................│──► Intellectual
     ╱            ╲ Poor diet .........................│    deficit of child
    Poor            Low birthweight ...................┘
 communities
    ╲              ┌ Poor diet ...........┐
     ╲  Children  ╱─ Multiple infections │
      ╲    in    ╱── Inadequate medical care ──► Intellectual
         poverty ╲── Poor schooling .....┘      deficit of child
```

Figure 4.1. Some confounding variables that may affect birthweight and intellect

to brain impairment and mental retardation. But the nature of the links are far from clear. Figures 4.1 and 4.2, taken from Stein and Kassab (1970), illustrate possible connections.

In Figure 4.1 are listed some common attributes of mothers and children living in poverty that might contribute to low birthweight or to mental retardation. A "case" either of low birthweight or of mental retardation is more likely to have the listed attributes than a "control." A case of low birthweight is therefore also more likely than a control to be mentally retarded. Conversely, a case of mental retardation is more likely than a control to be of low birthweight. Thus, an association of low birthweight with mental retardation may be found in the presence of any of their shared attributes and could have a common cause in that attribute. For the present, low birthweight cannot unequivocally be assigned a causal or even a mediating role in mental retardation.

Low birthweight itself has heterogeneous causes, known and unknown. Its

```
1. Maternal undernutrition ───► low birthweight ───► intellectual deficit

2. Maternal undernutrition ───► low birthweight
                            ╲──► intellectual deficit

3. Low social class ═══► maternal undernutrition ───► low birthweight
                    ╲──► verbal poverty ────────────► intellectual deficit
```

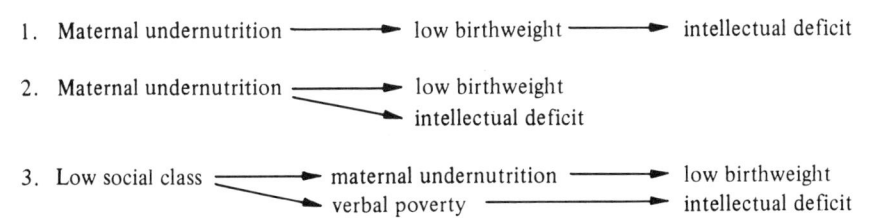

Figure 4.2. Diagram of three among many possible causal paths between maternal undernutrition, low birthweight, and intellectual deficit

association with mental retardation is reduced when those cases are excluded in which the causes of mental retardation are known to antedate birthweight and retard development, as with Down's anomaly. When *very low birthweight* (under 1500 grams) is the precursor of mental retardation, pre-existing congenital defects seem largely to account for both the low birthweight and the mental retardation (Drillien, 1970). Where congenital defect does not accompany very low birthweight, one study suggests that brain damage may be a necessary intervening factor between small size and mental retardation, at least where the small size reflects a short period of gestation. The frequency of cerebral palsy was high among those with short gestation periods, and the frequency of mental retardation was raised only among those with cerebral palsy (McDonald, 1964). A presumed causal sequence is thus premature birth → very low birthweight → cerebral damage → mental retardation, but others are possible.

With *moderately low birthweight* (1500 to 2500 grams), the nature of the association with mental competence is even less clear. The interconnectedness of the postulated causal factors of low birthweight and retarded mental development obfuscates the causal sequence among them (Birch and Gussow, 1970). The consistent social class gradients of birthweight and intelligence quotient are sharp and parallel, to the disadvantage of the lower classes. Yet when the closest possible control of social class has been applied, by making sib comparisons within families, only a small difference in intelligence quotient has been found between sibs of different birthweight (excepting the few sibships with gross weight differences between members) (Record, McKeown, and Edwards, 1970).

This finding suggests that among the complex of variables associated with social class, differences between families and not birthweight differences between individuals are the likely intervening link between social environment and measured intelligence. Similarly, it has been shown that within families with a mildly retarded child, the affected child is no more likely than his sibs to have been of moderately low birthweight or small for the period of gestation (Barker, 1966; Record, McKeown, and Edwards, 1969; Birch, Richardson, Baird, Horobin, and Illsley, 1970). These studies are in accord with the conclusion that cultural-familial retardation depends on membership in families of distinctive character and milieu (see Chapter 2).

The distinction between organic impairment and dysfunction may be at the root of the apparent incoherence of the relationship of mental performance with low birthweight. Many factors that limit or enhance function and influence levels of disability act postnatally. In Chapter 1 we noted that prenatal factors which cause mild impairment might be overshadowed or compensated for by acquired functional abilities.

Compensation may occur only in favorable circumstances—in other words, there would then be interaction between the prenatal factors and postnatal learning. Some studies, but not all, point to interaction between the effects of low birthweight and social class to produce mental retardation (Douglas, 1960;

Drillien, 1964, 1970; McDonald, 1964; Birch and Gussow, 1970). In these, moderately low birthweight was associated with mild mental retardation or lowered intelligence quotient only among the lower classes and not among the higher. In short, moderately low birthweight seems to be neither a sufficient nor a necessary cause of mild mental retardation, but it may well be a contributory cause in unfavorable circumstances.

A precise test of the hypothesis that birthweight is a contributory factor in mental performance should discriminate between prenatal phases in order to define critical periods. Analysis of the published data on birthweight from the Dutch famine shows that birthweight was measurably affected only by exposure to famine during the third trimester of gestation (Smith, 1947; Bergner and Susser, 1970). This exposure coincides with the postulated period of maximum brain growth during prenatal life derived from the studies of brain cell depletion described above. In addition, Smith's data suggested that exposure to famine early in gestation may have caused an excess of stillbirths and congenital anomalies, although the result did not reach statistical significance. This exposure coincided with a phase of growth critical for organogenesis.

We conclude that in humans direct evidence for an effect of prenatal nutrition on later mental development is lacking. In our current study of the Dutch famine, it will be possible to search for consequences of nutritional deprivation at postulated critical periods with some precision of timing. This search can be made because both the phase of development at which successive birth cohorts were exposed to famine, and the duration of their exposure, can be derived from the data.

5 Postnatal Nutrition and Mental Competence

We turn now to consider existing knowledge about the effects of early postnatal nutrition on mental performance. As in the case of prenatal nutrition, confounding of the effects of postnatal with prenatal nutrition presents equal difficulty. Studies of the effect of nutrition on mental competence in humans have most often taken malnutrition syndromes in infants and children as the measure of nutritional deficiency. Such syndromes are manifestations of a severe degree of nutritional deprivation but do not indicate levels of food intake antecedent to their onset. The nature of the nutritional experiences that precede the first clinical observations on the affected infants must be assumed. Even the records of the clinical episodes of malnutrition taken as the starting point may not yield data on time of onset, duration, and the nature and severity of food deficiencies at the time.

Social environment is a crucial determinant of diet at all ages. The nutritional experience of peasant societies is entirely different from that of industrial societies. Severe nutritional deficiencies are characteristic of preindustrial peasant or tribal societies. Even within preindustrial societies, urban and rural nutritional patterns are distinct. In the preindustrial societies of Africa, Asia, and South America, a common pattern of child-rearing, summed up in the phrase "protein-calorie-malnutrition culture," has been described (Jelliffe, 1968a, b). Among the rural poor of these diverse peoples, both infant feeding patterns and infant growth patterns have underlying similarities.

In protein-calorie-malnutrition cultures, pregnant women are often not given a free choice of diet, nor the privilege of special supplements. On the contrary, restrictions are common. Among the Zulu, for example, women may not drink milk nor eat eggs during pregnancy. After a child is born, the mother breast feeds it for many months, even years. In many societies, a child is denied foods regarded as "strong," like meat. The foods allowed are "bland" like soft porridge, the nutrient content of the cereal varying with the society. When the child is taken off the breast, typically at about two years, the child begins to partake of the more varied food of his elders.

Under the conditions of tribal and village life, most children between the ages of six months and two years are surely fed less than the optimum. The rate of growth, measured by height and weight, falls off after six months of age. By comparison with well-off children in industrial societies, many children are chronically short of protein, and some develop nutritional failure manifested in the kwashiorkor syndrome. Rates of child morbidity and mortality are high, and infants tend to suffer severely from infections like measles and gastroenteritis (Gordon, 1966). So dangerous is this age period of some societies that one out of two or three babies may not live through it. When the survivors go on to an unrestricted diet, they begin to gain weight and vigor and "catch up" a good deal in growth, although in comparison with better material conditions some stunting often persists in full-grown populations.

Infection is an extraneous confounding factor difficult to control in studies of the effect of nutrition on child development. Interaction between infection and food deficiency may contribute to stunting (Acheson and Hewitt, 1954; McGregor, Billewicz, and Thomson, 1961; McCance, 1962). Their interaction may also influence vitality and the severity of attacks of infectious diseases. Fatal summer diarrhea is particularly an affliction of malnourished infants (Kahn, 1952). Measles too, in Africa at least, has a higher mortality rate among the malnourished than among others (Savage, 1967; Morley, 1969). Finally, there is a suggestion of interaction in the possible effects of measles on mental performance. In the United States, scores on "reading readiness" tests in several populations of children were related to their previous history of measles. Among lower class children, those who had had measles scored lower than those who had not. Among higher class children, measles did not relate to reading readiness scores (Fox, Black, and Kogon, 1968).

Clinical observation amply confirms that acute nutritional failure has immediate effects on mental function. Children suffering from kwashiorkor are typically irritable, apathetic, and slow to react to their environment, and transient cerebral symptoms have been reported (Kahn, 1954). In addition, a number of reports and reviews of retarded mental development following on malnutrition in infancy have appeared (Scrimshaw, Taylor, and Gordon, 1968; Stein and Kassab, 1970; Birch, 1972b). In Cape Town, South Africa, 21 children, most of whom were identified as severely malnourished before their second birthday, were followed up to pubescence (Stoch and Smythe, 1963). On assessment at various ages during the follow-up, they were found to be inferior to controls in both physical and intellectual development. At 11 years of age, the average IQ was 61 for the cases, 77 for the controls. The malnourished children had smaller heads than controls and immature electroencephalogram rhythm.

This study illustrated the concurrence of execrable social conditions with malnutrition and retarded development. It did not demonstrate the causal connection between malnutrition and retardation, since the controls were not a comparable social group. The cases lived in conditions much inferior to the controls. The association of malnutrition and mental retardation could have been caused by any one of several factors in which the cases and controls differed. The concurrence of poverty, malnutrition, and retarded development is similarly illustrated, again without demonstrating a causal role for diet, by studies from Serbia, Peru, India, Uganda, and elsewhere that followed up malnourished children (Cabak and Najdanvic, 1965; Champakam, Scrikartia, and Gopalon, 1968; Pollitt, 1969; Hoorweg and Stanfield, 1972).

In Cape Town, a second follow-up study of the effects of acute nutritional failure on subsequent development used siblings of the same sex for comparison with cases, and in this way controlled for variation between families (Evans, Moodie, and Hansen, 1971; Hansen, Freesemann, and Moodie, 1971). The 40 index subjects had been admitted to the hospital between 10 months and 4 years of age. In this study, no noteworthy differences in mental or physical development were found between the 40 cases and their siblings in a 10-year follow-up. This result might not be unexpected in the light of the negative result in a similar sib comparison follow-up study of the effects that malnutrition syndromes in infancy have on height at later ages (Garrow and Pike, 1967).

In spite of the high degree of control of social factors inherent in sib comparisons, however, the results do not rule out the hypothesis that malnutrition in early childhood affects later development. One weakness of these studies lies in the measurement of nutritional experience of the index cases and their sibs. Indeed, the development of both sibs and controls might have been retarded. In the Cape Town study, intelligence scores of both sibs and controls were distinctly low.* The known difference between cases and controls, precisely considered, lies not in diet but in the fact that the cases and not the controls were admitted to the hospital with nutritional syndromes. The admission to a hospital of index cases with a nutritional syndrome may have been caused by factors other than diet in which the cases differed from their sibs. An infection that precipitates the florid nutritional syndrome, or maternal rejection, or social circumstances that prevent home care, might affect one child and lead him rather than an equally malnourished sib to the hospital.

Some of the design problems present in the Cape Town study were taken into account in a sib-comparison study in Jamaica (Hertzig, Birch, Richardson, and Tizard, 1972; Richardson, Birch, Grabie, and Yoder, 1972; Richardson,

---

*The mean score for both sibs and controls was 77 on a test similar to the WISC, but was not standardized for the Cape Coloured population from whom the cases were drawn.

Birch, and Hertzig, 1973). The subjects were 74 boys between 6 and 10 years of age who before the age of 2 had been selected for treatment of kwashiorkor with acute nutritional failure in a special metabolic ward. They were compared on the one hand with 38 brothers nearest in age and within the same age range who had not been admitted to the hospital for kwashiorkor and on the other hand with a non-familial comparison group of classmates (or yardmates for those not at school) matched for age and sex. The non-familial comparison group provided a match for each of 71 index cases.

On the WISC, the index cases scored lower than their sibs and lower than the matched comparison group. The sib scores were intermediate between the index cases and the matched comparison groups. A similar pattern was found on the independent measure of behavior at school as reported by teachers.

This study is highly suggestive of a nutritional effect on mental performance. It cannot yet be taken as conclusive, in view of other conflicting results. The conflict between the results in Jamaica and those found in Cape Town seems most likely to reside in the imprecision, common to both studies, with which the nutritional and other early experiences could be specified. In the Cape Town study the comparisons between index cases and sibs are not anchored in known differences in dietary intake; their similar outcomes could have been owed to a shared dietary pattern despite the apparent nutritional difference between them inferred from the hospital admission of the index cases.

In the Jamaican study too, comparisons between index cases and sibs are not anchored in known differences in dietary intake; their dissimilar outcomes could have been owed to non-nutritional differences in childhood experience that led to different experiences of medical care. If this same criticism of two studies with similar design and different results is to be sustained, however, those non-dietary experiences presumed to have influenced not only admission to the hospital but also later mental performance must necessarily have been present in Jamaica and not in Cape Town.

As noted above, admission to the hospital for the acute clinical state of kwashiorkor might have been precipitated by a variety of causes, such as supervening infection; maternal neglect, which is frequent among such cases (Sachs, 1952; Susser, 1957); or by some constitutional weakness of the individual child. These reasons for hospital admission could have differed in Jamaica and Cape Town and could have caused the difference in results in the two sib-comparison studies. Thus one known difference between the two studies is the rural residence of a part of the Jamaican sample, and the entirely urban residence of the Cape Town sample.* Indeed, in Jamaica significant

*The most obvious difference in experience between sibs and controls, namely, prolonged hospital stay and separation from the home, provides an attractive but untenable explanation for differences in outcome in the two studies. Cape Town and Jamaica children both had this separation experience, and in any case other studies of children, although in different environments, have failed to demonstrate long-lasting effects on IQ as a result of prolonged hospital stays (Bowlby, Ainsworth, Boston, and Rosenbluth, 1956).

differences between cases and their sib controls have been reported as confined to the country-dwellers (Birch, 1972a). Test scores were positively associated with an index of intellectual stimulation in the family (Richardson, 1972), and this index was also reported to be associated with urban residence (Birch, 1972 b). Social stimulation may overwhelm nutritional effects on mental competence in town families, or alternatively lack of stimulation and of nutrients may interact to depress mental competence in rural families.

In the comparisons involving matched non-familial controls in Jamaica, their superiority to both the index cases and their sibs points to a difference between families in which kwashiorkor arises and families in which it does not. These differences may be primarily nutritional but this can only be inferred. The superiority of the controls could reside in many other family characteristics that can affect the outcomes chosen for study. On the index of intellectual stimulation, for instance, the non-familial comparison cases are at an advantage over the index cases (Richardson, 1972). Yet in the Jamaican study, although each set of controlled comparisons has its own weaknesses, the gradient in the outcome measures from index cases rising through sibs to non-familial comparison cases has a coherence that favors the nutritional hypothesis.

No suggestion was found, however, of a critical period. The precise age within the first two years of life at which nutritional failure became manifest did not relate to mental competence. A study in Denver, Colorado, which also found persuasive evidence of developmental retardation following on malnutrition, also failed to identify a critical period. In this study 19 children admitted to the hospital with malnutrition in their first year of life were studied in their fourth year. The 10 children admitted to the hospital after four months of age were more retarded than 9 admitted before that age. The authors attributed the worse result among later admissions to a more prolonged exposure to malnutrition.

A similar result was reported by Hansen et al. (1971) in Cape Town; the mean IQ at follow-up of children admitted before the age of 18 months was considerably higher than that of children admitted later. That children admitted early were of different social background from those admitted later, however, is a more tenable explanation for the finding in this study, since the respective sib controls showed the same pattern.

The failure to demonstrate that growth is more critical early in postnatal life than later might be explained by the prolongation of rapid brain growth into the second postnatal year. Further specification of nutritional experience is called for: duration of deprivation should be added to the dimensions of timing and severity.

Our review of knowledge about the effects of postnatal nutrition on later mental development suggests to us that such effects do exist but that they are not large or easily detected. There are many areas of ambiguity. There is as yet no evidence to support the hypothesis that nutritional deprivation not only retards development but that its effects persist into adulthood and prevents the full realization of potential mental competence.

6 Specifying Nutrient Deficiencies

The measurement of nutrient intake is a besetting problem in all studies of the effects of diet on humans. So far we have considered some difficulties of interpretation that arise where dietary deficiency must be assumed although its timing, duration, and severity are not known. Even if intake were known, what constitutes adequacy and what deficiency would be somewhat arbitrary. Precision in research is surely enhanced, however, if constituents of diet can be specified. Although metabolic pathways exist by which each class of nutrients—carbohydrate, protein, and fat—can be converted into another, each class serves different primary metabolic functions. Thus deficiencies of each class, separately or in various combinations, can be expected to have dissimilar consequences. Most attention has been paid to differentiating the specific effects of protein deficiency from the effects of calorie deficiency (to which all three classes of nutrient contribute).

A number of animal experiments indicate that lack of protein during development can influence brain growth, behavior, and mental performance. In rats, the number of cells in the brain has been reduced by protein deprivation both during gestation (through restricting the mother's intake) and in the postnatal period. Behavioral abnormalities too have been produced by protein deprivation in pigs and dogs as well as in rats and in monkeys (Barnes, Reid, Pond, and Moore, 1968; Zamenhof, van Marthens, and Margolis, 1968; Platt and Stewart, 1968; Barnes, Moore, and Pond, 1970; Zimmermann, Strobel, Steere, and Geist, 1973).

The effects of simultaneous deficiencies in all dietary components have also been tested, in experiments that simulate famine and starvation. Pigs given a severely limited share of mother's milk performed poorly on conditioning tests. These animals were hyperactive and took food voraciously when it was offered; they improved after they were placed on full diet, and by the end of the experiment performed as well as controls on the conditioning tests. Among pigs reared on diets deficient specifically in protein (with fats either high or low), inferior performance persisted when full diet was introduced (Barnes, Moore, Reid, and Pond, 1968). Unfortunately, protein deficiency had effects on other aspects of behavior that muddied interpretation of the experiments. The animals were apathetic and lacked appetite. This made it difficult to maintain a high calorie intake concurrently with reduced protein intake, and also to rehabilitate the animals at the same rate as those on a balanced low calorie diet.

The theoretical difficulties of interpreting the relevance of these results to human nutrition are less easily dealt with than such practical difficulties of experimental design. The experiments with protein deficiency aimed to simulate the kwashiorkor syndrome (Williams, 1933; Brock and Autret, 1952; Trowell, Davies, and Dean, 1954). The syndrome has been ascribed to protein lack and distinguished from the marasmus ascribed to lack of all the foods that contribute calories. The distinction has recently become controversial, and both forms are now often subsumed under the heading protein-calorie malnutrition. The controversy indicates that the deficiencies that produce nutritional failure in humans are of doubtful specificity, and may not match the experiments.

Human analogies with the effects of protein deficiencies in animals must be made cautiously for other reasons too. Protein may be less important to primates than to other mammals. Primate fetuses are smaller in relation to their mothers than are non-primates, and after birth, primates grow at relatively slower rates. In keeping with this slower growth rate, the protein content of primate breast milk is relatively low. Thus the protein needs of primate young may be more easily sustained during gestation and lactation (Payne and Wheeler, 1967a, b). To add to the problems of analogy, in humans the contribution of postnatal learning to behavior is immeasurably greater than it is in other animals. On other grounds too, measures of intelligence in humans and of learning ability in other mammals cannot be considered comparable.

Some of these drawbacks do not apply to experiments with rhesus monkeys. In these animals induced kwashiorkor-like syndromes appeared to lead to behavior changes that persisted after they were put on rehabilitating diets. Effects on learning proved difficult to detect, as indicated previously, although the malnourished animals performed more poorly on tasks involving attention (Zimmermann, Strobel, Steere, and Geist, 1973).

In humans, such depressed intellectual function as may follow nutritional failure in infancy cannot yet be attributed to specific protein deficiency. The connections between the various findings on the effects of specific deficiencies of nutrients on the brain are tenuous. It is possible but not proven that during gestation or soon after birth either severe protein deficiency or severe starvation can lead to a sequence that begins with reduction in brain cell number, leads on even through cortical atrophy and reduced head circumference, and culminates in some degree of mental retardation. The study of the Dutch famine could enable us to examine a variety of possible effects of specified nutritional deficiencies in human beings. During World War II the official allocation of food rations was published every week, and these data can be related to the phase of development at which exposure occurred among successive birth cohorts. In this study we can hope to specify the severity, the timing, the duration, and the nature of the nutritional insult.

Conclusion

The studies reported in this book will consider what the long-term effects might be on the mental and physical state of those exposed to various degrees of famine at successive phases of prenatal development. In these short introductory chapters, we have reviewed areas of knowledge germane to these studies. Several of the hypotheses discussed will be put to test. It is not in question that starvation of mothers in the Dutch famine resulted in their infants having birthweights lower than they would have been otherwise (Sindram, 1945; Smith, 1947; Stroink, 1947; Kloosterman, 1966). The effect of famine on birthweight was a phenomenon of the third trimester of pregnancy (Smith, 1947; Bergner and Susser, 1970). Other effects, particularly on rates of stillbirths, neonatal deaths, and congenital malformations, may have been related to famine exposure in earlier phases of pregnancy. The number of post-famine births included in previous analyses was small, and the variation in rates was not statistically significant. Thus the data previously available could not do more than suggest that while the latter part of gestation affects the growth of the fetus, the earlier part affects development and the capacity for survival. We aim to re-examine these questions with data more extensive and better controlled, and to try and unravel the ultimate consequences of prenatal nutritional deprivation.

II The Context and Design of the Study

7 Famine in a Highly Developed Society

The Dutch People During World War II

The Netherlands, a small country 12,530 square miles in area, is customarily divided by the points of the compass into four regions, each comprising two or three administrative provinces. In the commercial and industrial West are the three provinces of Noord Holland, Zuid Holland, and Utrecht. The North, the "breadbasket of the country," is separated from the West by the IJsselmeer (the former Zuider Zee) and comprises the three agricultural provinces of Groningen, Friesland, and Drenthe. South of the great rivers of the Rhine estuary lies another agricultural region which comprises the three provinces of Limburg, Brabant, and Zeeland. The East comprises two provinces, Gelderland and Overijssel.

The estimated population of the Netherlands during the first half-year of 1945 was about 9,250,000.* About one-half lived in the forty-five cities with a population above 25,000 inhabitants; about one-fourth lived in seven cities located in the Western part of the country, which alone was affected by the famine. Five of these seven cities—namely, Amsterdam, Rotterdam, The Hague, Utrecht, and Haarlem—were the largest in the Netherlands; Leiden and Delft were somewhat smaller.

The population density of the Netherlands after World War II, 710 persons per square mile, was the highest reported in the world. In the West, density was twice as high as it was elsewhere; although this region has only one-fifth of the total land area, half the people in the country lived there. Because of its high

*Netherlands Central Bureau of Statistics, Population Estimate, 1945.

population density, the Netherlands in normal times depended on imports to maintain its food supply. Heavy imports of grain, oilseed, and cattlefeed went to the dairy farms, and these in turn produced milk, butter, cheese, meat, and eggs, much of which was exported (Breunis, 1946; Dols and van Arcken, 1946).

Standards of public health were high before World War II. The over-all mortality rate of 8.7 per 1000 in 1939 was low, and the infant mortality and tuberculosis mortality rates were among the lowest in the world (Banning, 1946). Food was plentiful, as indicated by the consumption of calories and protein (Dols and van Arcken, 1946). Social and health services were widely available, although they were entrusted in the main to voluntary associations. While these associations catered separately to broad religious groups (Catholics, Protestants, nonsectarians), they were financed by the central government and responsible to state health authorities. Community care for mental disorders, a movement pioneered in the Netherlands, had its beginnings before World War II.

The religious affiliations of the Dutch people require some comment. The religious organizations not only operated social, health, and educational institutions, but also played a major part in combating the famine. Furthermore, religious affiliation is a social and cultural indicator and hence an influence on the manifestations of mental development.

In 1947, more than 40% of the population belonged to two major Protestant sects, the Nederland-Hervormd (31.1%) and the Gereformeerd (9.7%). Thirty-eight per cent of the population was Roman Catholic. Seventeen per cent claimed no religious affiliation. Religion divides the Dutch people into groups with unequal concentrations in the regions and provinces of the country. The West and the North were predominantly Protestant. In these two regions, however, a substantial proportion of people had no religious affiliation (Noord Holland 34.2%, Zuid Holland 21.1%; Groningen 27.0%, Friesland 23.4%). In the southern provinces of Limburg and North Brabant, more than 90% of the population was Catholic; in the West only 30% was Catholic. Medical, social, and educational services were operated by the organizations of each of the three religious groups in accord with the geography of religious affiliations. In the Catholic South there were only Catholic-operated services. The services in the four regions were of about equal quality, with the exception of the South, which was thought to be somewhat underserviced.

Social class divided the Dutch population into horizontal strata. These strata did not fare equally in the famine. Social class is a powerful indicator of social environment and the command of resources, as well as of health and mental development. Social class membership will therefore have influenced not only the famine experience of the people but also those manifestations we intend to examine for marks of that experience.

Socioeconomic status in the Netherlands is largely determined, as elsewhere in the Western world, by three factors—namely, occupation, education, and income. The amount of social mobility is much the same as in some eight other

European countries and also the United States and Canada (Lipset and Bendix, 1958). We have no data on income distribution, and shall describe only the occupational and educational structure of the society.

With regard to occupational structure, we have used the national records of military induction for the birth years 1944 to 1946 to derive the distribution. Although these records refer only to the fathers of males examined from 1962 through 1965, they are germane to this description, for they refer precisely to the familial origins of that young adult population which is the subject of our study. The relevant information was missing in only 6%, either because the father had died more than six years before, or because it was not known or recorded.

A relatively large percentage of the population (11.5%) worked on farms, and many of them owned their own farms (9.5%). These farms are small compared with those of several other European countries. The percentage distribution of the main occupational groups was as follows:

Upper professional	2.0%
Lower professional	7.5%
Managerial and proprietary	11.6%
White collar workers (clerical and sales)	14.1%
Skilled workers (craftsmen, foremen, self-employed)	5.8%
Semi-skilled workers (operators, process workers, shop assistants)	27.3%
Miners	1.5%
Service occupations	1.1%
Laborers	11.4%
Farmers	9.5%
Farm Laborers	2.0%
Occupations unknown or not recorded	6.2%

The structure differed between regions. The West contained the large metropolitan centers in which a large percentage of persons were in professional, managerial, and white collar occupations. The rural provinces of the North (Drenthe, Friesland, and Groningen) and the South (Limburg, North Brabant), in contrast, had large percentages of farmers and agricultural workers.

The Dutch educational system is divided into four levels: elementary schools, secondary schools, high schools, and university. Since it is possible to leave school from any one of these levels, the type of school from which a pupil graduates can be used as a measure of school performance and of the standard of education attained. In publicly supported schools there are uniform standards of performance for each grade level; those who cannot meet the standards repeat the year. In consequence, at school-leaving age pupils may still be in lower education or in secondary education while their contemporaries are attending high schools and planning to enter the university. The highest grade attained, therefore, is a good measure of educational achievement.

The percentage of the study population in the three types of schools and the percentage in each type who had completed the curriculum and graduated on reaching the age of 19 years (the time of military induction) are given below:

Special school	3.1	
For the retarded		2.9%
For other handicapped		.2%
Lower school	50.7	
Failed		2.4%
Completed		14.2%
Completed, plus vocational training		34.1%
Secondary School	20.8	
More than one year from completion		7.6%
Completed, or less than one year from completion		13.2%
High School	21.2	
More than one year from completion		14.9%
Completed, or less than one year from completion		6.3%
University		3.2%
Attending or completed		
Unknown		.9%

The schools and institutions for the mentally retarded are of special interest to our study because they define a particular level of mental performance. There are 14 types of special school for the handicapped, for example the blind, the deaf, the physically impaired. The large majority are schools for the mentally retarded. The *Handbook for Mental Health in the Netherlands* for 1960 listed 300 schools for the mentally retarded. Almost 3% of the military induction sample attended these schools. In 1960 there were about 40 residential institutions for the mentally retarded. Most of these were small; only 4 had more than 500 patients. In addition there were 38 group homes (*tehuizen*) for children in need of care for a variety of reasons; because of parental neglect, for example. According to the 1967 census of patients in psychiatric institutions, approximately 18% of all patients had a primary diagnosis of mental retardation.

The Netherlands During World War II

The outbreak of World War II found the Dutch prepared with plans for the safeguard of their food supplies. In 1937 the Government Office for the Preparation of the Food Supply in Time of War had already begun preparing against the possibility that the Netherlands might be either neutral or isolated or occupied; plans were made to adjust agricultural production for each contingency and to introduce a system of rationing.

Immediately on the outbreak of war in September 1939, imports of animal feed stopped and the rationing of animal feed was begun. In May 1940 the Netherlands was occupied by the Germans. Rationing of foods for the Dutch people then began, and measures were taken to adjust agricultural production. The lack of feed for animals made it necessary to restrict dairy farming, and this in turn increased the need for cultivation of crops essential for nutrition. The stock of cattle was reduced by 75%, the stock of pigs and fowls somewhat less, and the supply of meat, butter, cheese, and egg products dropped sharply (Burger, Drummond, and Sandstead, 1948). The prewar acreage of 130,000 hectares* given over to potato growing was raised to 210,000 hectares so that potatoes might substitute for some of the deficient elements of the diet. Calculations had shown that under favorable circumstances the Dutch soil might supply a daily average of 2200 Calories per head. Virtually all foods were rationed from April 1941. In fact an average daily level of about 1800 Calories per adult was maintained through much of the time up to the end of 1943. In 1944, conditions deteriorated further, and by July 1944 the average daily ration for adults was down to 1350 Calories. The famine came at a time when food supplies were already marginal. Many unfavorable circumstances had conjoined (Bourne, 1943). Farm machinery and horses, requisitioned by the occupation forces, were scarce. Fertilizers were also in short supply. In 1938-39, the Dutch used 369 kilograms of nitrates per hectare, in 1944-45 only 9.1 kilograms. Similar declines in the use of other fertilizers led to a considerable reduction in productivity of the soil. Moreover, during the occupation much of the agricultural output was exported or used by the occupying forces (Dols and van Arcken, 1946).

The Nazi occupation was a period of continuous stress in many respects. Agricultural production in the Netherlands was encouraged and industrial production discouraged because of the food needs of the occupation forces and the German population (Burger, Drummond, and Sandstead, 1948, Part I, p. 5). The Nazis, at first, cultivated the cooperation of the Dutch population. Later, as the Occupying Authority encountered resistance and failed to elicit wholehearted cooperation, attitudes and methods hardened. Many hostages were interned in concentration camps. A number of hostages were shot in reprisal for the deaths inflicted by the Dutch underground movement. According to one estimate, 2774 hostages were executed during the war (Warmbrunn, 1963).

The greatest loss of Dutch manpower was to the German war industries, the needs of which became acute with the beginning of the German campaign in Russia in June 1941. The Nazis began with so-called voluntary methods to induce Dutch labor to work in German factories. From April 1942, they drafted skilled workers; those unwilling to go were rounded up into special

*One hectare=2.47 acres.

camps and transported to Germany. According to official statistics, 162,000 workers were deported to Germany in 1942 (Warmbrunn, 1963). In 1943, more forceful methods were introduced. 300,000 war veterans were drafted and the major cities were raided to provide forced labor. Because of effective Dutch resistance, however, the numbers deported actually declined; deportees numbered 148,000 in 1943 and still fewer after that. The number of Dutch workers in Germany at the end of the war, exclusive of "genuine" prisoners and deported Jews, was estimated to lie between 300,000 and 400,000. This made up a substantial proportion of all men of working age. About 20,000 are thought to have died in German labor camps.

The deportation of Jews on a large scale began in July 1942 and was virtually completed by September 1943. According to Maas (1970), there were about 140,000 Jews living in Holland at the beginning of the occupation. More than 100,000 were deported and died in concentration camps in Germany and Eastern Europe; fewer than 4000 survived deportation. About 22,000 resisted deportation. Some 2000 of these managed to flee the country. Another 20,000 went "underground" with forged identity cards; only 4000 of these survived.

The final episode of the war, which marks the beginning of the famine, dates from mid-September 1944. The Allied forces entered the Netherlands on September 14. Two large branches of the Rhine barred their advance on the main industrial centers of Germany in the Ruhr. Almost at once they attempted to seize the strategic bridges that spanned the river at Nijmegen and Arnhem. To support this attack and hamper the German defences, the Dutch government-in-exile in London broadcast an appeal for a general railroad strike. In response, and despite threats of reprisal, the Dutch rail workers brought rail traffic to a standstill. The German occupation forces then imposed the reprisal they had threatened, an embargo on all transport including food supplies. A British paratroop drop ended in disaster in the forests of Arnhem. As the fighting continued, both Arnhem and Nijmegen were severely battered and the people evacuated. By mid-November the Allied forces had liberated the Netherlands south of the Rhine, but they had failed to take the crucial bridges. Major fighting in that sector of the front ceased until the end of March 1945.

The food situation in the cities of the West, already difficult in September when the Allied drive on the Rhine began, had deteriorated sharply with the embargo on transport imposed in early October. Seyss-Inquart, chief of the Occupation Authority, relented a little and lifted the total embargo on November 8, 1944, to permit the use of water transport. By that time, the acute food shortage had become a famine. People were starving. More time passed before transport from the North across the IJsselmeer (Zuider Zee) could begin: most owners had hidden their vessels for fear of German confiscations. Those weeks were critical. Winter was both unusually early and unusually severe in 1944. Before much could be done, the canals had frozen and the barges could not move. The freezing of the canals prevented large-scale relief. What food came in from the North and the East was mainly shipped through the port of Amsterdam.

As the war continued, the means of transport were increasingly commandeered by the Occupation Authority. As a result a surplus of food accumulated in the North. Meanwhile, other circumstances exacerbated the shortage in the West. Many farmers were drafted. Large tracts of the country were inundated by the breaking of the sea dikes to delay an Allied invasion, and much farm land was given up to the construction of airfields and fortifications. Two hundred and thirty thousand hectares in all were rendered useless for agriculture. The famine conditions continued until the liberation of the Western Netherlands by the Allied forces on May 7, 1945.

The present study is more concerned with the extent and severity of the famine than with its causes. The famine was restricted to the half of the population residing in the West. The shortages in other parts of the country were of much briefer duration and did not amount to persisting famine with starvation. In the West, the famine was largely a phenomenon of the cities and towns. Rural people produced food for their own subsistence, even at the height of the famine. Some informants who were in the famine-stricken areas told the writers that while towns like The Hague and Leiden were starving, villages only two to three miles away were much better off.

Conditions were especially severe during the last four months of the famine, in spite of some relief supplies provided through the Swedish and the Swiss Red Cross organizations. The report of a survey of conditions in the Netherlands conducted by a team of specialist nutritionists recruited by Supreme Headquarters of the Allied Expeditionary Forces (SHAEF) well conveys the situation:

> Fall of bodyweight was progressive and rapid. All the characteristic signs of calorie-deficiency appeared: undue fatigue on moderate exercise, feeling cold, mental listlessness, apathy, obsession with thoughts of food, etc. In the beginning men especially were affected.
>
> It is easy to write now that each person got 400 calories a day. In practice it was quite another thing. Each Thursday there was published the list of the coupon-numbers that were valid for the next week's food. One planned to divide that food over the week. The ordinary person, however, often consumed in two or three days all that was given for the whole week. Consequently there was an enforced fast for 4 days until the next rations were available. This seriously aggravated the situation. People sought food everywhere in the streets and the surrounding countryside. Anything edible was picked up in this way and they were lucky who found a potato or two or a handful of greens.
>
> In January 1945 the first cases of hunger oedema appeared and were admitted to the hospitals. Soon the numbers multiplied. Little relief could be offered these patients. Even in the hospitals there was little food. The nurses and physicians worked day and night without supple-

mentary rations. Their menu for example was: one slice of bread and one cup of tea substitute for breakfast; two potatoes, a little bit of vegetables and some watery sauce for lunch; one or two slices of bread with a cup of coffee substitute and a plate of soup for dinner. This soup was frequently made with sugarbeets by the Communal Kitchen. For hospital patients, however, there was a little more food available, so something could be done for them.

In February, however, so many came complaining of starvation, that the hospitals could not admit them all. In several towns starvation-hospitals were established. With the aid of the underground forces schools were transferred into hospitals, complete with beds, blankets, sheets and other necessaries. Food too, was brought in by the underground forces. In spite of all these efforts enough beds could not be made available. The patients admitted were treated until they were able to walk and then were discharged. In many cases this remission was only temporary. There was always a waiting list of patients waiting for admission, and many of these were those who had been previously treated.

In addition, considerable help was given through polyclinics. Those who had lost 25% of their normal bodyweight received supplementary rations. At the beginning of 1945 this amounted to 400 g of bread, 500 g beans per day, and some milk, when it was available. Later on, this supplement was reduced to 400 g of bread alone, and it was only given when the decrease of weight was as great as 35% or 40%; too many people had reached the level of −25% (Burger, Drummond, and Sandstead, 1948, Part I, pp. 20ff.).

The newly organized Interchurch Bureau (IKB) was able to provide some extra food for people with overt signs of starvation like hunger oedema, and for the patients in the special starvation hospitals established to meet the emergency. The *SHAEF Report* continues:

In view of the large numbers of starving people, these polyclinics for starvation patients were set up in several towns. Here examinations were made, using the "sacratama" formula . . . ; the weights were taken and the patients inspected for oedema. The urine was examined to differentiate hunger-oedema from the frequently occurring nephritis. Then necessitous patients received a coupon for one meal per day from the I.K.B. for two or three weeks. If the patient was too ill to walk to the canteen, the meal was delivered to the home by volunteer-helpers. These volunteers were mostly children of about 14 years, because adults were in real danger of being "picked up" by the Germans for enforced work in the defence areas.

There was little opportunity to collect data at these polyclinics because of pressure of work: for example at Rotterdam 600 people were examined by 4 doctors each morning. After liberation many more such polyclinics were set up. When more food became available their aid became much more effective.

FAMINE IN A HIGHLY DEVELOPED SOCIETY

In spite of this local organisation and effort, conditions became worse. People dropped from exhaustion in the streets and many died there. Often people were so fatigued that they were unable to return home, before curfew; so they hid in barns or elsewhere to sleep and there died. Older people, who lacked the strength to go searching for food, stayed at home in bed and died. The worst cases were hidden in the homes and being unknown to the physicians could not be treated.

Famine took its course with all its consequences. Vermin became common; there was no soap; frequently there was no water, gas or electricity. Many people had skin-infections and frequently abscesses and phlegmones.

The exact number of hunger-oedema patients is unknown. Only an estimate can be made from data from some of the large towns. In May 1945 some 200,000 cases required additional food.

During the four weeks before the liberation on May 7, 1945, when the advance of the Allied forces had completely separated the West from the rest of the country, the famine reached its greatest intensity.

Reports of severe famine in Holland had reached the Allied forces. In anticipation of the relief of the occupation, the Supreme Headquarters of the Allied Expeditionary Force collected a team of expert nutritionists, food supplies, and transport facilities. The experts prepared to carry out, immediately upon liberation, a survey to determine the extent and the effects of the famine, and the best means of providing relief.

The SHAEF surveys, together with some other reports of the time, make possible a quantitative assessment of the severity of the famine. The amount of official rations assigned each week to each community is on record. Actual food intake was not precisely reflected by the ration. The food was not always and everywhere available for purchase, and not all had the money to buy what was available. The more fortunate got sporadic extra supplies from the black market and from forages into the country (hongertochten); those in special need, from the Interchurch Bureau and foreign relief.

Conditions differed from city to city. Extra food was more difficult to find in The Hague, with few nearby farms, than in Amsterdam or Rotterdam. The opportunities for foraging depended on many individual circumstances. A successful hongertocht required knowledgeable contacts who could supply addresses of farmers who might have and sell food, a bicycle, and valuables to barter for the food. Knowledgeable contacts could come from occupational and family connections. More than one doctor informed us that his patients had provided him with contacts denied to other professionals, such as teachers. In Rotterdam kin networks, according to another informant, were especially important to the large number of recent migrants from rural areas. As time went on and the famine continued, hongertochten became less and less rewarding:

> People went out as best as they could from the towns into the countryside in search of food: a few potatoes or sugarbeets. Anything

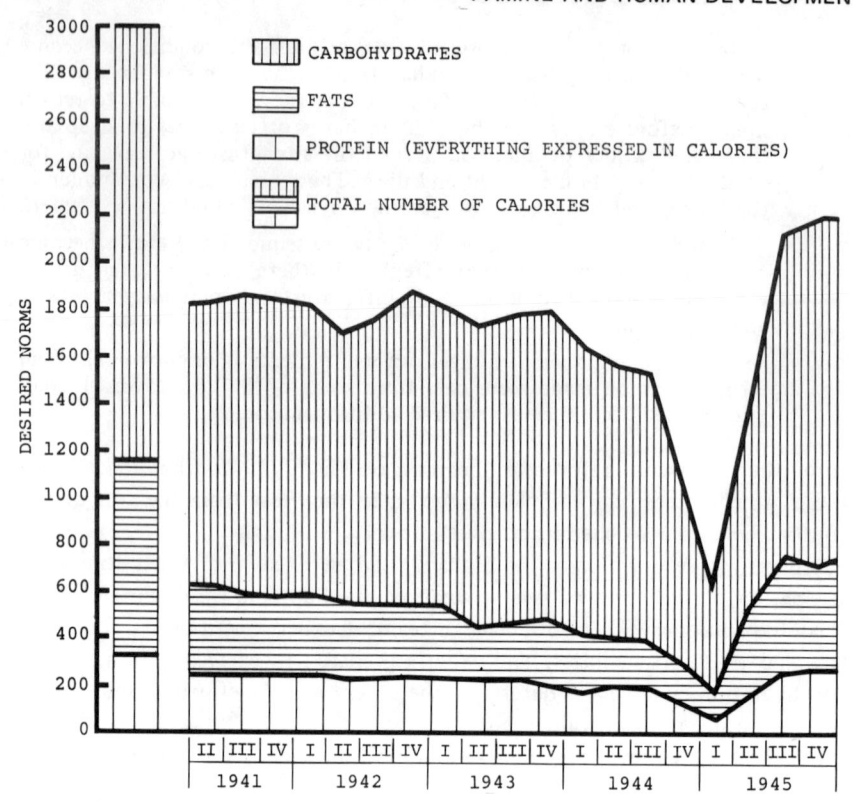

Figure 7.1. Average quarterly distribution of food rations in Calories, protein, fats, and carbohydrates in the western Netherlands, 1941 through 1945.
Source: Reproduced from Burger, Drummond, and Sandstead, 1948, Part I, p. 6.

that could be eaten was sought after. Before long the cold of the winter and the declining strength of people made the search for food increasingly difficult. Many died from exhaustion by the roadside (Burger, Drummond, and Sandstead, 1948, Part I, p. 9).

Figure 7.1, taken from the *SHAEF Report,* shows the constituents of the official food rations for the Western Netherlands throughout the period of occupation, and compares these rations with the standards of the prewar period.* At the beginning of the occupation the average daily ration for anyone not falling into a special category was about 1800 Calories. Rations were maintained at the same level in all three regions (West, North, and South) until

---

*Current standards of the Food and Agriculture Organization for these constituents are 40 grams of protein, 340 grams of carbohydrate, 119 grams of fat. This gives a total intake of 2570 Calories allowing 4.1 Calories per gram of protein, 3.75 Calories per gram of carbohydrate, 9.5 Calories per gram of fat (McCance and Widdowson, 1940).

September 1944. By that time, the average daily ration had fallen to about 1400 Calories. With the onset of famine in the West, rations were down to 1200 Calories in November, and by the turn of the year to less than 800 Calories (Table 7.1). Toward the end of February 1945, the food ration had dropped to 580 Calories. Between February and April 1945, bread and potatoes formed almost the entire ration. Rations elsewhere were lower than in previous years of the occupation, but did not reach the low levels of the West. In the North, the average daily ration varied between 1350 to 1400 Calories, and in the South between 1375 and 1700 Calories. Table 7.1 shows the average daily caloric ration in three-month averages for each region of the country.

The SHAEF nutrition teams made estimates of the *total* food supplies available at different places and periods during the famine over and above the official ration. They did this by combining data from several sources, including interviews with individual survivors. Samples, while not systematic, were made as representative as possible. Table 7.2 shows the amounts and sources of caloric

Table 7.1. Rations of Calories in three-month averages for the period June 1944 through August 1946

Area	June–Aug. 1944	Sept.–Nov. 1944	Dec.–Feb. 1944–45	Mar.–May 1945	June–Aug. 1945	Sept.–Nov. 1945
West	1512	1414	740	670	1757	2083
North	1512	1450	1345	1392	1755	2083
South	1512	1403	1375	1692	1864	2083

Table 7.2. Estimated daily Calorie intake by sources of supply for adults living in Amsterdam during four selected periods

Source of Supply	Oct. 1944	Feb. 1945	Apr. 1945	June 1945*
Official rations	1283	479	659	2045
Central kitchens**	29	86	105	–
Interchurch Bureau**	–	1	33	–
Extra-legal (Black market, forages, etc.)	564	724	446	–
Total	1876	1290	1243	2045

*The figures for June reflect only the first week of June 1945, i.e. the fourth week after liberation.
**The central kitchens fed 87,721 in October, 254,836 in February, and 224,852 in April out of a total population of 775,000. The Interchurch Bureau provided supplementary food for about 13,000 persons in February and 58,000 in April 1945.
Source: Burger, Drummond, and Sandstead, 1948, Part II, p. 153.

intake for individuals in Amsterdam estimated by the team for four separate months. These estimates suggest that at the height of the famine supplements and particularly extra-legal sources doubled the extremely meager official ration. The estimates do not reflect the experience of a large segment of the population who could not afford black market food and could not forage. The SHAEF team reported on the six cities of Amsterdam, Delft, The Hague, Leiden, Rotterdam, and Utrecht as follows:

> The average food intake from all sources, including extra-legal, in October 1944 was approximately 1600 calories. This was reduced to 1400 calories in February 1945 and 1300 calories or lower in April 1945. The official ration was reduced at a much more rapid rate and to maintain total intake levels at the figures quoted, it was necessary to use stocks of food which had been hidden away, and to make frequent forage trips into the more fertile provinces to the East. In addition, sugar beets and tulip bulbs were widely eaten during the six months prior to liberation and represented food sources not normally used. Also the development of very large central kitchens used by a high percentage of all inhabitants made for more economic use of food as well as fuel. However, these factors could only be maintained for a limited period of time. Stocks of hidden food were rapidly used; foraging expeditions were, of necessity, longer and more difficult and the Germans became more inclined to confiscate food obtained in this fashion. In addition, this average food intake did not apply to all people. The elderly who could not forage for food, the very poor who could not buy it or exchange goods for it and the occupants of institutions who received only the legal ration were very much worse off than the average individual.
>
> The situation was deteriorating rapidly in the period immediately before the German surrender, and intake of food from all sources was quickly reduced to extremely low levels, in some instances to the order of 500 to 600 calories (Burger, Drummond, and Sandstead, 1948, Part I, pp. 76-77).

Throughout the German occupation, official rations were adjusted for type of work, age, and special circumstances. Men doing heavy work qualified for more than those in sedentary work. The experiences of pregnant women are a focal point in this study. Supplements were given to pregnant women, mothers with young infants, and the sick. During the famine, however, the *SHAEF Report* states that "it was not always possible actually to provide these rations." Referring to conditions in The Hague, the team reports: "In the middle of November, 1944 the additional supplies for mothers who were feeding their babies stopped . . . the allowances for pregnant women were not met. Calories and almost every nutrient were below the standard allowances through the whole winter" (Burger, Drummond, and Sandstead, 1948, Part II, p. 265). Informants who were responsible for managing the estimation and distribution of rations for the Ministry of Agriculture during the war confirmed to the writers that during the famine pregnant women could not be protected from starvation. Some women pregnant during the famine weighed less at term than they had at the beginning of gestation.

Infants did not suffer as severely as other age groups. Special arrangements for them seemed to have been maintained throughout the famine in most Western cities. Table 7.3, adapted from the *SHAEF Report* for The Hague and Leiden, assesses the adequacy of official rations for infants and pregnant women. "Adequacy" is expressed as a percentage of the Oxford Nutrition Survey Standard Allowances.

Some people, we have noted, had more to eat than others. The lower social classes were at a disadvantage, although the SHAEF team reported no consistent correlations between weight loss and social class. On the other hand, other effects of famine did discriminate among the social classes. We shall show later, for example, that fertility was more affected in the manual than in the non-manual classes. In addition, there were distinct disparities among the social classes in deaths from malnutrition. During the first quarter of 1945 in The Hague malnutrition accounted for 28.7% (2346 cases) of all working class deaths, 26.1% (1479 cases) of all middle class deaths, and 13.8% (173 cases) of all upper class deaths (Banning, 1946).

The effects of the famine were immediately obvious to the SHAEF team of observers:

> The result of the physical examinations revealed that the reduced food intake had already produced evidences of starvation. Less than half of the people examined in the representative surveys presented an

Table 7.3. Adequacy of official Calorie and protein ration expressed as percentage of Oxford nutrition survey standard allowances, September 1944, February 1945, and April 1945

	Caloric Ration	Adequacy	Protein Ration	Adequacy
Children under 1 year				
September 1944	1380	138	46.0	128
February 1945	1233	123	53.0	148
April 1945	1621	162	64.0	178
Pregnant women				
September 1944	1924	64	61.0	73
February 1945	836	28	35.0	42
April 1945	862	29	35.0	41

Source: Adapted from Burger, Drummond, and Sandstead, 1948, Part II, p. 272.

appearance which could be considered as normal. Most could be classed as thin, some as very thin and a few as emaciated (Burger, Drummond, and Sandstead, 1948, Part I, p. 77).

The same report estimated that weight loss averaged about 15-20% of total body weight. Hunger oedema appeared in January 1945 and by May 1945 had affected an estimated 10% of the city populations. Menstrual irregularities, retarded menarche, or amenorrhea were reported in 50% of all women examined.

Figure 7.2 shows the rise in general mortality rates in three major cities during six months of famine compared with the rates for the same months of the previous year. Deaths from malnutrition were estimated at about 10,000 in the Western Netherlands. Table 7.4 refers to The Hague, and shows the sharp rise in number of deaths attributed to malnutrition as well as in the total number. Deaths attributed to malnutrition are likely to be underrepresented because of the rules for certifying deaths then in force. The malnutrition rubric would include only those deaths that the physician attributed to malnutrition as the primary cause and not deaths in which malnutrition was only a contributing factor.

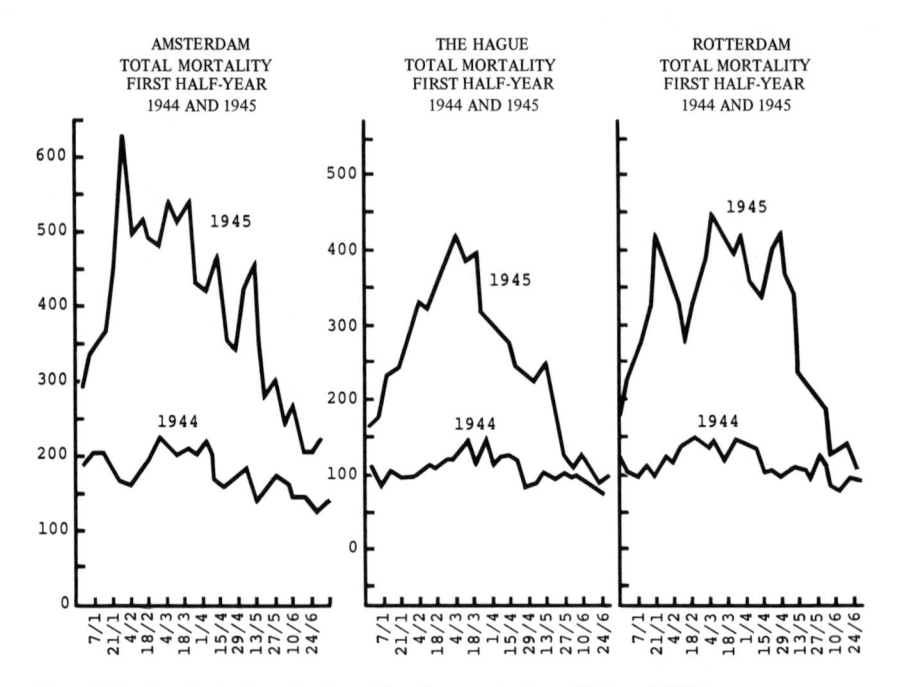

Figure 7.2. Deaths in three famine cities, January to June 1944 and 1945
Source: Reproduced from Burger, Drummond, and Sandstead, 1948, Part I, page 23.

FAMINE IN A HIGHLY DEVELOPED SOCIETY

This chapter has used historical sources to describe the impact of war-time famine on the well-organized, economically developed society of the Netherlands. We shall now proceed to describe how this tragedy enabled us to study some of those critical social issues of our day that center on nutrition, health, and mental competence.

Table 7.4. Reported deaths during selected weeks in The Hague*

Week Ending	Total Number		Per Cent Increase: from 1944 to 1945	Numbers of Deaths by Cause, 1945		
	1944	1945		Malnutrition	War	Other
January 6	124	168	35.5	27	32	109
January 20	113	239	111.5	52	0	187
February 3	104	288	176.9	108	7	173
February 17	126	320	154.0	131	17	172
March 3	130	389	200.0	141	80	168
March 17	158	378	139.2	121	71	186
March 31	139	312	124.5	127	31	154
April 14	134	281	109.7	146	9	126
April 28	91	239	162.5	80	5	154

*During the famine, the groups with an increased risk of dying were males, those at either extreme of age, and the less prosperous classes.
Source: Abstracted from Table 5, C. Banning, 1946, "The Food Supply," *Annals of the American Academy of Political and Social Sciences* 245, p. 102.

8 The Design of the Study

The essential object of this research is to trace the effects in mature individuals of prenatal exposure to famine. About 40,000 individuals were exposed to the hunger winter during gestation. The clear demarcation of the famine in time and place provided a key to identifying exposed individuals. Any individual could be classed in the group exposed to famine prenatally if he was born within a given calendar period in the famine-stricken areas. This calendar period could be determined from the known duration of the famine and the normal duration of pregnancy, taken together. By the same token, all those born outside these limits of time and place could be classed as unexposed.

The research task, reduced to its elements, is to isolate the relationship between the prenatal experience of famine and its manifest consequences for health and mental competence, and to throw this relationship into relief by appropriate comparisons. The developmental processes of the life stages that intervene between the prenatal experience and adult manifestations are many and various. These processes can have a profound influence on the manifestations under study and on the chances of detecting them within the given research design. For the sake of clarity, we shall present a simplified model that for the moment ignores the intervening processes. The core of the problem can be set out in a fourfold table familiar to epidemiologists:

		manifestation		
		+	−	
exposure	+	a	b	a + b
(famine)	−	c	d	c + d
		a + c	b + d	

THE DESIGN OF THE STUDY

The letters a, b, c, d represent the numbers of individuals falling into each cell. The question of whether, in this table, exposure to famine is associated with an excess of some manifestation can be approached in two ways, each arrived at by a different research design. In the case-control design one begins with a manifestation and selects an appropriate comparison group without the manifestation. One would then seek to discover whether the proportion exposed to the famine in those with the manifestation (that is, $\frac{a}{a+c}$) significantly exceeds the proportion exposed to famine in a comparison group without the manifestation (that is, $\frac{b}{b+d}$). While this strategy is parsimonious and often efficient, from our point of view its limitations were serious. We found no easy way of identifying sufficiently large numbers with the manifestations of central interest (mild mental retardation, or depressed IQ) who were in the right age group. Second, if we had found a ready source of cases, to choose controls who were truly comparable would have been an uncertain and laborious undertaking. Third and most important, the method provides no means of relating either cases or controls to the populations from which they were drawn. It seemed to us that if the processes of biological and social selection by which surviving adults entered the study population were not thoroughly understood, unknown bias in mortality and selective survival might seriously distort the outcome and lead to misinterpretation.

These reasons led us to choose the alternative cohort design. The design is superior in theory, since the starting population from which those with the manifestations of interest are drawn is known. In practice, the design may be less satisfactory; often years of laborious, prospective observation are required. For our purposes, the design promised advantages in practice as well as in theory. The cohort design begins with a study group which has experienced the hypothetical causal factor; the proportion among them which develops the manifestation of interest is then identified, that is, a/a+b. Another group, which has not experienced the causal factor, is selected for comparison; among them, too, the proportion who develop the manifestation is identified (that is, $\frac{c}{c+d}$). A significant excess of the manifestation in the study group over the comparison group, an excess of $\frac{a}{a+b}$ over $\frac{c}{c+d}$, confirms the hypothesis.

It might have been possible to determine famine exposure from date and place of birth through the community population registers maintained throughout the Netherlands, and to follow up each individual exposed. Yet to use the cohort design on a group thus identified, followed, and individually evaluated had limitations as serious as the case-control design. The only manifestations it would have been feasible to study in this manner were such continuous variables as IQ and height. No sample large enough could have been convened to study pathological conditions and mortality. Pathology and early death are of low frequency; a condition such as severe mental retardation requires populations in the tens of thousands to detect significant differences between groups. Even with more common conditions, such as mild mental retardation, the samples required for follow-up studies that must include clinical evaluation are unmanageably large.

The strategy we adopted aimed to avoid follow-up work that was bound to prove laborious and, quite likely, impractical. We searched among the institutions of the Netherlands for completed and stored data sets that could serve as epidemiological check points in the life cycle of all the affected individuals. The criteria for these checkpoints were three: (1) The members of the cohort at risk who passed through the checkpoint had been systematically rated in terms of an outcome variable of interest to the study. (2) Date of birth was recorded for each individual. (3) Place of birth was recorded for each individual.

Given date and place of birth, we could assign individuals to exposed and unexposed groups. By far the best checkpoint proved to be military induction procedures of males at age 18. We were fortunate to obtain the cooperation of the Dutch military authorities who agreed to make available to us information, already coded and transferred to computer tapes, on all Dutch men born in the years 1944 to 1946 and seen at induction centers. They also made available, upon request, raw data for selected cases stored on microfilm.

As noted above, the identifying attributes of date and place of birth entered into the basic design of the study. These attributes identified both those cohorts exposed to the famine prenatally, and those that were not so exposed and selected for comparison. We decided to use two forms of comparison: One form was a time comparison, and it compared exposed cohorts with cohorts whose gestation either preceded or followed the famine; the other was a place comparison, and it compared exposed cohorts with those born at the same time, but in unaffected areas.

No single comparison group could yield unimpeachable control. A before-and-after comparison has the virtue of comparing populations having the same origin, background, and place of residence. It has the weakness of leaving uncontrolled historical change through the period of study that could influence the postulated outcomes of the exposure to famine. A cross-sectional place comparison controls possible confounding by historical change; this design leaves uncontrolled differences between areas that might influence the postulated outcomes of exposure to famine. Thus with both time and place controls the strengths and weaknessess of one can complement those of the other.

The elements of the time control in the design are shown in Figure 8.1. Each horizontal bar represents a cohort of births from a one-month period; the beginning of the bar represents the month of conception; the end of the bar, the month of birth. The dates of conception are inferred from dates of birth. The average error in these estimates is bound to be small because the average reduction in the duration of gestation during the famine was about four days.

The monthly birth cohorts were grouped into large cohorts of unequal size by the criterion of stage of gestation in relation to famine exposure. These cohorts are defined below.

THE DESIGN OF THE STUDY

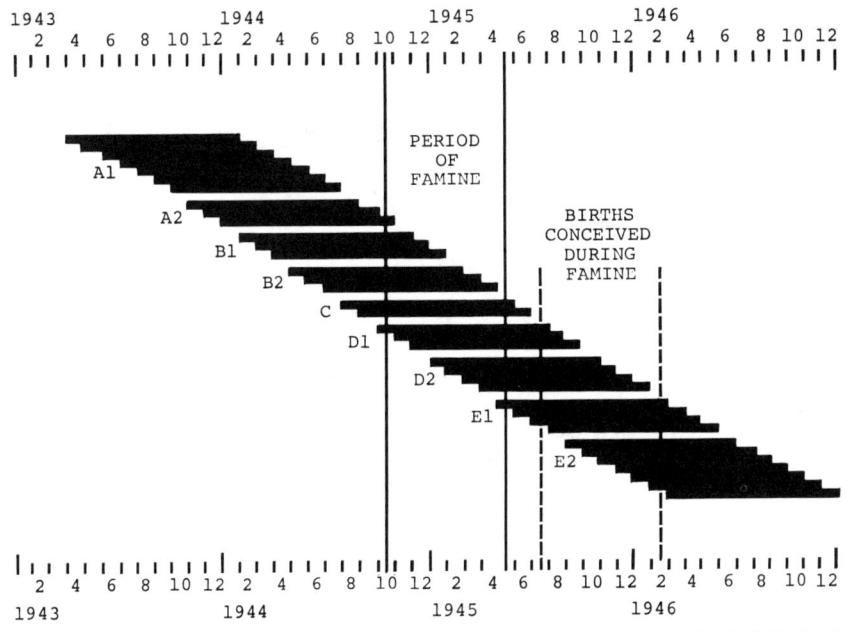

Figure 8.1. Design of study. Cohorts by month of conception and month of birth, in the Netherlands, 1943 through 1946, related to famine exposure. Solid vertical lines bracket the period of famine, and broken vertical lines bracket the period of births conceived during famine.

A1 (births from January through July 1944) and A2 (births from August through October 1944) were *conceived* and *born* before the famine.

B1 (births from November 1944 through January 1945) and B2 (births from February through April 1945) were *conceived* before the famine and *born* during the famine; B1 was exposed to famine for the third trimester of gestation only, and B2 was exposed for the second trimester as well as the third.

C (births from May through June 1945) was *conceived* before and *born* after the famine. C was exposed to famine during the middle six months of gestation.

D1 (births from July through September 1945) and D2 (births from October 1945 through January 1946) were *conceived* during the famine and *born* after it; D1 was exposed to famine during the first and second trimester of gestation, and D2 was exposed only during the first.

E1 (births from February through May 1946) and E2 (births between June through December 1946) were *conceived* and *born* after the famine and never exposed.

In theory, early postnatal exposure to famine could also be examined by comparisons of the A1 and A2 cohorts with the cohorts of the postwar period and unaffected areas as controls. In practice, it turned out that infant diets were usually maintained at an adequate level (see Chapter 7, p. 51).

Figure 8.2. The Netherlands

The elements of the geographic control are shown in Figure 8.2. This figure, a map of the Netherlands, depicts the famine-stricken area, and the location and size of the cities selected for study. The famine affected the large cities of Western Holland. As noted in Chapter 2, the people in the small towns and rural areas were better off because they lived within reach of food producing areas. We therefore confined our comparisons to cities defined by a census grouping of populations greater than 40,000 in 1944. In the famine area 6 such cities* are

---

*The seventh and smallest city in the famine area that was eligible by the population criterion, Delft, has been omitted from the main study reported here because we failed to obtain certain necessary data from that city.

included in our analyses. They are Amsterdam, The Hague, Haarlem, Leiden, Rotterdam, and Utrecht. In the unaffected areas we included 10 cities, * 5 from the North (Groningen, Leeuwaarden, Zwolle, Enschede, and Hengelo) and 5 from the South (Breda, Tilburg, Eindhoven, Heerlen, and Maastricht).

The structure of the time comparisons in terms of cohorts and of the place comparisons are maintained throughout the analysis of all the sets of data used in the study with one exception. The exception is the set of data on hospital maternities, which was drawn from teaching hospitals in 5 cities, 3 in the famine area, 1 in the North, and 1 in the South.

Military Induction

In the Dutch military draft system at the time of our study the names of all men, when they reached the age or 18, were sent forward from the population registers kept by each community to the military authorities. With the exception of a few statutory exemptions, amounting to about 3% of men in each age group, every man was called up for a medical and psychological examination in his nineteenth year. Men institutionalized for mental disorder or other handicaps did not have to appear in person, but they too were entered into the military record. Each institution with a resident population was required to notify the military authorities about the health and mental status of male inmates of requisite age and to provide documented support for the clinical opinions and diagnoses proffered.

The draft board examinations took place in one of seven centers. The medical examinations were conducted (as we observed) by doctors in a uniform manner that included a symptom inventory. The psychological tests were carried out by trained personnel under the guidance of psychologists. Procedures for the induction examination were set out in a special manual. Each record was reviewed by the medical officer in command of the induction center, who made the final decisions on the coding of the medical conditions elicited and on the category of fitness for service.

The records were stored on magnetic tape for processing by computer. To preserve confidentiality, records were assigned serial numbers and names were not used. In addition to date and place of birth, demographic items on the computer-stored record of the individual included duration and level of education, subject's occupation, and father's occupation at the time of induction.

The record of each individual contains details of the induction examination in respect of psychological and educational tests, of physical attributes, and of clinical status. Among the psychological and educational tests are the Raven Progressive Matrices Test (a standardized IQ test used in many Western countries), tests of language and arithmetic ability, and tests of clerical and mechani-

---

*Arnhem and Nijmegen were excluded because at the time of the famine they were disrupted by battle (see Chapter 7).

cal aptitude. The record of each medical examination was coded in three ways. First, diseases or impairments were coded by the International Classification of Diseases.* Second, a rating was made for each of 7 entities, described as ABOHZIS:

A. general condition and body build (*lichaamsbouw*)

B. upper extremities (*bovenste extremiteiten*)

O. lower extremities and back (*onderste extremiteiten, wervelkolom en rug beweeglijkheid*)

H. hearing (*oren*)

Z. vision (*visus*)

I. mental state (*intellect*)

S. social adjustment (*sociaal*)

Third, specific attributes such as height and weight were recorded. Further details are given in the notes at the end of this chapter.

Validation Study

The validity of the design so far outlined depends in part on the completeness with which military induction covers the entire male population of the relevant birth cohorts. Loopholes could introduce a systematic bias into the study population. Bias would follow if there were selective loss of individuals from certain areas or religious and social groups. We therefore undertook to validate the study in regard to such potential bias. Two thousand records of births were extracted in an unbiased sample from each of the population registers of the affected city of Amsterdam, and of the unaffected city of Tilburg in the South. We then tried to trace from birth to age 18 through the record systems of military induction, death registration, and emigration, all of the 2000 names of males thus extracted.

The Dutch system for collecting vital statistics is founded on population registers kept by local communities. These registers are a consequence of Napoleon's conquests and administration. The registers maintain local statistics autonomously, and supply selected material to the Central Bureau of Statistics for central compilation and analysis of national statistics. At the birth of a child, information is entered in the local register about the names of the child and his parents, place of birth and place of residence of the parents, the number of siblings, and the occupation of the father and mother. From the birth register is generated a so-called "personnel" card which follows the individual from town to town throughout his life. Whenever the individual changes addresses, a copy of the original personnel card is kept in the town thus left; this record makes the

---

*For the coding of military data the Dutch used the 1948 version of the ICD (International Classification of Diseases) (World Health Organization, 1948). Causes of deaths recorded by the Central Bureau of Statistics used the ICD 1938 version (World Health Organization, 1938) for the coding of deaths up to and including 1950, after which year the 1948 version was used for deaths.

tracing of any person possible, once a dwelling place, at any one time of life, is known. As well as the names and dates of all past places of residence, the individual personnel card contains information on three generations. This includes the names of parents and children, and their marital status, occupation and religion, and date of death.

In the validation sample deaths accounted for 3% of the total on the birth register, emigration for 2%, and exemption from the induction process for a further 3%. The military record was successfully matched with the local register for 85%; in a further 4% of births we were informed by the military authorities that military records existed, but deficiencies or errors in one or other record did not allow us to claim a certain match. We could thus satisfy ourselves that 97% in all of the 2000 male births that we followed either appeared in the induction records or had died, had emigrated, or had been exempted. The remaining 3% for whom we could not account came in equal proportions from the 2 cities and from the birth cohorts studied.

Developmental Process

We now turn to data that relates to the developmental processes intervening between the point of entry to the study, at conception, and the point of evaluation, at induction. These data cover three aspects: fertility, maternity and birth, and death.

In prospective cohort studies where the investigator observes the aging process (while he himself ages), the acquisition of data on each phase of development is a natural benefit of the method. Yet only a small proportion of such studies have exploited the analytic possibilities of linking more than one developmental phase with a later phase. The main obstacle to extracting the potential advantage of such analysis has probably been their conceptual, logical, and technical complexity. In retrospective cohort studies, the collection of data necessary to extend the observations to earlier developmental phases is likely to be a difficult undertaking. Much depends on the chance preservation of relevant sets of records. Hence, it is not surprising that to extend retrospective studies back to earlier developmental phases is a rare procedure, if indeed it is not unique to our study. The data bearing on the several stages of the life course were linked by various statistical techniques.

When we came to consider the culminating effects of famine among cohorts which had reached their adult endpoint, the backward extension of our study enabled us to take account of the antecedent effects of famine at early stages of the life course. To add this accounting served two purposes. One purpose was to incorporate a view of famine effects in terms of a continuous developmental process that begins at conception and ends in young manhood. Another purpose was to secure our interpretations of famine effects among men at induction against bias created by famine effects during early development. Some of the ways in which the impact of famine in early stages of development might have obscured or distorted the residual impact in men at induction will become apparent as the study unfolds.

Another purpose of backward extension to early developmental phases was no less important to the research design. Many observational studies of the effects of a specified historical experience are at a loss for the means to demonstrate the actual exposure of the study population to the experience. A drug may be prescribed and a program for health care may be funded and set up, but in either instance the prescribed treatments may not be delivered to the subjects in whom their postulated effects will be studied. Patients often do not comply with advice, and health organizations often do not do what they suppose they do. Our documentation of effects of the famine that were evident at the time of the famine or soon after is also a documentation of the reality of the famine experience for the exposed populations. Unequivocal famine effects at the time of the famine leave no doubt that the severity of the experience was of an order sufficient to test the initial hypotheses of the study.

Fertility

A requirement of the birth cohort design is that the numbers that comprise the cohorts at the outset are known. These numbers provide the denominators essential to calculating accurate rates of the outcomes under study. It will be evident that owing to the completeness of their coverage, the induction records could be used as an estimate of births at various times and places. Yet these estimates referred only to males, and there was the possibility of bias in the induction records for other reasons. The estimate of births could have been distorted by differing patterns of mortality among cohorts. Such distortion could have been minimized by supplementing the military records with records of death and migration. Unfortunately, the centralized death record of the Central Bureau of Statistics did not include place of birth, and the central records of emigration were also not maintained in a form that could serve our purposes. For these reasons, we had to turn to each local register at the 16 study cities to ensure that our estimates of the numbers of births in each cohort was unbiased. A simple numerical count of numbers born (live and stillborn) by month and by sex was carried out for the period 1944-46 in the study cities (see Appendix).

Our earlier estimates of births based on survivors at induction turned out to be trustworthy in practice and have been used for certain purposes.*

---

*For Rotterdam in the famine area and Hengelo in the North we could not obtain a count of births for the last 18 months of the war and estimates from the inducted population were substituted.

Maternities

The hypothesis that prenatal malnutrition depresses mental competence interposes, by analogy with animal studies, retarded intrauterine growth as an intervening process through which the nutritional effect is mediated. Low birthweight serves as an indicator of retarded fetal growth, and the stimulus which led us to conceive of the bitter experience of the Dutch famine as an experiment of opportunity was C. A. Smith's seminal report of lowered birthweight as a result of prenatal famine experience. In an undertaking of this scale, however, we deemed it unwise to take for granted the effect of prenatal famine exposure in retarding fetal growth, since it was crucial to the hypothesis.

We chose to confirm and extend the earlier reports in three aspects. First, we sought to test the finding of fetal growth retardation by replicating it in a number of famine-stricken cities. Second, we sought to complement the rigor of the before-and-after time control used in previous studies with cross-sectional geographic controls from areas unaffected by the famine. Third, we sought to measure other dimensions of fetal growth than birthweight alone, and so to achieve a fuller perspective of the nature of the growth process.

Records of maternities and of the characteristics of infants at birth could not be obtained from any central source. For this purpose, we resorted to such teaching hospitals as we could locate which had kept systematic and detailed records through the famine period in a form accessible 25 years later. Hospitals which satisifed these conditions in varying degree were found in Amsterdam, Leiden, and Rotterdam in the famine area, in Groningen in the Northern control area, and in Heerlen in the Southern control area.*

These data suffer from a problem of unrepresentativeness besides the fact that they represent only 5 of the 16 study cities; at that time, more than half the births took place outside the hospitals. This source of bias is potentially serious, since hospital births may have been selected by social and biological attributes that could influence the manifestations we hoped to study. The bias is to some extent controlled by analyses within each hospital population over the relevant time period. Control of the bias relies in part on the fact that, as far as we could discover, none of the hospitals changed their admission procedures during the time of the study and there is no reason to suspect a change in the nature of the populations they served during the study period. The social attributes of the patients admitted are reported to be quite different for each hospital in the famine area; consistency of results across these hospitals therefore can provide a

---

*In Leiden, Groningen, and Heerlen records of consecutive births were abstracted. For the sake of economy, in Amsterdam and Rotterdam where numbers were large, alternate pages of the records were abstracted. In these cities a complete abstract of the records was made only for those months in which fertility was low (the D2 cohort).

protection against the presence of bias due to social selection. Further details of these data are given in Chapter 10.

A limitation of the design with regard to maternities is that no link could be made between the records of *individuals* at military induction and at birth. The limitation applies much less, however, to the link between *cohorts* at induction and at birth, because average values of the attributes of each birth cohort at different life stages could be calculated and related to each other without risking the ecological fallacy (Robinson, 1950).

Deaths

High death rates are associated with some of the attributes and states of health that comprise the dependent variables in this study. We have already indicated that for this reason an excess of deaths among those exposed to the famine might be capable of changing the distribution of these attributes among survivors. A large enough change could distort comparisons with cohorts not exposed to famine. To check this possibility the compilation of a full record of deaths among the cohorts under study was required. This record would enable us also to examine a question important in its own right, if subsidiary to the main hypotheses of the study—namely, the influence of prenatal exposure to famine on subsequent survival. Low birthweight has a strong association with perinatal mortality. The famine provides a test of whether prenatal maternal nutrition could be an antecedent causal factor in this association.

Few of those who died outside the 16 study cities were in fact born in one of those cities; all such cases were included in our death record. A larger number who died within the study cities were born outside the cities; all such cases were excluded from our death record. The laborious process of linking the central and local records to obtain this information was carried out for all those dying over the age of 1 year, but on only 10% of the much greater number of deaths in infancy.*

Food Rations

In this study the postulated causal factor is prenatal nutritional deprivation due to maternal exposure to famine. The design outlined so far treats the famine as a single global factor, a dichotomous variable that distinguishes qualitatively between those exposed or unexposed. Individuals or cohorts can be classed in these two categories only. This dichotomy is not an entirely true reflection of experience in the Dutch famine. On the one hand, the famine was not equally severe at all times but increased in intensity as the months passed. On the other

---

*The number of infant deaths amounted to 15,000 from which a sample of 1500 was drawn. The number of later deaths, at one to 18 years, amounted to 6000. The linking of central records was carried out by the staff of the Nijmegen Institute of Social Medicine.

THE DESIGN OF THE STUDY

hand, the control areas were not always supplied with adequate food; they too experienced periods of hunger if not of starvation.

The use of this dichotomy also places restrictions on the study that are general to all dichotomous variables. The limited number of categories makes some techniques cumbersome and reduces their power; other techniques cannot be used at all. This applies particularly to multivariate correlation methods. If we were to fulfil our intention of exploring the interrelated effects of several variables at succeeding stages of the life cycle, these methods were likely to be our most powerful analytic instruments.

For these reasons, we paid special attention to the problem of quantifying the famine experience. Quantification would allow us to convert the postulated causal variable into a variable of continuous values, with the number of intervals determined by the range of the experience. We were able to accomplish this conversion by resort to the weekly announcements of official food rations published in every locality of the country throughout the period of gestation of the birth cohorts chosen for study.

As a quantified index of the independent study variable we averaged the official daily food ration over each month separately by each of the three regions (the values are given in the Appendix). The rationed amount of protein, fats, and carbohydrates, as well as their combined values converted into Calories, were highly correlated over the period of the famine. Hence any one measure serves well for all. Calories is the measure presented.

The independent study variable based on food rations was refined by creating separate variables, one each for the rations assigned during first, second, and third trimesters of pregnancy. The three variables were derived by relating each trimester of gestation of each monthly birth cohort to the average level of rations distributed during the relevant period.* These conversions into quantitative terms facilitated the use of a battery of statistical methods, in particular correlation matrices, partial correlations, regression coefficients, multiple regression analysis, and path analysis. By these means we could express a complex set of results and test them in many different ways.

Summary

The research task was to isolate the effect of prenatal famine experience on mental competence and health. The research design adopted to accomplish this

---

*Full term gestation is necessarily assumed in defining food intake during each trimester. The calendar month of birth was numbered 10, the preceding month 9, the one before 8, and so on, until 1 was the month of last menstrual period. Then

$C_1 = (1 + 2 + 3) \div 3$
$C_2 = (4 + 5 + 6) \div 3$
$C_3 = (7 + 8 + 9) \div 3$

Thus the calendar month of birth is not included in these indices.

task was of the historical or retrospective cohort type. That is, a population defined by a given point of entry was selected for study only after the period of observation required to cover the relevant stages of the life course had ended. In this instance, investigation was executed over the years 1969 to 1973. Entry of the cohorts to the study was at birth over the three years 1944 to 1946.

The strength of this design was enhanced by four particular features. First, the entry cohorts covered by the central body of data were complete populations and not samples, and these populations remained almost fully accounted for from birth to the endpoint at examination for induction. In a validating sample only 3% of 2000 births from two cities were finally considered untraced from birth through emigration, military induction, and death. The core data were culled from the information collected at the military induction examination and coded and stored on magnetic computer tape. Other major data sources included national and local registers of births, emigration, and deaths that covered the complete study population, and less representative records on maternities from five teaching hospitals.

Second, the comparisons of the cohorts exposed to famine prenatally with cohorts that escaped the famine were made doubly rigorous. Two concurrent controls that complemented each other were used: a before-and-after time control and a cross-sectional place control. To set up these two types of control, study and comparison populations were assigned by date of birth and place of birth. Thus a prerequisite for all sets of data used in the study was that date and place of birth were either recorded or could be established by other means.

Third, in interpreting comparisons of effects of famine among cohorts who had reached their adult endpoint, account was taken of the impact of the famine on intervening stages of the life course. These backward extensions of the study served to provide a view of the impact of famine in terms of a developmental process that began at conception and culminated in manhood. They served also to ensure that our observations in young men were not obscured or biased by the effect of the famine on what had gone before. Finally, the backward extensions served to document that the reality and severity of the famine experience were sufficient for testing our initial hypotheses. For these purposes, we studied fertility, maternity and gestation, and mortality. The data bearing on each of these stages of the life course were linked and studied by techniques of multivariate analysis.

Fourth, the postulated causal factor, prenatal nutritional deprivation due to maternal exposure to famine, was expressed in quantitative form as continuous variables reflecting food rations during each trimester of gestation. The conversion facilitated the use of a battery of statistical methods. These methods enabled us to construct multivariate models that controlled many variables simultaneously and that sharpened our powers of inference about the interrelations among variables, both at the same life stages and among different life stages.

Notes

Information from Military Medical Examinations. Magnetic tapes containing precoded information from the medical examinations of more than 400,000 men in their nineteenth year, after they were called up for military induction, were obtained from the military authorities. All Dutch citizens were registered with the civil authority at their place of residence, and each male upon turning 18 was notified to the military. Residential institutions for the mentally ill and the mentally retarded made this notification for all patients who reached the induction age. A few men were examined after their nineteenth year because of temporary deferment or because they were abroad. No one was entirely exempt from call-up procedures; the 3% exempt from induction examination were clergymen, policemen, long-term prisoners, emigrants, and men who could document that 3 older brothers had been in the service.

The information recorded and coded includes social and demographic variables, biological and medical data, psychological and aptitude measures.

Psychometric Data. Over 90% of all subjects completed written tests on five separate intellectual measures yielding 6 scores: (1) Raven Progressive Matrices (completed by 94.2% of all subjects); (2) language test; (3) arithmetic ability; (4) clerical ability; (5) Test of Mechanical Comprehension; (6) combined scores on all tests. Fewer than 5% did not take any of the tests; medical reports are available for them.

The data coded on the computer tapes for the Raven Test were grouped into a six class scale. The raw scores of the military examinations are stored in The Hague in the form of microfilms. We examined the distribution of raw scores from photocopies of the microfilm records of over 2000 cases. This enabled us also to check other variables of concern. Individuals were identified only by the army serial code number to avoid any breach of confidentiality.

Demographic data. For all cases in the military induction sample, information was available for the subject's date and place of birth and religion. For 95% or more information was available on education, occupational status, and father's occupation.

Different classifications of occupation were in use in the three data sets used in the study, namely, (1) subject's occupation at military induction; (2) father's occupation at military induction; (3) father's occupation on death records. These three classifications differed in scope and structure, and it was necessary to synchronize them for coding.

The two most extensive classifications were the three digit codes of the Central Bureau of Statistics (3, above) and the three digit military code for son's occupation. The Central Bureau of Statistics code describes the various occupations listed and is useful for stratifying them socially. The military code for son's occupation puts emphasis on skills that can be used for assignment to various army jobs. The two digit military code for classifying father's occupation had deficiencies when used for classifying middle level occupations.

For purposes of our study, classifications were translated into an eleven point scale which has proved useful for international studies (Broom and Jones, 1969; Hill, 1969; Richardson and Leslie, 1970; Lopreato, 1970).

Birth, Development, and Death

9 Fertility

Little is known of the relations between nutrition and fertility in human beings. *Fertility* is the demonstrated capacity of women for reproducing. In populations, fertility is described by age-specific birth rates among women.

Fertility and fecundity are terms that overlap in common usage. We shall need to be precise in our usage in order to discuss the consequences of the famine on reproduction and population. *Fecundity* is a predisposition or latent capacity for reproducing; it is a precondition for fertility. Fecundity is an attribute of couples, but in populations, fecundity can be crudely indicated by the distribution of women in age groups potentially capable of childbearing (usually 15 to 45 years).

Preconditions for fecundity in couples include the capacity for ejaculation and insemination, ovulation, fertilization, and nidation (Ryder, 1965). The preconditions on the woman's side are summed up by the awkward term *fecundability*. The ovum is fecundable only after ovulation, the release of mature ova from the ovary. The anterior pituitary hormone, gonadotrophin, plays a part in stimulating ovulation (Fowler and Edwards, 1973). The hormonal relations between pituitary and ovary are mediated by homeostatic mechanisms; the ovarian hormones whose production is stimulated by gonadotrophin in turn inhibit the production of gonadotrophin. It is difficult to assign cause and effect among such reciprocal relationships.

Susceptibility to fertilization varies among individuals, and in the same individual at different times. The greater the number of ovular cycles a woman experiences, the greater is the likelihood of fertilization. With amenorrhea there is no ovulation and, thus, infecundability. Menstruation does not always signify fecundability; some cycles may be anovular. In addition, ovulation does not occur during pregnancy nor in the immediate postnatal period, and lactation retards the resumption of ovulation. Thus with every pregnancy from the time of conception, and to a varying degree during lactation, a woman is rendered insusceptible to pregnancy. To that extent, her total lifetime fecundability is reduced. Developmental age also affects total fecundability in that it sets absolute limits on susceptibility to pregnancy. Women become fecundable after the menarche and remain so until the menopause. Developmental age is not entirely synchronous with chronological age; hence with an early menarche and a deferred menopause, for example, there will be a long period of fecundability.

Good evidence about the effect of nutrition on reproduction in humans is hard to find (Keys, Brožek, Henschel, Mickelson, and Taylor, 1950). With regard to fecundability, its duration is shorter in the women of developing countries than in those of developed countries. The menarche occurs later, the menopause probably earlier (Kark, 1943; Burrell, Healy, and Tanner, 1961; Harrison, Weiner, Tanner, and Barnicot, 1964; Bojlen and Bentzon, 1968; World Health Organization, 1969). Malnutrition, common in such countries, may be the cause.

In Europe during the past century, there was a gradual extension of the period of fecundability (Susser and Watson, 1971). There has been progressively an earlier onset of puberty in girls and boys, and a deferred menopause among women. A likely explanation is better nutrition.*

With regard to the effect of nutrition on fertility, chronic malnutrition in populations has not been shown to be a limiting factor on fertility. Fertility rates among humans depend in the first instance on the proportion of fecundable women in the population, second on their opportunities for mating, and ultimately and overwhelmingly on social norms expressed in individual decisions about birth control and family size.

In the extreme famine situation, however, the physiological preconditions of fecundity might assume importance in fertility. Some data relating to fecundability have been reported, in World War I from blockaded European cities, in the Spanish civil war, and in World War II from concentration camps, from the Leningrad siege, and from the Dutch cities affected by the hunger winter. Women evinced amenorrhea and also, it is believed, anovular menstrual cycles (Knack and Neumann, 1917; Peraita, 1946; Valaoras, 1946; Antonov, 1947; Boerema, 1947; Holmer, 1947). Similar changes have been reported in a clinical series of 26 young Finnish women who had starved themselves in order to lose weight. Their ovarian function was reduced to menopausal level and restored to normal through treatment with gonadotrophin (Klatskin, Salter, and Humm, 1947; Keys, Brožek, Henschel, Mickelson, and Taylor, 1950).

The male contribution to fecundity may also be affected by starvation. Men released from Japanese prison camps of World War II, who had been semi-starved,

---

*The rise in fecundity has not led to a rise in fertility, for economic forces and social institutions like marriage have overriding effects on voluntary mating behavior and its consequences in fertility. Indeed, the smaller families resulting from control of fertility have probably contributed to greater fecundability through raised standards of living and better nutrition.

evinced oligospermia. In young American men who volunteered to undergo experimental starvation, sperm were fewer, less motile, and shorter lived than normal (Keys, Brožek, Henschel, Mickelson, and Taylor, 1950). While starvation depresses the function of the sex organs, the need to find food and conserve energy evidently predominates over sexual activity: men appear to lose potency, and both men and women appear to lose libido.

In the reported war-time famines, including the famine in the Netherlands, factors besides starvation depressed fertility and could have depressed fecundity. The fear of death and destitution from war accompanied the famine, and many husbands were deported to forced labor camps or worked in the underground resistance movement. The confounding of nutritional deprivation with such factors has usually been insuperable. In the Dutch famine, the confounding can be controlled to some degree, because many of the factors co-existing with the famine were not confined to the famine-stricken cities. Thus fertility at those times and places where starvation was superimposed on the other factors can be compared with fertility at those times and places affected by the other factors alone. Yet famine itself inevitably carries with it the psychological dimensions of hunger and fear of death. This factor may be controlled to some extent if groups can be found who were exposed in similar degree to these fears but in different degree to lack of food. As a possible control we aim to examine social class differences.

Fertility and Famine

Fertility is more accessible to measurement than fecundity, and we shall consider it first. Our findings confirm the earlier reports that nutritional deprivation of sufficient severity causes infertility in human populations. The numbers born each month over the period 1944-46 in each of the 16 cities included in the study (6 designated famine cities and 10 control cities) were obtained from the local population registers of the cities. We assumed constancy in the number of women in each age group, which is reasonable over the short period of the famine.

Fertility varied closely with food rations at the time of conception through most of the years 1944-46. In the famine area (Fig. 9.1A), nine months after the onset of acute starvation, a distinct fall in the number of births began. The number of births did not return to pre-famine levels until the end of the famine. Assuming normal length of gestation to estimate date of conception from date of birth, there was a small decline in the total number of births conceived in November and December 1944, a moderate decline in those conceived in January 1945, and a marked decline in those conceived from February to April 1945. In May, with relief of the famine midway through the month, the number of births conceived at that time rose at once, and by June the number was at the pre-famine level. Had the famine continued with increasing severity so that none escaped the worst, it is likely that fertility would have been reduced even more.

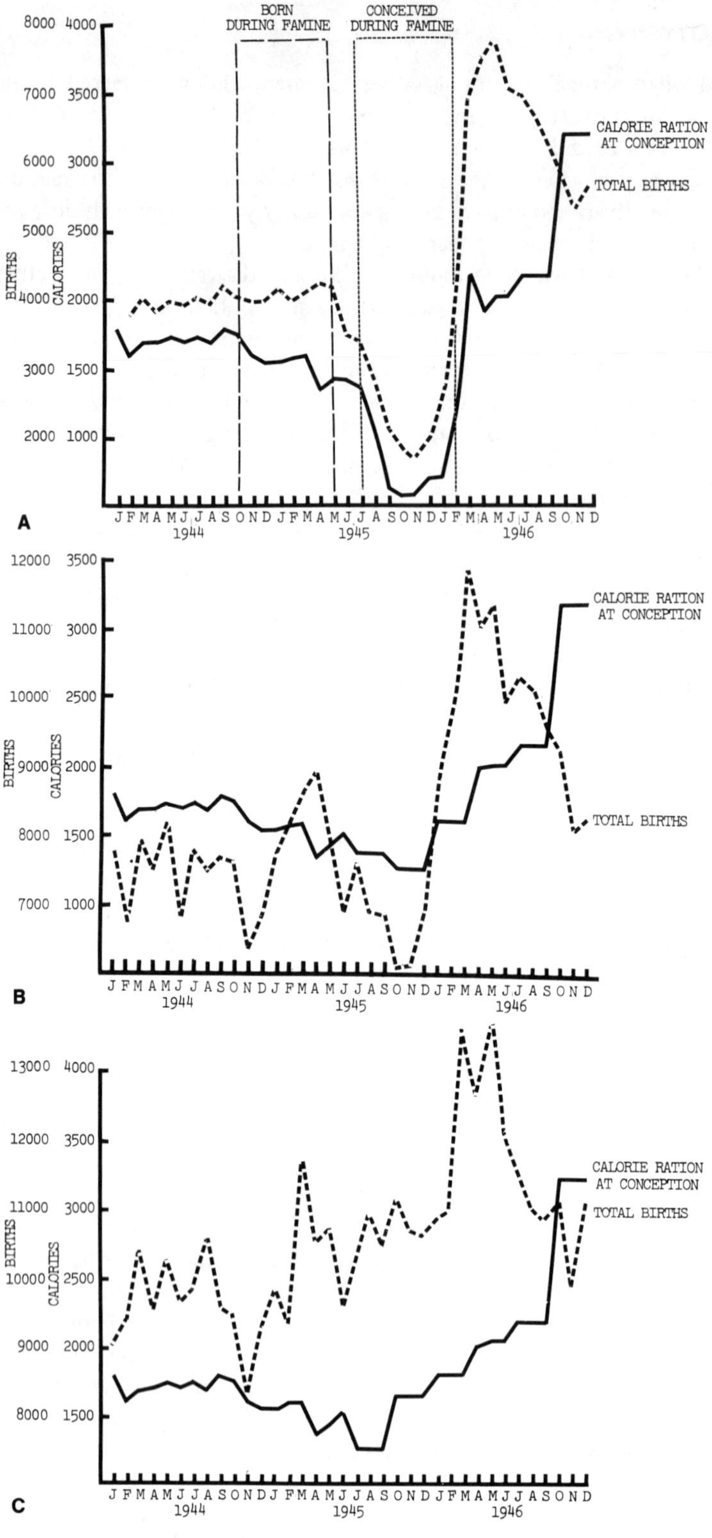
BORN
DURING FAMINE
CONCEIVED
DURING FAMINE
CALORIE RATION
AT CONCEPTION
TOTAL BIRTHS
BIRTHS
CALORIES
8000 4000
7000 3500
6000 3000
5000 2500
4000 2000
3000 1500
2000 1000
J F M A M J J A S O N D J F M A M J J A S O N D J F M A M J J A S O N D
1944
1945
1946
A
CALORIE RATION
AT CONCEPTION
TOTAL BIRTHS
BIRTHS
CALORIES
12000 3500
11000 3000
10000 2500
9000 2000
8000 1500
7000 1000
J F M A M J J A S O N D J F M A M J J A S O N D J F M A M J J A S O N D
1944
1945
1946
B
CALORIE RATION
AT CONCEPTION
TOTAL BIRTHS
BIRTHS
CALORIES
13000 4000
12000 3500
11000 3000
10000 2500
9000 2000
8000 1500
J F M A M J J A S O N D J F M A M J J A S O N D J F M A M J J A S O N D
1944
1945
1946
C

FERTILITY

In Leningrad, where famine continued for much longer, infertility became virtually total (Antonov, 1947).

Although the decline in the number of births coincided with conception at the onset of famine, a decline in the official caloric ration to below 1500 Calories per day had begun about two months before. This asynchrony of onset suggests that it took some time to exhaust nutritional reserves that maintained the fertility of couples. By contrast, recovery of fertility was immediate and sensitive to an increase of rations even at very low caloric levels, which indicates that with the provision of nutrients the preconditions of fertility, that is sexual activity and fecundity, were met at once.

In the Northern control cites (Fig. 9.1B), numbers of births each month exhibited the same sensitivity to local rations where they fell below about 1500 Calories per day. Again, there was asynchrony, with a lag of two months between the onset of a decline in rations and births and immediate recovery as rations increased. In the Southern control cities (Fig. 9.1C), numbers of births do not exhibit the same sensitivity to the level of food rations. We believe that this is because these smaller cities, many of which were already freed from the occupation, obtained food supplies additional to the ration from the surrounding countryside and the liberating armies.

The causal effect of the famine in depressing conceptions is hardly in doubt, for in control areas exposed at the same time to similar conditions of war and weather, fertility did not undergo the same changes. The strong association between fertility and the availability of food continued in the postwar period as the number of births soared. Unlike depressed fertility with famine, however, this rise in fertility cannot be attributed with any confidence to a causal effect of nutrition. During the postwar period, all three study areas experienced similar historical as well as nutritional conditions, and we have no means of identifying which of a large complex of associated factors all changing in the same direction is responsible for changes in fertility.

Collateral evidence suggests that above a minimal threshold level nutrition is not a critical factor in fertility. Indeed, the postwar rise in fertility occurred throughout the Western world, including the United States, where there had been no war-time nutritional deprivation. In the Netherlands, moreover, some of the rise in numbers of births must have been the result of a physiological rebound from the effects of the famine. Those women rendered infertile by a short-term event like the famine become susceptible to fecundation on recovery after the event, as after a period of latency. As a corollary, those few who conceived, carried a fetus, and lactated during the famine were rendered insusceptible to pregnancy after the famine ended. Thus after the famine, with recovery of the population from infecundity, a number of women greater than

---

Figure 9.1. Fertility and caloric ration (number of births and official average daily caloric ration at estimated time of conception for the period June 1944 to December 1946 inclusive in (A) famine cities, (B) Northern control cities, and (C) Southern control cities)

normal were rendered susceptible to pregnancy. Given normal sexual activity after the famine, therefore, the rise in fertility in the post-famine cohorts was a mirror image of the fall in the cohorts conceived during the famine. This rebound in number of births is plainly visible in Figure 9.1A, especially for the months February to May 1946.

The associations between fertility and food have been quantified in terms of correlation and regression coefficients. The correlation coefficient of monthly rations in the first trimester (summarized as average daily allowance of Calories) with number of births in the famine cities was $r = .76$, in the North, $r = .45$, and in the South, $r = .27$. In the famine cities the regression coefficient of number of births on caloric rations is $b = 1.79$, that is a change of 100 Calories in the ration yielded a change of 179 in number of births per month. In these cities caloric rations could account for 58% of the variance in monthly number of births. These results suggest that fertility may have been affected by nutrition only where there was marked food deprivation. A more valid set of numerical values is probably obtained from the estimates for periods when average daily rations fell below a threshold of about 1500 Calories. Below this threshold, the correlation coefficient of monthly rations as average daily Calories and number of births in the famine cities is $r = .92$. The regression coefficient indicates that a change of 100 Calories yielded a change of 241 in number of births. Caloric rations could account for 81% of the variance in monthly number of births. The three constituents of the diet—protein, fats, and carbohydrates—were closely correlated with each other. Their effects could not be separated, one from another, by statistical techniques (multiple regression analyses and partial correlations).

Fecundity and Famine

At the height of the famine, births in the affected Dutch cities were reduced to about one-third of the expected number. Was this infertility a result of changed sexual behavior, of infecundity, or of infecundability? Sexual behavior could have changed with many factors; declining libido in men and women, or unavailability of mates, or voluntary restraint and contraception among couples. On the other hand, fecundability was surely affected, although to an unknown extent. Clinicians reported amenorrhea among women subjected to famine during both world wars, including the women in the Netherlands during the hunger winter.

One way of separating the effects of sexual behavior from those of fecundity is to consider how far variations in fertility are compatible with variations in factors associated with sexual behavior on the one hand and with factors associated with fecundity or fecundability on the other. The age and parity of mothers, the size of their completed families, and their social class, are factors available in our data which we shall examine from this point of view.

Age and Parity

A number of facts point to a relation between the age and parity of women and fecundability. In the third and fourth decades of life, most physiological functions deteriorate, or at best sustain a plateau (Riley and Foner, 1968). Gonadotrophin excretion increases steadily with age and at the time of the menopause, when the pituitary is no longer inhibited by the secretion of ovarian hormones, excretion rises markedly. Parity is also involved; the menopausal rise occurs in all women but is sharpest in the nulliparous (Bulmer, 1970). Age and parity, through these associations with the hormonal influences on ovulation, are presumably also associated with changes in fecundability, and hence may influence it. Animal experiments also suggest that parity is a factor in fecundability; in mice, rats, and pigs of the same age, both ovulation and litter size increased with parity.

Some reports of depressed fecundability in countries whose food supplies were blockaded during World War I seem to support these suppositions, although data are meager. Under the blockade in Germany and Sweden, clinicians most frequently reported amenorrhea among nulliparous women in their twenties. In Sweden, the nulliparous women of the cohort in which frequent amenorrhea was reported also later seemed to have fewer births than expected (Nilsson, 1920; Sanders, 1934; Hytten and Leitch, 1971b).

During famine, it seems reasonable to assume that the least fecund women would have least reserve and be most susceptible to loss of fecundability. It would follow that fertility should be diminished most at the least fecund ages and parities, and that the births that did occur should be concentrated at the most fecund ages and parities. Thus, should the famine in the Netherlands have caused changes in the distribution of births by age and parity, the changes should point to the age and parity pattern of fecundity, and perhaps of its prerequisite, fecundability. Changes in distribution of births by age and parity could also point to changes in fertility brought about by the mating behavior of couples, since age and parity undoubtedly affect this behavior. There seems less reason to suppose that voluntary changes in mating behavior during the famine would be particular to age and parity groups, and good reason to suppose that any involuntary changes in fertility particular to parity groups would relate to the mother—in other words, to fecundability. Age changes might relate equally well to either spouse.

In pursuit of evidence that famine had particular age or parity effects, the records of women who gave birth at the maternity hospitals of three famine cities (Amsterdam, Leiden, and Rotterdam) and two control cities (Groningen and Heerlen) have been examined (Table 9.1). The cohort in which the number of births fell to the lowest level (D2 in the famine area, conceived at the height of the famine) shows slight famine effects on age and parity. Thus, in the famine cities but not elsewhere, the D2 cohort has the lowest mean age and the lowest percentages of births at ages above 30 years. In this cohort also, mean parity is lowest and births at high parity are fewest, again only in the famine area.

Since age and parity are highly correlated, we tried to separate effects of age and parity among mothers in each birth cohort. These data show no famine effect on the distribution of conceptions by mothers' age when parity is held constant. When age is held constant, there is a suggestion of a weak famine effect on the distribution of conceptions by parity; the proportion of births at parities five and over in the D2 cohort is reduced.

Numbers are rather small for the purpose and the analysis lacks power. In the military records, where numbers are large, maternal age was not recorded but birth order was recorded. Birth order represents the mother's parity transferred to her child. Although parity is highly correlated with maternal age, the analysis of maternities above suggests that variation of fertility with parity in these data is more likely attributable to parity than to maternal age.

In the cohort most affected by the decline in fertility (D2), a relative increase over earlier and later cohorts is seen in the proportion of first born in the famine area as compared with control areas (Table 9.2). Women of parity 5 and more are not under-represented as they were in the hospital data. Thus from the military data we can only say that women having their first child were less affected by the decline in fertility than were multiparous women. While aware of the strain on evidence, we infer that the famine selectively reduced fecundity, and probably fecundability, of higher parity women; this reduction may be an indicator of fecundability in general.

Despite this postulated lower level of fecundability among high parity women, upon recovery after the latent infertile period of the famine they can be supposed to have been relatively more susceptible to pregnancy as a population than those groups that conceived during the famine. As noted above, conceptions during the famine would have rendered a larger proportion of the less affected age and parity groups insusceptible to pregnancy after the famine. This rebound phenomenon leads us to expect a decline in the relative proportion of first births in the immediate post-famine cohort of the famine areas, and this is demonstrated in Table 9.2.

Size of family is a direct outcome of fertility and is largely a measure of social behavior. Yet since fecundability is a precondition for such behavior, it is possible that the most fertile women are also the most fecundable. Such women, mothers of large families, might for that reason have sustained a relatively high level of fecundability during the famine. With few exceptions, men inducted at 19 years of age belong to completed families, and an analysis of the military induction data is not subject to the problems introduced by incomplete families. To examine this hypothesis, therefore, the men registered for military induction were compared by size of family and by date and place of birth. Table 9.2 shows no changes in mean family sizes specific to cohorts most affected by the decline

FERTILITY 79

in fertility during the famine. In terms of our data, therefore, variations in fecundability cannot be inferred from its secondary effects on family size.

Social Class

Social class is a determinant of nutrition through its influence on dietary habits and access to food. Social class is equally a determinant of fertility through its influence on mating behavior. If the famine influenced fecundity and fertility, therefore, social class might have modified this influence. Social classes might have differed either in their experiences of famine because of the use of food and access to it, or in host response to famine in terms of sexual behavior, or both.

Figure 9.2 shows that social class was a more powerful predictor of changes in fertility during the famine than any of the other factors that have been discussed. The higher the occupational category of the father, the more likely was the couple to retain fertility during the famine. The most readily available measure of social class was the occupation of the father at the time of military induction. Inferences about fertility that rely solely on this source could be rendered unreliable by social mobility in the years subsequent to the famine. Occupation of father at the time of birth of the son, rather than 19 years later, provides a check on the effect of such mobility. We have this information on the substantial sub-sample of the validation study drawn from the local population registers; the sample comprised 2000 births in Amsterdam and 2000 in Tilburg, of both sexes. This independent source replicates the result in the military induction data.

Infertility in the famine cities was by no means confined to families in the lower social classes. All social classes suffered a sharp decline in births and the timing of the decline in fertility was concurrent in all social classes (Fig. 9.2A). In all classes the decline in birth indicated a decline in conceptions that began gradually in November 1944, and reached a low point in February 1945. This fall was steepest among the lowest social classes. In all classes, the numbers of births indicate that a slight recovery in number of conceptions began in April, and grew marked in May.* This early rise was steeper among the higher social classes. After liberation, in May and June, there was a much steeper rise in conceptions. This post-famine rise, like the fall during the famine, was steeper among the lower classes.

Our data indicate the known minimum of women whose fecundability was unaffected by famine. They show that the percentage of such women was larger in the higher than in the lower social classes, and remained so throughout the

---

*That these social class differences are not likely to be accounted for by seasonal effects is apparent from Figure 9.2.

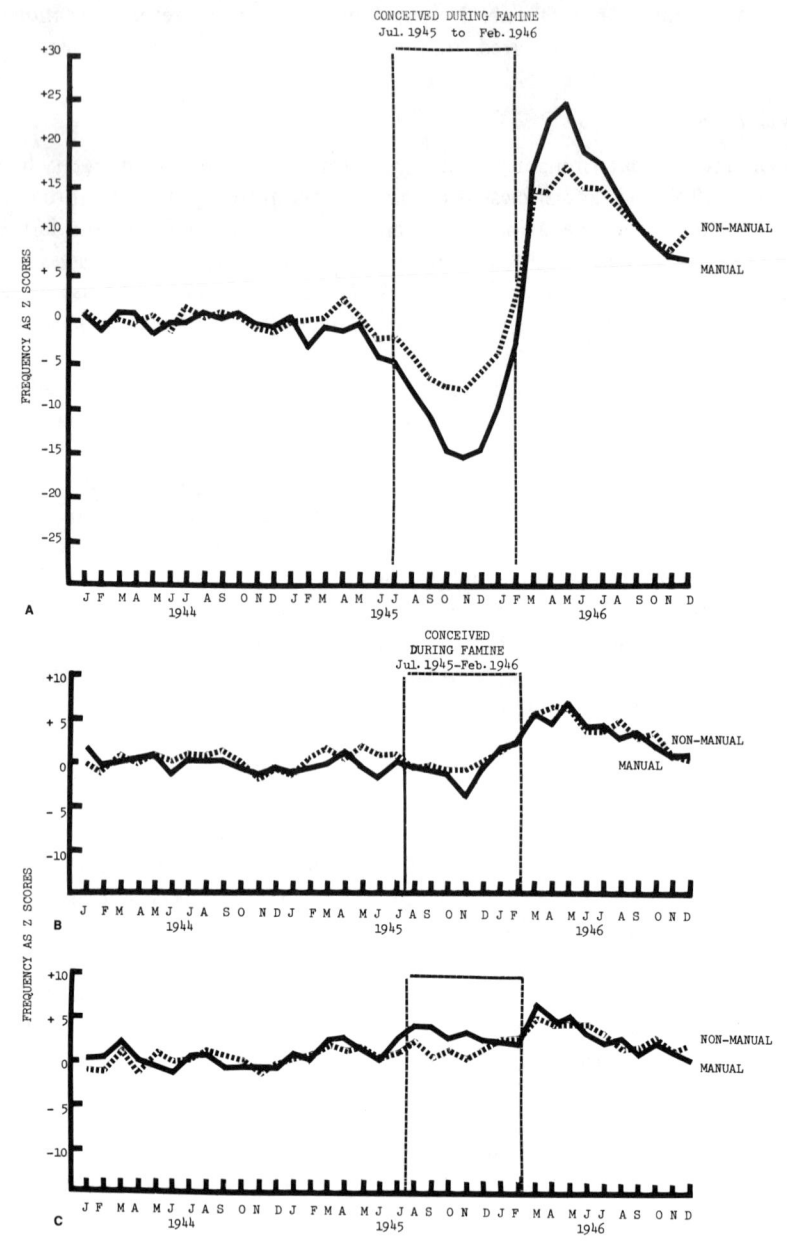

Figure 9.2. Fertility and social class (frequency of births, expressed as Z scores based on the number of male survivors at age 19 by social class according to father's occupation for the period January 1944 to December 1946 inclusive, in (A) famine cities, (B) Northern cities, and (C) Southern cities. Means and SD's for Z scores are based on births from January 1944 to December 1944).

famine. We weighed three interpretations of the differences in fertility between the social classes during the famine:

1. voluntary control of fertility;
2. physiological resistance to infecundity; and
3. access to food.

We cannot distinguish between these three interpretations with certainty.* The first seems least likely, the third most likely.

1. The social controls (sexual taboos, age at marriage, contraception, abortion) that differentiated the fertility of the classes before and after the famine might have been reversed during the famine, so that the upper classes relaxed their control of fertility, or the lower classes increased theirs.

This explanation is rendered unlikely because it requires a reversal of the usual pattern of fertility control among the social classes. Studies of family planning and sex behavior show that among the generations involved, higher social classes normally exercised stricter and more conscious controls on reproduction than the lower classes. In line with this behavior, many studies of class values have described an upper and middle class orientation toward deferring gratification for the sake of future reward, and a lower class orientation, in the absence of such anticipation, toward accepting the gratifications of the present (cf. Susser and Watson, 1971). Yet during the famine, in a time of great uncertainty when controls on fertility might be expected to have been all the stricter among the majority of the higher classes, there was a relatively greater decline in lower class births.

2. At the onset of the famine the higher social classes may have been in better health, and in particular better nourished, than the lower classes. This advantage might have sustained relative fecundity in the upper classes in the face of the famine. This explanation runs counter to some reasonable assumptions. If physiological resistance were crucial, we would expect that the onset of a decline in fertility would be delayed among the higher social classes and that persisting famine would eventually exhaust the bodily resources of all including the higher social classes and cause the rates of fertility of all classes to converge. The onset of infertility was simultaneous in all social classes, as we have seen, and convergence of fertility rates did not occur. The low ration levels of the worst famine period continued for at least 4 months. During these months, the fertility rates of each social class persisted at a low level, but the gap between them widened.

3. Those who obtained more food would have been protected against the most severe effects of starvation on fecundity. During the famine the higher

*Another explanation, that men of different classes were absent in different proportions, seems unlikely, although we have no data to indicate whether or not this is a valid explanation. Whatever the correct interpretation, our findings lend no support to the idea that the lowest classes are more fecund than others and thereby maintain the frequency of mild mental retardation in the population (Penrose, 1939).

social classes, having resources in money, property, and influence, may have obtained more food than the lower social classes. This explanation has most to commend it. The lower classes were worst hit by the famine in many respects. During the famine the lower classes suffered a disproportionate increase in deaths, and clinical signs of malnutrition were most common in the poorer sections of the cities (Burger, Drummond, and Sandstead, 1948). This third explanation of the social class differences in fertility during the famine emphasizes the effects of current nutritional state on fecundity.

Our analysis of birth order by social class provides evidence of an effect on fecundity. In the cohorts showing a decline in fertility, the excess of first births was most marked in the manual classes, and was not evident among the non-manual classes. This rise in the proportion of first born could be the complement of a decline in the proportion of later born, a change that could follow from poorly sustained fecundability among lower class women of high parity. Like the miner's canaries once used to detect noxious gases, their sensitivity could have signalled the special food deprivation of the lower classes.

We may now summarize our inferences about fecundity. On the basis of the changes in distribution of conceptions during the famine by mother's age and parity and father's social class, we infer that the famine probably did affect fecundity. One or more of the several preconditions for fecundity may be involved.

One precondition, nidation of the fertilized ovum, can probably be ruled out as a major cause of the infecundity for two reasons. The first reason is that if exposure to famine prevented effective nidation and resulted in abortion, the timing of the rise in births in relation to the restoration of adequate diet should be different. The end of the famine was an abrupt transition; the number of births nine months later indicates virtually no lag in the rise of conceptions when rations were restored. A nutritional effect acting at the time of nidation—say, during the first eight weeks of gestation, when abortions are most frequent— would require a shorter interval before the effect became apparent in a change in the number of births.

The second reason which inclines us to rule out nidation as a cause of infecundity during the famine is based on an examination of sex ratio among live births in affected cohorts. We detected no consistent changes in the sex ratio among live births. Most writers have assumed that there is a regular excess of male over female conceptions that diminishes during gestation, that is, there is a disproportionate loss of males between conception and full term live births (Stevenson, 1962).* Most also suggest that the presumed male excess diminishes more rapidly under harsh conditions than in good conditions, presumably because of an increased rate of male abortions (Teitelbaum and Mantel, 1971). Any effect of famine on nidation might thus be expected to reduce the proportion of males in affected birth cohorts, and this did not occur.

*Carr (1965), however, did not find consistent support for a male excess among spontaneous abortions.

Interpretations

Several propositions follow from acceptance of the hypothesis that starvation had a direct and current effect on fecundity:

1. Infertility and infecundity caused by starvation is rapidly reversible. A steep rise in conceptions immediately after the liberation marked the restoration of susceptibility to fertilization. The main contribution to the rise in conceptions was made by couples both of whom were resident in Holland throughout the famine period. The rise preceded in time a more gradual rise that followed the return home of soldiers, prisoners, deportees, and refugees. The immediate recovery of fertility indicates that there was also immediate physiological recovery of sexual activity, normal ovulation, and fecundity in general.

Indeed, one of the chief lessons to be learned from the famine is the resilience of human beings exposed to the harshest environmental forces. Early in May 1945, the people were so weakened that their very survival was in doubt. The liberating armies were supported by emergency nutrition teams and brought plentiful supplies of food. Within one month of liberation from the Nazi occupation, the people were restored to the normal activities of everyday life and to the business of rebuilding their families and their shattered cities.

2. Where conditions for reproduction are marginal because of severe nutritional deficiency, conceptions and births might be supposed to occur in two mutually exclusive ways. One way implies an all-or-none threshold, another a continuum of reproductive casualty.

On the all-or-none principle, when reproduction occurs, it occurs normally. Ovulation, fertilization, nidation, and birth are either possible or impossible, and the generation that ensues after exposure to nutritional insult is not damaged thereby. The hypothesis can be tested against the pattern of developmental anomalies among birth cohorts. The hypothesis would gain support if among the birth cohorts affected by infertility an increase in anomalies in the offspring were not detectable. The hypothesis would have to be rejected if such an increase were detectable.

If an increase in anomalies related to some stages of reproduction but not to all, the hypothesis would have to be modified. The reproductive process might operate on the all-or-none principle at some stages, and on the continuum principle at other stages. Severe radiation from Hiroshima and Nagasaki atomic bombs provides an analogy. There was a marked deficiency in numbers in the birth cohorts exposed in the first 8 weeks of gestation, but no increase in the incidence of mental retardation and microcephaly. In the birth cohorts exposed to radiation after 8 weeks' gestation there was no deficiency of births but an increase in mental retardation and microcephaly (Yamazaki, Wright, and Wright, 1954; Miller, 1956).

On the principle that nutritional deficiency results in damage to the developing fetus on a continuum of severity (Pasamanick and Lilienfeld, 1955), abnormal reproduction can proceed. The generation that ensued would be damaged thereby, and added anomalies in the offspring would be expected. Maternal rubella provides an analogy for this hypothesis. Among the offspring exposed to the famine, such outcomes as late fetal deaths, congenital anomalies, and unfitness for military service should be more frequent than in other cohorts. Since the severe conditions that made reproduction marginal persisted for only 4 months, conceptions under those conditions (the D2 cohort) would have been affected mainly during the first trimester of gestation.

3. The aftereffect of a phase of infertility will be expressed in an increment in fecundity. This increment will reflect the variations between groups in previous fertility, variations that have consequences for the distribution of manifestations that may be used to detect effects of exposure to famine during gestation on the outcome of pregnancy.

One consequence of the relative fertility of the higher social classes during the famine will be an altered social class composition of cohorts conceived during the infertile months. The altered class composition of the famine cohorts will contrast particularly with the cohorts conceived immediately after the famine, on the rebound from famine infertility. The different "mix" of social classes in successive cohorts can confound analyses of outcome measures in which social class differentials exist. Hence the altered mix is likely to be of import in studying the effect of the famine on mental performance.

Another consequence may bear on the frequency of congenital anomalies. Some researchers hold that birth defects and premature births occur more frequently among the less fecund (Warburton and Fraser, 1964). If, as we suggested, the women who conceived during the famine were more fecundable than others, then after the famine such women will have been transferred to the class of insusceptibles and will be underrepresented during the post-famine fertile period. Less fecundable women will have been transferred to the class of susceptibles and would be overrepresented. In that case, congenital anomalies could be overrepresented among conceptions that occurred after the famine, and they could be underrepresented among conceptions that occurred at the height of the famine. If fecundity and fertility, as measured by ability to reproduce during the famine, are not linked with subsequent fitness of the offspring, then no such differences should be found in the rate of birth defects among famine and post-famine cohorts.

Summary

In this chapter we have shown that the number of conceptions (estimated from the number of births) was immediately and markedly affected by severe nutritional deprivation. Recovery, too, was immediate with the relief of famine. These effects were not linear. Above a threshold value of food rations, nutrition seemed to be unimportant to fertility. The infertility during the famine, we infer, stemmed in part from a reduced capacity of couples to reproduce—that is, infecundity. Famine effects on fertility and presumably fecundity were most

FERTILITY

marked among the laboring classes. Older women of higher parity were more affected than younger women of lower parity, a distribution we attribute primarily to effects of famine on parity, especially high parities. The data analysis is based on three sources: registered births; maternity hospital records, which do not include all births; and military records which represent male survivors at age 19. The results are consistent for the three sources.

The changes in fertility substantially affected the social class composition of famine-born generations; birth order composition was slightly affected at the highest ranks; family size composition was not affected.

Table 9.1. Parity and age of mothers among hospital maternities by birth cohort and city (famine cities are Amsterdam, Leiden, and Rotterdam; Northern control city is Groningen; Southern control city is Heerlen. D2 cohort oversampled in famine cities)

	Birth Cohorts						
Group	A2	B1	B2	C	D1	D2	E1
	Mean age (and standard deviation) in years						
Famine	28.3(6.6)	28.2(6.5)	28.9(6.4)	27.7(6.4)	28.0(6.1)	27.5(6.2)	27.7(6.4)
North	28.1(6.2)	27.8(6.4)	27.5(6.4)	28.8(6.2)	27.0(6.7)	27.6(6.8)	27.8(6.4)
South	27.7(5.8)	30.5(6.1)	30.4(6.7)	29.6(6.5)	27.9(5.9)	29.1(6.5)	31.0(7.0)
	Per cent 30 years and over						
Famine	40.0	38.4	41.8	36.0	38.7	34.8	35.9
North	39.1	40.3	34.8	44.3	30.8	33.8	36.1
South	30.8	53.7	51.8	48.2	34.9	45.1	54.6
	Mean parity (and standard deviation) in years						
Famine	2.3(1.6)	2.4(1.8)	2.7(2.1)	2.4(1.8)	2.7(2.0)	2.2(1.7)	2.5(1.9)
North	2.3(1.7)	2.5(2.1)	2.4(1.9)	2.7(2.1)	2.4(2.0)	2.3(1.9)	2.2(1.7)
South	2.2(1.7)	3.1(2.3)	2.5(2.0)	2.5(1.9)	2.2(1.6)	2.4(1.9)	2.9(2.3)
	Per cent high parities (5 and over)						
Famine	10.7	10.2	14.8	11.7	14.8	9.7	14.3
North	9.8	11.5	10.9	13.9	13.2	12.5	10.3
South	8.3	22.0	13.7	13.4	9.0	13.8	19.3
	Numbers at risk						
Famine	345	333	325	197	297	528	496
North	164	174	230	122	182	255	329
South	133	123	168	112	221	275	264
	Per cent high parities (5 and over) among women of each age group (famine area)						
< 20	0	4.2	11.1	0	18.7	4.4	6.1
20–29	2.3	2.8	4.9	3.6	4.2	1.3	4.1
30–34	13.9	13.7	18.6	16.7	21.7	19.2	19.8
⩾ 35	34.8	32.7	36.4	41.4	41.3	31.0	46.3

Table 9.2. Birth order and family size among Netherlands men examined for military service, by birth cohorts and city, in the famine area (Amsterdam, Rotterdam, The Hague, Leiden, Utrecht, Haarlem), the Northern control area (Groningen, Enschede, Leeuwaarden, Helmond, Hengelo), and the Southern control area (Heerlen, Breda, Tilburg, Eindhoven, Maastricht)

Group		A1	A2	B1	B2	C	D1	D2	E1	E2
						Birth Cohorts				
				Birth order distribution (column per cent)						
Famine	1	41.1	39.8	36.7	34.8	35.3	35.2	38.2	33.8	36.1
	2–4	50.2	52.4	55.0	56.6	56.8	55.9	53.8	59.4	56.8
	5+	8.7	7.9	8.3	8.6	7.9	8.9	8.0	6.8	7.1
North	1	38.1	37.7	38.8	32.7	33.8	34.6	34.9	33.5	35.5
	2–4	52.4	53.3	52.7	58.6	57.5	56.1	56.1	58.0	55.9
	5+	9.5	8.9	8.6	8.7	8.7	9.4	9.0	8.5	8.6
South	1	32.0	29.6	28.4	27.8	30.8	28.4	25.3	28.0	29.1
	2–4	52.5	51.9	56.0	55.9	51.8	54.3	58.3	57.1	54.8
	5+	15.5	18.5	15.6	16.3	17.5	17.3	16.5	14.9	16.1
				Mean family size (and standard deviation)						
Famine		3.8(2.0)	3.7(2.0)	3.8(2.1)	3.8(2.0)	3.8(2.0)	3.9(2.1)	3.7(2.0)	3.6(2.0)	3.6(1.9)
North		3.9(2.0)	3.9(2.0)	3.8(1.9)	3.9(1.9)	3.8(2.0)	3.8(2.0)	3.8(2.0)	3.6(1.9)	3.7(1.9)
South		4.7(2.3)	4.9(2.3)	4.7(2.2)	4.7(2.2)	4.6(2.2)	4.6(2.2)	4.6(2.2)	4.5(2.2)	4.5(2.2)
				Per cent firstborn, by manual/non-manual class (famine cities only)						
Manual		37.7	37.6	34.8	32.2	31.9	33.3	37.7	31.9	35.5
Non-manual		44.7	42.8	39.2	37.5	38.8	37.0	38.2	35.3	36.8

10 Indices of the Reproductive Process

Ancient medical texts hint at a relationship between maternal nutrition and fetal development, and by the nineteenth century the role of maternal nutrition was given serious thought (Bernard, 1859). Epidemiological observations are more recent. Suspicion aroused by experience in Germany during the British blockade of World War I was confirmed during World War II. Thus the effects on birthweight of the siege of Leningrad of 1941-43 and the Dutch hunger winter of 1944-45 provoked the present study. Such effects stand as a crucial link in the postulated causal chain that runs from maternal nutrition, through fetal growth and the capacity for infant survival, to postnatal growth and development.

In this chapter, as a first step in examining the validity of this causal sequence, we assess the role of acute nutritional deprivation as a cause of changes in the outcome of the reproductive process among live births. To make this assessment, we shall examine the effects of prenatal famine exposure on six separate indices of the birth process. The indices are birthweight, placental weight, infant length at birth, head size at birth, duration of gestation, and maternal weight.

Each index is treated as a separate measure of outcome. In the next chapter we shall develop a model of how all these indices of the birth process relate to one another. The data on births used in this and the next chapter were obtained from teaching hospitals in 3 cities of the famine area (Amsterdam, Leiden, and Rotterdam) and in 1 city from each of the 2 control areas, Groningen in the North and Heerlen in the South. A brief description of the data sources is given in Chapter 8.

Methods

Chapter 8 describes how the cohort design treats prenatal famine exposure identified by time and place of birth as a dichotomous variable, and thereby provides an indirect measure of nutrition. Another measure of nutrition is based upon the weekly report of the official food ration in the three regions of the Netherlands during the period of this study. For this purpose, the official weekly ration was converted into a quantified independent variable. The conversion involves procedures and assumptions that should be kept in mind in the interpretation of those analyses that are based upon this measure.

First, there is no way of knowing how closely the official ration approximates the intake of individuals; rations may have been supplemented or depleted in many ways. The error in estimating individual intake from official rations could be substantial, and effects of nutrition would be to that degree more difficult to detect. The error will be much smaller where the rations are used to measure the average food intake of groups, or cohorts. Second, the variability in the war-time ration was not large outside the famine period. Lack of variation in the independent variable is translated into lack of effect in the dependent variable and will again make nutritional effects more difficult to detect. Third, in the postwar period rations were high. Hence individuals were not under the same necessity as during the war to consume what they were assigned. In the postwar period, therefore, rations are likely to be less accurate indicators of individual consumption than the war-time ration, and perhaps of group consumption as well.

As described in Chapter 8, the independent study variable based on the official caloric ration has been refined by creating three separate variables (C_1, C_2, C_3), one each for the average daily ration assigned during the first, second, and third trimester of pregnancy. Twenty monthly birth cohorts (August 1944- March 1946) were covered by our data, and therefore there were 20 X 3 trimesters under study in each area. We shall use the three variables based on caloric rations to try to assess the effects of food intake during each stage of gestation on the six outcomes in turn. Analyses based on the separate constituents of the food ration do not add to the results or deviate from them.

In interpreting the results for each dependent variable, a caution is necessary about two problems in addition to those inherent in the measure of the independent variable. The first is a problem of the reliability of the data for each outcome, and the second is a problem of inference general to all six outcomes.

Problems of reliability in these data arise from two sources. Variability of methods in the different hospitals at different times is one source of unreliable measurement. We have no direct control over this problem. From an examination of the means and standard deviations of the dependent variable within hospitals, however, we can obtain some sense of the comparability of measurement between hospitals. When allowance has been made for famine-induced

INDICES OF THE REPRODUCTIVE PROCESS 89

fluctuations, the means and standard deviations for each outcome from each hospital should be similar. This criterion has led us to reject some of the data on head circumference at birth.

The second source of unreliability is not special to these data but intrinsic to the methods used to measure each dependent variable. The unreliability arises from the varying precision with which each index of the reproductive process can be measured. The errors built into the measurements of birthweight and of maternal weight are probably the smallest among the six dependent variables. The variations in placental weight with different procedures of weighing are notorious, and both infant length and head circumference are difficult to measure accurately. Duration of gestation must often be guessed at because of uncertainties about reported dates of the last menstrual period, although with large numbers these reports have proved more reliable than many observers had believed (Hammes and Treloar, 1970; Erhardt, Joshi, Nelson, Kroll, and Wiener, 1964; Lin and Emanuel, 1972; Wiener, 1970). It must be anticipated that some of the apparent differences in famine effect among the six dependent variables could arise as a consequence of these differences in reliability. The most reliable measures will give the best chance of detecting effects.

The problem of inference arises from the common time of measurement of all the indices of reproduction at or around birth. Measurements made at birth can tell us about effects at an early stage of gestation on a particular outcome only if the effects persist through later stages and can be detected at birth. If no effects of exposure early in gestation can be detected at birth, we cannot be entirely sure that there were none; by the time of birth they may have disappeared or they may have been reversed by experience later in gestation. For lack of any data, we are obliged to ignore this possibility in our interpretations.

Analysis

The essential concept of the initial study design, we have explained, was to identify cohorts exposed to famine during gestation and to compare them with unexposed cohorts in terms of effects that might have been induced by the famine. The two measures of nutrition—namely, the dichotomous variable famine exposure and the continuous variable estimated average daily food ration by trimester—were used to analyze each of the six outcome variables in three ways described below.

A. Cohort Analysis by Time and Place

In graphic presentations, the mean values of the outcome variables are given for birth cohorts in famine-stricken and in control areas. Variations in outcome can be seen in relation to the progress of the famine through time, and thereby to exposure to known levels of official rations during each month of gestation. The contingency tables from which the figures accompanying the text derive are given in the Appendix. The Appendix groups the data in twenty single months of birth from August 1944 through March 1946; for the sake of clarity the figures group the months into seven larger birth cohorts. The seven cohorts are defined by the relation of famine experience to stage of gestation, as described in Chapter 8. Among the several forms of analyses we have undertaken in this chapter, these graphs and the Appendix tables are in our opinion the closest to reality, for they have been the least subject to manipulation and make the fewest assumptions.

B. Multiple Regression Analysis Under Different Nutritional Conditions*

In successive multiple regression analyses, we aim to elicit any unique or combined effects that food intake during each trimester of pregnancy might have upon each index of the reproductive process. The analyses rely on the quantified indices of nutrition, mentioned above, which yield independent variables for caloric rations in each of the three trimesters of pregnancy. The multiple regression analyses have been carried out for births under two conditions, those exposed to levels of nutrition below and those exposed to levels of nutrition above a "famine threshold." These we term the famine condition and the non-famine condition. In the event that variation in outcome connected with nutrition differs in the two conditions so defined, this refinement of the analysis is intended to enable more of that variation to be explained. The analysis also enables us to discover special relations between variables that may obtain only in one of the two nutritional conditions.

In defining the two nutritional conditions, we tried to locate a threshold value above which food intake sustains both the basal metabolic needs of the mother and the gestational growth of herself and her child in the womb. The threshold was chosen empirically by the inspection of scattergrams.** Caloric rations had definite relationships with the dependent variable only in the third trimester and these were non-linear. The breakpoint for birthweight was selected as the most reliable of the indices. This value was 1500 Calories average daily official ration in the third trimester of pregnancy.

Hytten and Leitch (1971a) give theoretical values for the basic metabolic needs of pregnant women in each trimester; the value of 1750 Calories per day for the metabolic rate of women in the latter half of pregnancy is above our empirical threshold. The basal metabolic rate underestimates need because it is taken at rest. The offical ration, on the other hand, underestimates intake because of unmeasured unoffical supplementation. Thus the theoretical and empirical values could be in good agreement.

The use of third trimester rations to fix two nutritional conditions imposes limitations on some aspects of the analysis. Because of the short famine period

---

*Procedures and assumptions of these multiple regression analyses are described in Notes on Method at the end of this chapter.

**These are not shown; they can be reconstructed from the data given in the Appendix.

INDICES OF THE REPRODUCTIVE PROCESS   91

and the fixed relation in time of each trimester of pregnancy, the range of variation of caloric rations in the first and second trimesters of pregnancy is limited by the condition imposed in the third trimester. After thorough exploration of all these variations in relation to the dependent variables, however, we believe that this limitation is not an important one.

More important is the contrast with the cohort analysis by time and place in the variables controlled and in the inferences that can be drawn. The grouping in the multiple regression analyses of two nutritional conditions around a famine threshold value for rationed Calories is made without regard to time and place, on which our graphic presentations were based. The analysis takes account of the fact that food rations fell to a low level outside of the famine period; two to three months before mid-October, the date of onset of the famine often given in previous reports and used by us, rations fell below 1500 Calories daily average. Similarly, the analysis also takes account of food rations that fell below the selected famine threshold in designated control areas.

Thus the structure of the comparisons used in the multiple regression analysis departs altogether from the contingency table and graphic analysis by time and place, and pivots solely around food supply. In ignoring time and place the results can be expected sometimes to differ from, rather than to complement, analyses that control time and place. Analyses hinged only to different nutritional conditions may suffer also from a loss of precision in crossing areas. The data are more heterogeneous and dispersed than those for single areas and they incorporate more "noise," in the form of variation unrelated to the hypothetical cause under study. Uncontrolled variation damps the strength of associations that exist in the data.

The multiple regression analysis is given in terms of the mean values of the specified dependent variable for each monthly birth cohort. These mean values are related to the average caloric ration during the specified periods of gestation. We term these "analyses of groups."* Where sufficient information was recorded the analysis includes data from all five hospitals whose records were extracted. Three were in the famine area (Rotterdam, Amsterdam, and Leiden) one in Groningen in the North, and one in Heerlen in the South. Where insufficient information was recorded, omissions are noted in the text.

C. Correlation of Differences Between Areas in Independent and Dependent Variables.**

In a further analysis which we shall term the "analysis of differences," we quantified the differences in outcome between famine and control areas illustrated graphically by time and place. This was done by correlating the *differ-*

---

*See Notes on Method at the end of this chapter for comment on analyses based on individuals.

**Further discussion of the interpretation of this analysis is given at the end of this chapter in Notes on Method.

ences between famine and control cohorts in the independent study variable with the *differences* in the specified outcome variable. The independent variables in these analyses were again derived from average caloric rations in each trimester. By means of this analysis, we aimed to exploit the dual strength of the research design. The simultaneous comparisons of the cohorts with controls for both time and place are summarized in a single statistic for each outcome.

This is the most rigorous of the analyses we have devised. In the multiple regression analysis of groups under famine and non-famine conditions, confounding of nutritional deprivation with season, temperature, war-time disorganization, and peace-time reorganization of services is possible. Thus the effects attributed to nutritional deprivation might in truth be the effects of these other uncontrolled factors associated with changes in nutrition. In the analysis of differences, all time-related factors that affected the whole country are controlled, and there is much less opportunity for confounding. One may anticipate that the amount of variation in the reproductive processes explained by nutrition will be less and statistical significance will be more difficult to attain in the analysis of differences than in the analysis of groups.

We turn now to present the analysis of the indices of the reproductive process. A section is devoted to each of the six dependent variables; each section reports results and ends with a summary. The dependent variables are presented in an order more or less arbitrary. First we deal with the group of four variables (birthweight, placental weight, infant length, and head size) that derive from fetal dimensions and measure fetal growth; they are treated in order of size of effects. Then we deal with two variables, duration of gestation and maternal weight, that reflect maternal change as much as or more than fetal change. Each of these variables in turn is subjected to the three types of analysis: (A) cohort analysis by time and place, (B) Multiple regression analysis under different nutritional conditions, and (C) Correlation of differences between areas in independent and dependent variables.

Birthweight

The potential biological significance of changes in birthweight is considerable. For instance, in New York City in the 1960's, birthweight differences of 150 grams could account for the whole of the disparity in perinatal mortality between whites, with a rate of 26 per 1000, and non-whites, with a rate of 44 per 1000 (Bergner and Susser, 1970). The potential significance of birthweight as a crucial mediating factor in infant survival and child development has several times been alluded to. In before-and-after studies of the Dutch famine, Sindram (1945), Smith (1947), and Stroink (1947) all found a fall in birthweight coincident with the famine (Kloosterman, 1966). As Smith suggested and we have confirmed, the fall was related to mothers' exposure to famine during the

INDICES OF THE REPRODUCTIVE PROCESS

third trimester. We could perceive in Smith's data no added effect from exposure during the first and second trimesters (Bergner and Susser, 1970). Smith also found an excess of "premature" infants of very low birthweight among births conceived during the famine and exposed to it early in gestation. This result did not reach conventional levels of statistical significance.

The standard deviations and the means in each hospital suggest acceptable levels of reliability in measurement.

	Mean	*SD*	*Number*
Amsterdam	3211	665	1148
Leiden	3331	607	457
Rotterdam	3245	654	806
Groningen	3311	659	1290
Heerlen	3345	551	1149

A. Birthweight Among Cohorts by Time and Place (Figure 10.1)

Our data show a distinct fall in mean birthweight related to exposure to famine. In the two non-famine areas at the same period, the fall in mean birthweight was moderate in the North and slight in the South. The decline in birthweight in the non-famine areas affected monthly birth cohorts differently from those in the famine area, but also to some extent followed a decline in rations.

Visible effects of famine on birthweight are confined to exposure during the third trimester. In the famine area the most affected cohorts are B1, B2, and C.

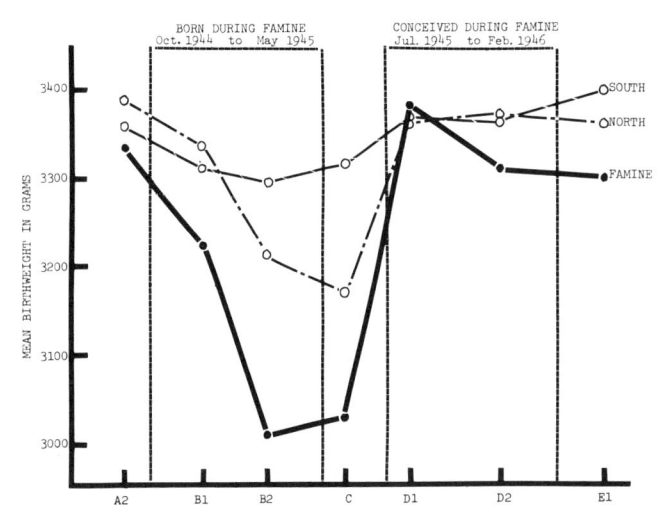

Figure 10.1. Birthweight by time and place (mean birthweight in grams for births in maternity hospitals for seven birth cohorts: famine, Northern control, and Southern control areas compared for the period August 1944 to March 1946 inclusive)

Mean birthweight in the B2 cohort fell 327 grams or 9% from a level of 3338 grams in the A2 cohort, and on recovery rose 297 grams or 8.9% to 3308 grams in the E1 cohort. Exposure solely during the third trimester (cohort B1) coincided with a fall in birthweight. Exposure solely during the first trimester (cohort D2) or solely during both first and second trimester (cohort D1) produced no detectable effect on birthweight. The greater apparent effect of exposure during both second and third trimesters (cohort B2), therefore, can best be attributed to the greater severity of famine during the third trimester of the affected cohort. The low mean birthweight of the C cohort indicates an effect of early third trimester famine exposure not reversed by a period of access to normal nutrition in the very last weeks of gestation. The changes in birthweight in the two control areas are consistent with this interpretation. They have somewhat similar relations with changes in rationed calories, but the fluctuations in birthweight between cohorts are less marked in accord with the less marked variation in rations.

Although there was no reduction in the mean birthweight of the D2 cohort, in the famine area this cohort has a wider standard deviation for birthweight than have other cohorts (see Appendix). This was caused by an excess of infants of birthweight under 2000 grams: 27 were expected, and 37 were observed. There is reason to consider the excess biologically significant because of its coincidence with other manifestations in the D2 cohort (see Chapters 12, 13, 16, 17).

B. Multiple Regression Analysis of Group Means of Birthweight Under Different Nutritional Conditions (Tables 10.1.1, 10.1.2)

The two nutritional conditions of this analysis were derived from a clear break, at the threshold value of 1500 Calories average daily rations, in the linear relation of rations and birthweight. The large contribution of the square of C_3 (22%) to variance in mean birthweight across all nutritional conditions confirmed the non-linearity. In the famine condition, caloric rations can account for 64% of the variance in mean birthweight, at a high level of statistical significance (Table 10.1.1). In the non-famine condition caloric rations can account for no more than 3% of the variance, a result without statistical significance (Table 10.1.2).

Table 10.1.1 confirms that in the famine condition virtually the whole of the association between famine and birthweight can be accounted for by caloric rations in the third trimester (C_3). C_1 and C_2 have lesser correlations with mean birthweight, and can account for much less variance; even these small correlations can be explained by their intercorrelations with C_3. This we infer from the three alternate forced sequences in the multiple regression analysis. In the sequence where C_3 is entered first, the variance added by C_2 is negligible. C_1 still accounts for the small amount of 1% of the variance.

INDICES OF THE REPRODUCTIVE PROCESS

This result can still accommodate two alternative causal chains: The first sequence

$$C_2 \longrightarrow C_3 \longrightarrow \text{birthweight}$$

implies that C_2 has an independent effect and acts in some fashion through C_3 as an intervening variable. While, in normal circumstances, caloric intake in the second trimester of pregnancy may serve to predict the intake in the third, it cannot be said to cause it. The intake during the two periods are merely the elements of a common complex without organic connection; thus during the Dutch famine the limits of caloric intake were dictated by circumstances quite independent of intake during a previous period of pregnancy. We therefore reject this causal model.

The alternative sequence

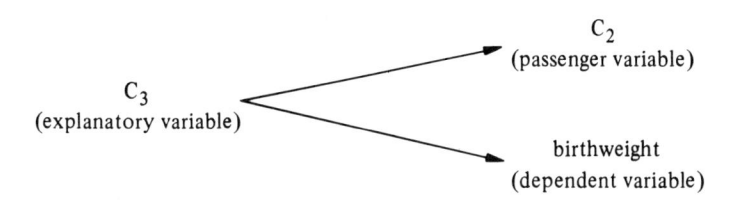

$$C_3 \text{ (explanatory variable)} \longrightarrow \begin{array}{l} C_2 \text{ (passenger variable)} \\ \\ \text{birthweight (dependent variable)} \end{array}$$

implies that C_3 is the common cause of the association between C_2 and birthweight. In this model, C_3 is associated with C_2 and is also a cause of variation in birthweight. For that reason only, C_2 comes into association with birthweight.*

This is a tenable causal model given one modification. Our argument that the association of C_2 and C_3 is part of a common complex of factors means that their relationship is symmetrical and without direction. We therefore modify the model as follows:

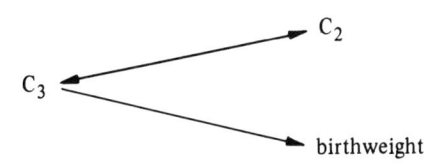

$$C_3 \begin{array}{l} \longleftrightarrow C_2 \\ \\ \longrightarrow \text{birthweight} \end{array}$$

In the multiple regression analysis with caloric rations in each trimester as separate independent variables the b values indicate that a change of 100

---

*C_3 is an explanatory variable that "explains" their association; C_2 can be described as a passenger variable that merely rides with the dependent variable birthweight, and does not cause it (cf. Susser, 1973).

Calories of daily rations in the third trimester of pregnancy predicts a change of 40 grams in mean birthweight below the famine threshold (Table 10.1.1). Table 10.1.2 shows no statistically significant effects of caloric rations under the non-famine condition.

C. Correlation of Differences Between Areas in Group Means of Caloric Rations and Birthweight (Table 10.2)

The analysis of differences confirms again the predominant effect of caloric rations in the third trimester: the correlations of differences between the famine area and the Northern control area ($r = .49$), and between the famine area and the Southern control area ($r = .60$) are both statistically significant.

Summary

This analysis shows unequivocally and quantitatively that the effect of food deprivation on birthweight occurred in the third trimester. The effect was to shift birthweight fairly evenly to the left throughout the weight range. An excess of very low birthweight infants was present among those conceived at the height of the famine and exposed early in gestation, but the result was not statistically significant.

The effect of food intake on birthweight was not linear. Below a threshold value of caloric rations chosen to demonstrate famine conditions (1500 Calories daily average in the third trimester) there was a significant effect of food rations on birthweight; above the threshold, there was none.

Placental Weight

Placental weight is correlated with birthweight (Gibson and McKeown, 1950, 1951; McKeown and Gibson, 1951; Solth, 1961; Gerlach, 1962; Armitage, Boyd, Hamilton, and Rowe, 1967; Thomson, Billewicz, and Hytten, 1969). In animals, a loss of placental weight follows on nutritional deprivation. We know of no studies among humans that relate the mother's nutrient intake to placental weight at birth. Mothers from populations that suffer chronic malnutrition, however, tend to have babies of low birthweight and also to deliver lighter placentae. Biochemical changes are associated with these weight changes (Winick, 1967, 1971; Winick, Coscia, and Noble, 1967; Laga, Driscoll, and Munro, 1972a, b).

In the present study, the data on placental weight were drawn from Rotterdam only in the famine area; data were not available from Amsterdam and Leiden. We have no information on the way in which the placentae were weighed. The standard deviations and the means in each hospital suggest substantial variation between hospitals in reliability of measurement.

INDICES OF THE REPRODUCTIVE PROCESS

	Mean	S.D.	N
Rotterdam:	573	130	775
Groningen:	641	147	1236
Heerlen:	572	142	1108

We now turn to the detailed analysis of placental weight.

A. Placental Weight Among Cohorts by Time and Place (Figure 10.2)

In the famine-stricken city of Rotterdam, mean placental weight declined in a manner concomitant with changes in food rations and with changes in birthweight; the B2 and C cohorts were chiefly affected. In the cities of the control areas, the fluctuations in placental weight were also compatible with changes in rations, although less so. In the control area of Heerlen in the South, the B2 cohort was most affected; in the control area of Groningen in the North the C cohort was most affected. The curious fall in mean placental weight in Groningen to the low value of the C cohort, however, cannot be explained in terms of the official caloric ration.

The main changes in placental weight, like birthweight, relate to exposure to low food rations in the third trimester, despite the fact that in normal circumstances placental growth probably reaches a maximum somewhat earlier in

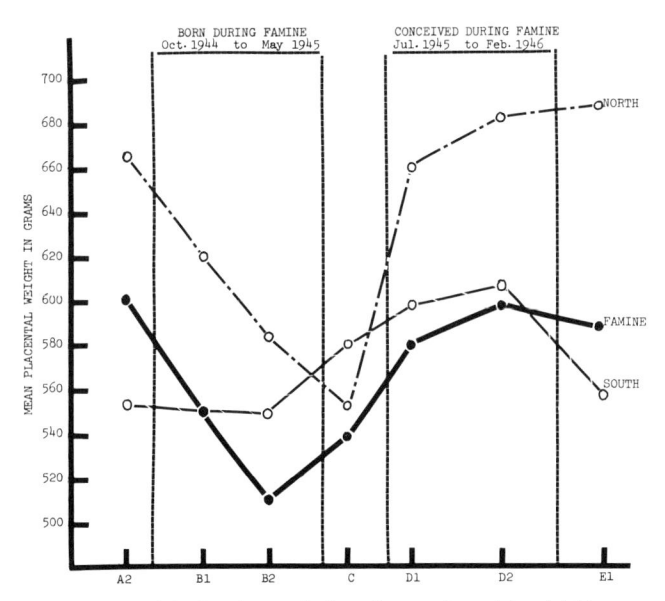

Figure 10.2. Placental weight by time and place (mean placental weight in grams for births in maternity hospitals for seven birth cohorts: famine, Northern control, and Southern control areas compared for the period August 1944 to March 1946 inclusive)

pregnancy than does birthweight (Gruenwald, 1963; Thomson, Billewicz, and Hytten, 1969). The inferences from which this conclusion derives are the same as for birthweight. In Rotterdam, the mean placental weight, 601 grams in the A2 cohort born before the famine, declined by 15% to 511 grams in the B2 cohort born during the famine, and on recovery rose by 14% to 592 grams in the E1 cohort conceived after the famine.

B. Multiple Regression Analyses of Group Means of Placental Weight Under Different Nutritional Conditions (Tables 10.3.1, 10.3.2)

Significant associations between caloric rations and mean placental weight appear, as with birthweight, only in the famine condition. Thus from the outset of this analysis we are obliged to recognize the non-linear and conditional nature of the relationship.

The quantitative analysis under the famine condition confirms the conclusions from Figure 10.2 that caloric rations in the third trimester can account for the whole of the association of rations with mean placental weight. C_3 has the strongest correlation (r = .59). Thus caloric rations in the third trimester can account for 36% of the variance, or 90% of the total of 40% "explained" variance in mean placental weight. The contribution of C_3 to the variance in mean placental weight overlaps with and can explain that of C_1 and C_2; when in this equation C_3 is entered first, the smaller contributions of C_1 and C_2 become negligible.

On exactly the same grounds as in the case of birthweight, we adopt as a tenable model of these associations the following.

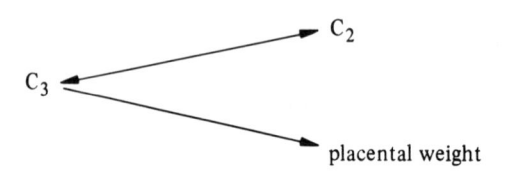

$$C_3 \rightarrow C_2$$
$$C_3 \rightarrow \text{placental weight}$$

Under the famine condition this relationship is linear; a quadratic transformation of the variable caloric rations in the third trimester (C_3^2) adds nothing to the variance. The values in this multiple regression analysis indicate that below the famine threshold, a change of 100 Calories of rations in the third trimester of gestation predicts a change of 10 grams in placental weight (Table 10.3.1). Above the famine threshold, a change in rations in any of the trimesters does not predict a change in placental weight (Table 10.3.2).

C. Correlations of Differences between Areas in Group Means of Caloric Rations and Placental Weight (Table 10.2)

The analysis of differences in relation to placental weight is less consistent than in the case of birthweight, and none of the correlations are statistically significant. The only positive association that approaches the level of statistical significance is that with C_3 in the comparison between the famine area and Heerlen in the South.

Summary

Our data show that the effects of nutritional deprivation on placental weight in humans are similar to the effects on birthweight. Low caloric intake caused a decline in placental weight. The relation of caloric rations with placental weight was not linear, and the effect was again much more marked in the famine than in the non-famine condition. This effect was confined to prenatal exposure in the third trimester.

Infant Length at Birth

C. A. Smith noted changes in infant length at birth during the Dutch famine, although they were not statistically significant; the reduction was less marked and consistent than changes in birthweight (Smith, 1947). In the famine of the 21-month Leningrad siege during World War II, Antonov (1947) also found a decrease in length among infants at birth. Shortness is associated with the more severe forms of fetal growth retardation (Gruenwald, 1966) but the reports of Antonov and Smith provide the only direct evidence in humans of a nutritional effect on growth in fetal length. The reliability of measurement between the five hospitals seems adequate:

	Mean	*S.D.*	*Number*
Amsterdam	49.6	4.1	973
Leiden	50.0	3.9	457
Rotterdam	49.6	3.6	794
Groningen	49.3	3.5	1272
Heerlen	49.6	2.8	1129

A. Infant Length at Birth Among Cohorts by Time and Place (Figure 10.3)
Infant length varied among the seven birth cohorts in a manner similar to but less marked than birthweight and placental weight. A famine effect can be localized to exposure during the third trimester of pregnancy. In the famine area the B1 and B2 cohorts, which suffered chiefly third trimester exposure, showed a relatively steep decline in length at birth. This low level continued through the C cohort, as it did for other fetal dimensions. Infant length fell 2½% from 50.2 cms in the A2 cohort born before the famine to 48.9 cm in the B2 cohort born during the famine, but rose only 1½% to 49.7 cms in the E1 cohort.

B. Multiple Regression Analysis of Group Means of Infant Length at Birth Under Different Nutritional Conditions (Tables 10.4.1, 10.4.2)

Associations of infant length at birth with caloric rations, as with birthweight and placental weight, are non-linear and much stronger under the famine condition than under the non-famine condition. Under the famine condition, caloric rations can account for about 25% of the variance in mean infant length at birth; under the non-famine condition, the partial regression coefficients for caloric rations are not statistically significant.

Once again, caloric rations in the third trimester exerted the main influence on variation in infant length at birth. Under the famine condition, when C_3 is entered first in the regression equation, it alone contributes 22% of the variance compared to 24% of the variance explained by C_1, C_2, and C_3 combined, and the regression coefficient is statistically significant. The partial correlation of C_3 with mean infant length at birth (r = .4) is also statistically significant. The unstandardized partial regression coefficients (b values) indicate, however, that under the famine condition a change of 100 Calories in third trimester rations predicted a change of only .1 centimeters in mean infant length at birth.

C. Correlation of Differences Between Areas in Group Means of Caloric Rations and Infant Length at Birth (Table 10.2)

The correlation of differences between famine and control areas is coherent with the preceding analysis. Differences in caloric rations in the third trimester of gestation correlate at the level of r = .52 in the comparison of the famine area

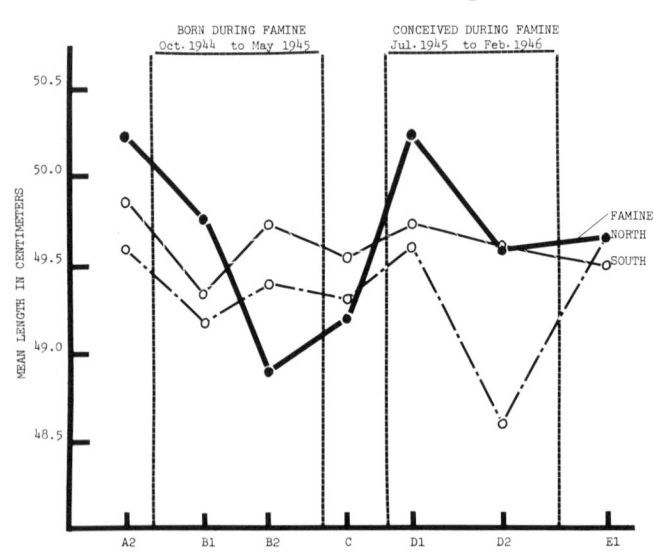

Figure 10.3. Infant length by time and place (mean infant length in centimeters for consecutive births in maternity hospitals for seven birth cohorts: famine, Northern control, and Southern control areas compared for the period August 1944 to March 1946 inclusive)

with the North and r = .54 in the comparison of the South. These correlations reach statistical significance.

In the famine-North comparison, the negative correlation of differences in C_1 and mean infant length produces a distorter effect. On common-sense grounds, we are not inclined to accept a high maternal intake of food as a cause of shortness in infants, and we interpret the result as a consequence of the extreme outlying value of the D2 cohort in the North, and thus an artifact of the construction of the caloric intake variables from a limited number of cases and times.

Summary

We conclude that an effect of prenatal nutrition on infant length at birth was present, although slight compared with that on birthweight.

As with birthweight and placental weight, the effect was both non-linear and confined to exposure to famine during the third trimester. Thus below the famine threshold, but not above, caloric rations accounted for a substantial amount (24%) of variation in group means of infant length. Statistically significant associations were demonstrated by the partial regression coefficient, by the partial correlation of third trimester rations with infant length, and by the correlation of differences in third trimester rations and infant length.

Head Size at Birth

Head size has been shown to be smaller in malnourished children than in comparison groups (Stoch and Smythe, 1963; Monckeberg, 1968; Chase and Martin, 1970). In such children small head size occurs conjointly with other small body measurements, particularly height and weight. Small head size also seems to accompany retarded fetal growth (Gruenwald and Minh, 1961; Gruenwald, 1966; Naeye, 1970; Nelson and Deutschberger, 1970; Baum and Searls, 1971). Conversely, an increased rate of growth in head size in premature infants after birth has been attributed to improved nutrition brought about by changed hospital feeding practices. In premature infants born at the Hammersmith Hospital in London in 1965 through 1968, head size grew more rapidly than in those born 4 years earlier (Davies and Davies, 1970).

Small head size has been invested with biological significance as an index of brain growth and later development. In East African autopsy studies, the brains of malnourished children weighed less than others (Brown, 1965). In a small number of children who died of malnutrition and were compared at autopsy with children who had no signs of malnutrition, small head size has been found to relate also to reduced cell number in the brain (Winick and Rosso, 1969).

Other evidence points to an association between head size and mental function and behavior. Apart from the "primary" condition of microcephaly itself, small heads are characteristic of many forms of mental retardation (Penrose, 1962; Martin, 1970) including those with chromosomal anomalies as in mongolism, and with enzyme deficiencies as in phenylketonuria. Intrauterine exposure to the irradiation of the atomic bomb at Hiroshima caused a reduction in mean head size, often accompanied by mental retardation; the effect was related to the intensity of exposure and to the stage of gestation (Miller and Blot, 1972). Finally, in a follow-up of a large series of births from a number of hospitals in the United States, head size at birth has been found to be associated with IQ measured at age 4 (Nelson and Deutschberger, 1970).

In presenting the Dutch data we have chosen, from the five or six indices of head size recorded in each hospital series included in our analysis, to use "median head circumference." This measurement is the one most commonly reported in the literature. In our data, it is highly correlated with most of the other head measures ($r = .7$ to $r = .9$) and seemed to be one of the most sensitive to prenatal nutritional deprivation.

The data on head size comprise consecutive births recorded in three hospitals, one in Rotterdam in the famine area, one in Groningen in the North, and one in Heerlen in the South. In Rotterdam and Groningen data were available over a period of 20 months; in Heerlen the records were incomplete for the last 4 months. Agreement between hospitals is far from good:

	Mean	S.D.	Number
Rotterdam	34.9 cm	2.1	644
Groningen	33.7 cm	1.5	1179
Heerlen	35.1 cm	1.7	760

An F statistic rejected the hypothesis of the equality of the estimated regression lines of the famine and the Northern control areas ($F_{2, 19} = 49$: $p < .001$). The disparity between Groningen in the North and other areas is most likely a measurement problem since among measures of fetal growth, the low mean value in Groningen is unique to this measure. Agreement between Heerlen in the South and Rotterdam in the famine area is better, despite the missing data for 4 months of the observation period in Heerlen.

A. Head Circumference Among Cohorts by Time and Place (Figure 10.4)
In the famine area, the decline in head circumference among births during the famine period (B1, B2, and C cohorts) again suggests that prenatal exposure to famine in the third trimester of gestation affected this dimension of fetal growth. Head circumference declined 2.7% from 35.3 cm in the A2 cohort born before the famine to 34.3 cm in the B2 cohort, and rose 2.4% to 35.2 cm in the E1 cohort born after the famine. The pattern in the famine area is fairly distinct from that in the South for the period in which data were available. For the

INDICES OF THE REPRODUCTIVE PROCESS

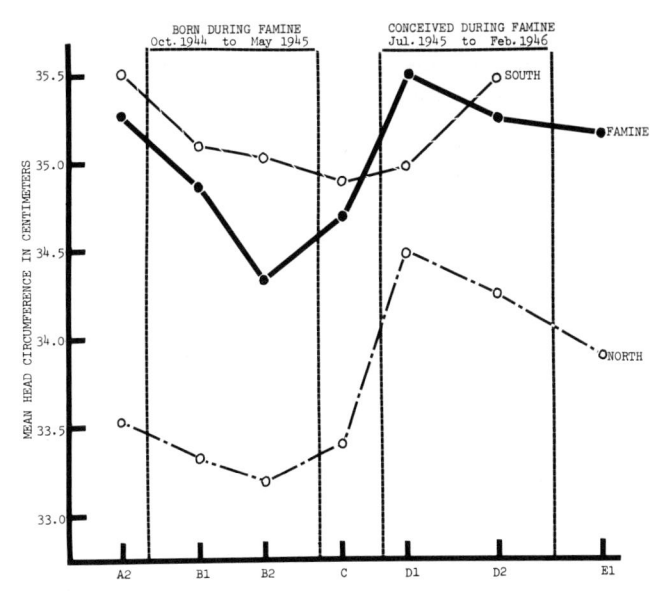

Figure 10.4. Head circumference of infants by time and place (mean head circumference of infants in centimeters for consecutive births in maternity hospitals for seven birth cohorts: famine, Northern control, and Southern control areas compared for the period August 1944 to March 1946, inclusive)

period covered by the cohorts B2 through E1, the pattern in the famine area resembles that in the North. Among the crucial cohorts that exhibit an apparent famine effect, however, the Northern area does not show the sharp reduction in head circumference seen in the famine area.

B. Multiple Regression Analysis of Group Means of Head Circumference at Birth (Table 10.5)

In the instance of head circumference, multiple regression analysis of the data for all three areas at once suffers distortions because of the incompleteness of the Southern data and even more because of the aberrant low mean value of the Northern data. The correlations and coefficients for the combined data do not clearly reflect either what appears in the graphic presentation or in the analysis of each area taken singly. It seemed safe to proceed only with a statistical analysis of the famine area. This decision eliminates the analysis of differences and makes analysis under different nutritional conditions statistically impractical. The number of monthly mean values available under the famine condition is too small for useful analysis. An analysis under different nutritional conditions for Rotterdam individuals (not presented) confirmed that an effect of prenatal nutritional deprivation on head circumference is present, as for other fetal dimensions, only under the famine condition. Table 10.5 refers to monthly means of Rotterdam births taken alone.

The analysis presented in Table 10.5 confirms the evidence of Figure 10.3 that average daily caloric rations in the third trimester alone can account for the whole of the association of rations with mean head circumference. The correlation of C_3 is the strongest ($r = .55$): C_3 alone can account for 31% of the variance in mean head circumference; C_1, C_2, and C_3 taken together account for 38% of the variance. A causal effect on head size of rations in the third trimester can be inferred in the same manner as for birthweight, placental weight, and length at birth.

The partial regression coefficient is significant but small. Under all conditions over the 20 months in Rotterdam, a change of 100 Calories average daily rations in the third trimester predicts a change of .05 cm in head circumference. Given a sufficiency of cases under the famine condition, a larger effect can be predicted. In the analysis of individuals, a change of 100 Calories predicts a change of .13 cm in head circumference under the famine condition. There is no significant change under the non-famine condition ($b = -.03$).

Summary

We conclude that an effect of prenatal nutrition on head circumference at birth was present in our data. The effects of nutritional deprivation on head circumference at birth are similar to the effects on other fetal dimensions. Incomplete and unreliable measures in hospitals in the two control areas limit the validity of combined data. When measures from the single hospital in the famine area were taken on their own, the relation of caloric ration to head size was significant, non-linear, and confined to prenatal famine exposure in the third trimester.

Duration of Gestation

The reported variation in average duration of gestation between human groups has been relatively small—for instance, between social classes or ethnic groups (Butler and Bonham, 1963; Henderson, 1967). Sindram (1945) reported a mean reduction in length of gestation during the Dutch famine of 4 days, about 1%. We have found no other reports of a direct effect of nutrition on length of gestation.

Our data were taken from hospitals in Amsterdam and Rotterdam in the famine area, Groningen in the North, and Heerlen in the South. Reliability of measurement (weeks from last menstrual period to birth) seemed adequate.

	Mean	*S.D.*	*Number*
Amsterdam	39.4	2.3	1144
Rotterdam	39.4	2.9	791
Groningen	39.5	2.4	1021
Heerlen	39.5	2.5	1085

INDICES OF THE REPRODUCTIVE PROCESS 105

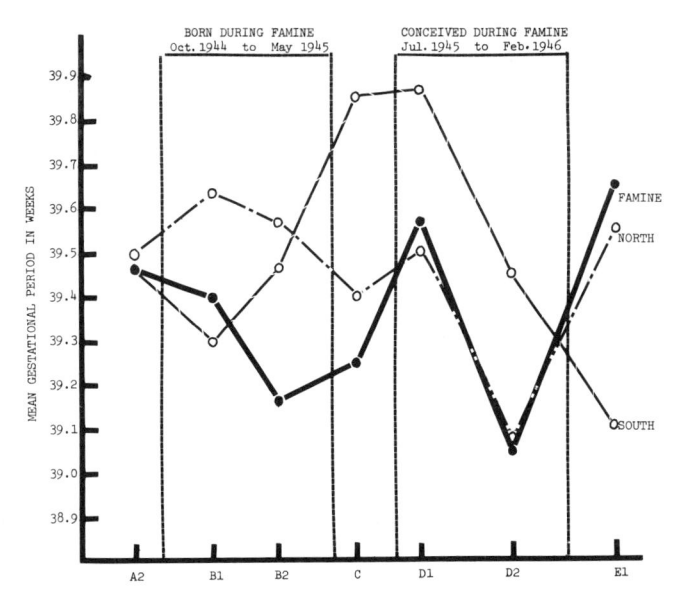

Figure 10.5. Length of gestation by time and place (mean weeks of gestation for births in maternity hospitals for seven birth cohorts: famine, Northern control and Southern control areas compared for the period August 1944 to March 1946 inclusive)

A. Duration of Gestation Among Cohorts by Time and Place (Figure 10.5)

The pattern of changes in lengh of gestation for births during the period of famine is similar to that of the outcome variables previously analyzed. Hence, the pattern is consistent with an effect of famine exposure during the third trimester of pregnancy. Mean length of gestation fell by .8% from 39.5 weeks in the A2 cohort to 39.2 weeks in the B2 cohort, and rose by 1% to 39.7 weeks in the E1 cohort.

Changes in length of gestation cannot be convincingly attributed to prenatal famine exposure, however, because of inconsistencies in the common variation through time of the two study variables in the famine area. The most striking contraction of the average period of gestation occurred in the D2 cohort, exposed to famine only in the first trimester.* Famine exposure alone cannot explain this effect, since the Northern control city experienced a similar contraction in the D2 cohort. Moreover, the D1 cohort was also exposed to famine at conception and early in pregnancy, and duration of gestation was not shortened. In the Southern control city of Heerlen, length of gestation fluctuated widely without evident relation to food rations.

*This finding needs to be considered in relation to the increased number of births under 2000 grams in weight in the same cohort.

B. Multiple Regression Analysis of Group Means of Duration of Gestation Under Different Nutritional Conditions (Table 10.6)

Under the famine condition, no correlations of caloric rations with length of gestation are statistically significant. Under the non-famine condition, there is a statistically significant partial regression coefficient, mainly contributed by C_1 and C_2. A nutritional hypothesis does not yield a coherent explanation of these results.

C. Correlation Between Areas in Differences in Caloric Rations and Length of Gestation (Table 10.2)

None of the correlations of differences between the famine and the two control areas are statistically significant.

Summary

There was a reduction in length of gestation from the norm in the most affected birth cohorts similar to that previously reported by others, although the reduction was not of statistical significance. Mean length of gestation was shorter with third trimester famine exposure and is not inconsistent with a nutritional explanation. The greatest reduction in length of gestation, however, occurred in the D2 cohort in both famine and Northern cities. A nutritional explanation is not consistent with these results for first trimester famine exposure.

Maternal Weight

Estimated caloric intake has been found to correlate with maternal weight during pregnancy in a study in Aberdeen, Scotland (Thomson, 1959). The relationship was demonstrated in the course of an attempt to establish the connection between nutrition and birthweight. In that observational study the direction of the relationship between nutrition and maternal weight could not be determined with certainty, for both the index of nutrition and the index of maternal weight were based on observations made at one point in pregnancy (mostly in the seventh month). The partial correlation between caloric intake and birthweight disappeared when maternal weight was introduced into the analysis, and the investigator inferred that maternal weight must be the antecedent variable and common cause of both caloric intake and birthweight. Maternal height appeared to be the determinant of this association, for caloric intake increased with height and was similar for overweight and underweight women of the same height (Thomson and Billewicz, 1961).

With regard to maternal weight if not stature, another interpretation is possible—namely, that caloric intake is the antecedent variable and maternal weight the intervening variable. All the data required to test these interpretations are not available, since they involve both height and weight gain during pregnancy. One point of interest in the Dutch data, however, is that the direction of

INDICES OF THE REPRODUCTIVE PROCESS

nutritional effects on maternal weight during the famine can be inferred with a high degree of certainty. A second point of interest is that maternal weight may also provide a criterion by which to judge the severity of the famine at different periods.

Our raw data for maternal weight are more limited than for other outcomes; they are available only for hospital births in the city of Rotterdam. With this variable, the problem of the time of measurement may be relevant to interpretation of effects at different stages of pregnancy. A single measurement was made just before discharge home, 9 or 10 days after delivery. About earlier stages of pregnancy, we can say only that any effects of food intake that may exist were overshadowed or reversed by the third trimester experience. The reliability of the measurements is difficult to estimate since our data were drawn from a single hospital, and we have located no other published series weighed at this same stage in the puerperium.

A. Maternal Weight Among Cohorts over Time (Figure 10.6)

At the onset of the famine, war-time maternal weights were low in comparison with the immediate postwar norm. In this respect the variable differed from the other indices of the reproductive process. A sharp decline from this relatively low level of postpartum maternal weight quickly followed the reduction in food rations. The average decline from the pre-famine level in the most affected

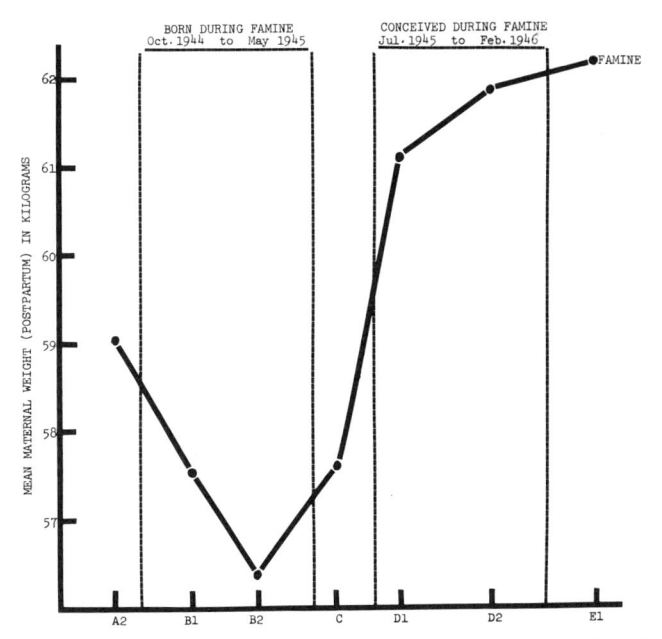

Figure 10.6. Maternal weight by time and place (mean postpartum weight of mother in kilograms for births in maternity hospitals for seven birth cohorts for famine area only for the period August 1944 to March 1946 inclusive)

cohort (B2) was 2.6 kilograms or 4.3% and the rise with recovery was 5.9 kilograms, or 10.5%. Both the rise and fall of the curves for postpartum maternal weight were closely related to that of caloric rations toward the end of pregnancy. Thus mothers of the C cohort, who had an average of only 3 weeks to enjoy the more favorable conditions after liberation, had begun to recover.

B. Multiple Regression Analysis of Group Means of Postpartum Maternal Weight (Table 10.7)

The number of cases, or months, in this series from one area is too few to dichotomize a statistical analysis around the famine threshold. Caloric rations had a higher correlation with maternal weight than with other outcome variables and explained 83% of the variance. Caloric rations in the third trimester had the highest correlation ($r = .9$) and could account for by far the most variance (77%) in mean maternal weight. In the sequence of Table 10.7 when C_3 is entered first in the equation, the contribution of C_2 is only 5% and that of C_1 only 1%. Moreover, the bivariate correlation of C_1 with maternal weight is negative, the partial correlations of C_1 and C_2 are both negative, and none reach levels of statistical significance. Following the same procedure of inference as was done for birthweight and other outcomes, we accept a causal model in which C_3 accounts for the main changes in postpartum maternal weight.

The partial regression coefficients indicate that a change of 100 Calories of average daily rations in the third trimester predicts a change in mean mothers' weight of .37 kilograms. The relation between caloric rations and postpartum maternal weight seems to be a linear one (a quadratic transformation of C_3 adds practically nothing to the proportion of variance explained).

Summary

Our data show a clear effect of food rations on postpartum maternal weight. The effects were entirely confined to famine exposure in the third trimester of pregnancy. Unlike all other indices of the reproductive process, the effect of third trimester food intake on maternal weight was linear and there was no evidence of a threshold above which the effect was absent. Indeed, the correlation of caloric rations and postpartum maternal weight was slightly weaker under the famine condition. This was probably a result of weight loss in mothers before the onset of the famine; during the famine, maternal weight early reached a floor, and did not continue to fall as the famine progressed to maximum severity.

Summary and Conclusions

Exposure to famine during late gestation retarded fetal growth. Food intake measured by official rations in the third trimester surely affected three of six indices of the reproductive process, namely, birthweight, placental weight, and maternal weight at the end of pregnancy. Food intake affected infant length at birth to a smaller degree. It also affected head circumference; the effect is less clear in certain of the analyses because in some hospitals the measure was unreliable. While duration of gestation was possibly affected, changes were small and difficult to interpret.

First trimester effects of nutritional deprivation were equivocal. A first trimester effect on length of gestation was present, but common to the famine and Northern control areas. This first trimester interaction relates also to a proportion of infants of very low birthweight; they had shortened periods of gestation and were born prematurely. The increase in births of very low weight was not statistically significant; later analyses will show, however, that it has probable biological significance.

All the unequivocal effects of low food intake in slowing fetal growth could be localized to the third trimester of gestation. Among third trimester famine effects, only that on maternal weight was linear. All the unequivocal third trimester effects on fetal growth were non-linear. Non-linearity was well demonstrated by conditional relationships. The famine condition was defined as occurring below an empirical threshold of 1500 Calories average daily official ration in the third trimester of gestation. Effects on fetal growth were plainly present under the famine condition, and were minimal under the non-famine condition.

In the end result, our data show that infants exposed to famine late in gestation were lighter than pre- or post-famine norms; to a lesser degree they were also shorter and had smaller heads. The smallness of these infants at birth was not mediated through shortened gestation and can be attributed to a slowed rate of fetal growth. By contrast, the intimation of an effect on birthweight of famine exposure in early gestation did seem to be mediated by length of gestation. Unknown differences in the reliability with which each index was measured could have contributed to differences in their capacity to reflect effects of famine exposure. We have no way of estimating this contribution.

To cull these results from the data, complex procedures were undertaken: analysis by time and place, quantification of food rations, analysis under different nutritional conditions, and the determination of causal relations among independent variables including the control of exposure at different stages of gestation. We can now put the results and the understanding gained to use in further analysis of the developmental process. Our first step will be to try and determine the structure of relationships among these six indices of the reproductive process.

Notes on Method

Multiple Regression Analysis
These analyses relate quantified indices of nutrition in each trimester of pregnancy to each of the six indices of the reproductive process. Analyses were

carried out, wherever possible, for births occurring under two nutritional conditions, famine and non-famine.

Regression analysis yields statements about the average amount of change produced in a dependent variable for each unit of change in an independent variable. Where there are several independent variables, as with nutrition in each trimester, multiple regression analyses are used. To infer unique or combined effects of the independent variables, we have used what we shall term "forced sequences" of variables in the regression equations. In the typical procedure of stepwise multiple regression incorporated in packaged computer programs, the entry of independent variables into the regression equations is ordered by the sizes of the partial correlations between the dependent and the independent variables, the largest being entered first. In "forced sequences" analysis, however, the analyst rules the order in which the variables are entered into the regression equations according to the logical needs of his analysis (Cohen, 1968).

The *combined* effect of all the independent variables on the dependent variable is given by the square of the multiple correlation coefficient (R^2), which is that fraction of the total variance explained by the regression. This value is not affected by the order of entry of variables. The *unique* effect of an independent variable is given by the increase in explained variance that accrues when the variable is added to the regression equation. This increment, however, varies according to the order in which the independent variable is added to the regression equation. The effect solely attributable to a particular variable can sometimes be logically inferred when alternative sequences of variables are compared, provided we have some knowledge of the time order of the variables. In other words, a causal relation can be inferred. The forced sequences are permutations selected to aid inference as to what the causal sequence of variables might be. These procedures of inference are illustrated in the course of the report of results.

The regression coefficients specify the average amount of change to be expected in the dependent variable for a unit change in the independent variable. These are stated in the units of the initial measurement (*b* values) and in the standardized form (beta values). The multiple regression analyses are supported by other statistics. Partial correlations indicate the strength of the correlation between two variables when other specified variables are controlled, or held constant. They offer another way of estimating the unique effect of an independent variable. F values help in evaluating the statistical significance of the multiple regression and of the partial regression coefficients. The F values express the ratio of the variance in a dependent variable explained by a specific set of independent variables to the total unexplained variance; the probability with which the F values obtained might occur by chance can be estimated.

Transformations of the variables by squaring and cubing have been used routinely. Our multiple regression analyses have assumed the associations between variables to be linear; that is, as the value for one variable changes, the values for the other variables change proportionately. Where the assumption of linearity is violated, transformations of the variables can give a more accurate estimate of the true relationships between them. They are not given except when helpful or appropriate.

In these multiple regression analyses, the strength of the associations is likely to be diluted by combining, as we have done, the data from three separate areas. In the combined data the amount of variance to be explained is greater and the proportion accounted for is less. Despite this sacrifice of statistical power, results for single areas usually did not differ materially from those for the three areas combined, and we present the combined data for the sake of simplifying the large number of tables. In one exception, head circumference, the variability of the measure in different areas was great enough to obscure an association; the data are presented for the famine area only.

The analyses relate the grouped mean values of each variable. These analyses of groups confer benefits in this study. One benefit is that each variable is an attribute of the same unit, namely, a one-month period. In consequence average food rations for any period of one month are properly related to mean values for the birth cohort of the same period. The weakness of the official ration as an index of individual nutrition referred to in the text of Chapters 7 and 8 is avoided, and the dilution of associations between average rations over a period and individual values of an outcome does not ensue. A second benefit is that the uncontrolled variance in the dependent variable owed to individual but unmeasured factors—for instance, genetic endowment—is likely to be balanced among cohorts. To the degree that they are so balanced, such unmeasured factors will be eliminated as a source of variation in the dependent variable when comparisons are made between cohorts. Thus the practical advantage of the use of group means over individuals as units is to tighten the analysis. Irrelevant variation is removed from consideration through this quasi-matching. The variation in the dependent study variable remaining among the birth cohorts defined for this study is bound to be less than among individuals, and our design ensures that this variation includes any which is relevant to the independent study variable. We may therefore anticipate that a much larger proportion of variance in the dependent variable will be accounted for by the independent study variable.

The advantages of control over irrelevant variation obtained by the use of monthly means are sufficient, we believe, to risk the problems known to attend the use of means in correlational and regression analysis. Larger correlations between variables are obtained from mean values than from individual values based on the same populations. In addition, with multiple regression the proportion of variance explained (R^2) increases as the number of independent variables increases and approaches the number of cases. In our analysis of monthly cohorts, the number of cases is reduced from many individuals to a few monthly groups (n = 20).

We have compared our analyses of groups with analyses of individuals. The two types of analysis have proved consistent in the direction of effects revealed and also roughly in the size of regression coefficients. They differ chiefly in the amount of variation accounted for and in the levels of significance reached. As with group means, the analysis of individuals was made for births occurring under two conditions—those exposed to levels of nutrition below and above a "famine" threshold—and in this respect too the results of the two sets of analyses were consistent. This congruence reinforces confidence in the many substantial correlations found in the analysis of groups, although they were so much larger than in the analysis of individuals for the reasons given above.

Analysis of Differences

In this analysis, the differences between famine and control areas in the mean monthly values of the independent study variable, official rations, were correlated with the differences in the mean monthly values of each dependent study variable. Thus time and place controls are brought to bear in a single result.

One may anticipate that the amount of variation in the reproductive processes that can be explained by nutrition will be less and statistical significance will be more difficult to attain in the analysis of differences than in the analysis of groups. One desirable reason for the diminution of effect will be the greater rigor of the analysis in removing the effects produced by confounding variables from those produced by nutrition. A second and less desirable reason is that the amount of variance in the specified dependent variable irrelevant to nutrition is increased. This follows from the fact that the dependent variables in the three areas each have their own norms expressed in terms of means and variation about these means. When dependent variables from different areas are compared, the differences between them are incorporated in the variance that we aim to account for by the independent variable. Thus we must expect that the proportion of variance that nutrition as an independent variable can account for will be reduced.

Tables

These tables summarize successive multiple correlation analyses among groups and the correlated differences between famine and control areas for each of the six separate outcomes of the reproductive process in turn. The data are taken from the famine cities of Rotterdam, Amsterdam, and Leiden, and the control cities of Groningen (North) and Heerlen (South), except where the tables indicate otherwise.

The contents of the multiple correlation tables (Tables 10.1, 10.3, 10.4, 10.5, 10.6, and 10.7) for each outcome are arranged as follows:

Average daily rations by trimester as independent variables, and mean values of the dependent variable among birth cohorts for each of 20 months from August 1, 1944, through March 31, 1946, in the famine and control cities combined, under famine and non-famine conditions analyzed separately, to show:

1. proportion of variance (R^2) of mean birthweight explained by three variables, namely, rations in the first (C_1), second (C_2), and third (C_3) trimesters, under different orders of entry in the regression equation;
2. analysis of variance;

INDICES OF THE REPRODUCTIVE PROCESS

3. *partial regression coefficients:* unstandardized *(b)* with standard errors *(s.e.)*, and standardized *(beta)* with F values;
4. *correlation coefficients (r):* bivariate, between dependent and each independent variable, and partial, holding all other variables constant.

The content of the *analysis of differences* table for each outcome (Table 10.2) is arranged to show:

Differences between famine and control cities in average daily calories in first (C_1), second (C_2), and third (C_3) trimesters, correlated with differences in mean monthly values for the outcome variable over the 20 months August 1944 through March 1946. The famine cities are compared with the control cities of Groningen (North) and Heerlen (South) taken separately.

The levels of significance for the F-values and for the bivariate and partial correlation coefficients are coded as: $*p < .05, **p < .01, ***p < .001$.

Table 10.1.1. Calories and birthweight under the famine condition

Mean: 3236 grams   S.D.: 146   N: 26

Proportion of Variance $(R^2 = .6439)$

C_1	.1768	C_2	.2625	C_3	.6254
C_2	.0878	C_1	.0021	C_2	.0049
C_3	.3793	C_3	.3793	C_1	.0136

Analysis of Variance

Source	df	Mean Square	F
Regression	3	115469	13 ***
Residual	22	8709	

Independent Variable	Mean Calories	Partial Regression Coefficients			Correlation Coefficients	
		b (se) in grams/Cals	Beta	F	Bivariate r	Partial r
C_1	1524	.2416 (.2636)	.2414	< 1	.42 *	.19
C_2	1357	−.0747 (.1516)	−.1460	< 1	.51 **	−.10
C_3	1236	.3978 (.0822)	.7804	23 ***	.79 ***	.71 ***

Table 10.1.2. Calories and birthweight under the non-famine condition

Mean: 3350 grams   S.D.: 86   N: 34

Proportion of Variance ($R^2 = .0329$)

C_1	.0010	C_2	.0025	C_3	.0037
C_2	.0079	C_1	.0064	C_2	.0181
C_3	.0240	C_3	.0240	C_1	.0111

Analysis of Variance

Source	df	Mean Square	F
Regression	3	2693	<1
Residual	30	7914	

Independent Variable	Mean Calories	Partial Regression Coefficients			Correlation Coefficients	
		b (se) in grams/Cals	Beta	F	Bivariate r	Partial r
C_1	1448	.0309 (.0527)	.1364	<1	.03	.10
C_2	1676	−.0699 (.0736)	−.2961	<1	−.05	−.17
C_3	2018	.0500 (.0579)	.2250	<1	.06	.15

Table 10.2. Differences by area in Calories and outcome variables

Famine-North Comparison

Calories in Trimester	Birthweight	Placental Weight	Length	Gestation
C_1	−.33	.27	−.51*	−.27
C_2	−.18	−.32	.14	−.19
C_3	.49*	−.42	.52*	.43

Famine-South Comparison

Calories in Trimester	Birthweight	Placental Weight	Length	Gestation
C_1	−.36	.18	−.22	.31
C_2	−.13	.31	−.11	.31
C_3	.60**	.42	.54*	.30

INDICES OF THE REPRODUCTIVE PROCESS

Table 10.3.1. Calories and placental weight under the famine condition†

Mean: 572 grams   S.D.: 46   N: 26

Proportion of Variance ($R^2 = .3980$)

C_1	.1124	C_2	.1237	C_3	.3598
C_2	.0151	C_1	.0038	C_2	.0120
C_3	.2705	C_3	.2705	C_1	.0271

Analysis of Variance

Source	df	Mean Square	F
Regression	3	6951	4.8*
Residual	22	1433	

Independent Variable	Mean Calories	Partial Regression Coefficients			Correlation Coefficients	
		b (se) in grams/Cals	Beta	F	Bivariate r	Partial r
C_1	1524	.1262 (.1069)	.4043	1.4	.33	.24
C_2	1357	−.0603 (.0615)	−.3777	<1	.35	−.20
C_3	1236	.1048 (.0333)	.6591	9.8***	.59**	.55**

† Excluding Amsterdam and Leiden.

Table 10.3.2 Calories and placental weight under the non-famine condition†

Mean: 600 grams   S.D.: 53   N: 34

Proportion of Variance ($R^2 = .1951$)

C_1	.0090	C_2	.1010	C_3	.1247
C_2	.1288	C_1	.0367	C_2	.0079
C_3	.0573	C_3	.0573	C_1	.0625

Analysis of Variance

Source	df	Mean Square	F
Regression	3	6196	2.4
Residual	30	2556	

Independent Variable	Mean Calories	Partial Regression Coefficients			Correlation Coefficients	
		b (se) in grams/Cals	Beta	F	Bivariate r	Partial r
C_1	1448	−.1499 (.0983)	−.3735	2.3	.09	−.02
C_2	1676	−.0706 (.1307)	−.3408	<1	.31	−.11
C_3	2018	.0931 (.0638)	.9598	2.1	.35	.03

† Excluding Amsterdam and Leiden.

Table 10.4.1. Calories and length at birth under the famine condition

Mean: 49.4 cms S.D.: 0.5 N: 26

Proportion of Variance ($R^2 = .2437$)

C_1 .0530	C_2 .0565	C_3 .2168
C_2 .0059	C_1 .0024	C_2 .0014
C_3 .1848	C_3 .1847	C_1 .0255

Analysis of Variance

Source	df	Mean Square	F
Regression	3	.49	2.4
Residual	22	.21	

Independent Variable	Mean Calories	Partial Regression Coefficients			Correlation Coefficients	
		b (se) in cms/Cals	Beta	F	Bivariate r	Partial r
C_1	1524	.0011 (.0013)	.3303	<1	.23	.18
C_2	1357	−.0006 (.0007)	−.3618	<1	.23	−.17
C_3	1236	.0009 (.0004)	.5447	5.37*	.46*	.44*

Table 10.4.2. Calories and length at birth under the non-famine condition

Mean: 49.6 cms S.D.: 0.6 N: 34

Proportion of Variance ($R^2 = .0924$)

C_1 .0134	C_2 .0831	C_3 .0321
C_2 .0762	C_1 .0065	C_2 .0524
C_3 .0028	C_3 .0028	C_1 .0079

Analysis of Variance

Source	df	Mean Square	F
Regression	3	.38	1.0
Residual	30	.37	

Independent Variable	Mean Calories	Partial Regression Coefficients			Correlation Coefficients	
		b (se) in cms/Cals	Beta	F	Bivariate r	Partial r
C_1	1448	.0002 (.0004)	.1151	<1	−.11	.09
C_2	1676	−.0007 (.0005)	−.4150	1.8	−.28	−.24
C_3	2018	−.0001 (.0004)	.0772	<1	−.17	.05

INDICES OF THE REPRODUCTIVE PROCESS   117

Table 10.5. Calories and head circumference: Rotterdam only

Mean: 35 cms   S.D.: 0.5   N: 20

Proportion of Variance (R^2 = .3768)

C_1	.0863	C_2	.0227	C_3	.3106
C_2	.0824	C_1	.1460	C_2	.0557
C_3	.2081	C_3	.2081	C_1	.0105

Analysis of Variance

Source	df	Mean Square	F
Regression	3	.70	3.2*
Residual	16	.22	

Independent Variable	Mean Calories	Partial Regression Coefficients			Correlation Coefficients	
		b (se) in cms/Cals	Beta	F	Bivariate r	Partial r
C_1	1327	−.0002 (.0003)	−.1284	<1	−.29	−.12
C_2	1382	−.0002 (.0003)	−.2019	<1	.15	−.16
C_3	1524	.0005 (.0002)	.6630	5.34*	.55*	.50*

Table 10.6.1. Calories and length of gestation under the famine condition†

Mean: 39.4 weeks   S.D.: 0.3   N: 26

Proportion of Variance (R^2 = .2008)

C_1	.0165	C_2	.0017	C_3	.1108
C_2	.0922	C_1	.1070	C_2	.0341
C_3	.0921	C_3	.0921	C_1	.0559

Analysis of Variance

Source	df	Mean Square	F
Regression	3	.13	1.84
Residual	22	.07	

Independent Variable	Mean Calories	Partial Regression Coefficients			Correlation Coefficients	
		b (se) in weeks/Cals	Beta	F	Bivariate r	Partial r
C_1	1524	−.0009 (.0007)	−.4893	1.54	−.12	−.25
C_2	1357	.0002 (.0004)	.2428	.30	.04	.11
C_3	1236	.0004 (.0002)	.3846	2.54	.33	.32

† Excluding Leiden.

Table 10.6.2. Calories and length of gestation among groups under the non-famine condition†

Mean: 39.5 weeks   S.D.: 0.4   N: 34

Proportion of Variance ($R^2 = .3386$)

C_1	.0239	C_2	.1156	C_3	.1197
C_2	.3102	C_1	.2184	C_2	.0175
C_3	.0046	C_3	.0046	C_1	.2014

Analysis of Variance

Source	df	Mean Square	F
Regression	3	.47	5.12**
Residual	30	.09	

Independent Variable	Mean Calories	Partial Regression Coefficients			Correlation Coefficients	
		b (se) in weeks/Cals	Beta	F	Bivariate r	Partial r
C_1	1448	.0005 (.0002)	.5817	9.13***	.15	.48***
C_2	1676	−.0006 (.0002)	−.6314	5.99**	−.34	−.40*
C_3	2018	−.0001 (.0002)	−.0984	<1	−.34	−.08

† Excluding Leiden.

Table 10.7. Calories and maternal weight among groups: Rotterdam only

Mean: 59.45 Kilograms   S.D.: 2.5   N: 20

Proportion of Variance ($R^2 = .8334$)

C_1	.1175	C_2	.1220	C_3	.7673
C_2	.2739	C_1	.2694	C_2	.0526
C_3	.4420	C_3	.4420	C_1	.0136

Analysis of Variance

Source	df	Mean Square	F
Regression	3	33.34	26.68***
Residual	16	1.25	

Independent Variable	Mean Calories	Partial Regression Coefficients			Correlation Coefficients	
		b (se) in Kg/Cals	Beta	F	Bivariate r	Partial r
C_1	1327	−.0009 (.0007)	−.1462	1.30	−.34	−.27
C_2	1382	−.0009 (.0008)	−.1802	1.27	.34	−.27
C	1524	.0037 (.0006)	.9661	42.45***	.87	.85***

11 Interrelations Among Indices of the Reproductive Process

In our study of the reproductive process in relation to famine, the time order and the logical priority of the variable "caloric intake" in relation to each separate outcome was secured by the retrospective cohort design. Caloric intake during the period under study resembled an experimental or test variable. The design enabled us to isolate this variable as if it were the result of purposeful intervention. Where associations were found, there was no doubt about the direction of change and the sequence of events in the causal chain.

The dimensions of the infant, placental weight, and the end-point of gestation, however, were necessarily measured at the same time. In principle, measures of related outcomes made at the same point in time can in themselves tell us nothing about their order in time. With these dependent variables, therefore, no design could confer certainty either about their ordering in time or about the directions of change among them. This knowledge is essential to secure inferences about causes and determinants. To accomplish the difficult task of judging among many alternatives about time order and direction of change, we drew on existing knowledge of human biology as well as on quantitative analyses of multivariate models.

We took successive steps in the analysis of the connections and sequences among all the outcomes of the reproductive process. First, we made a graphic representation to show the changes through time of all the variables concurrently. These graphs suggested a number of conclusions. We then turned to multiple regression analysis to test, elaborate, and add to these conclusions. Our object was to arrive at a tenable model of the direction and strength of the paths between all the variables for which we had measures. We hoped to construct our models from observed data by means of path analysis.

Graphic Presentation

We first graphed the six variables of the reproductive process for the famine area against calendar time (Figure 11.1). Only the data for the famine area are discussed, since the cogency of our analysis depends on the severity as well as the timing of the nutritional changes during the famine. The sources of data are the same as for the separate analyses of each index of the reproductive process reported in Chapter 10.

The pattern of time-related changes in the six outcome variables before, during, and after the famine leads us to a number of interpretations. Some of these inferences are more secure than others. All must be seen in the context of the firm conclusions of the previous chapter. Thus we know that nutritional deprivation caused intrauterine growth retardation with little change in length of gestation, that all the notable effects of the famine on maternal weight and intrauterine fetal growth related to exposure during the third trimester of pregnancy, and also that the effects on birthweight, placental weight, infant length, and head circumference at birth were not linear like those on maternal weight, but more marked in the famine condition. Our graphic analysis (Fig. 11.1) suggests the following:

1. *There is a threshold value of maternal nutrient intake around which the strength of nutritional effects change.*

Above the threshold value, the growth of the products of conception is to a large degree buffered from nutritional deprivation, presumably by maternal food stores. Below the threshold, the distribution of nutrients between mother and products of conception changes: maternal needs gain more priority than they have above the threshold; this is to the detriment of fetal and placental growth but to the advantage of maternal survival.

The level of nutritional deprivation imposed by war-time rations before the famine affected maternal weight mainly and in our data had no noticeable effect on placenta and fetus.* Only when famine supervened did a sharp fall in placental weight and birthweight follow the further fall in maternal weight. Maternal weight loss reached a maximum with this initial sharp fall in the second month of famine, and there was no further loss, although the famine continued severe. By contrast, placental weight and birthweight continued to fall concomitantly with the decline in rations for a further two months before reaching their maximum weight loss. Thus, below the famine threshold, there seemed to be a reallocation of nutritional priorities. We surmise that this distribution of nutrients continued into the early phase of recovery. For in the recovery phase maternal weight rose, if not more sharply than placental weight, distinctly more sharply than birthweight did.

---

*The data of C. A. Smith (1947) collected from clinics in Rotterdam and The Hague suggest that the median levels of birthweight might have been up to 150 grams lower in the war-time pre-famine period than in the peace-time post-famine period.

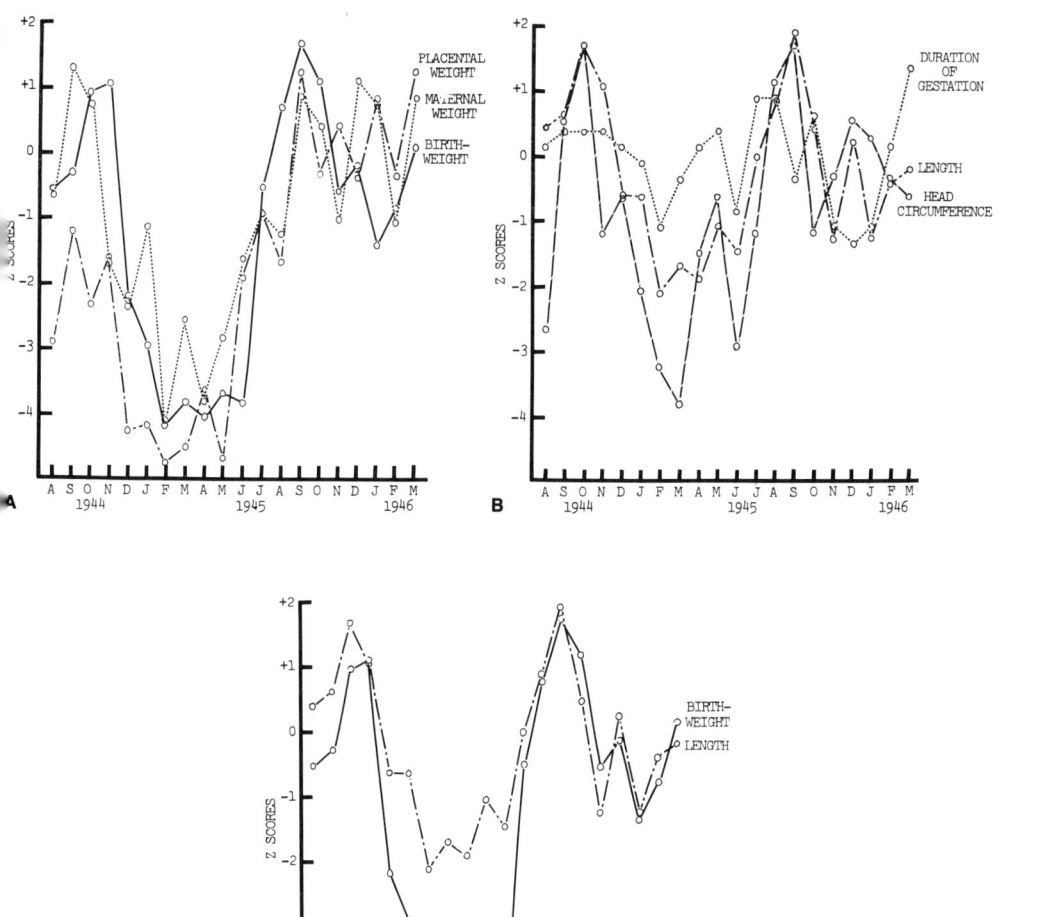

Figure 11.1A. Birthweight, maternal weight, and placental weight in the famine cities for the months August 1944 through March 1946 expressed as Z scores based on the average values of the post-famine period (July 1945 through March 1946)

Figure 11.1B. Duration of gestation, length, and head circumference at birth for the months August 1944 through March 1946, expressed as Z scores based on the average values of the post-famine period (July 1945 through March 1946)

Figure 11.1C. Birthweight and length at birth in the famine cities for the period August 1944 through March 1946, expressed as Z scores based on the average value of the post-famine period (July 1945 through March 1946)

2. *As between placenta and fetus, the metabolic needs of the placenta seem to have first call on circulating nutrients.*

The famine retarded the growth in weight of fetus and placenta almost simultaneously, but the fall in birthweight lagged a little behind the erratic course of placental weight in timing and degree. On recovery from the nadir of the last famine months fetal growth lagged a full month behind placental growth. This lag in fetal weight, modest during decline and more marked during recovery, might indicate the presence of a placental barrier in the direct line of supply of nutrients from mother to fetus. The placenta is bathed in maternal blood, and its needs can be met before the nutrients are transmitted to the fetus (Dawes, 1968).

3. *The growth of the bones that determine fetal length was less affected by nutritional deprivation than the growth of the other tissues that determine fetal weight, such as fat and muscle.*

The changes in infant length at birth, while responsive to famine exposure in the third trimester, were less marked than the changes in birthweight and placental weight, and also lagged behind them somewhat. A significant reduction in infant length associated with exposure in the third trimester did not appear until the famine reached its height. After that, the pattern for infant length at birth was synchronous with that for birthweight. Thus most birth cohorts, in accord with the usual "small-for-dates" syndrome, had lost weight while maintaining length. Infants were shorter as well as lighter only after severe and prolonged maternal food deprivation. These results are consistent with those of autopsy studies of intrauterine growth retardation (Gruenwald 1966).

Although the lag in changes in length at birth seem most likely to reflect lesser effects than on weight, it could imply a second threshold value for nutrient intake, lower than the threshold value for fetal weight, above which growth in length is buffered. This hypothesis is not supported by scattergrams of caloric rations against length. Alternatively, length at birth could have been affected only by the interaction of famine and another factor, such as temperature. The maximum effect on length occurred among births of the two coldest months, and fluctuations in the control areas were not entirely dissimilar. The synchrony of length changes with birthweight changes, however, is against this hypothesis, since birthweight changes did not require the interaction of both factors. Another alternative, that length at birth was affected by exposure in the second trimester of pregnancy and therefore deferred, can also be ruled out by the absence of second trimester effects; there was no deferral of recovery in length at birth after the famine. The statistical analysis of changes in infant length with changes in caloric rations reported in the previous chapter supports the interpretation of an effect limited to the third trimester.

4. *Changes in head circumference at birth were clearly related to nutritional deprivation in the third trimester, although less regularly than infant length.*

The changes in head size, while more erratic than changes in length, exceeded them in magnitude. The irregularity of the pattern may be a function of the smaller numbers of cases included in the analysis. The erratic behavior of the head size curve makes determination of a threshold value difficult, although there is no doubt that it exists as for other fetal dimensions and may be higher. If brain growth is a determinant of skull growth (Gruenwald and Minh, 1961), a higher threshold is in accord with autopsy studies which suggest that with intrauterine growth retardation the brain is spared, in that it is among the organs least diminished in size (Gruenwald, 1966; Naeye, 1970).

5. *The effects of famine on fetal growth were neither mediated nor confounded through the shortening of gestation.*

We concluded in the previous chapter that nutritional effects on length of gestation were equivocal; at most, they were small. Simple inspection of the graphs is sufficient to show that reductions in the mean period of gestation could not have accounted for the main changes in other reproductive indices during the famine.

A detailed interpretation of Figure 11 from which these conclusions derive is given in the section on Notes and Methods appended to this chapter (pp. 141-43).

Foundations for a Model of Interrelations

In order to test and extend the inferences made from the analysis by inspection, we now turn to quantitative analysis of the interrelations between variables. We shall do so with the help of multiple regression and finally, path analysis.

Path analysis imposes on investigators the salutary discipline of making explicit at the outset the hypotheses underlying their conception of the relations between variables. By taking one step at a time, we tried to establish a sound basis for the necessary assumptions of direction and time order. We took combinations of sets of three variables and examined their relations in two ways: by contingency table analysis, illustrated in diagrams in the text, and by the method of "forced sequences" of multiple regression analyses previously described (see Chapter 10, Notes on Method). The regression analyses are given in tables at the end of this chapter. The unit of analysis throughout is the individual birth and not group means. Analysis of individuals best serves the logic of a study of interrelations within the maternal-fetal unit.

We shall show that provided the position in time or logical priority of any one variable among three associated variables is known, in some instances these analyses can lead to inferences which permit us to place the other two in logical order. Only after we had strengthened our grasp of the logical priorities among all the available variables did we test path models incorporating the whole set.

The literature on human reproduction is ambiguous about the direction of change among some of the seven variables included in our analysis so far. In particular, there are doubts about the relations between caloric intake, maternal weight, and fetal weight, and about the relations between placental and fetal growth. We shall consider these two problems first.

Caloric Intake, Maternal Weight, and Birthweight

We have found the quantitative relations between caloric intake, maternal weight during reproduction, and birthweight analyzed in only one previous study (Thomson, 1959). All three variables are related. The associations between them, avoiding assumptions about time order and direction of effect, can be represented in our data as follows.

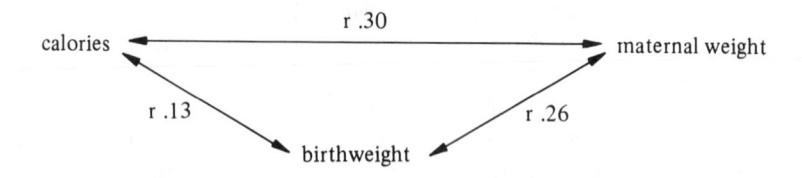

```
                    r .30
    calories ←————————————————→ maternal weight
         ↘                    ↙
        r .13              r .26
             ↘            ↙
              birthweight
```

The sizes of Thomson's correlations were similar to ours. For our purposes birthweight is the dependent variable among these three. There has been doubt, however, about the direction of change between the remaining two independent variables. As we observed in the previous chapter, Thomson found that the partial correlation between caloric intake and birthweight disappeared when maternal weight (in height categories at about 20 weeks of pregnancy) was introduced into the analysis. On the other hand, the partial correlation between caloric intake and maternal weight persisted when birthweight was introduced into the analysis. He chose to interpret this result as meaning that maternal size, indicated by weight for height, "explained" the association—that is, it was the common cause of both caloric intake and birthweight. Thomson's causal model can be represented as follows.

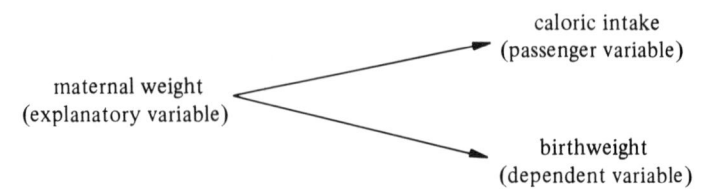

```
                                    caloric intake
                                 ↗  (passenger variable)
    maternal weight         ————
    (explanatory variable)      ↘
                                    birthweight
                                    (dependent variable)
```

This interpretation, buttressed by other surveys, brought into disfavor the hypothesis that maternal nutrition during pregnancy influenced birthweight, or fetal growth and development in general. The hypothesis remained outcast through the succeeding decade of the 1960s. Together with the association Thomson found between maternal height and birthweight, his interpretation led him to the view that the nutrition of mothers during their own growth, rather than during pregnancy, was an important determinant of birthweight.

As we indicated in the previous chapter, however, when a third variable is introduced into an analysis of an association between two other variables, and the association then disappears, an alternative hypothesis remains (Lazarsfeld and Kendall, 1950). Such a third variable may be an intervening variable between the two variables of the initial association. A causal chain equally plausible on logical grounds, therefore, would be as follows.

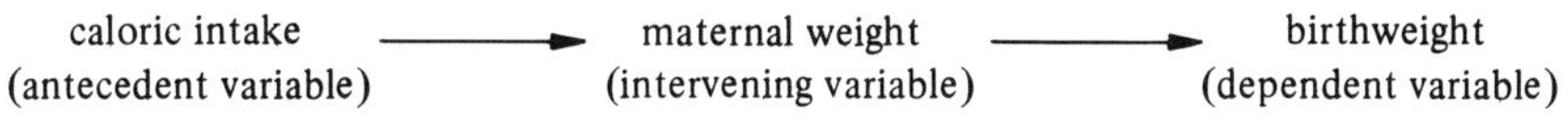

caloric intake ⟶ maternal weight ⟶ birthweight
(antecedent variable)　(intervening variable)　(dependent variable)

We have been able to clarify this question somewhat in a multivariate analysis of births in Harlem Hospital, New York City. In our own and other data, gestation, smoking, and history of previous low birthweight have strong independent associations with birthweight (Rush, Davis, and Susser, 1972). But we found that other long-established associations with birthweight, such as those of height, parity, and age, were not direct. On introducing maternal weight and weight gain in pregnancy into the analysis, these associations disappeared. Height, parity, and age are all logically antecedent to maternal weight; hence we concluded that they acted only through maternal weight as an intervening variable. A model of these causal links can be constructed as follows.

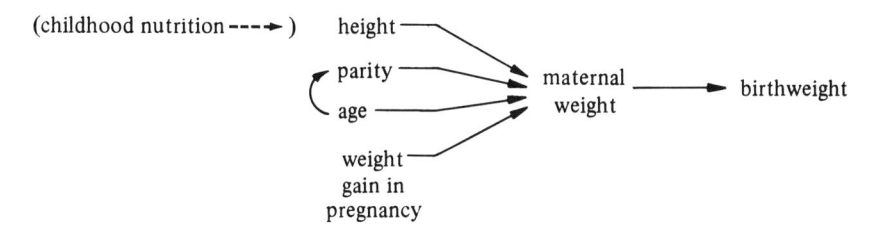

(childhood nutrition ---→)　height ⟶
　　　　　　　　　　　　　parity ⟶　maternal ⟶ birthweight
　　　　　　　　　　　　　age ⟶　　weight
　　　　　　　　　　　　　weight ⟶
　　　　　　　　　　　　　gain in
　　　　　　　　　　　　　pregnancy

This model revived the hypothesis that nutrition during pregnancy is a factor in birthweight; the persistent association of birthweight with maternal weight gain, especially, points to the mother's diet (Bergner and Susser, 1970). We lacked a direct demonstration of this relationship in the above analysis, however, and our model could stand only as follows (the broken lines indicate untested paths):

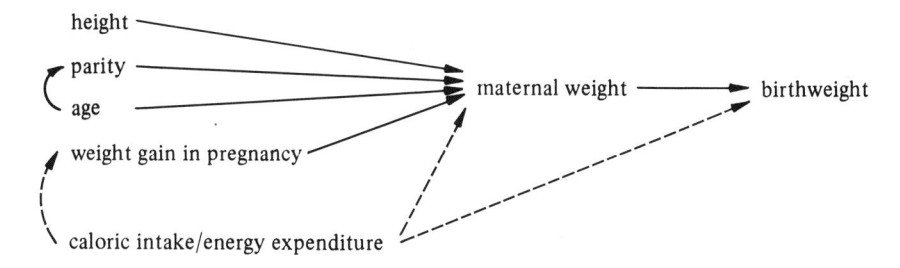

height ⟶
parity ⟶
age ⟶　　　　　　maternal weight ⟶ birthweight
weight gain in pregnancy ⟶
caloric intake/energy expenditure

The data from the Dutch famine enable us to argue, at least under the special condition of nutritional deprivation, that caloric intake *produced* the changes in the outcomes of the reproductive process. Rations determined caloric intake, which can safely be considered an antecedent of the changes that accompanied it, provided there was no confounding by other factors.* These time changes, and their localization and magnitude in the famine areas, leave no doubt that deficient caloric intake reduced both maternal weight and birthweight.**

Two pathways, one direct and one indirect, remained viable between caloric intake under the famine condition and birthweight:

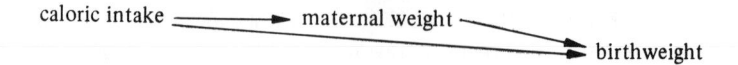

```
caloric intake ─────────▶ maternal weight ─╮
                                            ╰─▶ birthweight
```

Upon the introduction of maternal weight into the analysis of the association between calories and birthweight, in our data as in Thomson's, the association disappeared (Table 11.1). As an intervening variable, therefore, maternal weight accounts for all the variance in birthweight that can be attributed to caloric rations. This sequence leaves no place for a direct effect of caloric intake separate from that acting through maternal weight. Thus in considering our data overall we might retain only the indirect path of the two in the diagram above—that is, caloric intake acts through maternal weight.

We shall use the foregoing analysis to buttress our assumptions about the position of maternal weight in relation to caloric intake and other indices of the products of conception under circumstances of nutritional deprivation. That is, we conceive maternal weight as consequent on caloric intake and antecedent to measures of fetal and placental dimensions. We have noted that caloric rations were related to birthweight under famine rather than non-famine conditions, and we shall see later that the paths may be modified under famine conditions. Our path models will take care of these contingencies.

Birthweight and Placental Weight

Now we turn to consider the nature of the associations between fetal and placental weight. This question has been posed before but not resolved (McKeown and Record, 1953; Armitage, Boyd, Hamilton, and Rowe, 1967; Thomson, Billewicz, and Hytten, 1969). The question about the causal sequence of fetal and placental weight has significance for the interpretation of studies of

---

*This is not as safe an assumption under non-famine conditions. Thomson's assumption that mother's size determined both her caloric intake and baby's weight cannot be ruled out, especially in the absence of significant association, in the data given in Chapter 10, between caloric intake and birthweight under the non-famine condition.

**The reader will recall that the maternal weight measure in these data is based on a sample of postpartum weights from the single famine-affected city of Rotterdam. This weight to some degree subsumes both the mother's pre-pregnant weight and her weight gain during pregnancy. It need hardly be emphasized that weight change ascribed to caloric intake always implies a change in the metabolic balance between caloric intake and energy expenditure.

the placenta in relation to measures of fetal growth and nutrition. A number of such studies have recently appeared (Winick, 1971; Laga, Driscoll, and Munro, 1972a, b; Rosado et al., 1972). If placental growth is a determinant of fetal growth, measures of placental dysfunction would point to the presence of placental insufficiency as a potential cause of fetal dystrophy but not necessarily to the presence of fetal dystrophy itself. If fetal growth is a determinant of placental growth, or if both are the result of a common cause, then measures of placental dysfunction would be an index rather than a determinant of fetal dystrophy and would point to the presence of fetal dystrophy. Hence, depending on which inference is correct, the import of such measures for research or clinical work is different.

In the first concept, the placenta is a mediating organ between mother and fetus (McKeown and Record, 1953; McLaren and Michie, 1963; McLaren, 1966; Payne and Wheeler, 1967a, b; James, 1967). In keeping with this view are the physiological hypotheses of placental barriers in the exchange of gas, nutrients, hormones, and immune bodies, and the pathological hypotheses of placental insufficiency in the function of transmitting nutrients. On these hypotheses a reduction in placental weight might be reflected in a reduction in placental function, including nutrient transmission. In other words, maternal support for fetal growth could be reduced by placental insufficiency and lead to an associated reduction in birthweight.

In the alternative concept, the placenta is a fetal organ that is adaptive to the needs of the fetus (*cf.* Aherne, 1966). Anatomically the placenta is indeed a fetal organ inserted into the uterus (Boyd and Hamilton, 1967). The size and function of the placenta are held to respond to the needs of the fetus; as the fetus grows so the placenta grows, and thus fetal growth governs the association of placental weight with birthweight. Dawes (1968) has argued for the concept of a more active fetus than the passive recipient implied by the analogy of the fetus as spaceman isolated in an externally controlled environment; he attributes more of the metabolic processes of growth to fetal reactivity, and less to an active placental barrier between mother and fetus.*

The morphology of the placenta has not been shown to be either cause or consequence of fetal growth. Both the dispersal of placental arteries studied in a series of over 1000 births (Armitage, Boyd, Hamilton, and Rowe, 1967), and the amount and distribution of placental villi minutely studied in a comparison of 18 Boston and 20 small Guatemalan infants (Laga, Driscoll, and Munro, 1972a, b), were unrelated to birthweight.

Although morphological comparisons proved equivocal, metabolic compari-

---

*Adjustments of the fetal circulation can be shown to influence partial gas pressures in the blood. In contrast with this, the sharp differential in partial oxygen pressure between the maternal and fetal circulations can be accounted for simply by placental metabolic needs, and by disjunction ("inhomogeneity") between the terminal villi of the maternal and fetal circulations where nutrient exchange takes place.

sons of the Boston and Guatemalan series were consistent with the hypothesis that placental function is determined by the fetus. Birthweight, but not gestational age or placental weight, served to differentiate the capacity of placentae for synthesizing protein.* Partial correlations of an array of indices of protein metabolism with gestational age and placental weight were negligible with birthweight held constant.

The authors themselves concluded that fetal weight determines placental metabolism without discussing the contrary explanation. Armitage, Boyd, Hamilton, and Rowe (1967) obtained a similar result and implicitly reached a similar conclusion. They noted that although the total effect of length of gestation on placental weight is positive, "the more premature infants tend to have lower birthweights and hence lower placental weights."

In further support of the concept that fetal needs determine placental function, Aherne (1966) constructed equations to represent the relationships between growth rates of placenta and fetus. He found chorionic villous surface area of the placenta varied as the placental weight. Since fetal metabolism varies with fetal weight in approximately the same manner as does placental weight, Aherne deduced from his formula, as he put it, that throughout gestation the chorionic surface is matched to fetal metabolism.

There is nothing in Aherne's work to exclude the reciprocal formulation of this relationship, however, and Payne and Wheeler (1967a, b) do indeed use similar equations to support the alternative concept that fetal growth is directly dependent on the supply through the placenta of nutrients from the mother. They constructed a mathematical model general to fetal growth across species in which two asumptions were made: (1) weight gain is decided by the rate of nutrient supply to the fetus across the placenta, a rate dependent on the area of vascular surface; (2) the area of this vascular surface remains in constant proportion to the total surface of the fetus itself. (This condition fits well, in humans, with the data of Aherne (1966) and Laga, Driscoll, and Munro (1972a,b).)

The model was tested on a series of fetal weights at different periods of gestation taken from a variety of species. It proved to be compatible with the experimental data, and it conforms with a model in which the rate of nutrient supply determines differences in the size of offspring in a constant relationship to the power of three, which the authors name "a cubic law of growth." As we have noted, it remains compatible with the reciprocal model; the model assumes, but does not establish, the direction of relations between fetus and placenta.

Here we approach the question first through an analysis of the interrelations between the three variables fetal weight, placental weight, and fetal age (i.e. length of gestation). The diagram below sets out the associations in our data between all the pairings in the first set of three variables, without assumptions of time order or direction of effect.

*Detailed data provided by the authors at our request are coherent with their published conclusions.

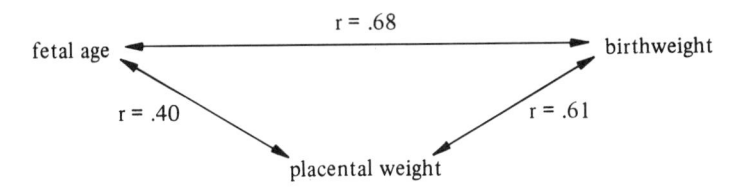

```
                           r = .68
        fetal age  ◄─────────────────────►  birthweight
                ◄                        ▲
                 ╲                      ╱
              r = .40                r = .61
                   ╲                ╱
                    ▼              
                    placental weight
```

The correlations conform quite well with the other data to be found in the literature (Solth, 1961; Armitage, Boyd, Hamilton, and Rowe, 1967; Thomson, Billewicz, and Hytten, 1969). Fetal age at birth has a stronger association with birthweight than with placental weight. With regard to ordering the three variables, this finding is suggestive of a closer relation of fetal age with birthweight than with placental weight. To some extent, however, this pattern of correlations could arise from the concentration of birth data toward the end of the third trimester, in consequence of the inaccessibility to measurement of the growth process at earlier stages of gestation. In good circumstances, the rate of gain in fetal weight continues in linear fashion until late in the third trimester, when absolute weight gain is at a maximum (Hosemann, 1949; Karn and Penrose, 1951; McKeown and Record, 1953). By contrast the placental-fetal weight ratio declines in the third trimester, and the rate of gain in placental weight reaches its peak somewhat earlier (Gruenwald and Minh, 1961; Thomson, Billewicz, and Hytten, 1969). Hence the association of placental weight and duration of gestation may be stronger earlier in pregnancy when increase in placental weight is probably linear. No representative data are available for early pregnancy.

In consideration of possible causal paths, a crucial step is to determine the logical position of at least one variable. We shall argue here that fetal age at birth is logically and biologically an antecedent condition for the remaining two variables. Without the passage of time, measured by fetal age, there can be no growth. We therefore reject at the outset all major pathways based on the opposite assumption.* With fetal age in a known position in our three-variable analysis, three plausible models remain to be considered.

---

*In actuality, the existence of a reversed relationship of the weight of the products of conception with length of gestation, which we use as a measure of fetal age, is plausible. In rats, elegantly designed experiments have shown that the more rapid placental and fetal growth are, the shorter the period of gestation is (McLaren, 1965). In humans, in a multiple regression analysis, an inverse relation between placental weight and length of gestation was found for given values of the other variables included in the analysis (Armitage, Boyd, Hamilton, and Rowe, 1967); from another contingency table analysis (Thomson, Billewicz, and Hytten, 1969) one can infer that this inverse correlation occurs specifically toward the end of gestation. In our own data, too, a small negative partial correlation was found under the famine condition.

These various findings and others (McKeown and Record, 1953) suggest that placental or fetal size or both combined may trigger parturition on reaching a certain threshold. Growth of the products of conception may thus influence length of gestation.

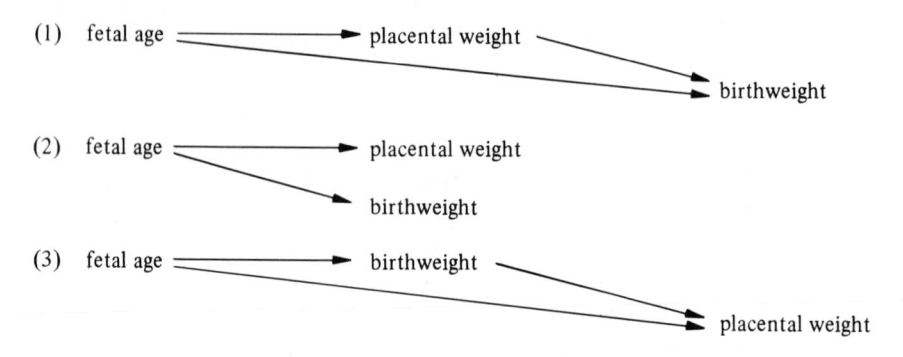

(1) fetal age ⟶ placental weight ⟶ birthweight
    fetal age ⟶ birthweight

(2) fetal age ⟶ placental weight
    fetal age ⟶ birthweight

(3) fetal age ⟶ birthweight ⟶ placental weight
    fetal age ⟶ placental weight

On the basis of the analysis that follows, we conclude that we should reject the first two paths. In multiple regression analyses we have used "forced sequences," and also partial correlations and contingency table analysis (see Notes and Tables, Chapter 10, pp. 109 ff). The multiple regression sequences, taking placental weight as dependent variable, show that the introduction of birthweight can account for the whole of the variance in the association between fetal age and placental weight (Table 11.2). In other words, fetal age adds nothing to the explained variance in placental weight when birthweight has been entered before it in the regression equation.

Such a result is compatible with only one interpretation. Since logically birthweight cannot be conceived as an explanatory variable antecedent to fetal age, it must be an intervening variable as in Model 3 above. At the same time in this model, a direct path between fetal age and placental weight that bypasses birthweight can be rejected, because birthweight leaves none of the explained variance in placental weight unaccounted for. The tenable model then stands as follows.

fetal age ⟶ birthweight ⟶ placental weight

In the association of fetal age with birthweight as dependent variable, on the contrary, the introduction of placental weight does not account for all the variance in the association, and is therefore compatible with either Model 1 or Model 2. That is, fetal age accounts for added variance over and above that

---

Such negative correlations with the size of the products of conception must be interpreted in the context of length of gestation as an index of *fetal age at the time of birth*. In other words, a fast-growing large fetus may trigger its birth at an earlier fetal age than a slow-growing small fetus. For the purposes of our analysis, however, we use length of gestation as an index of chronological *fetal age irrespective of time of birth*. Whether a particular fetus and placenta grows fast or slow, the older the fetus is the larger will be their size, and the logic of the argument that fetal age is biologically antecedent to fetal and placental weight is not affected.

contributed by placental weight. Both models 1 and 2 require, however, that fetal age must be associated by a direct link with placental weight in addition to its direct link with birthweight. In this regard, neither Model 1 nor Model 2 is readily compatible with the small negative partial correlation of fetal age with placental weight controlled for birthweight ($r = -.08$). Model 3 meets this requirement.

It remains possible that unusual distributions of placental weight by fetal age—for instance, in opposite directions for different categories of birthweight— could produce the negligible or negative partial correlations found in several sets of data (Solth, 1961; Zschiesche and Gerlach, 1963; Armitage, Boyd, Hamilton, and Rowe, 1967).

This possibility can be rejected on examination of our own data, and the data of Thomson, Billewicz, and Hytten (1969). Figure 11.2A shows a consistent linear relationship of mean birthweight with fetal age, when placental weight is held constant. By contrast Figure 11.2B shows that there is no clear relationship of mean placental weight with fetal age, when birthweight is held constant. If anything there is a slightly negative slope of placental weight with increasing fetal age in most discrete birthweight categories.

We conclude that Model 3 correctly represents relations among the three variables under consideration insofar as length of gestation represents fetal age. In other words, fetal age is a determinant of fetal growth (as indicated by birthweight) and fetal growth is in turn a determinant of placental growth (as indicated by placental weight). In addition, it seems likely that in accord with experimental evidence cited in the footnote on page 129, length of gestation is influenced by placental growth. Thus, in late pregnancy, for given values of birthweight, the higher the placental weight the shorter is the duration of gestation.

The analysis of these three variables alone can be accepted as establishing one sequence among the determinants of fetal growth. In relation to independent variables other than fetal age, the analysis does not exclude a reversed sequence between placental weight and birthweight. Nutrient intake, say, might contribute to fetal growth through differently ordered pathways. Moreover, one can assume that the integrity of the placenta must be a condition for adequate fetal nutrition and growth. Under extreme limiting conditions—for instance, when placental function is insufficient to transmit essential nutrients—the damaged placenta will interpose a barrier to fetal nutrition that could reverse the normal pathway. To demonstrate such effects of placental pathology would require a special investigation.

With starvation, however, one might anticipate a similar modification. Inspection of the changes through the famine in the variables relating to reproduction in our data, it will be recalled, suggested that maternal and placental weight reflected nutritional deprivation before birthweight did; on recovery, after

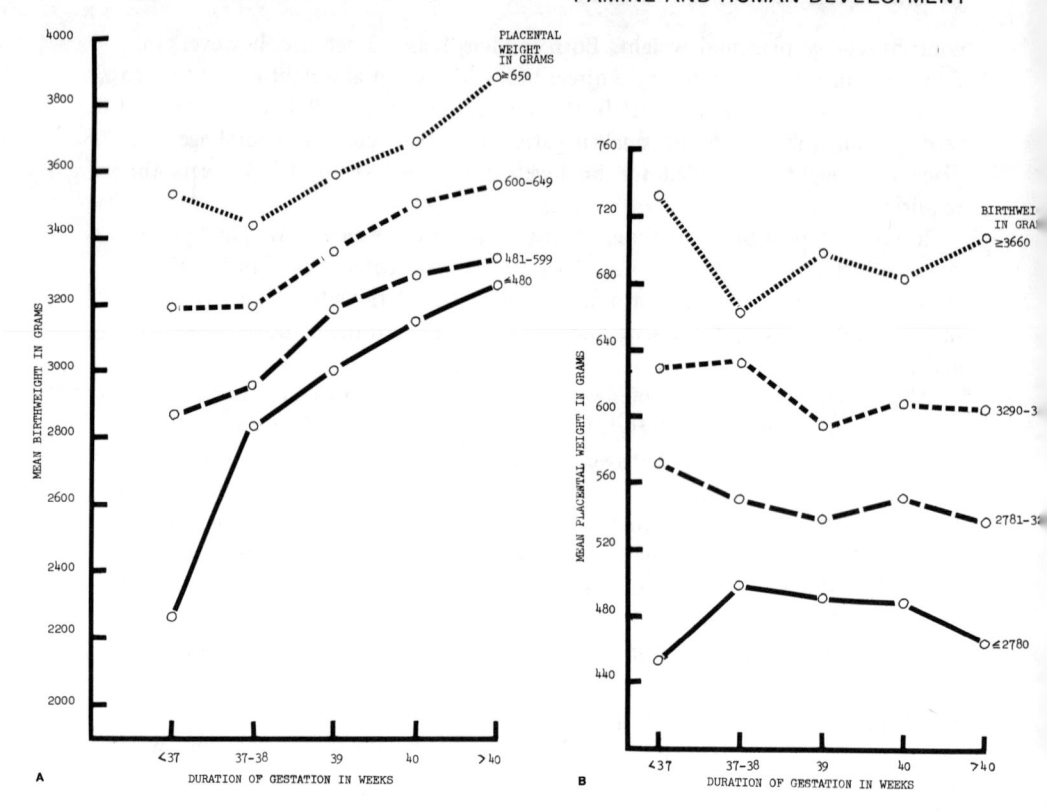

Figure 11.2A. Mean birthweight by duration of gestation within four placental weight categories among children born in the cities of Rotterdam (famine area), Groningen (Northern control area), and Heerlen (Southern control area) between August 1944 and May 1946

Figure 11.2B. Mean placental weight by duration of gestation within four birthweight categories among children born in the cities of Rotterdam (famine area), Groningen (Northern control area), and Heerlen (Southern control area) between August 1944 and May 1946

nutrient stores had been severely depleted, the placenta together with the mother had first call on the nutrient intake. These changes too would constitute a reversal of the direction of the path between placental and fetal growth under the famine condition. In this situation, there is presumably reciprocal alternation of the paths between birthweight and placental weight; at the point at which the needs of placental metabolism were satisfied, fetal growth would resume and determine further placental growth. This model seems closest to the data analyzed so far.

To pursue this question, we turn our attention to the relations of caloric intake with the reproductive process. Another three-variable analysis, of caloric rations in the third trimester with birthweight and placental weight, suggests that there is indeed a direct path between caloric intake and placental weight. Caloric rations in the third trimester contribute 2.4% of the variance in placental weight, of which 1% is unique and over and above the contribution of birthweight (Table 11.3). The simple correlation of caloric rations in the third trimester with placental weight (r = .15) is not much reduced when controlled for birthweight (partial correlation = .12). Figure 11.3A confirms that with placental weight held constant the small association of caloric rations with birthweight disappears, except perhaps at the lowest levels of rations. By contrast (Fig. 11.3B) with birthweight held constant, the association of caloric rations with placental weight persists under conditions of nutritional deprivation below an average daily ration of 2500 Calories. These results suggest that while fetal growth determines placental growth, under conditions of nutritional deprivation the placenta mediates the nutrient supply of the fetus.

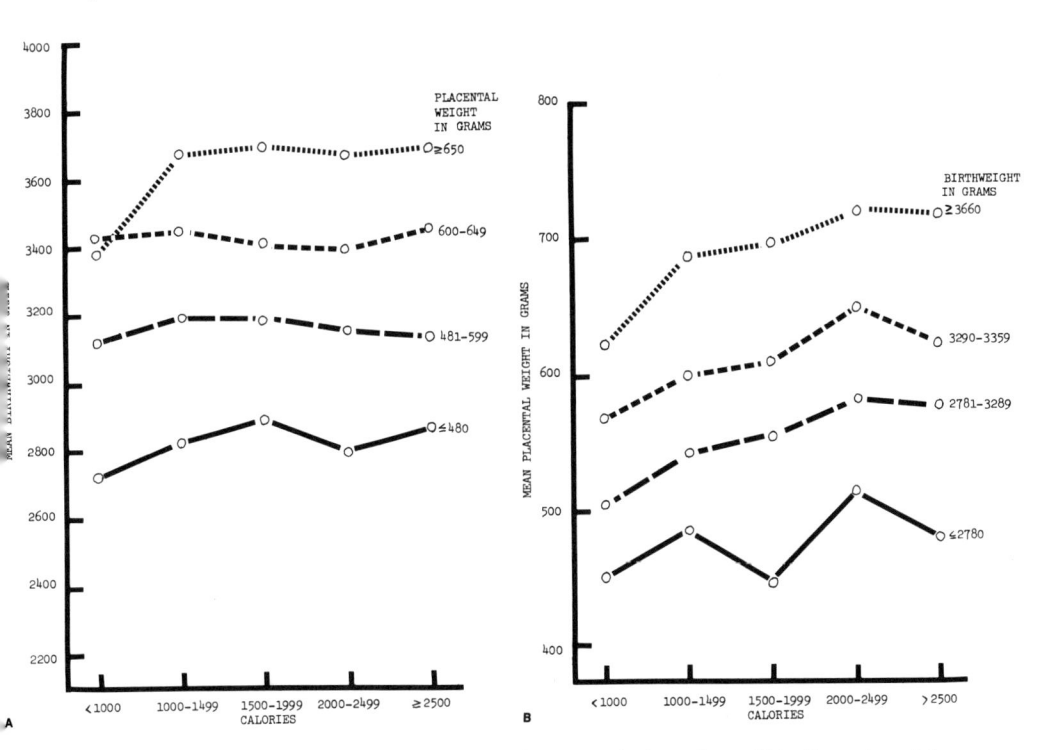

Figure 11.3A. Mean birthweight by third trimester caloric ration within four placental weight categories among children born in the cities of Rotterdam (famine area), Groningen, (Northern control area), and Heerlen (Southern control area) between August 1944 and May 1946

Figure 11.3B. Mean placental weight by third trimester caloric ration within four birthweight categories among children born in the cities of Rotterdam (famine area), Groningen (Northern control area), and Heerlen (Southern control area) between August 1944 and May 1946

To go further, we are obliged to carry out a more complex path analysis. We have seen that the relations between the available variables changed with nutritional conditions and that the changes affected several variables at once. Path models enable us to include all the plausible paths between variables that can be constructed from the available data, as well as the shifts among them under different conditions (Blalock, 1964; Heise, 1969; Land, 1969).

For the purpose of setting up these path models, we now neeed to fix the relative position of all the variables to be included. Caloric rations in the third trimester have been placed as an antecedent variable throughout, since we have demonstrated the effects of famine and war-time rationing on the reproductive process by separate analysis of each outcome variable. In essence, caloric intake is the test variable in a cruel experiment. Fetal age we have taken, on logical grounds, to be antecedent to the fetal dimensions of length, head circumference, and weight at birth. Fetal age is placed antecedent to postpartum maternal weight on logical grounds also; length of gestation, by which fetal age is measured, is a necessary logical antecedent to maternal weight change in pregnancy. Maternal weight was established by previous analysis as an intervening variable between caloric intake and fetal dimensions, at least under the famine condition. With regard to fetal dimensions, we argue, again on logical grounds, that the weight of the infant is consequent on its length. Added length is bound to add mass, while added mass is not bound to add length.

That the fetal dimension of length at birth is logically antecedent to placental weight follows from the previous inference that fetal growth determines placental growth. This postulated structure of variables is coherent with another three-variable multiple regression analysis of infant length at birth, birthweight, and placental weight. When birthweight is entered first in the equation, it can account for the whole of the variance in placental weight, so that infant length adds no variance over and above that accounted for by birthweight (Table 11.4). Stated otherwise, the partial correlation between infant length and placental weight disappears when controlled for birthweight. Finally, contingency table analysis shows no relationship between infant length and placental weight within birthweight categories (Fig. 11.4B), while infant length and birthweight retain their relationship within placental weight categories (Fig. 11.4A).

It remains to assign a position to the dimensions of the head in relation to the other variables measured simultaneously at birth. We shall assume that head circumference at birth has the same position relative to other variables as infant length, since both are skeletal structures, although different types of bone are involved. A main problem unresolved by this assumption resides in the position of head circumference in relation to infant length. There seems little logical reason to assume that either of these two variables give rise to the other; we prefer to assume that the bony structures of the head will behave jointly with the bony structures that give rise to length. In our path model head circumference will therefore be placed alongside length in a common complex without direction between them. That is, head circumference is treated as a separate but associated outcome of the same set of antecedents as is ascribed to length.

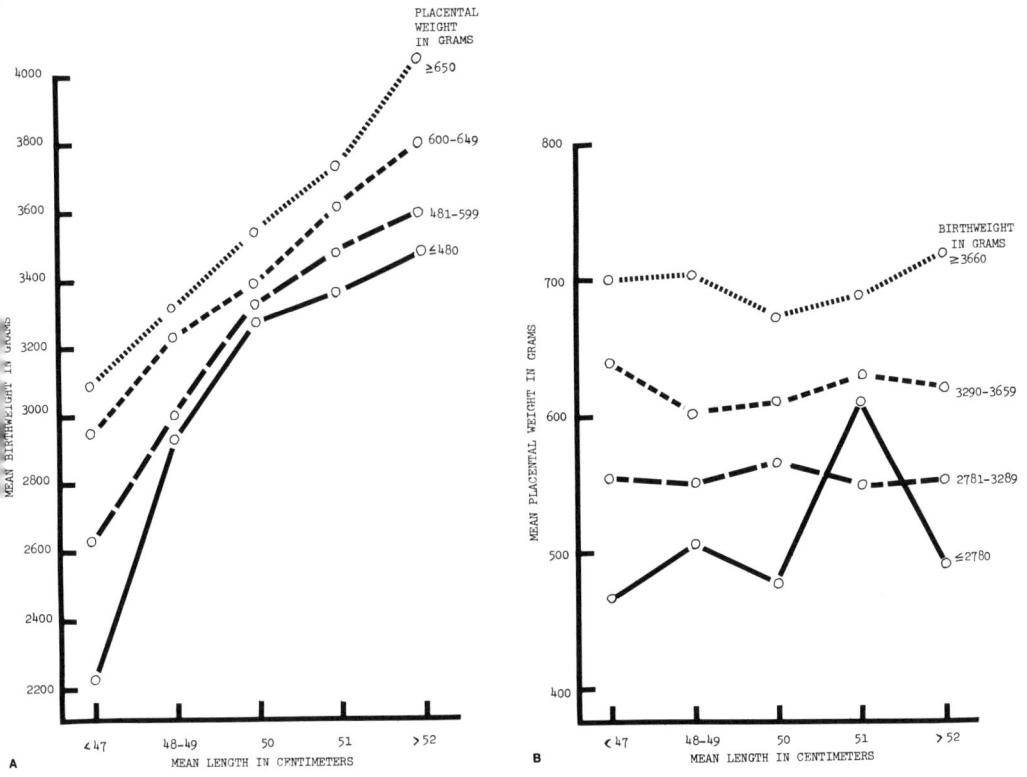

Figure 11.4A. Mean birthweight by length at birth within four placental weight categories among children born in the cities of Rotterdam (famine area), Groningen (Northern control area), and Heerlen (Southern control area) between August 1944 and May 1946

Figure 11.4B. Placental weight by length at birth within four birthweight categories among children born in the cities of Rotterdam (famine area), Groningen (Northern control area), and Heerlen (Southern control area) between August 1944 and May 1946

Path Models

We are now ready to set up path models of the available variables. The correlations on which the models are based are given at the end of this chapter (Table 11.5). The data are for individual births from Rotterdam.*

Models have been constructed for the Rotterdam population defined under each of two conditions:

---

*These include all seven variables. Maternal weight, which we regard as one that may have great biological significance, appears solely in the Rotterdam data. Moreover, to use a homogeneous population for a single city seemed to us a sounder course than to extrapolate. Nonetheless, models based on the much larger numbers taken from those sources that comprise only six variables excluding maternal weight are remarkably consistent with the Rotterdam results.

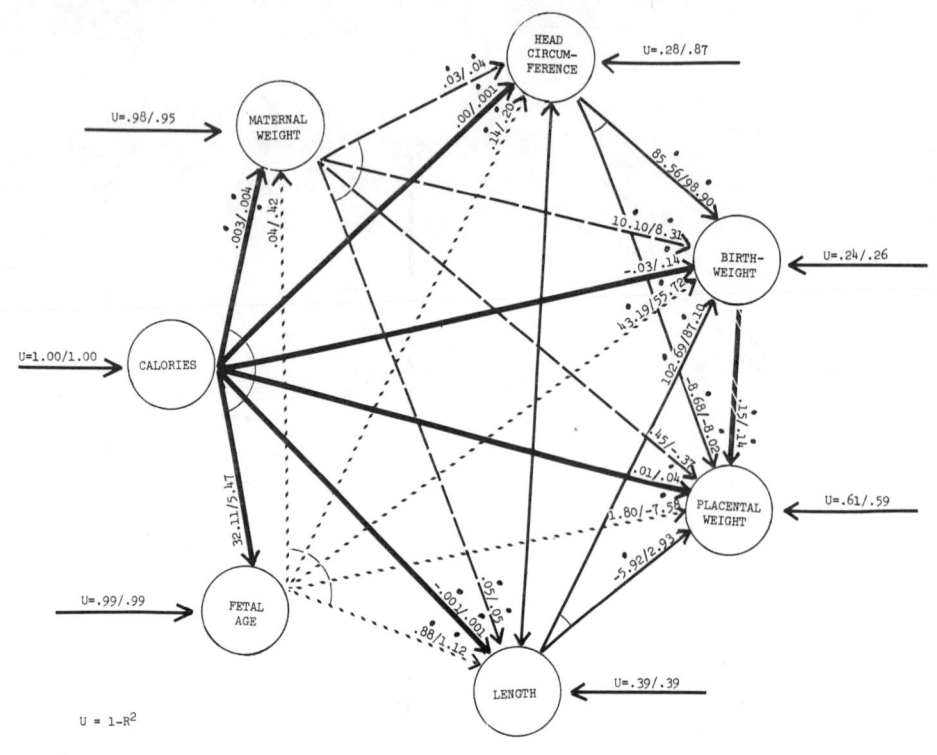

Path diagram of reproductive process: Model A
Caloric rations and indices of the reproductive process among individual births in Rotterdam under two nutritional conditions: famine, non-famine. In this model, *fetal growth is assumed to be a determinant of placental growth*. B values for each condition are given along the appropriate paths with the non-famine condition given first. A dot above the B value indicates statistical significance at the 5% level of probability. U indicates unexplained variance.

1. the population exposed to the non-famine condition: daily rations average 1500 Calories or more during third trimester of pregnancy;

2. the population exposed to the famine condition: daily rations average less than 1500 Calories during the third trimester of pregnancy.

Each condition has been analyzed with two different structures of paths among the variables:

Model A with birthweight antecedent to placental weight;
Model B with placental weight antecedent to the dimensions of the fetus.

On the basis of the analyses leading up to this point, we think it likely that Model A is the more appropriate to the non-famine condition, Model B to the famine condition.

Model A is a path diagram to illustrate the first model, with birthweight a determinant of placental weight, and Model B illustrates the second model with

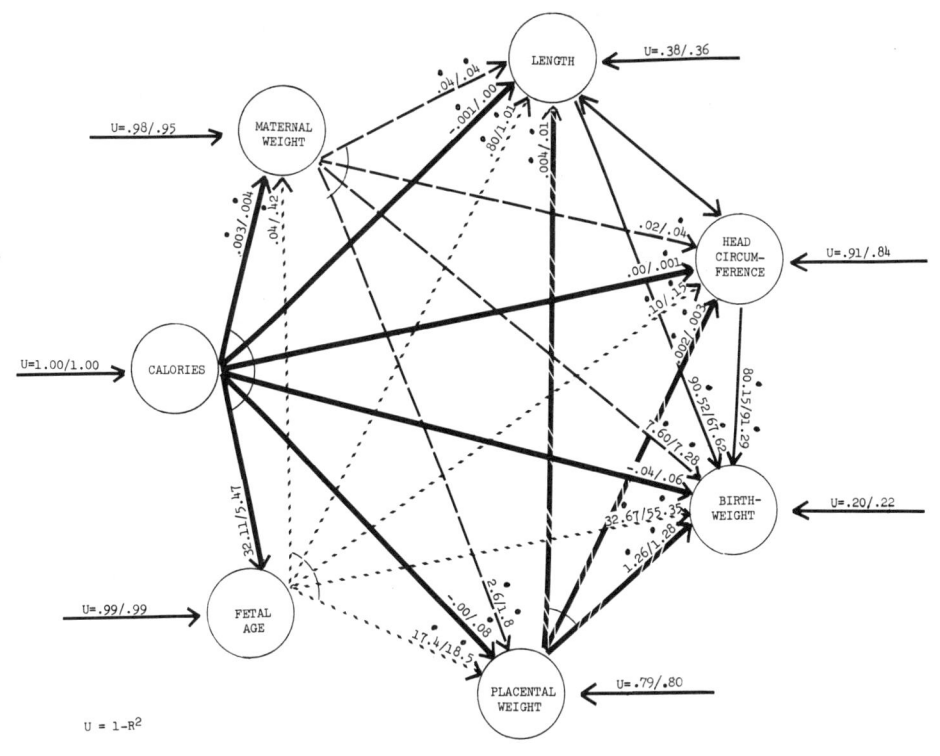

Path diagram of reproductive process: Model B
Caloric rations and indices of the reproductive process among individual births in Rotterdam under two nutritional conditions: famine, non-famine. In this model, *placental growth is assumed to be a determinant of fetal growth*. B values for each condition are given along the appropriate paths with the non-famine condition given first. A dot above the B value indicates statistical significance at the 5% level of probability. U indicates unexplained variance

placental weight the determinant of fetal dimensions. Along each path in the diagram is shown the value for the regression coefficient derived from successive multiple regression analyses. Taking in succession all the variables in the path model excepting exogenous variables (in this case caloric rations alone) these multiple regression analyses indicate the proportion of variance in each variable that can be accounted for by the variables antecedent to it in the path model. The regression coefficients indicate the amount of change in the dependent variable that can be expected per unit change in the independent variable. Two regression coefficients are given for each path, one value for each of the nutritional conditions on either side of the 1500 Calorie ration level in the third trimester.

The path models show significant changes between the famine and non-famine conditions in the magnitude of the coefficients of a number of paths.

Although the magnitude of the changes differ, in both models the changes tend to be in the same direction. Several changes are in accord with the expectations from the preceding graphic analyses of time changes through the famine.

In brief, both models show the effect of caloric intake on the fetus to be mediated primarily through other variables, and particularly through maternal weight, with rather small direct effects. Model A with placental weight as the final outcome explains about twice as much of the total variance in placental weight (39% in the non-famine condition and 41% in the famine condition) as Model B with birthweight as the final outcome (which explains 21% and 20% of the variance in placental weight, respectively). On the other hand, Model B, explains respectively under the two conditions 5% or 6% more variance than Model A in birthweight, 1% or 4% more in length, and 1% or 2% more in head circumference.

Interpretations

In our path models, fetal age is treated as an antecedent condition logically necessary to fetal growth, and can be conceived as an index of the mechanisms intrinsic to the fetus which act together with such extrinsic factors as may affect the rate of growth. The fetal growth process is a determinant of the size of skeletal structures. On logical grounds, skeletal structure in turn is necessarily a determinant of fetal weight. In these terms, the placenta can be considered a fetal organ. Fetal length and fetal weight can be taken as indices of the fetal growth process; hence they are determinants of placental weight.

Fetal age is measured by length of gestation. This inferred gestational age marks the transition of birth. By analogy with other developmental processes, chronological age may be more or less advanced at the time of the transitional event of birth. That accelerated fetal growth may advance the time of birth and reduce age at birth is a limitation on the use of length of gestation as an index of fetal age. On the other hand, the insensitivity of length of gestation to the extrinsic factor of nutrition, as well as to such extrinsic factors as social class (Butler and Bonham, 1963), encourages us to use it as an index of fetal age.

Nutrition is the main exogenous variable in this study, and like fetal age it is another necessary condition for fetal growth. The fetal supply is transmitted through the mother and involves her metabolism and her stores. Under normal nutritional conditions, almost the whole of the influence of current caloric intake on fetal weight is in some manner mediated by maternal weight. With the decline of maternal weight under famine conditions, a more direct path of fetal supply that bypasses maternal weight is added, although the mediation of maternal weight in fetal weight continues almost unchanged. We suggest that this mechanism interprets, in our path models, the shift seen in the famine condition towards stronger direct paths between caloric intake in the third trimester and birthweight and placental weight. It seems as though in nutritional extremity maternal reserves were exhausted and maternal weight had reached a lower limit. Now a larger share of caloric intake was needed to sustain the mother's metabolic processes. At the same time, the fetus continued to draw on the mother as under normal conditions.

A degree of deficiency in nutrients that failed to sustain normal fetal weight sustained normal growth in length. Where fetal weight is thus diminished without diminution in fetal length, the relative contribution of infant length to the variation in birthweight naturally diminished, while that of the intrinsic growth process indicated by length of gestation increased.

Fetal growth is a determinant of placental growth. Under normal nutritional conditions, the placenta seems to act like a passive channel of transmission; it lies like a dam in the direct line of supply of nutrients from mother to fetus. Thus, in the non-famine condition, nutrient supplies were sufficient to sustain the needs of fetus and placenta for continuing growth as well as for the maintenance of their current metabolic state. The placenta, bathed in the blood of the maternal villi, has first access to nutrient supplies. From these supplies, we postulate, the placenta obtains directly the nutrients to maintain the current metabolic state determined by the development achieved up to that time. The remaining nutrients are transmitted to the fetus, where they are used to maintain the current metabolic state of the fetus, to sustain the further growth of the fetus, and thus in turn to sustain the further growth of the placenta.

In normal nutritional conditions, the amount of nutrients transmitted to the fetus after the placenta has satisfied its current metabolic needs are evidently adequate for the further needs of fetal growth. Hence path models show an indirect pathway from caloric intake through maternal metabolism (indicated by maternal weight) without diversion of caloric intake to the placenta. In famine conditions, however, the nutrients transmitted to the fetus after passage through the placenta are presumably insufficient to sustain normal rates of fetal growth. The appearance of a direct path from caloric intake to placenta then makes evident the placenta's absorption of nutrients and its potential role either as a barrier in the path of the fetal supply, or even as an active agent for the transmission of nutrients.

Summary

A graphic analysis was made of the variation of indices of the reproductive process through 20 months before, during, and after the famine. The interrelations of famine with the indices of the reproductive process were further elaborated in a path model. Assumptions about the direction of change among these indices were first tested in analyses of sets of three variables. The method developed in these analyses enabled us to infer precedence among the three variables in each set, provided the position of one of the three was known. On this foundation, two path models with different structures of causal paths were analyzed. Model A placed birthweight antecedent to placental weight; Model B placed placental weight antecedent to dimensions of the fetus. Each of these models was examined under two conditions, "non-famine" and "famine."

The graphic analysis indicated that maternal weight was low before the famine. Maternal weight also absorbed the first impact of the famine. Only after a lower threshold limit of maternal weight was reached did nutritional deprivation seem to affect the products of conception, especially placental weight, by direct paths. On reaching this threshold, mean maternal weight did not continue to fall as the famine progressed. On the other hand, mean placental weight, and then mean birthweight—both of which began to fall later than mean maternal weight—continued to fall and reached their lower limit later than maternal weight. From these circumstances we inferred a reallocation of nutritional priorities between mother and fetus under the famine condition, a reallocation regulated by the placenta. In recovery, the priorities of the normal condition were again restored. With the provision of food after liberation, it seemed likely that the mother and placenta first supplied their own metabolic needs, before the fetus was supplied; maternal weight and placental weight recovered together, but birthweight began to rise, as it had fallen, only after a time lag.

The path models A and B are in general consistent with such changes. Model A seems appropriate to the nonfamine condition, Model B to the famine condition (although some shifts under the famine condition were not anticipated and have no ready explanation). Under the famine condition, there was a shift in the distribution of caloric rations in the third trimester which brought into play direct paths to birthweight and placental weight. The pathway from caloric intake to maternal weight was strengthened under the famine condition. At this point mothers had priority in the allocation of nutrients, we presume, because they had reached the lower weight limit compatible with survival, and little further weight could be lost. At the same time, the path from maternal weight to birthweight was sustained. Coherent with these relations, the paths between maternal weight and both length and head size at birth were sustained at the same level throughout the famine.

Under the famine condition the paths from infant length at birth to birthweight diminished in strength. These shifts are consistent with the fact that the famine affected length at birth much less than birthweight; in most affected cohorts, infants at birth were thin but not short. A compensatory strengthening can be seen in the path from fetal age to birth weight. This presumably reflects a relatively larger contribution of intrinsic growth process to fetal weight as the contribution of fetal length diminished.

Notes and Tables

Detailed Interpretation of Figure 11.1

For the sake of legibility, we chose three sets of graphs to illustrate the findings. Figure 11.1A shows the three curves for maternal weight, placental weight and birthweight. Figure 11.1B shows three additional curves, for length of gestation, infant length, and infant head circumference. Figure 11.1C shows only two curves, birthweight and length at birth. The data, based on the famine cities as specified in Chapter 10, are set out in the Appendix.

The units of measurement for each variable have been converted from the absolute values of recorded measurement units into standard deviations from a norm, known as standardized normal deviates or Z scores. By this means, all the outcomes can be seen against each other in terms of a common scale.* Z scores should be used with caution. The size of the fluctuations for any variable vary according to the dispersal of the values in the population that is used as the norm; the reference norm governs the shape of the curve. We have chosen, as a reasonable reference population, births during the post-famine period July 1, 1945, to March 31, 1946. In comparing these curves with previous diagrams, the reader should note that values are plotted not by grouped cohorts, but in more refined form by months of birth. It is common practice to take a value of more than two standard deviations from the norm as being statistically significant, since 95% of observations fall within that limit. In reading these continuous time curves, however, we do not ignore the possible biological significance of trends and gradients, even if less dispersed than two standard deviations, where they are coherent with other data and concepts.

Mean maternal weight (Fig. 11.1A), at the onset of the famine, was clearly at a lower level than the norm for the postwar reference population. This level was sustained through the first six weeks of steadily increasing nutritional deprivation during the famine, and fell sharply to reach its virtual lower limit, more than three standard deviations below the norm, in a single step during the month of December 1945, that is, among births occurring seven to ten weeks after the onset of the famine. Maternal weight continued at this low level (between three and four standard deviations below the norm) through May when the famine ended, but in June quickly rose to within two standard deviations of the norm. This recovery occurred among births three to six weeks after the liberation; seven to ten weeks after liberation, mean maternal weight was within one standard deviation of the post-famine norm.

Mean placental weight (Fig. 11.1A) was similar among pre- and post-famine cohorts, although the pre-famine cohorts are rather few to judge by. The placental weight curve is irregular and difficult to interpret with precision. Mean placental weight fell sharply to two standard deviations below the norm in December, that is, seven to ten weeks after the onset of famine and in the same

---

*The control cities show no consistent patterns, as would be anticipated from the analyses of Chapter 10, and the figures are not given. Z scores can be derived from the data on monthly means given in the Appendix.

period as the sharp fall in maternal weight to more than three standard deviations below the norm. Possibly the fall in mean placental weight had begun earlier. In the previous month of November, the level of mean placental weight was more than one standard deviation below the norm. On the other hand, in the succeeding month of January 1945, placental weight rose again to within one standard deviation of the norm. The curve turned down again to fluctuate around its lowest levels (two to four standard deviations below the norm) from February, at the height of the famine, until recovery began. Recovery was concurrent with that of maternal weight; in June, three to six weeks after liberation, both maternal weight and placental weight had recovered to within two standard deviations from the norm, and in July they were within one standard deviation from the norm.

Mean birthweight (Fig. 11.1A), like placental weight, seems to have been at similar levels among pre- and post-famine cohorts. Birthweight began its decline in December, seven to ten weeks after the onset of the famine, the same month as maternal weight, and possibly a little after placental weight. This point was less than two standard deviations below the norm. The low point was reached only in February at the height of the famine, the same month as placental weight. Recovery in mean birthweight was slower than with maternal and placental weights; in June mean birthweight was still at a level more than two standard deviations below the norm, and then rose sharply during July, seven to ten weeks after the famine had ended.

Mean infant length (Fig. 11.1B), like the other dimensions of fetal growth, seems not to have differed between pre- and post-famine cohorts. Infant length was definitely affected only late in the famine. In December 1944 and January 1945, mean infant length was below the norm, however, but still within one standard deviation. A decline to almost two standard deviations below the norm was first apparent in February 1945, about fifteen to eighteen weeks after the onset of the famine. From this low point, the trend was slightly upward until June, three to six weeks after the famine, in the main between one and two standard deviations below the norm. Infant length, like birthweight, recovered fully in July. Excepting January, the directions of the changes in infant length are synchronous with those in birthweight, although of lesser magnitude. (We note in passing that the regression coefficients of infant length and birthweight showed that if length were controlled it could not account for the main part of the fluctuation in birthweight.)

Mean head circumference (Fig. 11.1B) shows no noticeable disparity between pre-famine and post-famine norms. A decline, evident in November, is consistent with a response to caloric deprivation. We assume that a definite famine-induced downward trend began in January 1945, when head size first fell two standard deviations below the norm. In April and May there is a rise to within less than two standard deviations, and a fall again in June. From July, mean head circumference, like length and weight at birth, again rises to the norm and beyond. Most of the fluctuations show a degree of synchrony with those of weight and length at birth, but there is less regularity, probably because of smaller numbers.

Mean length of gestation, depicted in Figure 11.1B, shows no definite effect of the famine. A dip of one standard deviation is coincident with the low points of other outcome variables during February at the height of the famine. This dip is transient as well as small. It is exceeded by the dips for the months November 1945 to January 1946 and almost equalled by that in June 1945. The fluctuations in length of gestation are difficult to interpret by inspection. If biologically significant the largest effects, around the end of 1945, relate to nutritional deprivation during the first and second trimesters of pregnancy.

The small regression coefficients of other outcome variables on length of gestation confirm that length of gestation cannot account for the main fluctuation in the other variables during the famine. To control length of gestation would smooth out the irregular decline in June 1945 in infant length and birthweight, and thereby strengthen their association with caloric rations.

Three Variable Sequences

Data sources are the same as in the analyses of separate indices of reproduction (Chapter 10) and of Z score graphs. That is, all the sources in famine and control areas where the necessary information for the variable was available were combined. The analyses are presented in terms of individuals only, since the interrelations concern the dimensions of individual infants, or at most of individual mothers and infants as units.

Each table presents the summary statistics of a multiple correlation analysis of an independent variable selected as logically antecedent and two indices of the reproductive process alternating as independent and dependent variables among single births from August 1, 1944, through March 31, 1946. The statistics given are the following:

1. proportion of variance (R^2) of the dependent variable explained by the independent variable selected as logically antecedent;

2. analysis of variance;

3. partial regression coefficients: unstandardized (b) with standard errors (s.e.), and standardized (Beta) with F values;

4. correlation coefficients (r): bivariate, between dependent and each independent variable, and partial, holding all other variables constant.

The levels of significance for the F values and for the bivariate and partial correlation coefficients are coded as follows: * $p < .05$; ** $p < .01$; *** $p < .001$. Total numbers of individuals used in each table (indicated by N) to derive means and standard deviations are greater than numbers used in the regression equations (indicated by df) because all attributes were not recorded for all individuals.

Table 11.1. Calories, maternal weight, and birthweight

Dependent Variable: Birthweight   Mean: 3244 grams   S.D.: 654   N: 806

Proportion of Variance ($R^2 = .0709$)

C_3	.0181	Maternal Weight	.0675
Maternal Weight	.0528	C_3	.0035

Analysis of Variance

Source	df	Mean Square	F
Regression	2	9108854	22***
Residual	598	399041	

Independent Variable	Mean	Partial Regression Coefficients			Correlation Coefficients	
		b (se)	Beta	F	Bivariate r	Partial r
C_3	1628 Cal.	.0581 (.0389)	.0617	2.2	.13**	.06
Maternal Weight	59 Kg.	21.3281 (3.6877)	.2411	34.0***	.25**	.23***

Table 11.2. Fetal age, birthweight, and placental weight

SEQUENCE A. Dependent Variable: Placental Weight Mean: 600 grams S.D.: 151 N: 3108

Proportion of Variance ($R^2 = .2948$)

Fetal Age	.0615	Birthweight	.2895
Birthweight	.2333	Fetal Age	.0053

Analysis of Variance

Source	df	Mean Square	F
Regression	2	7762993	480***
Residual	2297	16166	

Independent Variable	Mean	Partial Regression Coefficients			Correlation Coefficients	
		b (se)	Beta	F	Bivariate r	Partial r
Fetal Age	39.4 weeks	−5.2554 (1.2558)	−.0895	17***	.24***	−.08***
Birthweight	3305 grams	.1431 (.0052)	.5893	760***	.53***	.49***

SEQUENCE B. Dependent Variable: Birthweight Mean: 3305 grams S.D.: 623 N: 3233

Proportion of Variance ($R^2 = .4951$)

Fetal Age	.3280	Placental Weight	.2894
Placental Weight	.1671	Fetal Age	.2056

Analysis of Variance

Source	df	Mean Square	F
Regression	2	220953010	1126***
Residual	2297	196202	

Independent Variable	Mean	Partial Regression Coefficients			Correlation Coefficients	
		b (se)	Beta	F	Bivariate r	Partial r
Fetal Age	39.4 weeks	113.2224 (3.7019)	.4681	935***	.57***	.53***
Placental Weight	600.7 grams	1.7370 (.0630)	.4219	760***	.53***	.49***

Table 11.3. Calories, birthweight, and placental weight

SEQUENCE A. Dependent Variable: Placental Weight Mean: 600 S.D.: 151 N: 3108

Proportion of Variance ($R^2 = .3009$)

C_3	.0237	Birthweight	.2895
Birthweight	.2772	C_3	.0114

Analysis of Variance

Source	df	Mean Square	F
Regression	2	7921960	494***
Residual	2297	16027	

Independent Variable	Mean	Partial Regression Coefficients			Correlation Coefficients	
		b (se)	Beta	F	Bivariate r	Partial r
C_3	1759 Calories	.0311 (.0051)	.1073	37.5***	.15**	.12***
Birthweight	3305 grams	.1284 (.0043)	.5286	910.7***	.53***	.53***

SEQUENCE B. Dependent Variable: Birthweight Mean: 3305 S.D.: 623 N: 3233

Proportion of Variance ($R^2 = .2895$)

C_3	.0078	Placental Weight	.2895
Placental Weight	.2817	C_3	.0000

Analysis of Variance

Source	df	Mean Square	F
Regression	2	129196570	467***
Residual	2297	276095	

Independent Variable	Mean	Partial Regression Coefficients			Correlation Coefficients	
		b (se)	Beta	F	Bivariate r	Partial r
C_3	1759 Calories	.0066 (.0212)	.0055	09	.08**	.00
Placental Weight	600 grams	2.2115 (.0733)	.5372	910.75***	.53***	.53***

Table 11.4. Length, birthweight, and placental weight

SEQUENCE A. Dependent Variable: Placental Weight Mean: 600 S.D.: 151 N: 3108

Proportion of Variance ($R^2 = .2908$)

Length	.1546	Birthweight	.2895
Birthweight	.1362	Length	.0014

Analysis of Variance

Source	df	Mean Square	F
Regression	2	7657514	470***
Residual	2297	16758	

Independent Variable	Mean	Partial Regression Coefficients			Correlation Coefficients	
		b (se)	Beta	F	Bivariate r	Partial r
Length	49.4 cms	−2.6861 (1.2748)	−.0585	4.4**	.39***	−.04**
Birthweight	3305.8 grams	.1417 (.0068)	.5833	441.2***	.53***	.40***

SEQUENCE B. Dependent Variable: Birthweight Mean: 3305 S.D.: 623 N: 3233

Proportion of Variance ($R^2 = .6642$)

Length	.5997	Placental Weight	.2895
Placental Weight	.0645	Length	.3747

Analysis of Variance

Source	df	Mean Square	F
Regression	2	296417330	2271***
Residual	2297	130495	

Independent Variable	Mean	Partial Regression Coefficients			Correlation Coefficients	
		b (se)	Beta	F	Bivariate r	Partial r
Length	49.4 cms	125.8223 (2.4853)	.6658	2563***	.77***	.72***
Placental Weight	600.7 grams	1.1375 (.0541)	.2762	441***	.53***	.40***

Table 11.5. Descriptive statistics and correlations for path models

Famine Condition
(<1500 Calories in third trimester)

	Birth-weight	Maternal Weight	Fetal Age	Length	Head Circumference	Placental Weight	Calories 3
Birthweight		0.31***	0.67***	0.78***	0.58***	0.62***	0.22***
Maternal Weight			0.13**	0.22***	0.22***	0.19***	0.18***
Fetal Age				0.77***	0.26***	0.36***	0.02
Length					0.39***	0.49***	0.11*
Head Circumference						0.30***	0.21***
Placental Weight							0.25***
Mean	3183 grams	57.8 Kg.	39.5 wks.	49.6 cms	34.8 cms	553 grams	1040 Calories
S.D.	595	6.9	2.2	3.3	1.8	120	338
N	402	367	393	395	345	377	404

Non-Famine Condition
(>1500 Calories in third trimester)

	Birth-weight	Maternal Weight	Fetal Age	Length	Head Circumference	Placental Weight	Calories 3
Birthweight		0.19***	0.70***	0.83***	0.54***	0.61***	0.02
Maternal Weight			0.03	0.10*	0.12*	0.15***	0.15**
Fetal Age				0.77***	0.25***	0.43***	0.08
Length					0.43***	0.47***	-0.01
Head Circumference						0.24***	0.04
Placental Weight							0.05
Mean	3306 grams	61.6 Kg.	39.2 wks.	49.5 cms	35.2 cms	592 grams	2212
S.D.	703	7.3	3.4	3.8	2.0	137	404
N	404	381	398	399	298	398	408

12 Deaths From Infancy to Adulthood

During the famine there was a rise in deaths at all ages in the affected areas (de Haas-Postuma, and de Haas, 1968).* Around that time and in the months that followed, however, there was also an extraordinary rise in infant deaths over the whole country (de Groot, 1947; Pasma, 1947). A main question we shall seek to answer is how much of this excess mortality was caused by prenatal exposure to famine. The effects of postnatal exposure to famine or of other circumstances of the time was not the focus of our inquiry, and our design and analysis aims to exclude these effects rather than to determine their contribution. Another question we shall address is the degree to which the influence of prenatal exposure to famine is direct or mediated through intrauterine growth retardation. In later chapters we shall also try to see if deaths among those exposed to famine altered the distribution of states of health among survivors in a manner that could have distorted the results of comparisons with cohorts not exposed to famine.

Forms of Analysis

The analysis in this chapter will proceed roughly on the model familiar to the reader from our analysis of the reproductive process (Chapter 10). The deaths at successive ages are subjected to a similar statistical battery. The specific age categories include stillbirths, the first week of life, 7 to 29 days, 30 to 89 days, 90 to 364 days, and over 1 year. As before, we shall take the contingency tables and graphs as the touchstone for the analysis. The quantification of food rations

*Notes on data sources and on methods are given at the end of this chapter.

and the statistics that derive from the use of these variables elaborate the results in many respects, but they are derivatives of the contingency tables. The derivative analyses do not respect every assumption required by the methods used, and are subject to error for these reasons. Wherever they do not cohere with our interpretation of the tables and graphs, therefore, they are treated as less cogent.

A. Cohort Analysis by Time and Place

Death rates at the given ages are presented graphically by birth cohort, with a separate curve for each of the three areas. The point on the graph for each cohort is located at the midpoint of all the months of birth included in that cohort. The reader will recall that the birth cohorts were grouped in the initial design with regard to intrauterine famine exposure. The smallest birth cohort in the famine area comprised 3141 births, and in a control area 1677 births. The graphs are constructed from the contingency tables of death rates for monthly birth cohorts shown in the Appendix. Because numbers at risk in the monthly birth cohorts are smaller than in grouped cohorts, death rates based on them are less stable, especially in the control areas. In the descriptive text, we present grouped cohort death rates and where necessary refer to the more detailed monthly cohorts. For the same reason, analyses of death rates are presented for both sexes combined, although they have also been carried out for males and females separately. We have not alluded to the sex differences in the text: the reader can check on the data presented in the appendices.

Such prenatal effects as were revealed by birth cohort analysis may understate the true effects. Erhardt and his colleagues (1964) have shown that, counting age from birth as we did, a prenatal effect on fetal death may be difficult to detect. When age is counted from conception, approximated by last premenstrual period, the relevant births are scattered over a time span as wide as six months.

Analyses of periodic death rates are given in the Notes and Tables section at the end of this chapter (pp. 165 ff). These supplement the cohort analyses.

B. Quantitative Analyses of Food Rations

The quantified food ration variables for each trimester of pregnancy (C_1, C_2, C_3) have been applied to two different sets of data:

1. Correlations of food rations with age-specific mortality over the *36 months,* January 1, 1944, to December 31, 1946 (Table 12.1).

2. Correlations of fetal growth with food rations and age-specific mortality over the *20 months,* August 1, 1944, to March 31, 1946 (Table 12.2).*

For both sets of data the forms of analysis comprised the following: by area (famine, North, South, all areas combined); by nutritional condition (famine,

---

*Hospital data on maternities were collected only for that period.

non-famine). Differences between famine area and each control area are shown in Table 12.3. Multiple regression analysis and partial correlations were carried out and where useful are referred to in the text.

An assumption that follows from the fact that the data on fetal growth and on mortality do not relate to conterminous populations should be noted. The data on maternities derive from 5 hospitals: 3 in the famine area, 1 in the North, and 1 in the South. The data on deaths derive from all 16 study cities in the 3 areas, including those where the hospitals were sited. Thus we make an assumption of representativeness when we extrapolate fetal growth data for 20 monthly cohorts of births in the 5 hospitals to death data for cohorts comprising all births in all the 16 cities, albeit they occur over the same period of time. This assumption, we believe, is likely to dilute existing associations rather than introduce spurious ones. The correlations of food rations with death rates for the 36 monthly cohorts do not make the same assumption, since the rations covered exactly the same groups as were defined by the birth cohorts. For the rest, the same questions of interpretation discussed in Chapter 10 (pp. 175 ff) apply to each form of analysis.

Stillbirths

A. Cohort Analysis by Time and Place

Figure 12.1 shows an effect of prenatal exposure to famine early in gestation among birth cohorts conceived during the famine and born after it (D2). There is no effect of the famine on stillbirth rates among birth cohorts conceived before the famine and exposed in late gestation (B1, B2, C). In general, the stillbirth rate is stable in the famine cities around a rate of about 20 per 1000, except for the marked rise in the D2 cohort to a rate of about 35 per 1000.

The rise reflected in cohort D2 began among births in October 1945, reached a peak in December, and continued high into February 1946. The rise in the D2 cohort draws suspicion on an effect of exposure to famine early in gestation. Assuming a normal length of gestation, this cohort was conceived at the height of the famine. Most members of the affected cohort, including prematures, would have been conceived between January and May 1945 and therefore were not exposed to famine during the second and third trimesters of gestation.

The curves for the stillbirth rates in the North and South may be thought to detract from the supposition of a famine effect during early gestation. Compared with the famine area, both North and South have stillbirth rates that are much higher and fluctuate around 35 per 1000.* The pattern of fluctuations among the cohorts was similar in the North and the South; this pattern was dissimilar

---

*The high levels of stillbirth rates in the North and the South maintained throughout the period of observation are not easily explained. The data on stillbirths were extracted directly from local records, and a check on their validity was provided from the Central Bureau of Statistics. The results from the two sources compared well.

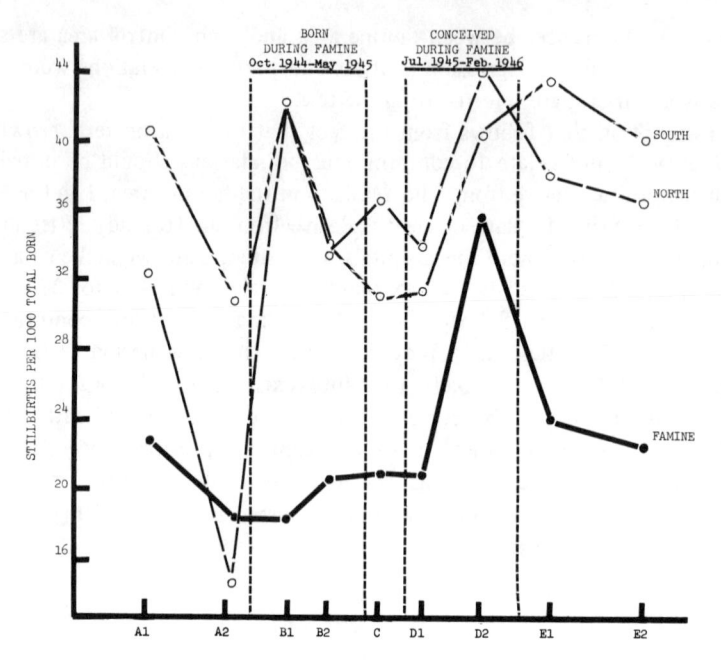

Figure 12.1. Stillbirths by time and place (stillbirths per 1000 total births: famine, Northern control, and Southern control areas by cohort for births January 1944 to December 1946)

from that of the famine area, except in one respect. In all three areas the D2 cohort experienced a rise in stillbirth rates. The rise in the D2 cohort in the North and South was not as sharp as it was in the famine area and not strictly concurrent by month, but it was nonetheless distinct. Hence the rise in the famine area, we conclude, was not an effect of famine alone, but was exacerbated by some other agent, perhaps infective. On the other hand, the singular sharpness of the rise in stillbirths in the famine area points to the strength of the contribution of the famine exposure.

B. Quantitative Analysis of Food Rations and Stillbirths

Correlations of stillbirth rates with caloric rations among 36 monthly birth cohorts were not statistically significant in any trimester of pregnancy, nor in any specification of the analysis by area or by the threshold of caloric value for famine.

Correlations of stillbirth rates with indices of fetal growth and caloric rations among the 20 monthly birth cohorts for whom the data were available also produced no significant negative correlations. Our quantitative analysis of food rations thus fails to demonstrate a famine effect on stillbirths, whether direct or moderated by fetal growth. The absence of association of stillbirths with birthweight is against expectations from previous studies of other populations (Bergner and Susser, 1970; Susser, Marolla, and Fleiss, 1972). The strong associations found in other studies must presumably be accounted for by forms of low birthweight owed to causes other than maternal starvation in late pregnancy.

Summary

Prenatal exposure to famine in early gestation appeared to produce a rise in stillbirth rates. The apparent effect occurred in interaction with some other unknown factor, since a lesser rise in the same birth cohort occurred in the control areas. Against expectation, stillbirth rates were not raised among the cohorts that exhibited lowered birthweight and other features of fetal growth retardation as a consequence of famine exposure late in gestation. Correlations of average daily caloric rations in each trimester of pregnancy with stillbirth rates were not statistically significant.

First-Week Deaths

A. Cohort Analysis by Time and Place

Figure 12.2 shows that first-week death rates in the famine area rose among the cohorts born during the famine (B1, B2, C) in a manner consistent with the

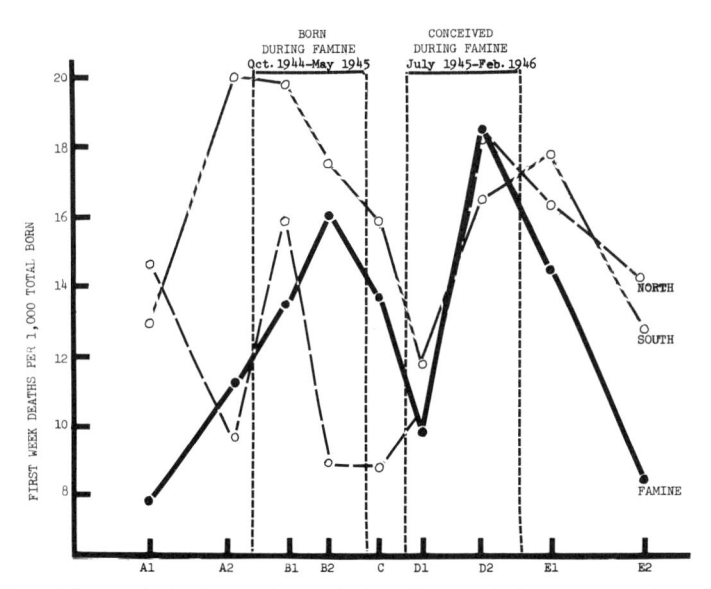

Figure 12.2. First-week deaths by time and place (first-week deaths per 1000 total births: famine, Northern control, and Southern control areas by cohort for births January 1944 to December 1946)

effects of exposure to the famine in late pregnancy. This pattern was unlike either first-week death rates in other areas, or stillbirth rates in any area.*

In the D2 cohort of the famine area, first-week death rates rose sharply; the rate is more than double that of cohorts with the lowest death rates (Fig. 12.2). Yet we cannot attribute this rise among births conceived during the famine to the famine alone. The rise in the first-week death rate in the D2 cohort appears in the North and the South as well. The pattern resembles that of the stillbirth rate, and as with stillbirths, the peak is sharpest in the famine area.

The configuration of *monthly* cohort rates in the three areas (Appendix) suggests that the D2 phenomenon is compatible with the spread from area to area of a maternal infection that had greater impact in nutritionally deprived areas. A rise in stillbirth rates first appeared in the North, to reach a peak in the month of October 1945; it appeared next in the famine area, to reach a peak in the month of December 1945; it appeared last in the South, where the peak was ultimately reached in May 1946, after a more gradual rise. This configuration, moreover, is similar to that found in monthly analysis of stillbirths in the three areas, except that in the South a peak was reached earlier.**

B. Quantitative Analysis of Food Rations and First-Week Deaths

Among 36 monthly birth cohorts, the single statistically significant correlation of first-week deaths with food rations was for C_1 in the famine area. The correlation is consistent with the indication, in the graphs above, of a famine effect in early gestation on first-week deaths in the D2 cohort. The finding is also consistent with the analysis of differences between the famine area and the South, although not the North. The indication in the graphs of a famine effect in late gestation on first-week deaths in the B1, B2, and C cohorts also is given some support by the correlation of differences in C_3 and first-week deaths. The correlation of differences between the famine area and the North is statistically significant, that between the famine area and the South small but in the same direction.

The correlations of first-week deaths with indices of the reproductive process, as well as the analysis of differences between the famine area and the North, point only to a significant effect of duration of gestation. It is a reasonable speculation that shortened gestation was a variable intervening between food rations and mortality; the D2 cohort, which suffered first trimester exposure to famine, also experienced reduced length of gestation and a high first-week death rate.

---

*Deaths during the first week of life and stillbirths correlated significantly in all three areas: $r = .47$ in the famine cities, $r = .50$ in the North, and $r = .33$ in the South.

**The peak for stillbirths in the South was in January 1946 as compared with May 1946 for first-week deaths: the stillbirth rates remained high until May 1946, but at a level lower than the peak rate.

Summary

Prenatal exposure to famine in the *first* trimester of gestation was followed by raised first-week death rates, as with stillbirths. There again appeared to be interaction between famine experience and another prenatal factor, possibly maternal infection, that was common to both famine and control areas. Prenatal exposure to famine in the *third* trimester led to a rise in first-week deaths. The results in this respect appear transitional; the rise was less striking than at later ages, as we shall see.

These conclusions, based on the graphs, could be supported from the quantitative analysis only with regard to the first trimester effects. Thus there was a significant correlation of first-week deaths with food rations only in the first trimester. Also, among indices of the reproductive process, there was a significant correlation of first-week deaths only with length of gestation. Shortened gestation was a likely mediating factor in the association between first-week deaths and prenatal famine exposure in the first trimester.

Deaths at 7 to 29 Days

A. Cohort Analysis by Time and Place

Figure 12.3 shows a clear famine effect on the death rate at 7 through 29 days of age among cohorts born during the famine (B1, B2, and C) in the famine area. In the C cohort (births in May and June 1945) in the famine area, the death rate is much lower than in the B2 cohort (births in February through April 1945).

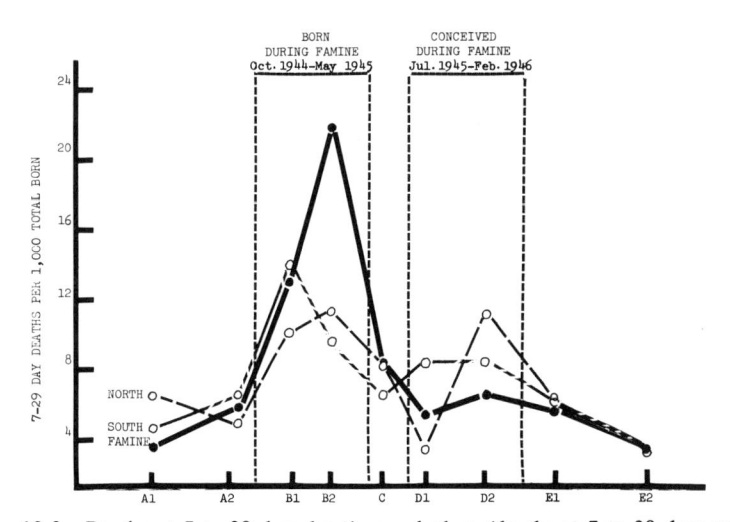

Figure 12.3. Deaths at 7 to 29 days by time and place (deaths at 7 to 29 days per 1000 total births: famine, Northern control, and Southern control areas by cohort for births January 1944 to December 1946)

Analysis of monthly cohorts (Appendix) shows that the decline in deaths in the C cohort (births through May and June 1945) is entirely accounted for by June births, after the famine had ended. This June decline suggests some dissociation between fetal growth retardation and the death rate at 7 to 29 days, because mean birthweight and length among June births remained at the same reduced level as among those born during May.

The Northern and Southern control areas also show raised death rates in this age group for the B1 cohort (births November 1944 through January 1945). The rise in the B2 cohorts is much less in the control areas than in the famine area. Unlike the famine area, moreover, in the control areas the death rate in the C cohort is not raised in comparison with post-famine cohorts. These dissimilarities point to an independent nutritional effect in the famine area, over and above any other factor such as severe winter cold. The rise in B1 and B2 cohort death rates in the control areas as well as the famine area, however, suggests the presence of a non-nutritional prenatal factor active in all areas, and interacting with famine exposure in the famine area.

A close examination of the fluctuations in the monthly cohorts both in the North and South (Appendix) reveals the presence of four successive winter peaks in the mortality rates at 7 to 29 days. In the famine area, the winter levels apart from the hunger winter of 1944-45 are only slightly raised. The seasonal patterns normal to the different areas emphasize the singularity of the hunger winter.

B. Quantitative Analysis of Food Rations and Deaths at 7 to 29 Days

The analysis combining data across the country for 36 monthly birth cohorts shows a strong inverse correlation of deaths at 7 to 29 days with food rations in all three trimesters. The correlations rose in a gradient through the three trimesters (to $-.5$ for C_3). Under the famine condition, only the correlation with C_3 persisted ($r = -.6$). The same was true for the analysis of differences. These results indicate the presence, under the famine condition, of an effect of food rations in the third trimester on mortality at 7 to 29 days.

Under the non-famine condition, correlations of deaths at 7 to 29 days with food rations in all three trimesters persist. A causal association of nutrition and deaths under less extreme conditions than famine must therefore be considered. Confounding factors other than prenatal nutrition that were associated with the improving secular trend in the post-war period, however, cannot be ruled out.

The analysis of indices of fetal growth and mortality at 7 to 29 days among 20 monthly birth cohorts from August 1944 to March 1946 under the famine condition shows a statistically significant negative correlation with birthweight. Correlations with placental weight and length at birth are consistent with the result and close to statistical significance. Under the non-famine condition, the correlations of fetal growth measures with mortality were all small.

In the analyses for the famine area under all nutritional conditions maternal weight is available as an additional variable. These analyses for the famine area yield strong and significant inverse correlations of mortality at 7 to 29 days with all indices of the reproductive process except duration of gestation.

The analysis of differences conforms in general but not in detail with the over-all pattern.

The relations of fetal growth indices and food rations with mortality at 7 to 29 days were explored by means of partial correlations. The more homogeneous data of the famine area as a whole were used. In this partial correlation analysis, the research design assures us of the order of precedence of the three variables in the causal chain; caloric intake is antecedent to birthweight, and birthweight antecedent to mortality at 7 to 29 days. When C_3 was held constant, the association of birthweight with deaths at 7 to 29 days was reduced only a little (from $r = -.7$ to $r = -.5$). When birthweight was held constant, the association of C_3 with the deaths was reduced substantially (from $r = -.6$ to $r = -.3$). Given the known precedence among the variables, on this model third trimester nutritional deprivation acts primarily through fetal growth to increase mortality, and only to a small degree directly:

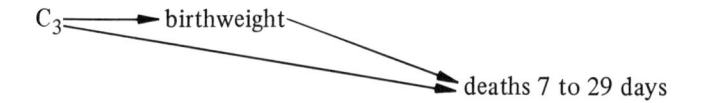

$$C_3 \longrightarrow \text{birthweight} \longrightarrow \text{deaths 7 to 29 days}$$

The famine area analysis fits well with our anticipations from previous work and with the current frame of thought in this field.

Summary

Famine exposure in late gestation had an unequivocally adverse effect on death rates in the age group 7 to 29 days. In the famine area, the pattern of mortality was quite different from that of stillbirths. It was also different from that of first-week deaths, although less so. Regression coefficients (not reported in the text above) show that under the famine condition a change of 100 Calories in the average daily food ration in the third trimester predicts a change of 1.2 deaths per 1000 in the cohort at this age.

Retarded fetal growth (particularly in the dimensions of weight and length at birth) was associated with a raised death rate. Partial correlations of food rations, fetal growth, and mortality in the famine area taken as a whole fit a model in which food deficiency acts to raise mortality indirectly through retarded fetal growth, and to a smaller degree directly.

Under the non-famine condition, food rations in all three trimesters of pregnancy correlated significantly with cohort mortality at 7 to 29 days. We cannot infer causality for these associations because of the limitations of our research design, but incline to reject a causal association. Fetal growth indices did not correlate significantly with mortality under the non-famine condition.

Deaths at 30 to 89 Days

A. Cohort Analysis by Time and Place

In this age group much of the excess of deaths among infants born during the famine occurred in the aftermath of the famine. In view of the focus of this study, our analysis must try to determine to what extent deaths in the post-famine period were a deferred consequence of prenatal experiences or a current consequence of postnatal experiences, or both. To determine which provides the most plausible explanation of the pattern of mortality, cohort and periodic rates must be compared. Given the use of monthly birth cohorts, the 30 to 89 day age group is the youngest in which cohort and periodic death rates diverge. The age intervals and the time units of the periods of observation are not fine enough to separate the two rates in younger age groups.

The comparison of cohort and periodic rates proved arduous, but left us in little doubt that prenatal and not postnatal experiences determined the cohort mortality pattern of this age group. The relevant analysis is given in the Notes and Tables section at the end of the chapter, and we show in the text only the more salient cohort analysis. Figure 12.4 illustrates death rates at 30 to 89 days for the nine grouped cohorts in the three study areas. A clear famine effect on the death rate in the famine area is evident among cohorts born during the famine

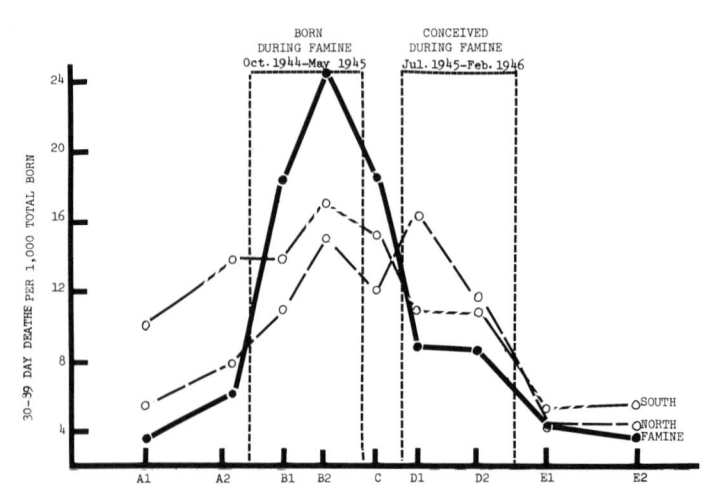

Figure 12.4. Deaths at 30 to 89 days by time and place (deaths at 30 to 89 days per 1000 total births: famine, Northern control, and Southern control areas by cohort for births, January 1944 to December 1946)

(B1, B2, C). The maximum effect occurred with maximum third trimester exposure at the height of the famine, in the B2 cohort. In the Northern and Southern control areas, death rates for this age group were raised for the cohorts born during the famine period (B1, B2, C), but not by any means to the same degree as in the famine area. As with younger age groups, the fact that famine-period birth cohorts had high death rates across the whole country suggests the interaction of some mortal factor common to all areas with prenatal nutritional deprivation in the famine area only. Among cohorts conceived during the famine, no famine effect is detectable. Mortality in all three areas was higher for these cohorts than for cohorts whose gestation did not impinge on the famine period, but among the three areas it is least in the famine area.

B. Quantitative Analysis of Food Rations and Deaths at 30 to 89 Days

Death rates at 30 to 89 days share a pattern of correlations closely similar to that for death rates at 7 to 29 days. The analysis combining data across the country for 36 monthly birth cohorts shows a strong inverse correlation of deaths at 30 to 89 days with food rations in all three trimesters, and the correlations rose in a gradient through the three trimesters (to $r = -.62$ for C_3). Under the famine condition, only the correlation with C_3 persisted, and again the same was true for the analysis of differences. Correlations for fats, protein, and carbohydrates were much the same as for calories. These results indicate the presence, under the famine condition, of an effect of food rations in the third trimester of gestation on mortality at 30 to 89 days.

Under the non-famine condition, correlations of deaths at 30 to 89 days with food rations in all three trimesters persist. Hence a causal association of nutrition under less extreme conditions than famine must be considered. As with deaths at 7 to 29 days, however, confounding factors other than prenatal nutrition cannot be ruled out.

The analysis of indices of fetal growth and mortality among 20 monthly birth cohorts under the famine condition shows statistically significant inverse correlations with birthweight ($r = -.6$) and placental weight ($r = -.4$). Correlations in the same direction with infant length at birth ($r = -.2$) and length of gestation ($r = -.24$) did not reach levels of statistical significance. In the more homogenous data of the famine area taken separately under all nutritional conditions, all indices of fetal growth had significant negative correlations with mortality at 30 to 89 days, and so too did maternal weight. Again the correlation of length of gestation did not reach the level of significance. The direction of associations in the analysis of differences is in accord with these results, although only the negative correlation with birthweight in the comparison between famine and Southern control areas is statistically significant. The vagaries of placental weight and head circumference in the analysis of differences point to unreliability of the data collected for certain periods and areas.

Partial correlations of food rations, indices of the reproductive process, and mortality at 30 to 89 days were carried out for the famine area data under all nutritional conditions. The association of birthweight with deaths was reduced a little, from $r = -.8$ to $r = -.6$, when C_3 was held constant. Conversely, the association of C_3 with deaths was reduced a little more, from $r = -.8$ to $r = -.5$, when birthweight was held constant. The correlation was reduced substantially, to $r = -.3$, when all fetal growth indices were held constant. In a logical causal model capable of fitting these results, C_3 acts on mortality both directly, and with somewhat greater strength indirectly through retarding fetal growth.

The results of the analysis of indices of fetal growth and mortality among 20 monthly birth cohorts under the non-famine condition have still to be considered. The correlations of fetal growth measures with mortality were all small, with the exception of birthweight. Since food rations and fetal growth do not correlate significantly under the non-famine condition (see Chapter 10), any causal interpretation of this result must point to independent effects of rations and fetal growth.

The quantitative analysis leads us to conclusions about the determinants of death at 30 to 89 days identical with those at 7 to 29 days. Famine raised the cohort death rate at age 30 to 89 days. Fetal growth retardation was a mediating factor in the causal sequence. Outside the famine condition, food rations and birthweight had independent associations with mortality; from our research design we cannot determine whether these associations are causal.

Summary

Famine exposure in late gestation had an unequivocal effect on deaths at 30 to 89 days, as it did at 7 to 29 days. From a comparison of cohort with periodic death rates it was inferred that the pattern of mortality could well be accounted for by prenatal exposure to famine and not by postnatal exposure to famine. Under the famine condition, regression coefficients (not reported in the text above) indicated that a change of 100 Calories in the average daily food ration in the third trimester predicted a change of 1.5 deaths per 1000 in the cohort at this age.

Under the famine condition, birthweight and placental weight correlated inversely and significantly with mortality. In the more homogeneous data of the famine area under all conditions, all indices of fetal growth and also maternal weight had significant inverse correlations with mortality. The causal model constructed to fit the relationships of food rations, fetal growth and mortality was closely similar to that for deaths at 7 to 29 days. In the famine area taken as a whole, food rations appeared to act primarily by retarding fetal growth to raise mortality, and to a smaller degree directly.

Under the non-famine condition both caloric rations and birthweight had significant inverse correlations with mortality. Causality cannot be determined for these associations, as is always the case within the limits of our research design. If either food or fetal growth is causal, their effects are independent of each other.

DEATHS FROM INFANCY TO ADULTHOOD

Deaths at 90 to 364 Days

A. Cohort Analysis by Time and Place

Figure 12.5 illustrates mortality among the nine grouped cohorts in the three study areas. The existence of closely similar patterns of cohort mortality in both the famine and control areas confutes arguments for a prenatal famine effect on mortality at this age. The patterns do suggest the presence of a prenatal effect not caused by famine that is common to the cities of all areas. They also suggest the presence of a postnatal famine effect. In the famine area particularly, the A2 cohort born before the famine experienced a sharp rise in mortality. A similar explanation can account for the peak death rate of the B1 cohort. The prenatal but not the postnatal experience of this cohort preceded the full blast of the famine; during the first half-year of life after birth the B1 cohort experienced the worst rigors of the hunger winter.

The peaks in *periodic* mortality in both famine and control areas in the summer after liberation (Notes and Tables, pp. 165 ff) confirm the reports of several observers that fatal gastrointestinal and respiratory infections of mysterious origin were rampant among infants. Explanations offered include the movement of populations and the distribution of infected dried milk. The periodic mortality analysis, however, shows a most irregular rise in mortality.

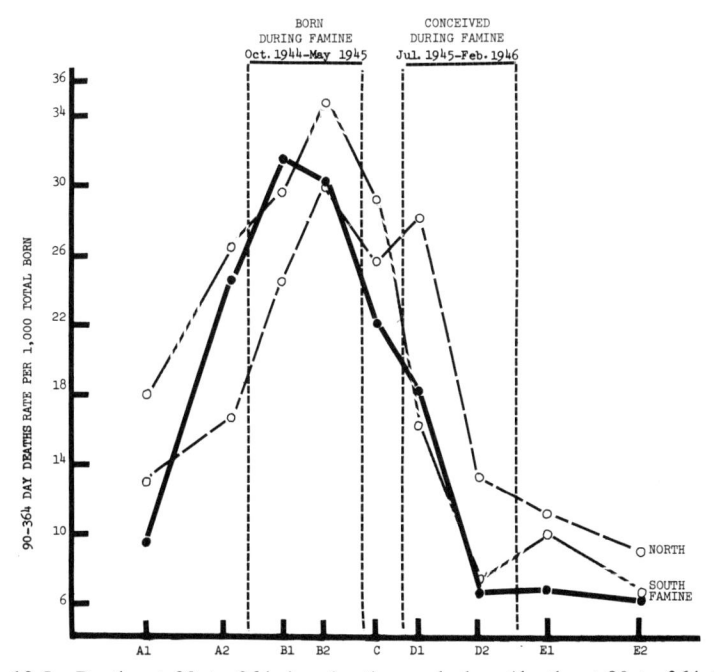

Figure 12.5. Deaths at 90 to 364 days by time and place (deaths at 90 to 364 days per 1000 total births: famine, Northern control, and Southern control by cohort for births January 1944 to December 1946)

The excessive rates extended over a period of more than a year and showed no obvious relation to known environmental factors. By contrast, the cohort mortality patterns match a period of known environmental stress quite well and locate it at the stage of prenatal development. Taken together with the reports of rampant infection, these patterns suggest that debility produced by prenatal stressors predisposed infants to succumb to the postnatal infections current at the time of epidemic mortality. We are in no position to suggest what the nature of the postulated prenatal stressors might be; thus we do not exclude poor nutrition at a level less than famine.

B. Quantitative Analysis of Food Rations and Deaths at 90 to 364 Days

Cohort death rates at ages 90 to 364 days for the 36 months January 1944 to December 1946 correlate inversely with food rations in a rising gradient from the first trimester to the third. Under the famine condition, however, as well as in the analysis of differences, the correlations are negligible. These results accord with the graphic presentations in that they yield no evidence of a prenatal famine effect.

Under the non-famine condition, negative correlations with food rations in all trimesters persist. A forced sequences multiple regression analysis suggests that, were the association causal, C_3 would account for almost the whole of it. It is unlikely that these associations of mortality with food rations could be causal when they were not present in the extreme famine condition. The correlations presumably reflect the known improvement in infant mortality through time which accompanied the improvement in general conditions of life after the war. A specific cause of the declining trend in mortality cannot be isolated within the confines of our research design.

The analysis of fetal growth and mortality through the 20 monthly birth cohorts of August 1944 to March 1946 under the relevant famine condition shows no significant negative correlations.* Partial correlations and multiple regression analysis have little further to contribute.

We conclude that there is no demonstrable effect specific to prenatal famine exposure among death at ages 90 to 364 days, although the cohorts born during the famine have a markedly raised mortality.

Summary

While the cohorts born during the famine had an unprecedented high death rate at 90 to 364 days, an effect of prenatal exposure specific to famine could not be isolated from other general effects that occurred across the country. Cohort mortality is much more in harmony with the pattern to be anticipated from the stresses of war-time shortages and disorganization than is periodic mortality. The

*We take two aberrant positive correlations in the analyses of differences to be chance findings created by errors of measurement and representativeness.

cohort pattern points to prenatal stressors, environmental but not owed to the famine; these may have interacted with postnatal stressors such as infection to produce the high periodic death rates that afflicted the whole country in the summer after liberation. Effects attributable to postnatal exposure to famine seem to be discernible in some cohorts (A2, B1). There is no clear basis, however, for inferring strong postnatal effects in the mortality of this age group in later cohorts. We interpret the cohort mortality pattern as showing that the primary source of the extraordinary and mysterious epidemic of infant mortality interacted with the infections abroad in the summer—when most of the deaths occurred—and again in the winter, when there was also a high death rate for the age group.

Deaths at 1 to 18 Years

A. Cohort Analysis by Time and Place

Figure 12.6 illustrates the pattern of birth cohort deaths from 1 to 18 years. Numbers of deaths are small at these ages and deaths for the Northern and Southern control areas have been combined. There is no evident effect of prenatal exposure to famine: in the famine cities mortality was at a peak in the B1 cohort, born in the earlier and less severe stages of the famine, and declined irregularly in successive cohorts; in the control cities mortality was higher, but the pattern was similar.

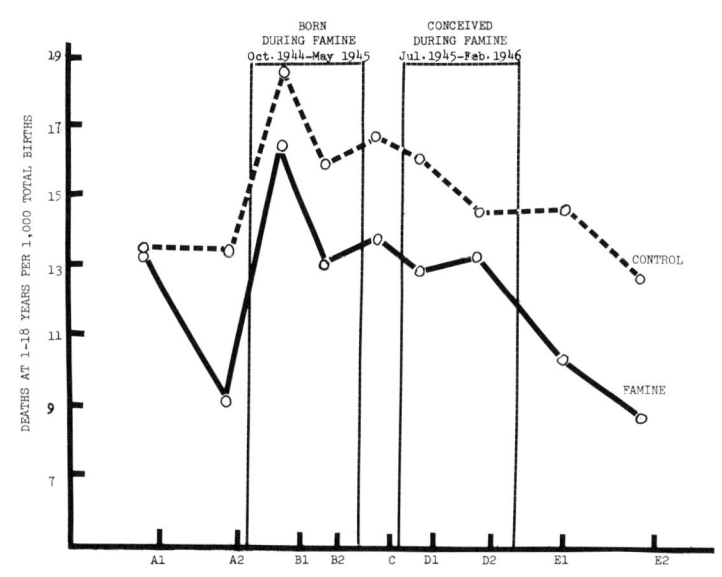

Figure 12.6. Deaths at 1 to 18 years by time and place (deaths at 1 to 18 years per 1000 total births: famine and combined control areas by cohort for births January 1944 to December 1946)

The sharp rise in the death rate of the B1 cohort in both famine and control cities reflects chiefly deaths during the second year of life, as we found in a periodic analysis of mortality. Although these deaths are distributed through the period November 1945 to January 1947, the peak can be accounted for by the high death rate in all areas among infants and young children in the winter of 1945-46, the year after the hunger winter.

B. Quantitative Analysis of Food Rations and Deaths at 1 to 18 Years

Cohort death rates at ages 1 to 18 years for the 36 birth months, January 1944 to December 1946, have moderate but statistically significant negative correlations with food rations in each trimester. Under the famine condition, and in the analysis of differences, however, the correlations are negligible and indicate the absence of a prenatal famine effect.

Under the non-famine condition, the negative correlations of death with food rations persist. As in other age groups it seems unlikely that these correlations with food rations could be causal when no causal effect is demonstrable under the extreme deprivation of the famine. Were the association indeed causal, a forced sequences multiple regression analysis suggests that C_1 would account for the whole of it.

One index of fetal growth, infant length, has a significant negative correlation with mortality at 1 to 18 years under the famine condition. This correlation is not supported by the analysis of differences. Whatever the source of the correlation may be, it must be unrelated to fetal growth retardation resulting from nutritional deprivation. Mortality in this age group was related to food rations in the *first* trimester under the *non-famine* condition whereas fetal growth was related to food rations in the *third* trimester under the *famine* condition (Chapter 10).

Death rates after infancy, then, show disparities among cohorts of almost two to one, but the disparities relate to no factors isolated by our design and analysis. For this reason, in further elaborating our analysis, we shall confine ourselves to mortality in the first year of life.

Summary

The pattern of mortality in the age group 1 to 18 years does not suggest any specific effect of prenatal exposure to famine. Periodic analysis indicates that a peak in mortality in the B1 cohort in both famine and control areas was accounted for by deaths in the second year of life in the winter of 1946, that is, the year following the hunger winter. Retardation of fetal growth caused by famine had no definite relation to mortality at these ages.

Notes and Tables

Data Sources

The sources of data for the analyses of deaths are two: the Central Bureau of Statistics of the Netherlands and the local registry offices throughout the country. The data of the Central Bureau of Statistics provided the fact of death, the date of death, the place of death, month of birth, age at death,* and the main contributory causes of death. In the analysis of deaths in infancy, place of birth could be adduced with some confidence from the datum "usual place of residence of parent," which was noted in the central record. A 10% sample of infant deaths, followed through local registers to test certain items of the data, satisfied us about the utility of the central statistics in this regard. For all deaths at over 1 year of age we supplemented the Central Bureau of Statistics data with information from the local registries on place of birth.

The central register provided the numerators for cohort death rates. To generate denominators, we obtained from the local registry a direct count of the number of liveborn (by sex) and the number of stillborn that were registered in the names of residents of the selected cities during each of the 36 months, 1944 through 1946.

We also had independent counts of stillbirths from both the central and the local records, and were able to check the data sets against one another. There were virtually no discrepancies.

Up to 1950 the Central Bureau of Statistics classified the causes of death by the Dutch version of the International Classification of Diseases (ICD), 1938 (World Health Organization, 1938). After 1950, the Dutch version of the 1948 ICD (World Health Organization, 1948) was used.

The "usual" occupation of the father at the time of death of the child was coded by our field workers on a three digit social class classification described in Chapter 7. This information, not recorded in central statistics, was obtained from local population registers, in the case of infants from the 10% sample mentioned above, and in the case of older ages for all deaths.

Quantitative Analysis of Food Rations and Mortality

1.1. We began the analysis of the quantitative effects of nutrition on death rates in each age group by correlating the average caloric ration of a cohort in each trimester of pregnancy (C_1, C_2, C_3) with the age-specific death rate for the 36 available monthly birth cohorts (Table 12.1, p. 176). Rations were also quan-

---

*For infants, exact age (in months) at death was not always recorded in the period 1944-45. This gave no real cause for concern, because an age group was nearly always recorded. Deaths were grouped as occurring at less than 7 days, 7 to 29 days, 30 to 89 days, 90 to 364 days. We adopted this grouping for classifying deaths in infancy.

tified in terms of protein, fats, and carbohydrates (as given in the Appendix). Six correlation matrices were obtained for each analysis—namely, one matrix for each of the three areas—and a fourth for all areas combined; a fifth for the famine condition defined by an average daily ration of 1500 Calories or less in the third trimester; and a sixth for the non-famine condition defined by an average ration of more than 1500 Calories.

1.2. A "correlation of differences" (see Chapter 10, p. 112) of food rations and death rates between the famine area and each control area, giving a combined total of 72 instances, was then carried out. In each analysis of differences three sets of cohorts, one for each area, are available. Two of the three sets are shown (Table 12.2, p. 177) since only the comparisons of the famine area with the South and with the North are strictly relevant to our search for famine effects.

1.3. Where the need arose to separate overlapping contributions of rations in the three trimesters (C_1, C_2, C_3) to variation in the death rates, we undertook a multiple regression analysis based on the "forced sequences" procedure described in the Notes and Tables to Chapter 10.

2.1. In the second set of analyses, we added indices of fetal growth for 20 monthly birth cohorts to the correlations of food rations with death rates (Table 12.3, p. 178). The power of this analysis is reduced by the reduction in the number of monthly cohorts, which determines the number of group means available. The use of group means was mandatory, because there was no way of linking the data on individual deaths with the data on individual births.

In these analyses, five correlation matrices were obtained: a matrix for each of the three areas under all caloric conditions and a matrix for each of the two nutritional conditions, famine and non-famine, for all areas combined. Since fetal growth retardation occurred only under the famine condition, the other condition is used merely to test the coherence of the results.

2.2. A correlation of differences between each independent variable and age-specific deaths in the famine area compared with the control areas was carried out for these 20 monthly birth cohorts in the same manner as for the 36 monthly cohorts, and for the same reasons.

2.3. Partial correlations of the age-specific death rates with each independent variable, with all other independent variables held constant, were calculated. The object of this analysis was to determine the unique effect of each independent variable. These correlations were made only in the famine area and selected results are given in the text.

Multiple regression analyses of each age-specific death rate are not presented. By this stage of the analysis, we had satisfied ourselves about the logical structure of the variables involved, as described in the path analysis of the reproductive process among individual births in the preceding chapter. To include death at given ages, this structure must be extended. Such extension cannot be accomplished without changing the measurement units of the analyses; only mean values of attributes of grouped births, not individual births, can be related to death rates. To use a structure of variables derived from the intra-individual processes of reproduction as if it reflected the relations of these variables among groups risks the pitfalls of the ecological fallacy without, it seems to us, a corresponding return in useful information.

Birthweight was the most sensitive and reliable indicator of famine effects on fetal growth. Where we seek to understand the interrelations of food rations, fetal growth, and mortality, we content ourselves with presenting partial correlations that use birthweight as an index of fetal growth.

The statistical significance of the correlations found in these data has been tested and the level of probability has been estimated for a two-tailed test. The choice is a conservative one, since a one-tailed test could be justified.

Periodic Death Rates

Cohort and Periodic Analysis Compared

Cohort death rates are plotted against the dates of birth of the cohorts under study. For any given age, cohort death rates take as numerators the numbers from that birth cohort who died at the given age. Cohort death rates take as denominator the total numbers born in the months assigned to the cohort. For instance, in a cohort infant death rate the numerator comprises those who died before the first birthday and whose date and place of birth place them in the appropriate cohort, whatever the calendar year might be. The denominator comprises all those born into that cohort. The period during which the deaths of any one cohort occur overlaps with that of adjacent cohorts. The period of observation for a cohort is determined by the span of time covered by the dates of birth taken together with the span of time covered by the age group. The observation period begins on the date at which the oldest cohort members reach the youngest age included in the specified age group; the observation period ends on the date at which the youngest cohort members reach the oldest age included. The larger the span of time covered by dates of birth of each cohort and by the specific age group under analysis, the greater is the period of time over which deaths from one cohort may occur and overlap with deaths from other cohorts. For instance, in an annual cohort, deaths under one year may occur at any time throughout a period of observation of two years.

Periodic death rates are plotted against the dates of death of the groups under study. For any given age, periodic death rates take as numerator the numbers of individuals who died during a specific period of observation. The period of observation is chosen for convenience and is most usually a calendar year. Periodic rates take as denominator the estimated number of those of given age living at some time conveniently related to the period of observation of the deaths. For instance, in a periodic infant death rate* calculated over a one-month period by the convention for older age groups, the numerator would comprise all those of the given age who died in that month, and the denominator all infants under 1 year of age alive at a particular date during that month, usually the midpoint. Such a denominator for a periodic rate covering one month would include no less than thirteen different monthly birth cohorts. In the present study, these denominators were calculated from the numbers in all the birth cohorts who reached the given age in the specified period of observation.

For stillbirths and first-week deaths in this analysis, cohort and periodic rates are identical, and up to the age of 1 month they are almost so. After this age, the rates begin to diverge; one must then look to cohort rates to decipher the effects of prenatal and other early experiences persisting into later life and to periodic rates to decipher the effects of experiences closer to the time of death.

Deaths at 30 to 89 Days **

Monthly periodic death rates for the 30 to 89 day age group in the famine and control areas are shown in Figure 12.7A. A famine effect cannot be isolated. The death rate in the famine area rises sharply through the famine period, but although in decline the rate continues high for some three months during the summer following liberation. The death rate in the control areas begins higher and rises as sharply to an earlier mid-winter peak. The only feature that suggests an effect distinct from that of the famine is that the level continues high somewhat longer after liberation.

Monthly cohort rates reveal a quite different configuration, one that concords better with a famine effect. In Figure 12.7B and 12.7C, the corresponding cohort curves are added to the graph. In the famine area (Fig. 12.7B) the curve is consistent with a third trimester famine effect for cohorts born during the famine or soon after; it is also consistent with a lesser first trimester effect for cohorts conceived during the famine and exposed only in the first trimester. In the control areas the cohort death rates, unlike the periodic rates, have a pattern distinct from that of the famine area. During the period of the famine the rates are elevated, but much less so than in the famine area, and in the period after the liberation, they continue elevated with a much less abrupt decline.

*The vital statistics convention for infant death rates is a compromise between cohort and periodic rates. These infant death rates are obtained from the ratio of the number of deaths among liveborn children under one year of age in a specified period to the number of live births in that period. The deaths in the numerator may thus be drawn from cohorts not included in the denominator.

**Our population of birth cohorts begins in January 1944. A developed 3-month-old population at risk is therefore not available before April 1944, when the rates in Figure 12.7A begin. The denominators of the rates have been standardized for age in months because of the substantial variations in numbers born each month during the study period. Northern and Southern control areas have been grouped because of the small numbers of deaths in many months.

DEATHS FROM INFANCY TO ADULTHOOD

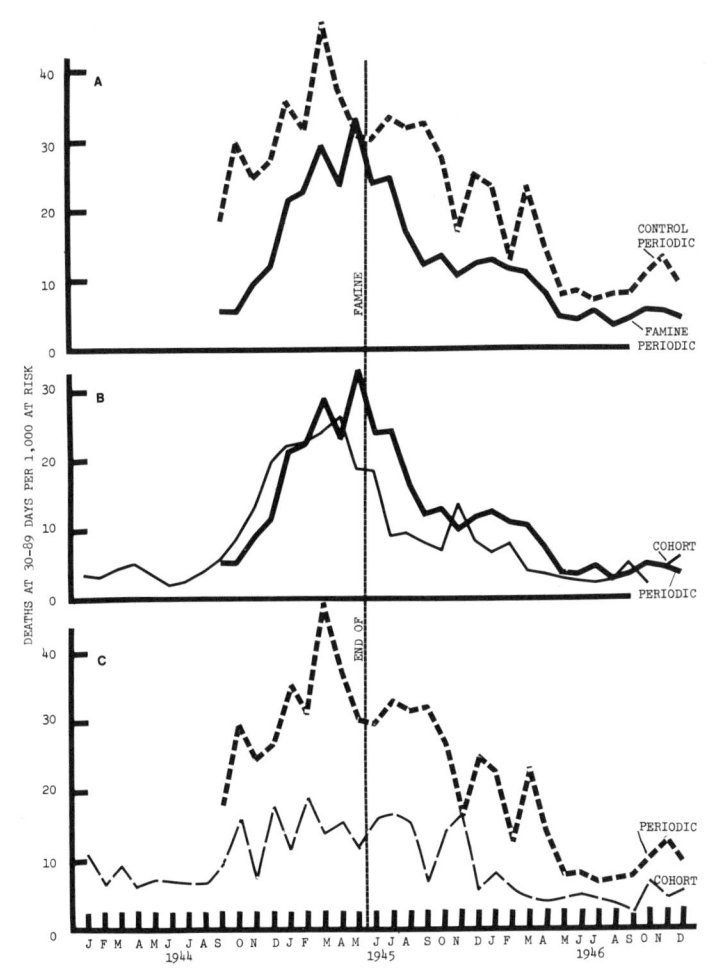

Figure 12.7. Cohort and periodic death rates at 30 to 89 days (cohort and periodic monthly rates for deaths occurring at ages 30 to 89 days among births from January 1944 to December 1946, inclusive, arranged to show: (A) periodic rates by famine and control cities, (B) cohort and periodic rates in the famine cities, and (C) cohort and periodic rates in the combined control areas)

The concord of the cohort rates and the discord of the periodic rates with a prenatal famine effect can be illustrated quantitatively by a simple calculation. The birth cohort of April 1945 was the last to be exposed throughout the third trimester; the whole of this exposure occurred in the most severe period of famine, and no cohort suffered greater deprivation. In the birth cohorts of May, June, and July, some or all members escaped exposure to famine, in the last stage of gestation, for a period that coincided with the interval between the time of liberation until the day of birth. From these facts we have crudely estimated the reduction of nutritional deprivation in the three later born cohorts, as compared with April.* The tabulation below of the estimated amount of third trimester deprivation against the death rates of the relevant cohorts shows reasonable agreement between them.

Birth Cohort	March	April	May	June	July	August
Estimated Nutritional Deprivation (%):	100	100	90	50	10	0
Death Rate 30 to 89 days:	80	100	70	71	34	35

By contrast, the pattern of periodic death rates in the 30 to 89 day age group is not consistent with a current postnatal effect during or soon after the famine. For convenience, we shall assume that a current postnatal effect requires a one-month exposure. April 1945 is the last month of famine in which all those who died were exposed for a full month. For those who died in May and in June 1945, we have estimated the average current exposure to famine in the same manner as for cohorts. For those who died in July 1945 or after, there was no current exposure.

Month of Death	March	April	May	June	July	August
Estimated Current Famine Exposure (%)	100	100	75	2½	0	0
Death rate, 30 to 89 days:	123	100	142	106	97	58

The agreement between periodic death rates and current exposure to famine is poor.

Deaths at 90 to 364 Days

Monthly periodic death rates for the 90 to 364 day age group in the famine and control areas are shown in Figure 12.8A.** No famine effect can be distinguished. The extremes of infant mortality that stand out in the summer after the liberation have not been known or recorded in the country at any other time within recent memory. As with the 30 to 89 day age group, the death rate in the

---

*The estimates are based on the product of the average number who escaped exposure and the duration of their escape, assuming equal effects of famine at all stages of the last trimester. Deprivation for any complete famine month is given equal weight and scored 100%.

**The population of the study, beginning with births in January 1944, determines that a complete population at risk for the 90 to 364 day age group does not become available before September 1944, when the curves in the chart begin.

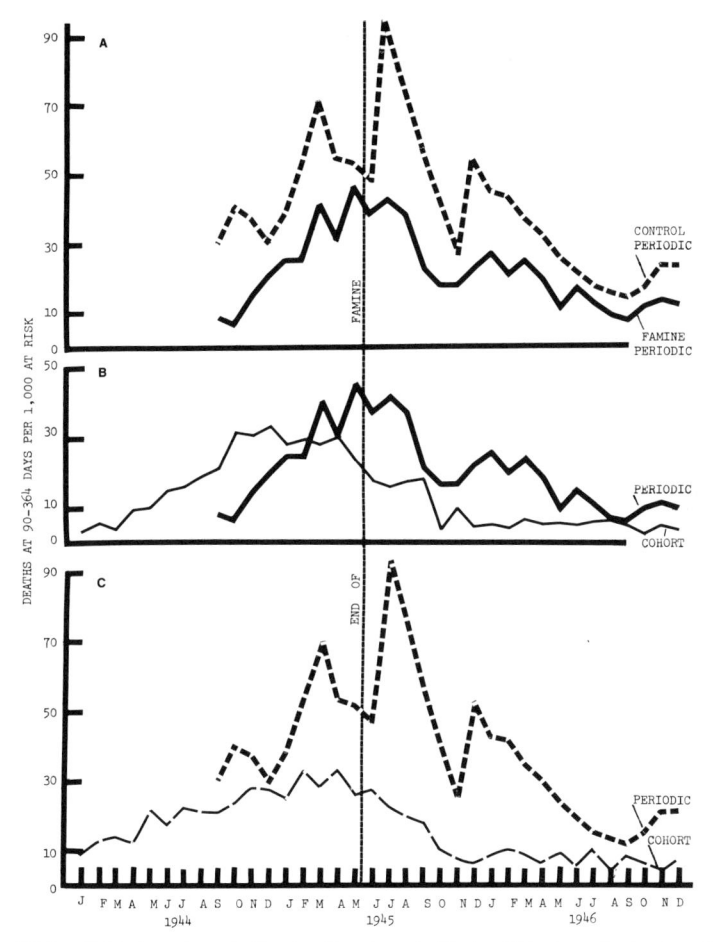

Figure 12.8. Cohort and periodic death rates at 90 to 364 days (cohort and periodic monthly rates for deaths occurring at ages 90-364 days for births January 1944 to December 1946 arranged to show: (A) periodic rates by famine and control cities, (B) cohort and periodic rates in the famine cities, and (C) cohort and periodic rates in the combined control cities)

famine area rises by a factor of about six through the famine period, but continues high through the three summer months following before it declines. During the subsequent winter, too, the rate rises noticeably. The death rates in the control area follow a not dissimilar course through the famine period and after. They maintain a much higher level than in the famine area, and infants were literally decimated in the summer after liberation; mortality reached a peak of almost 10%. The proportional rise by a factor of about three, however, is less than in the famine area. The excessive but irregular rise in mortality rates over the period of more than a year, from the winter of 1944 to the end of the winter of 1945, points to no ready explanation.

The cohort curves for the famine-stricken and control cities, by contrast, can be made to fit the assumption that a harsh period of environmental stress was relieved at liberation. In Figures 12.8B and 12.8C cohort curves are added to the periodic curves for famine and control areas. The death rate for the famine area reached an early winter peak for cohorts born as famine fully declared itself; the rate then remained high for all cohorts born during the famine. For births from the months of liberation in May, a decline began. The decline in the cohort death rate was checked among late summer births but was rapid thereafter. The pattern is consistent with an environmental stressor active in late pregnancy that was removed at the time of liberation. Yet the stressor cannot be the famine alone. In the control areas (Fig. 12.8C), as we saw in Figure 12.5, p. 161, we find that the cohort death rate behaves in similar fashion. A more likely explanation of the cohort pattern of mortality, therefore, is that a factor common to both famine and control areas operated during the war-time period to render the exposed cohorts susceptible to death through the first year of life.

Age-Specific Death Rates Grouped by Area

Our object in what follows is to establish the validity of cohort patterns of mortality previously described. A concurrent pattern of cohort curves among age groups points to generational experiences that have affected population mortality at some stage *antecedent to the event of death,* and irrespective of age or current experience. A concurrent pattern of periodic curves among age groups points to current experiences that have affected population mortality *at the time of death,* and irrespective of age or generation.

Cohort Rates

Figure 12.9 groups the cohort death rates of each infant age group by area. The curves for stillbirths, first-week deaths, and 7 to 29 day deaths are drawn in thin lines, in contrast with the older age groups. They are thus distinguished because at these ages cohort and periodic curves are interchangeable. Only later, at 30 to 89 days and 90 to 364 days, can they be separated.

The famine cities (Figure 12.9A) show three distinct patterns of age-specific cohort mortality, with transitions between them. First, the pattern of stillbirths stands out on its own, its only possible relation to famine being early in gestation (the D2 cohort). Second, the three curves of death rates in the first three months of life share a common pattern that is congruent with an effect of famine exposure late in gestation; there is high mortality in the B1, B2, and C cohorts, with the peak in B2. The curve for first-week deaths appears transitional, in that it shows a rise in the D2 cohort as does the stillbirth curve, and it also shows a peak in the B2 cohort as do the curves for deaths at 7 to 29 days

Figure 12.9. Cohort death rates by area (age-specific infant death rates grouped by area for nine birth cohorts: (A) famine area, (B) Northern control area, and (C) Southern control area)

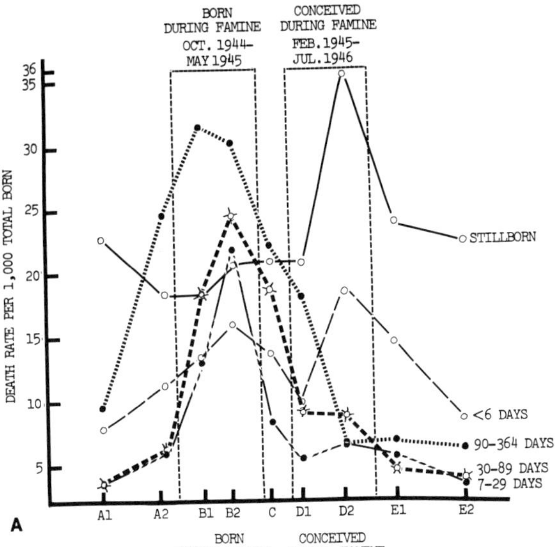
BORN
DURING FAMINE
OCT. 1944–
MAY 1945
CONCEIVED
DURING FAMINE
FEB. 1945–
JUL. 1946
DEATH RATE PER 1,000 TOTAL BORN
STILLBORN
<6 DAYS
90–364 DAYS
30–89 DAYS
7–29 DAYS
A1
A2
B1
B2
C
D1
D2
E1
E2

A

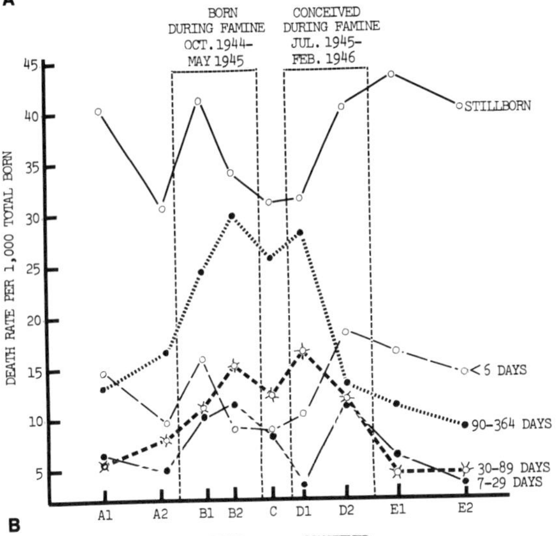
BORN
DURING FAMINE
OCT. 1944–
MAY 1945
CONCEIVED
DURING FAMINE
JUL. 1945–
FEB. 1946
DEATH RATE PER 1,000 TOTAL BORN
STILLBORN
< 5 DAYS
90–364 DAYS
30–89 DAYS
7–29 DAYS
A1
A2
B1
B2
C
D1
D2
E1
E2

B

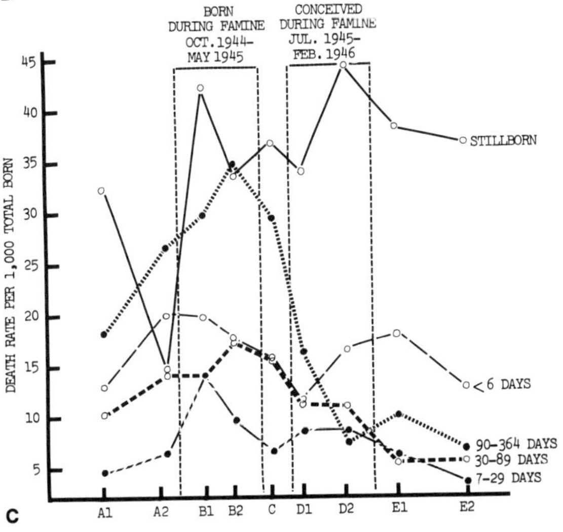
BORN
DURING FAMINE
OCT. 1944–
MAY 1945
CONCEIVED
DURING FAMINE
JUL. 1945–
FEB. 1946
DEATH RATE PER 1,000 TOTAL BORN
STILLBORN
< 6 DAYS
90–364 DAYS
30–89 DAYS
7–29 DAYS
A1
A2
B1
B2
C
D1
D2
E1
E2

C

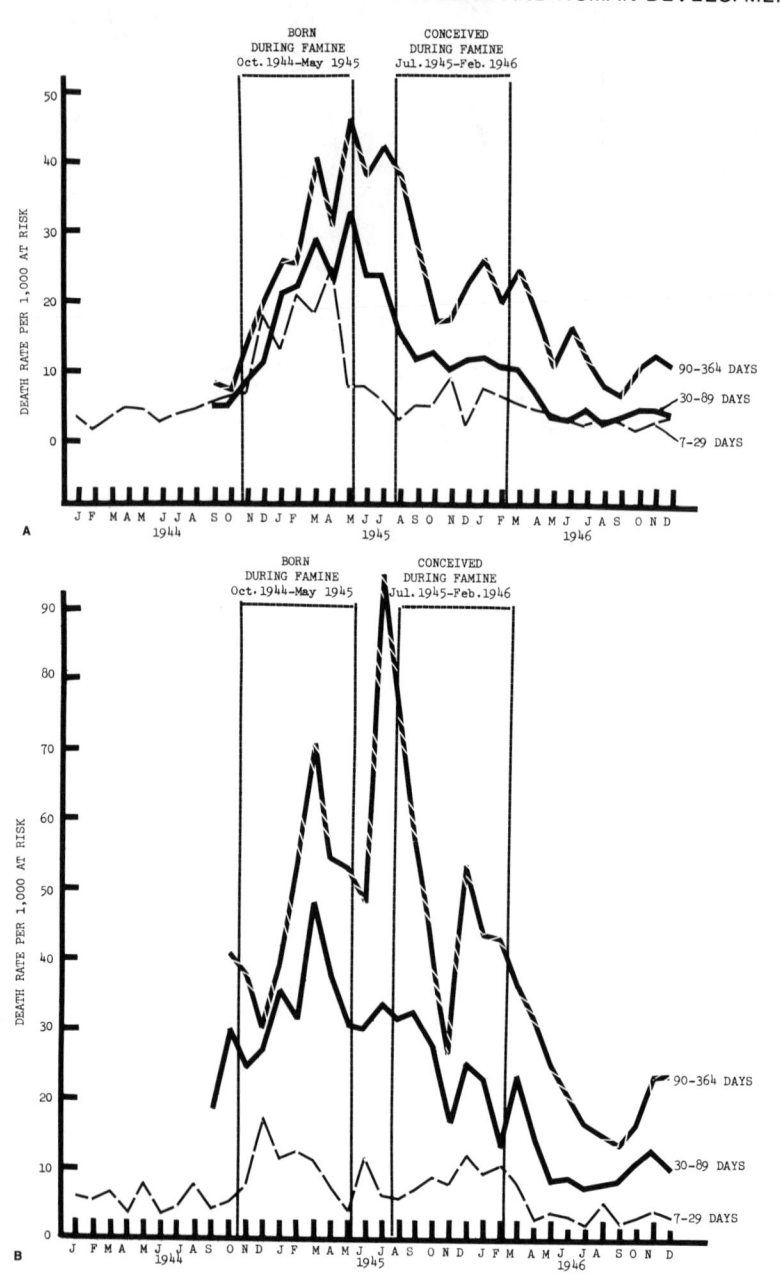

Figure 12.10. Periodic death rates by area (age-specific periodic infant death rates for each month from January 1944 to December 1946: (A) famine area and (B) combined control areas)

DEATHS FROM INFANCY TO ADULTHOOD

and 30 to 89 days. Third, the curve for the 90 to 364 day age group differs from the curves for deaths in the first three months of life, although it shares the high B2 rate and its subsequent decline.

It can be seen at a glance that the Northern and Southern control cities have patterns of cohort mortality that differ from the famine cities; in particular the curves for each age group are more dissonant with each other and the peaks less distinctly related to births during the famine period. The degree to which the pattern of mortality through the first year of life relates to the prenatal experience of each birth cohort is thus less pronounced than in the famine area. Taken together, the three sets of cohort curves emphasize the distinctiveness of the pattern of mortality in the first three months of life among those cohorts born at the height of the famine in the famine cities. This pattern suggests the deferred manifestation of a prenatal experience.

In order to test our interpretations of cohort death rates grouped by area, we carried out an analysis of periodic death rates similarly grouped (Fig. 12.10).

Periodic Rates

In the famine area in particular, the periodic curves shown in Figure 12.10 are less congruent with each other than the cohort curves shown in Figure 12.9A. The pair of curves for mortality after 1 month of age (30 to 89 days and 90 to 364 days) show some congruence during the famine period and diverge during the summer of 1945. In both famine and control areas, these divergences are informative. In the famine area, after liberation, the rates at 90 to 364 days maintain a high level. The high rate persists for 4 months, through August, while the rate at 30 to 89 days is in steady decline. In the control area, the 90 to 364 day rate rises to an extreme peak. This peak covers five months, through September, while the rates at 30 to 89 days maintain a steady level. The divergence between the two age groups in both areas is evidence against a current effect in the summer of 1945 as the primary source of the epidemic of infant death rates of the time. By elimination, the pattern supports the inference made from the analysis of the 90 to 364 day death rates (pp. 161-63), that in both famine and control areas, late *prenatal* environmental stressors acting during the famine period were the source of the 1945 summer epidemic. Consistent with this explanation, mortality at 7 to 29 days in both areas is at its highest during the famine period.

Table 12.1. Food rations and mortality (correlation matrices of age-specific death rates for 36 monthly birth cohorts from January 1944 through December 1946 with average daily caloric rations in each trimester of gestation, by area and nutritional condition)

Age at Death	Data Set	N	Calories First Trimester	Calories Second Trimester	Calories Third Trimester
Stillbirths	Famine	36	−0.12	0.18	0.24
	Southern Control	36	0.17	−0.11	0.16
	Northern Control	36	0.20	0.21	0.24
	All areas	108	0.13	0.18	0.19
	< 1500 Calories	26	0.18	0.33	0.38
	> 1500 Calories	82	0.07	0.05	0.04
< 7 days	Famine	36	−0.46**	−0.25	−0.24
	Southern Control	36	−0.19	−0.30	−0.25
	Northern Control	36	0.17	0.19	0.24
	All areas	108	−0.11	−0.07	−0.04
	< 1500 Calories	26	0.35	0.26	−0.01
	> 1500 Calories	82	−0.12	−0.05	0.06
7 to 29 days	Famine	36	−0.28	−0.42**	−0.61***
	Southern Control	36	−0.45**	−0.51**	−0.47**
	Northern Control	36	−0.43**	−0.41*	−0.40*
	All areas	108	−0.37***	−0.44***	−0.51***
	< 1500 Calories	26	−0.15	−0.10	−0.60***
	> 1500 Calories	82	−0.37***	−0.37***	−0.32**
30 to 89 days	Famine	36	−0.39*	−0.56***	−0.71***
	Southern Control	36	−0.53***	−0.67***	−0.67***
	Northern Control	36	−0.56***	−0.55***	−0.49**
	All areas	108	−0.46***	−0.57***	−0.62***
	< 1500 Calories	26	−0.19	−0.26	−0.71***
	> 1500 Calories	82	−0.45***	−0.49***	−0.44***
90 to 364 days	Famine	36	−0.34*	−0.61***	−0.76***
	Southern Control	36	−0.54***	−0.72***	−0.74***
	Northern Control	36	−0.60***	−0.68***	−0.67***
	All areas	108	−0.45***	−0.63***	−0.70***
	< 1500 Calories	26	0.15	−0.28	−0.14
	> 1500 Calories	82	−0.41***	−0.57***	−0.57***
1 to 18 years	Famine	36	−0.59***	−0.54***	−0.54***
	Southern Control	36	−0.10	−0.04	0.03
	Northern Control	36	−0.47**	−0.40*	−0.37*
	All areas	108	−0.30**	−0.24*	−0.23
	< 1500 Calories	26	−0.06	0.07	0.12
	> 1500 Calories	82	−0.31**	−0.23*	−0.20

Table 12.2. Fetal growth and mortality (correlation matrices of age-specific death rates, for the 20 monthly birth cohorts from August 1, 1944, through March 31, 1946, with six indices of the reproductive process [birthweight, infant length, head circumference, placental weight, fetal age, and maternal weight])

1. For births in famine cities, and Northern and Southern control cities.
2. For births with third trimester famine exposure (below 1500 Calories average daily ration)
3. For births without third trimester famine exposure (1500 and over Calories average daily ration)

Statistical significance at .05 level on two-tailed test is indicated by *, at .01 level by **, and at .001 level by ***.

Age at Death	Data Set	N	Birthweight	Length	Head Circumference	Placental Weight	Duration of Gestation	Maternal Weight
Still-births	Famine	20	0.15	−0.12	0.15	0.35	−0.43	0.41
	South	20	−0.003	−0.01	0.22	0.39	−0.11	
	North	20	0.20	−0.001	0.09	0.28	0.03	
	<1500 Calories	26	0.34	−0.13	+	0.29	0.15	
	>1500 Calories	34	−0.01	−0.23	+	0.32	−0.14	
0 Days	Famine	20	−0.25	−0.42	−0.01	0.02	−0.54*	0.06
	South	20	−0.05	0.17	0.06	0.001	−0.41	
	North	20	0.16	−0.38	0.23	0.42	−0.27	
	<1500 Calories	26	0.20	0.14	+	−0.18	−0.30	
	>1500 Calories	34	−0.24	−0.36	+	0.10	−0.33	
1 to 9 Days	Famine	20	−0.75***	−0.69***	−0.53*	−0.78***	−0.22	−0.65**
	South	20	0.10	0.02	0.27	0.23	−0.27	
	North	20	−0.18	0.001	−0.36	−0.07	−0.01	
	<1500 Calories	26	−0.47*	−0.31	+	−0.37	−0.25	
	>1500 Calories	34	−0.05	−0.19	+	0.08	−0.10	
10 to 29 Days	Famine	20	−0.83***	−0.68***	−0.57**	−0.85***	−0.30	−0.77***
	South	20	−0.55*	0.08	0.10	0.06	0.19	
	North	20	−0.32	−0.04	−0.01	−0.28	0.06	
	<1500 Calories	26	−0.61***	−0.23	+	−0.44*	−0.24	
	>1500 Calories	34	−0.41*	−0.20	+	−0.15	0.16	
30 to 364 Days	Famine	20	−0.40	−0.08	−0.27	−0.59**	0.08	−0.78***
	South	20	−0.26	0.04	0.01	−0.43	0.01	
	North	20	−0.27	0.38	−0.30	−0.61**	0.48*	
	<1500 Calories	26	0.06	0.28	+	−0.33	−0.11	
	>1500 Calories	34	−0.11	0.15	+	−0.20	0.40*	
1 to 18 Years	Famine	20	−0.27	−0.32	−0.32	−0.26	−0.32	−0.13
	South	20	0.12	0.02	0.12	−0.05	−0.36	
	North	20	−0.20	−0.09	−0.07	−0.21	0.02	
	<1500 Calories	26	−0.09	−0.42*	+	0.04	0.02	
	>1500 Calories	34	0.14	−0.17	+	0.52**	−0.24	

+Omitted because of heterogeneity of data by area.

178 FAMINE AND HUMAN DEVELOPMENT

Table 12.3. Differences by area in Calories, indices of fetal growth and mortality (differences between famine and control cities (famine-South and famine-North) in average daily Calories in first (C_1), second (C_2), and third (C_3) trimesters and in monthly means for birthweight, length, head circumference, placental weight, and duration of gestation, correlated with differences in age-specific death rates over 36 months in the case of Calories and over 20 months in the case of the indices of fetal growth)

Age at Death	Areas	N	C_1	C_2	C_3	Birth-weight	Length	Head Circumference	Placental Weight	Duration of Gestation
Still Born	F-S	36	−0.18	0.08	0.07					
	F-S	20	−0.30	−0.11	−0.09					
	F-N	36	−0.34*	−0.14	−0.18	−0.12	−0.12	0.08	0.06	−0.08
	F-N	20	−0.07	−0.19	−0.43**	0.05	0.20	0.10	0.21	0.01
7 Days	F-S	36	0.27	0.05	−0.60***	−0.27	−0.15	0.13	−0.02	−0.07
	F-S	20	0.17	−0.19	−0.52***	−0.43	−0.31	0.13	0.17	−0.46*
	F-N	36				−0.34	−0.50*	−0.47*	−0.26	0.01
	F-N	20				−0.29	−0.25	0.18	0.18	−0.21
7–29 Days	F-S	36	0.01	−0.09	−0.55**	−0.69***	−0.37	−0.22	−0.25	−0.05
	F-S	20	0.35*	0.07	−0.55***	−0.39	−0.17	0.19	0.27	−0.32
	F-N	36								
	F-N	20								
30–89 Days	F-S	36	−0.30	−0.13	−0.13	0.51*	0.43	0.20	0.09	−0.16
	F-S	20	0.36*	0.35*	−0.11	0.07	0.27	0.61**	0.28	−0.01
	F-N	36								
	F-N	20								
90–364 Days	F-S	36	−0.22	−0.16	−0.10	0.25	0.18	−0.005	0.01	−0.27
	F-S	20	−0.02	0.14	0.06	−0.36	−0.06	−0.26	−0.26	0.01
	F-N	36								
	F-N	20								
1–18 Years										

13 Death Rates Refined and Specified

Two elaborations of the analysis of mortality are considered in this chapter: (1) analysis by assigned causes of death, (2) analysis by social class of decedents.

Assigned Causes of Death

By examining certified causes of death, we hoped that we might identify those that accounted for the excess of deaths attributable to prenatal exposure to famine. Knowledge of the distribution of assigned causes of death should clarify the nature of famine effects and aid in the understanding of pathogenetic processes.

The famine area was compared with a control area made up of North and South combined, because within either of the control areas taken singly, numbers of deaths in each monthly cohort were small. For the same reason, in the diagrams infant deaths assigned to selected causes were grouped in only two age groups—under 90 days (Fig. 13.1A, B, C) and 90 to 364 days (Fig. 13.1D). The age intervals were chosen because of the common patterns of cohort death rates that exist on either side of the 90-day breakpoint. The tables given at the end of the chapter, however, show causes of death at ages 0 to 7 days, 7 to 29 days, 30 to 89 days, 90 to 364 days, and 1 to 18 years.

In general, whenever high death rates occurred in cohorts exposed to famine at ages less than 1 year, the rates of most of the more common causes of death, like gastrointestinal, respiratory, and other acute infections were also high.

Among deaths at ages under 90 days, one group of causes of death seemed special to the period of the famine. This group comprised the triad starvation,

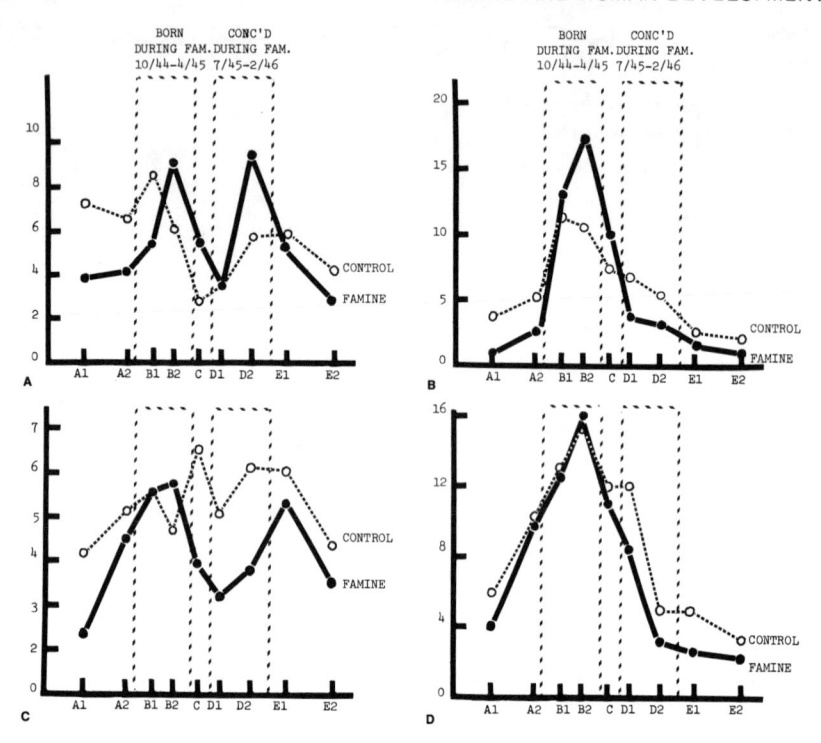

Figure 13.1. Cohort deaths by cause and area (selected causes of death per 1000 total births compared in famine and combined control areas: **A.** prematurity; **B.** starvation, atrophy, and sclerema; **C.** obstetric, all at ages under 90 days; and **D.** acute infections at ages over 90 days)

atrophy, and sclerema;* the rates for these conditions in the famine area were as much as 5 to 10 times as high in cohorts born during the famine (B1, B2, C) as in cohorts born before (A1) and after (E1, E2). These conditions were not peculiar to the famine area. In the control areas peaks for these conditions also appeared among the same cohorts. The peaks in the control areas were much lower, however, the changes in rates were less sharp, and the proportional increase considerably less (Fig. 13.2). Thus, while war-time conditions, a cold winter without fuel, and similar factors doubtless contributed to these inordinately high death rates in all areas, late prenatal maternal starvation surely made a major contribution to deaths assigned to this triad of conditions.

Two causes of death that usually cluster in the first week of life—namely, prematurity** and obstetric causes—also had famine-associated patterns. The control areas had dissimilar patterns. In the famine area both causes had two

*International Classification of Diseases (ICD), 1938, Codes 502, 750, 777, 911, 902.
**ICD code 774. Low birthweight of any origin as a cause of death, whether or not associated with shortened gestation, will have been assigned to the cause "prematurity."

peaks; for deaths assigned to prematurity the peaks were among the B2 cohort *born* at the height of the famine, and among the D2 cohort *conceived* at the height of the famine; thus the peaks were coincident with famine exposure in the third trimester and the first trimester, respectively. The peaks for obstetric deaths occurred among the B2 and E1 cohorts; only the B2 cohort peak, coincident with third trimester exposure, could be famine-related.

Age-group differences in the two peaks for deaths assigned to prematurity suggest that the peaks may reflect two different syndromes of low birthweight. In normal conditions, first-week deaths make the main contribution to deaths from prematurity. The D2 cohort, conceived during the famine and exposed early in gestation, conforms with expectation: the rate of death from prematurity was particularly high in the first week of life (Table 13.1). It will be recalled that this cohort also had shortened gestation without fetal growth retardation, and an excess, albeit not statistically significant, of infants of very low birthweight (Chapter 10). Thus the D2 cohort experience suggests a syndrome of premature birth with very low birthweight and a raised risk of first-week death. On the other hand, the B2 cohort, conceived before the famine and born at its height, departs somewhat from expectation; although the rate of first-week deaths from prematurity was high, the relative increase in the rate among deaths at 7 to 29 days was even higher. It will be recalled that this cohort suffered fetal growth retardation from third trimester exposure without shortened gestation (Chapter 10). The B2 experience suggests a syndrome of retarded fetal growth, delivery at full term with low birthweight, and a raised risk of death persisting through the first month of life.

In general, the array of causes to which cohort deaths were chiefly assigned in the first three months of life are coherent with effects to be expected from exposure to famine at different stages of prenatal life. The pattern of death is less coherent at later ages. In the 90 to 364 day age group, which was decimated by the summer epidemic of 1945, the outstanding causes to which death among cohorts with excess mortality were assigned were acute infections, especially gastrointestinal and respiratory conditions. Gastrointestinal infections, but not respiratory infections, are those to be expected in a summer epidemic of those times. Deaths due to the triad of starvation, atrophy, and sclerema also increased markedly in this age group, and persisted through the summer in both famine and control areas. These too are uncharacteristic of fatal epidemics of infectious diseases at this age. Deaths from sclerema are usually associated with cold. In this instance all of them cannot be attributed to a severe winter without fuel; a substantial proportion of the deaths occurred in the spring and summer of 1945 and there was no fall-off in the rate until September 1945.

None of the main causes to which deaths were assigned discriminated entirely between famine and control areas. In the light of our previous analyses, the pattern of mortality can best be accounted for by severe environmental stressors during prenatal life* that produced debilitated infants and rendered them susceptible in postnatal life to a variety of precipitating causes of death, particularly acute infections.

Acute infections also made the predominant contribution to certified causes of death after infancy. The patterns of mortality in famine and control areas followed each other closely in both magnitude and direction throughout, as they did for all causes (Fig. 12.6). Thus, the results of the earlier analyses are supported; the analyses by assigned cause of death after three months of age and up to eighteen years do not make a prenatal *famine* effect any more likely than did the analysis of all deaths without regard to cause. One feature of these data for deaths at later ages, which occurred throughout 17 postwar years, is the steady declining gradient in the porportion of deaths assigned to infections in successive cohorts in all areas.

Famine-related causes of death after infancy possibly occurred in the D2 cohort conceived at the height of the famine. Deaths from disorders of the central nervous system excluding malformations (ICD 1948, 330-399) were higher than expected in that cohort (10.9%, when 6.2% was expected). This is a heterogeneous category, but meningitis makes the main contribution to the excess. Congenital malformations (ICD 1948, 750-759) were also somewhat higher in the D2 cohort (10.9%, when 7.6% was expected). This too is a heterogeneous category, and we discern no specific pattern. Neural malformations, with or without cerebral palsy, do not stand out. Deaths assigned to mental retardation (ICD 1948, 325) are few in each cohort and exhibit no pattern consistent with a famine effect.

Summary

The findings of analyses of mortality in terms of certified causes of death were coherent with those of our other analyses. Among cohorts with high death rates, the rates for causes of death that are frequent at non-famine periods were high. Rates for some causes that could plausibly be viewed as specifically famine-related also had raised rates: among deaths in the first three months of life, the grouping of atrophy, sclerema, and starvation assumed prominence; in the first month of life deaths assigned to prematurity (defined by low birthweight) increased among cohorts exposed to famine in the first and in the third trimesters of gestation. The age distribution of deaths assigned to prematurity suggests the existence of two different syndromes, one governed by fetal growth retardation and low birthweight following third trimester famine exposure and raising the risk of death at 7 to 29 days of age, the other governed by short gestation and low birthweight following first trimester exposure to famine and raising the risk of death in the first week of life.

*We can only guess at the nature of the prenatal influences. They might have acted directly on the fetus (e.g., interference with immune responses) or indirectly through the mother (e.g., deficient lactation).

After the first three months of life, at 90 to 364 days of age, deaths assigned to gastrointestinal respiratory, and other acute infections increased markedly among cohorts born during the famine, but the increase was much the same in control and in famine cities. This age group was the main contributor to the summer epidemic of 1945. Some of the main causes of death among them were not usual for summer epidemics of infant mortality at that period. The aberrant causes can be accounted for by the susceptibility to death of infants debilitated by prenatal exposure to war-time stressors.

At 1 to 18 years of age, there was one famine-related cause of death, namely an increase of central nervous system disorders in the D2 cohort conceived at the height of the famine.

Specification by Social Class

By specifying the social class of decedents, we hoped to discover whether interaction between famine and social conditions exaggerated or diminished famine effects on mortality in particular social groups. The presence of such interaction would modify or elaborate the starting hypotheses of this study (see Chapter 1).

The following analysis uses only two classes, manual and non-manual. Numbers of deaths are insufficient for a more refined classification. A percentage of deaths (about 15%) could not be assigned to either of the two classes. About one-third of those not so assigned belonged to farming occupations; in the remaining unassigned cases, the occupation was not recorded (as, for instance, when there was no legal father). As a comparison population, we used the survivors called up at 19 years of age for military induction in 1964-66. The index of social class for deaths was the father's usual occupation at the time of his child's death. The index of social class for the comparison population was again the father's occupation.*

*Between birth and induction, there was almost bound to have been an upward shift in the social class of father's occupation, both because of mobility within the natural life course and because of the changing occupational structure of the society as a whole. Deaths would have shifted the surviving population in the same direction because of the higher mortality expected among the lower social classes. This effect is unlikely to be noteworthy; a skewed distribution even among the heavy 6% loss of the famine cohorts could not do much to skew the distribution among the 94% survivors. We attempted to check the possible extent of upward social mobility by comparing the occupational structure among fathers of the population at induction with the occupational structure among fathers at the time of birth in 1944-46. For this purpose, we used a sample of 2000 male births taken from the population registers of Amsterdam and Tilburg. The population register records of occupation were less complete than the military records; a greater proportion were entered as "unknown." The two sets of data were not much different, and conclusions about social class effects would not have been modified by using the data collected at birth to stratify the population. The validity of these data is enhanced by the larger percentage of older deaths in the non-manual classes in the D2 cohort; this is consistent with the social class composition of the cohort, as noted previously in both the military and population register data.

In Table 13.3, we compare social class in three sets of data: infant deaths, deaths at 1 to 18 years, and 19-year-old men at induction. As expected, the percentage in the non-manual class is lowest among the infant deaths, intermediate among older deaths, and highest among survivors. In these comparisons we sought and failed to find evidence of unequal impact of prenatal famine exposure on mortality in the social classes.

The criterion we chose was the ratio of the percentage of the non-manual among deaths to the percentage of the non-manual among survivors.* There was no indication that changes in this ratio related to prenatal famine exposure, either in comparisons of the successive birth cohorts, or of birth cohorts born in different areas.

For the reasons discussed, the social class comparisons must be crude, and they render inference insecure. It seems legitimate to conclude that the non-manual classes were not spared the raised mortality rates associated with the famine. The possibility that social class disparities went undetected by our data and methods, however, cannot be ruled out.

Conclusions About Mortality

The object of the analyses presented in this and the previous chapter has been to establish the effects of nutritional deprivation of mothers on the subsequent survival of their offspring. This task has been approached by considering death rates in specific age groups from birth to 18 years in many ways. Age-specific death rates have been considered in cohort and periodic analyses by time and place, and in relation to the effects of quantified food rations for each trimester under the famine and non-famine condition. We have also considered the place of fetal growth in a causal sequence between nutritional deprivation and mortality, the assigned causes of death, and the social class of those who died.

Among major conclusions, the most general is that prenatal experience produced a discernible, even a profound, impact on the infant mortality of an entire population. The fatal experiences were of more than one kind. Some were nutritional in origin, some were not, and some experiences required the combination of nutritional and other factors. Some occurred early in gestation and affected survival in the perinatal and neonatal period; some occurred late in gestation and affected survival beyond the neonatal period. The permutations of nutritional and non-nutritional factors acting at different stages of gestation to

---

*Collateral evidence from the military data shows that information on occupations recorded for the non-manual classes is more complete than for the manual classes. Thus, a large proportion of individuals for whom the datum was not recorded resembled the manual classes in other attributes. Because the proportion not assigned to any social class is not consistent across classes, the missing information takes on importance in comparison of cohorts. The proportion unknown could affect the ratios of occupational classes among deaths and survivors used as the criterion of comparison. We applied the ratio to the non-manual classes because they were less subject to this source of error than the manual classes.

produce effects at different stages of the life course resulted in a complex pattern that has proved difficult to unravel and difficult to describe with lucidity.

We have considered nutritional factors in terms of the severe deprivation of famine during early and during late gestation; also, coincidentally to the specific purpose of our research design, we have considered the effect of nutrition on mortality in terms of change over time outside the famine period.

Famine exposure *in the first trimester* related somewhat equivocally to perinatal mortality. There was a sharp rise in stillbirths and first-week deaths in the D2 cohort conceived at the height of the famine and exposed to famine only during the first trimester of gestation. The rise can be attributed only in part to severe nutritional deprivation. The rise in perinatal mortality appeared in the same cohort outside the famine area, and points to interaction between prenatal nutrition and an unknown factor common to all areas, possibly a spreading infection affecting pregnant women. Cause-specific cohort mortality curves further support the notion that first trimester famine exposure raised mortality in the D2 cohort. First-week deaths assigned to "prematurity" (for which the certifying criterion was low birthweight) were markedly increased in this cohort. Low birthweight in these infants is likely to have been the consequence of true prematurity; a shortened gestation period and very low birthweight coincided in the D2 cohort, as we saw in Chapter 10.

In relation to famine exposure *in the third trimester* the outstanding result was increase in death rates up to 90 days, but not thereafter. The increase in rates appared in a gradient rising with each successive age group; third trimester effects were absent among stillbirths, modest below the age of 7 days (an age group with a pattern transitional between first and third trimester effects), marked from 7 to 29 days, and at a maximum between 30 and 90 days of age. Partial regression coefficients indicate that a change in daily average ration of 100 Calories predicts a change of about 1.2 deaths per 1000 at ages 7 to 89 days. At 90 to 364 days the pattern of mortality in cohort and periodic death rates was in better accord with the effects of prenatal than of postnatal experience. Effects specific to famine, however, were absent.

In the third trimester, as in the first, the effects of famine exposure are not pure and isolated from other factors; interaction between famine and non-famine factors raised mortality. This interaction affected the B2 cohort born at the height of the famine; the famine factor appeared predominant. Assigned causes of death in age groups most affected by famine exposure in the third trimester were coherent with other results. Rates for causes that could be viewed as related to famine were raised as expected. Rates were also high for the more common causes of death not specific to famine, such as gastrointestinal and respiratory infections; these non-specific causes could best be interpreted as precipitating death in infants already debilitated by prenatal experience. Deaths assigned to prematurity were increased throughout the first month of life. (This increase in prematurity as a cause of death in the B2 cohort, persisting to a later age and as result of exposure at a later stage of gestation than the increase in the D2 cohort, suggests the presence of a low birthweight syndrome different from that of the D2 cohort and related to retarded intrauterine growth; it was not mediated by shortened gestation.) Through the whole of the first three months of life, the triad atrophy, sclerema, and starvation assumed prominence as a cause of death.

The role of retarded fetal growth in the causal sequence leading from nutritional deprivation to infant mortality proved unexpectedly elusive. To our surprise, we were unable to show that retarded fetal growth was associated with stillbirths and it was only weakly associated with first-week deaths. On the other hand, retarded fetal growth was strongly associated with death rates between 7 and 90 days of age. Fetal growth had the characteristics of an intervening variable in a causal chain between nutritional deprivation and mortality. The data fitted a model in which a part of the effect of nutritional deprivation was direct and a larger part was mediated through the retardation of fetal growth,

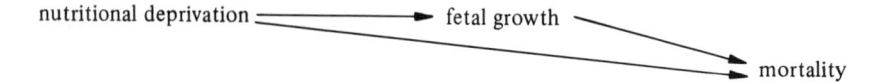

nutritional deprivation ⟶ fetal growth ⟶ mortality

The validity of the model must be qualified by regard for the assumptions involved with the use of second order correlations for aggregated data.

The effects on mortality of prenatal nutrition under less rigorous conditions than famine could not be conclusively settled, although it is improbable that there were notable effects. Under the non-famine condition (third trimester rations greater than 1500 Calories daily average), negative correlations of food rations during pregnancy were found with death rates in the age groups 30 to 89 days and 90 to 364 days. Within the limitations of a research design directed to another purpose, causality cannot be established for these correlations. We incline to attribute the correlations to postwar social improvements other than nutrition, because at 90 to 364 days the extreme prenatal nutritional deprivation of famine did not cause a rise in death rates over and above the rise that occurred in all areas.

Non-famine prenatal factors have been alluded to above in two instances of interaction with prenatal nutrition, one factor operating in early gestation (the D2 cohort) and another operating in late gestation (the B2 cohort). A major non-famine factor that produced the pattern of infant mortality in the 90 to 364 day age group is also postulated. The timing of this factor best fits late gestation, but in any event was not later than the first month of postnatal life. This factor is invoked to account for the extraordinary and mysterious summer epidemic of 1945. The epidemic, to which the 30 to 89 and 90 to 364 day age groups were the main contributors, spread throughout the country at a time when the people had been relieved of the rigors of war and famine. The primary source of the epidemic in our judgment is to be found in the antecedent prenatal war-time experience of the affected age groups rather than in the postnatal postwar experience which was current at the time of the epidemic. The epidemic cannot be attributed to prenatal or postnatal famine exposure, since it was common to all areas. The increase in deaths at 90 to 364 days of age assigned to gastrointestinal, respiratory, and other acute infections among cohorts born during the famine period conforms with the inference of a non-famine effect, since the increase in these causes was no less in control than in famine cities. The pattern of mortality was also not consistent with a postnatal effect acting on the affected age groups at the same points in time after the famine; it was consistent with an antecedent prenatal effect acting on all the affected age groups during the period of war-time stress and disorganization. Furthermore, the rise in heterogeneous causes of death, including respiratory and other acute infections and accompanied by such unusual causes for the affected age groups as atrophy, sclerema, and starvation, are highly uncharacteristic of the summer epidemics among infants that, in those times, could be attributed to specific infections or the like. The assigned causes of death are compatible, on the other hand, with factors that precipitated death among infants already debilitated by prenatal experience.

Analysis by social class added little to the understanding of famine effects. Differences in mortality between the social classes exist; they were apparent in the distribution of starvation and death during the famine, as noted in Chapter 7, and are sufficient to account for a good part of disparities between famine and control areas in the non-famine period. In our analysis, however, we found little departure from the expected ratios of the percentage of the non-manual among infant deaths to the percentage of the non-manual among survivors, either in successive cohorts or between famine and control areas. The absence of detectable effects might have been a result of weaknesses in data and analysis.

Table 13.1. Causes of infant deaths (rates of death per 1000 born by selected causes in grouped cohorts: famine and control cities compared A. first week, B. 7 to 29 days, C. 30 to 89 days, and D. 90 to 364 days)

A. FIRST-WEEK

FAMINE

Causes	A1	A2	B1	B2	C	D1	D2	E1	E2	All
Obstetric Causes	2.00	4.03	3.63	4.21	3.42	2.97	2.93	4.53	3.01	3.32
Congenital Neural	0.18	0.08	0.16	1.13	0.66	0.71	0.98	1.11	0.55	0.60
Congenital Other	0.80	1.31	1.73	1.46	2.89	1.54	1.96	1.96	1.13	1.44
Pneumonia	0.07	0.25	0.00	0.16	0.00	0.00	0.00	0.23	0.07	0.10
Other Acute Infections	0.03	0.00	0.00	0.00	0.00	0.00	0.00	0.04	0.00	0.01
Intestinal, Dysentery	0.00	0.08	0.00	0.08	0.26	0.12	0.00	0.00	0.00	0.03
Atrophy, Sclerema, Starvation	0.33	0.16	2.31	1.86	0.66	0.24	0.98	0.46	0.18	0.61
Prematurity	3.12	3.12	4.20	5.34	3.81	3.09	8.92	4.57	2.32	3.73
Neonatal Infection Pemphigus	0.00	0.16	0.08	0.00	0.13	0.00	0.00	0.00	0.02	0.03
Cot and Sudden death	0.65	0.58	0.74	0.65	0.39	0.36	0.49	0.65	0.25	0.51
All Other	0.62	1.40	0.58	1.05	1.44	0.72	2.20	0.84	0.83	0.93
All Causes	7.81	11.18	13.44	15.94	13.66	9.75	18.45	14.40	8.37	11.32

CONTROL

Causes	A1	A2	B1	B2	C	D1	D2	E1	E2	All
Obstetric Causes	3.80	4.20	3.93	4.01	5.70	4.52	5.33	5.26	3.77	4.37
Congenital Neural	0.74	0.57	1.03	1.57	0.85	0.56	1.26	2.00	0.98	1.09
Congenital Other	1.41	2.10	2.28	1.22	1.42	1.51	2.52	1.79	2.03	1.82
Pneumonia	0.33	0.19	0.21	0.35	0.00	0.00	0.14	0.00	0.28	0.19
Other Acute Infections	0.00	0.00	0.00	0.00	0.28	0.00	0.00	0.21	0.00	0.04
Intestinal, Dysentery	0.00	0.00	0.00	0.00	0.00	0.00	0.00	0.00	0.00	0.00
Atrophy, Sclerema, Starvation	0.25	1.14	1.66	0.52	0.28	0.19	0.84	1.05	0.56	0.68
Prematurity	5.71	5.15	7.04	4.36	3.99	2.64	5.05	5.05	3.63	4.63
Neonatal Infection Pemphigus	0.00	0.00	0.21	0.52	0.00	0.00	0.42	0.10	0.07	0.15
Cot and Sudden Death	0.83	0.76	0.62	0.35	0.85	0.38	0.84	0.84	0.70	0.71
All Other	0.58	1.33	1.03	0.70	0.85	1.32	0.70	0.73	1.26	0.93
All Causes	13.56	15.45	18.01	13.60	12.82	11.12	17.10	17.03	13.28	14.62

B. 7 TO 29 DAYS

FAMINE

Causes	A1	A2	B1	B2	C	D1	D2	E1	E2	All
Obstetric Causes	0.25	0.08	0.74	0.97	0.39	0.12	0.24	0.46	0.27	0.37
Congenital Neural	0.29	0.25	0.82	1.05	0.79	0.36	0.37	0.54	0.32	0.47
Congenital Other	0.05	0.57	0.82	1.46	0.79	0.71	0.73	0.84	0.48	0.69
Pneumonia	0.02	0.57	1.32	1.62	0.26	0.12	1.22	0.46	0.18	0.52
Other Acute Infections	0.04	0.41	0.49	1.46	0.79	0.36	0.48	0.61	0.27	0.51
Intestinal, Dysentery	0.00	0.08	0.08	3.07	0.39	1.07	0.37	0.12	0.07	0.39
Atrophy, Sclerema, Starvation	0.02	0.90	3.71	5.02	2.10	0.95	0.98	0.65	0.27	1.17
Prematurity	0.05	1.07	0.99	2.91	1.31	0.24	0.61	0.69	0.34	0.79
Neonatal Infection Pemphigus	0.03	0.74	0.99	1.05	0.39	0.47	0.48	0.42	0.38	0.51
Cot and Sudden Death	0.02	0.33	0.74	1.05	0.13	0.24	0.12	0.19	0.09	0.28
All Other	0.06	0.74	2.14	2.02	0.79	0.59	0.73	0.42	0.48	0.79
All Causes	0.35	5.76	12.86	21.69	8.15	5.23	6.35	5.41	3.17	6.50

CONTROL

Causes	A1	A2	B1	B2	C	D1	D2	E1	E2	All
Obstetric Causes	0.25	0.19	0.83	0.70	0.57	0.56	0.56	0.63	0.28	0.46
Congenital Neural	0.99	0.38	0.83	0.52	1.14	0.94	0.56	0.63	0.42	0.68
Congenital Other	0.41	0.95	0.83	0.52	0.57	1.51	0.56	0.73	0.28	0.62
Pneumonia	0.50	0.38	1.03	0.87	0.28	0.38	1.54	0.63	0.42	0.65
Other Acute Infections	0.58	0.00	1.66	1.05	1.14	0.19	2.38	0.31	0.14	0.71
Intestinal, Dysentery	0.08	0.57	0.21	0.17	0.57	0.00	0.28	0.21	0.14	0.21
Atrophy, Sclerema, Starvation	0.74	0.95	3.31	2.79	1.14	0.75	1.82	0.63	0.14	1.11
Prematurity	0.91	0.38	1.03	1.39	0.28	0.75	0.28	0.84	0.49	0.71
Neonatal Infection Pemphigus	0.41	0.19	0.62	0.87	0.57	0.00	0.28	0.42	0.49	0.43
Cot and Sudden Death	0.41	0.19	0.41	0.17	0.28	0.00	0.56	0.21	0.07	0.25
All Other	0.08	1.53	1.45	1.22	0.57	1.13	0.56	0.73	0.28	0.68
All Causes	5.37	5.72	12.21	10.28	7.12	6.22	9.39	5.99	3.14	6.50

C. 30 TO 89 DAYS

FAMINE

Causes	A1	A2	B1	B2	C	D1	D2	E1	E2	All
Obstetric Causes	0.11	0.41	1.24	0.57	0.13	0.12	0.61	0.31	0.25	0.35
Congenital Neural	0.14	0.08	0.16	0.24	0.00	0.36	0.85	0.50	0.14	0.25
Congenital Other	0.22	0.66	1.32	0.89	1.05	0.59	0.49	0.34	0.23	0.49
Pneumonia	0.33	0.99	1.90	1.78	1.18	0.95	0.73	0.54	0.48	0.79
Other Acute Infections	0.94	0.57	1.57	1.70	1.58	0.95	1.83	1.08	0.30	0.94
Intestinal, Dysentery	0.14	0.33	1.07	3.32	4.86	0.95	0.37	0.31	0.07	0.77
Atrophy, Sclerema, Starvation	0.40	1.56	7.01	10.36	7.23	2.61	1.22	0.58	0.62	2.36
Prematurity	0.25	0.00	0.33	0.89	0.39	0.24	0.00	0.08	0.23	0.25
Neonatal Infection Pemphigus	0.18	0.33	0.25	1.13	0.66	0.36	0.24	0.04	0.07	0.25
Cot and Sudden Death	0.22	0.49	1.57	1.70	0.66	0.59	0.61	0.27	0.39	0.58
All Other	0.65	0.74	1.98	1.94	0.92	1.18	1.71	0.34	0.87	0.97
All Causes	3.60	6.17	18.39	24.52	18.66	8.91	8.68	4.38	3.66	7.99

CONTROL

Causes	A1	A2	B1	B2	C	D1	D2	E1	E2	All
Obstetric Causes	0.17	0.76	0.83	0.00	0.28	0.00	0.28	0.21	0.35	0.30
Congenital Neural	0.08	0.38	0.21	0.12	0.85	0.11	0.56	0.42	0.21	0.30
Congenital Other	0.58	0.19	0.21	1.22	0.85	0.34	0.84	0.11	0.14	0.46
Pneumonia	0.99	2.48	1.24	1.92	0.57	1.13	1.26	0.74	0.70	1.18
Other Acute Infections	1.24	1.72	0.83	0.52	1.71	0.45	2.38	0.42	0.63	1.05
Intestinal, Dysentery	0.33	0.38	0.00	1.74	1.71	1.82	0.84	0.63	0.28	0.80
Atrophy, Sclerema, Starvation	2.65	3.05	6.21	7.15	5.98	3.52	2.66	0.95	1.47	3.25
Prematurity	0.58	0.95	0.41	0.35	0.28	0.11	0.42	0.00	0.21	0.35
Neonatal Infection Pemphigus	0.25	0.00	0.21	0.87	0.00	0.34	0.14	0.21	0.00	0.22
Cot and Sudden Death	0.50	0.19	1.66	0.87	0.28	0.00	0.98	0.52	0.49	0.59
All Other	0.74	1.14	0.83	1.39	1.42	0.11	0.84	0.63	0.49	0.77
All Causes	8.11	11.26	12.63	16.21	13.96	7.94	11.22	4.84	4.96	9.27

D. 90 TO 364 DAYS

FAMINE

Causes	A1	A2	B1	B2	C	D1	D2	E1	E2	All
Obstetric Causes	0.73	1.48	1.40	0.48	0.92	1.07	0.73	0.54	0.60	0.78
Congenital Neural	0.25	0.25	0.25	0.16	0.52	0.47	0.12	0.27	0.14	0.23
Congenital Other	0.36	1.23	0.41	0.73	1.31	0.47	0.12	0.30	0.60	0.57
Pneumonia	1.71	2.80	1.98	2.43	2.63	2.50	0.61	0.92	1.08	1.60
Other Acute Infections	1.63	2.96	2.47	5.50	4.73	5.11	1.95	1.42	0.87	2.21
Intestinal, Dysentery	0.62	4.03	8.08	7.93	3.55	0.71	0.61	0.27	0.21	2.00
Atrophy, Sclerema, Starvation	1.60	6.25	12.04	7.77	3.81	2.50	0.12	0.54	0.57	2.86
Prematurity	0.00	0.00	0.16	0.08	0.13	0.00	0.00	0.00	0.00	0.03
Neonatal Infection Pemphigus	0.00	0.08	0.16	0.24	0.00	0.00	0.24	0.04	0.00	0.06
Cot and Sudden Death	0.94	2.20	1.73	0.97	1.05	1.19	0.48	0.61	0.41	0.91
All Other	1.71	3.21	2.80	3.88	3.42	4.04	1.47	1.69	1.59	2.23
All Causes	9.56	24.59	31.50	30.19	22.07	18.07	6.48	6.68	6.07	13.48

CONTROL

Causes	A1	A2	B1	B2	C	D1	D2	E1	E2	All
Obstetric Causes	0.83	1.53	0.83	1.57	1.14	0.94	0.14	0.31	0.07	0.67
Congenital Neural	0.41	0.38	0.00	0.35	0.28	0.00	0.00	0.21	0.63	0.31
Congenital Other	0.58	0.19	0.21	0.70	1.99	0.38	0.28	0.52	0.42	0.52
Pneumonia	1.82	4.58	2.90	3.31	3.70	3.80	1.12	2.00	1.47	2.36
Other Acute Infections	2.98	4.58	4.35	5.58	4.84	6.41	2.52	2.00	1.12	3.21
Intestinal, Dysentery	1.07	1.14	5.80	6.45	3.42	1.69	1.40	0.84	0.70	1.97
Atrophy, Sclerema, Starvation	3.97	4.77	8.90	10.63	7.98	4.33	1.82	1.79	0.98	4.02
Prematurity	0.08	0.00	0.21	0.17	0.00	0.00	0.00	0.00	0.14	0.07
Neonatal Infection Pemphigus	0.00	0.19	0.21	0.17	0.00	0.38	0.00	0.00	0.00	0.07
Cot and Sudden Death	1.07	1.33	1.66	0.70	1.42	1.32	0.98	0.73	0.91	1.05
All Other	3.06	3.43	2.28	2.79	2.85	1.69	1.26	2.00	2.24	2.38
All Causes	15.88	22.13	27.33	32.43	27.64	20.92	9.53	10.41	8.66	16.63

Table 13.2. Cause of death at older ages (percentage distribution of deaths from selected causes by cohort in famine and control cities in age group 1 to 18 years)

	FAMINE									
Causes	A1	A2	B1	B2	C	D1	D2	E1	E2	All
Infections	37.2	38.4	33.8	35.6	27.4	28.4	23.6	25.8	20.5	29.6
Neoplasm	10.1	5.4	7.5	13.5	9.4	18.3	13.6	16.0	10.5	11.5
Allergy	0.3	0.0	0.5	0.0	0.9	0.0	1.8	0.0	0.0	0.3
Blood Disease	0.0	0.0	1.0	0.6	0.9	0.0	0.0	2.2	1.0	0.8
Mental Retardation	0.5	3.6	1.5	2.5	0.9	3.7	0.0	1.1	2.1	1.6
Central Nervous System	5.2	5.4	5.5	2.5	8.5	3.7	10.9	6.2	8.2	6.2
Respiratory	6.6	5.4	10.9	12.9	9.4	11.9	6.4	6.5	9.2	8.6
Gastro-intestinal	4.6	5.4	3.5	3.1	2.8	3.7	3.6	5.1	3.6	4.0
Urogenital	1.4	0.9	0.0	0.6	1.9	0.0	1.8	1.8	2.3	1.4
Skin	0.0	0.9	1.0	0.6	1.9	0.0	0.0	0.0	0.0	0.3
Muscle and Joint	0.3	1.8	0.0	0.0	0.0	0.0	0.9	0.4	1.0	0.5
Congenital	4.4	8.9	7.0	4.9	6.6	10.1	0.9	10.5	8.2	7.6
Accidental	25.1	18.8	24.4	20.2	22.6	16.5	20.9	22.5	28.2	23.6
Cardiovascular	1.6	1.8	2.0	1.2	0.9	0.9	2.7	0.4	2.1	1.5
Other	2.7	3.6	1.5	1.8	5.7	2.8	2.7	1.5	3.1	2.7
Total Number (100%)	366	112	201	163	106	109	110	275	390	1832
Total Death Rate per 1000 Born	13.37	9.21	16.57	13.19	13.93	13.07	13.44	10.52	8.97	11.60

	CONTROL									
Causes	A1	A2	B1	B2	C	D1	D2	E1	E2	All
Infections	31.3	25.7	35.6	28.3	33.9	23.3	19.2	16.1	19.5	24.8
Neoplasm	11.0	5.7	8.9	17.4	6.8	10.5	9.6	11.2	14.1	11.2
Allergy	0.6	0.0	0.0	0.0	1.7	0.0	1.0	1.4	0.5	0.6
Blood Disease	0.6	0.0	1.1	1.1	0.0	0.0	0.0	1.4	1.1	0.7
Mental Retardation	1.2	2.9	2.2	0.0	1.7	2.3	1.9	1.4	1.1	1.5
Central Nervous System	4.9	12.9	5.6	4.3	5.1	5.8	5.8	9.8	5.9	6.6
Respiratory	3.1	8.6	6.7	6.5	6.8	7.0	6.7	6.3	5.4	5.9
Gastro-intestinal	3.7	8.6	5.6	6.5	0.0	5.8	4.8	4.9	8.6	5.6
Urogenital	4.9	2.9	1.1	2.2	5.1	1.2	5.8	1.4	1.1	2.7
Skin	0.0	0.0	0.0	1.1	0.0	0.0	0.0	1.4	0.5	0.4
Muscle and Joint	1.2	0.0	1.1	1.1	0.0	2.3	1.9	0.7	1.6	1.2
Congenital	4.9	2.9	0.0	2.2	3.4	11.6	3.8	4.9	6.5	4.7
Accidental	24.5	27.1	24.4	19.6	30.5	24.4	34.6	31.5	26.5	27.0
Cardiovascular	4.3	1.4	4.4	5.4	1.7	2.3	2.9	3.5	4.3	3.6
Other	3.7	1.4	3.3	4.3	3.4	3.5	1.9	4.2	3.2	3.3
Total Number (100%)	163	70	90	92	59	86	104	143	185	992
Total Death Rate per 1000 Born	13.56	13.55	18.63	16.04	16.81	16.21	14.72	14.82	12.86	14.66

DEATH RATES REFINED AND SPECIFIED

Table 13.3 Mortality by social class (percentage of fathers in manual and non-manual occupations compared among those dying in the first year of life, those dying at 1 to 18 years, and surviving men at induction. [The category "other" includes farm occupations, unknown occupations, and no legal father])

FAMINE

Birth Cohort	Infant Deaths (row %)			Deaths 1 to 18 years (row %)			19 year olds, at induction (row %)		
	Manual	Non-manual	Other	Manual	Non-manual	Other	Manual	Non-manual	Other
A1	50.0	30.6	19.4	55.3	28.9	15.8	46.4	44.4	9.2
A2	68.4	22.8	8.8	56.8	29.7	13.5	46.8	44.9	8.3
B1	56.0	22.0	22.0	61.0	26.0	13.0	48.1	43.8	8.0
B2	55.1	34.6	10.3	51.9	32.7	15.5	44.6	47.4	8.0
C	55.9	14.7	29.4	56.2	32.4	11.5	46.6	45.7	7.6
D1	70.8	16.7	12.5	57.3	27.3	15.4	44.9	46.5	8.5
D2	52.4	28.6	19.1	39.1	48.2	12.7	39.3	52.5	8.3
E1	39.6	35.4	25.0	62.4	29.6	8.0	46.0	47.3	6.7
E2	63.0	23.9	13.0	56.9	29.0	14.1	44.6	48.4	7.0

CONTROL

Birth Cohort	Infant Deaths (row %)			Deaths 1 to 18 years (row %)			19 year olds, at induction (row %)		
	Manual	Non-manual	Other	Manual	Non-manual	Other	Manual	Non-manual	Other
A1	72.9	20.8	6.3	49.7	33.1	17.2	52.5	37.6	9.9
A2	79.3	17.2	3.4	56.3	29.6	14.0	51.2	40.0	8.8
B1	55.3	33.0	11.8	54.4	34.4	11.1	54.6	37.1	8.3
B2	61.3	22.6	16.2	54.3	28.3	17.4	50.3	39.4	10.3
C	50.0	18.8	31.3	54.2	22.0	23.8	48.0	41.6	10.4
D1	58.1	16.1	25.8	50.0	30.2	19.7	52.7	38.2	9.1
D2	41.4	31.0	27.6	58.1	22.9	19.0	50.3	38.8	10.9
E1	59.5	27.0	13.5	55.3	29.1	15.6	47.9	42.0	10.0
E2	66.7	21.4	11.9	49.5	27.2	23.4	47.8	41.0	11.2

RATIO OF PERCENTAGE NON-MANUAL
(a) infant deaths to adult survivors, (b) deaths 1-18 to adult survivors, in famine and control areas

Birth Cohort	Infant Deaths to Adult Survivors		Deaths 1-18 to Adult Survivors	
	Famine	Control	Famine	Control
A1	0.69	0.55	0.65	0.88
A2	0.51	0.43	0.66	0.74
B1	0.50	0.89	0.59	0.93
B2	0.73	0.57	0.69	0.72
C	0.32	0.45	0.71	0.53
D1	0.36	0.42	0.59	0.79
D2	0.54	0.80	0.92	0.59
E1	0.75	0.64	0.63	0.69
E2	0.49	0.52	0.60	0.66

IV Outcome in Young Adults

14 Mental Performance After Prenatal Exposure to Famine

The effect of prenatal nutritional deprivation on subsequent development is the central concern with which this study began. The review of the present state of knowledge in the introductory chapters of the book, therefore, will serve to place the substance of this chapter in context. We can turn at once to matters of method and results.

The techniques of statistical analysis used here are in all essentials the same as those used in earlier chapters. As before, we begin with graphs based on contingency table analysis. Detection of effect in these results depends on the relative risk of a particular outcome in exposed and non-exposed groups defined by time and place of birth, and to make our judgments we rely in the first instance on inspection of the graphs. To assign quantitative values to any associations that may exist in the data, we turn to correlations of the outcome variable under study with the average level of food rations available at each trimester of gestation. These correlations are made with individuals and not groups as the unit of analysis, and they are studied under famine and non-famine conditions.

The results are examined for possibilities of confounding and interaction. Social class has a known and strong association with both nutrition and mental performance. Moreover, in the chapter on fertility we found that the social class composition of birth cohorts had been altered by the famine. In all analyses likely to be affected, we deemed it wise to specify social class by occupation of the father at the outset. At later stages of the analysis, we also took into account the smaller effects of religion, family size, and birth order. The last and one of the most important analyses aims to discover what effect selective mortality in early life might have had on the configuration of results among adults. This analysis is treated in a separate coda at the end of the chapter.

The main data source for these analyses is the record of medical and psychological examinations made at the military induction of all males at 19 years of age. The population under study at induction comprised over 100,000 males born in the selected famine and control cities in the three-year period January 1, 1944, to December 31, 1946. Some severely handicapped men (0.6%) were excused from attending the induction examination in person, but they were entered on the induction records. In such cases, an assessment of their condition was made from the clinical record forwarded to the induction center by a medical practitioner.

Measures of Mental Performance

Mental capacities are reflected with more or less accuracy in several types of indices that can be used for epidemiological analysis. School progress affords educational indices; intelligence tests afford psychometric indices; diagnoses of mental retardation afford clinical indices. We give here a brief outline of our rationale for their use, for the distinctions we make between them, and for the assumptions we perceive as built into them.

Educational indices are in some respects crude measures of mental capacities. The indices may be derived from direct evaluation by teachers, from examinations, or from specially constructed achievement tests of special abilities, such as reading and reckoning. In our discussion of results, we shall treat achievement tests as psychometric indices. Duration of schooling and educational level reached provided one educational index for our purposes.

We examined assignments to schools for the backward and found that virtually all those so assigned were classed as retarded by psychometric and clinical indices, but not all the retarded attended schools for the backward. Hence, this measure added no new information to that obtained from other measures, and the data are not presented.

Psychometric indices have attracted passionate and persisting controversy over the last half-century. Some are controversies of taxonomy and inference between protagonists of conflicting theories about the nature and types of mental abilities. A particular taxonomic controversy is whether one or more innate cognitive abilities underlie the array of measurable abilities. Controversy over taxonomy leads on to controversy over inferences about the degree to which social experience overwhelms the expression of innate abilities. Other controversies are ethical and political. Contenders interpret variations in performance on psychometric tests observed among individuals and more particularly among groups as the consequence primarily of genetic superiority, or primarily of social and cultural advantage.

These controversies continually renew questions of the validity of psychometric tests as measures of differences in "intelligence." Tests of mental ability are more precise and objective than other educational indices, yet they engender more hostility. Simplistic genetic and racial interpretations have made them a sensitive political issue.

In the midst of this scientific and political turbulence, a necessary preface to our results is a discussion of our conception and use of these indices. In any society intelligence tests inevitably are vehicles for the concepts, the modes of thought and expression, and the values of the dominant social classes and ethnic groups. The tests relate to a limited and sketchy range of mental capacities. They are saturated with verbal, numerical, and logical elements. These are the building blocks of the scholastic abilities cultivated by the culture of the dominant social groups; in one sense, they are the instruments of that culture. They transmit the dominant culture to all social groups, including those who are dominated and whose position and attendant culture places them in objective contradiction to the values of the dominant culture. By a cumulative social process, the dominant culture and its educational instruments create in many of these dominated groups a trained incapacity for scholastic performance. Moreover, despite standard testing methods, intelligence tests are not free of those influences of motivation and the subjective perceptions of subjects and observers that contaminate educational indices.

The tests have other problems. For instance, their results are often reduced to a single global score such as the Intelligence Quotient. Many workers hold that the tests do not measure any single attribute that represents "intelligence" but a number of disparate abilities, or at the least two distinctive types that do not always go together (Spearman, 1927; Thurstone, 1935; Vernon, 1968; Cattell, 1963; Guilford, 1959; Jensen, 1969). By the nature of mental development, successive age groups are subjected to tests, such as the Wechsler series, which have been standardized for age, and that must be different in content at each age since they must be made progressively more difficult. That they measure the growth of the same abilities from one age to the next, therefore, can be only a plausible assumption.

All these limitations make the misuse of intelligence tests common, and attacks on such misuse deserved, and even necessary. Attacks on intelligence tests per se are not. Intelligence tests are standardized and reliable compared with many measures used by epidemiologists to describe the state of health of populations. As long as the limitations of IQ tests are borne in mind, they provide a relatively objective and available measure of an important attribute.

In this study, we place reliance on psychometric indices as the dependent variables most likely to detect a famine effect. We do so because of the objectivity of the tests, which were administered under standardized testing conditions with scores for each member of the population, and because they facilitate statistical manipulation. The psychometric index of greatest sensitivity and most importance in this study is the Raven Progressive Matrices. Although no psychometric test can be culture free, the Raven is a non-verbal test which depends less than most others on verbal and numerical learning. Scores were recorded for 95% of the population examined at induction. The data we used were scores grouped in six levels. Across the country the average percentages in each group, from highest to lowest scores, were 1, 17.7%; 2, 28.4%; 3, 20.2%; 4, 13.6%; 5, 9.9%; 6, 4.8%; and not known, 5.3%.

Other psychometric indices were available to us. The analyses of these indices are not presented in the text because in testing our hypotheses they add nothing to the results of the Raven Progressive Matrices. One score (Global Psychometric Score) that combines the results of five psychometric and educational tests is given in the Appendix. This score includes the Raven Progressive Matrices, the Bennett Mechanical Comprehension, Clerical Aptitude, Language Comprehension, and Arithmetic scores.

Clinical indices of mental performance likewise have limitations. By the nature of their origin and uses, they are designed to describe only the part of the distribution of states of health that encompasses disorder and abnormality, and they are insensitive to degrees of healthy functioning. Even with regard to malfunction, many clinical decisions are unavoidably subjective and unreliable. The diagnostic process is a pattern-seeking procedure. While these procedures include laboratory, psychometric, and sociological data that are relatively objective, they also include subtle clues that are not measurable. Disparate decisions among physicians flow from disparate training applied to subjective and unstandardized criteria.

A special problem in the epidemiology of mental retardation* is the definition of the case. Cases, to be counted, must be distinguished from non-cases, but the lines of demarcation are blurred by confused definition. Recognized mental retardation is a social attribute. Recognition is a consequence of failures to perform the social roles demanded of individuals at each stage of life. The order of society determines how taxing these roles shall be. What is expected in particular social roles, therefore, varies with time and among societies, and among the classes of a single society.

The manifestation of mental retardation as a social attribute contains at least three components: organic, functional, and social (Stein and Susser, 1971). A primary *organic* component refers to a structural or physiological disorder; this we shall term "impairment." A psychological or *functional* component, which

---

*Mental retardation is used here as in the classification of the American Association for Mental Deficiency. A number of terminologies are available and in use in different classifications. The term "retardation," not entirely satisfactory, was introduced to avoid the stigma that had been acquired by the terms mental deficiency and mental subnormality (the latter introduced, for the same reason, in the British legislation of 1959). Unlike these terms, retardation does not necessarily imply a permanent state of dysfunction. It describes better the particular syndromes of mild mental retardation from which recovery can occur, rather than all the conditions it has been made to designate. We have not been able to sustain this stance against the current, and we yield to common usage.

we shall term "disability," arises from the limitation imposed on an individual's function by organic impairment, as well as from the individual's psychological reactions to his impairment and his environment. In mental retardation, functional disability is expressed in intellectual deficit. The *social* component of mental retardation, defined by the special social roles assigned to the retarded individual, we shall term mental "handicap." Handicap describes the manner and degree in which primary impairment and functional disability limit the social roles an individual is expected or allowed to perform.

These organic, psychological, and social criteria yield different frequencies of mental retardation and make quite different contributions to our understanding of the condition. The components of mental retardation measured by each criterion do not have a one-to-one relationship with each other and are made apparent by different circumstances. Impairments that can be recognized at birth and for which a one-to-one relationship with functional disability and mental handicap can be predicted, as in Down's syndrome, are not common. Cerebral palsy is an impairment recognized by the signs of brain damage. Only about one-third of all cases of cerebral palsy suffer the functional disability of intellectual deficit, or are assigned the special social role of the handicapped person (Rutter, Graham, and Yule, 1970).

Conversely, recognized functional disability cannot always be related to definitive organic lesions. In a large proportion of cases of mental retardation, even with severe intellectual deficits, a specific clinical diagnosis cannot be made. In these cases of severe mental retardation, indeed, the presence of organic impairment is often merely assumed.* Severe mental retardation of unspecified diagnosis thus describes a residual class of mental handicap, cases that are heterogeneous in terms of the origins and types of organic impairment from which they suffer. Yet it is a homogeneous class in that all members share a similar and extreme degree of functional disability and social handicap. In cohort studies, this form of handicap presents difficulties because it is of low frequency, and numbers must be very large to provide enough statistical power to detect differences between cohorts in the frequency of the condition.

Mild mental retardation is far more frequent (up to ten times) than severe mental retardation and does not present the analytic difficulties of a condition of low frequency. The condition does present other difficulties of inference. Unlike severe mental retardation and like educational and IQ scores, the distribution of mild mental retardation is strongly related to social class and confounding is always possible. Social class biases can affect any level of organization, but it affects especially the levels of psychological function and social role performance.

In mild mental retardation, by contrast with severe retardation, the intellectual deficit and functional disability of the cultural-familial syndrome is pre-

---

*Brain lesions have been found in about 90% or more at autopsy (Crome, 1972).

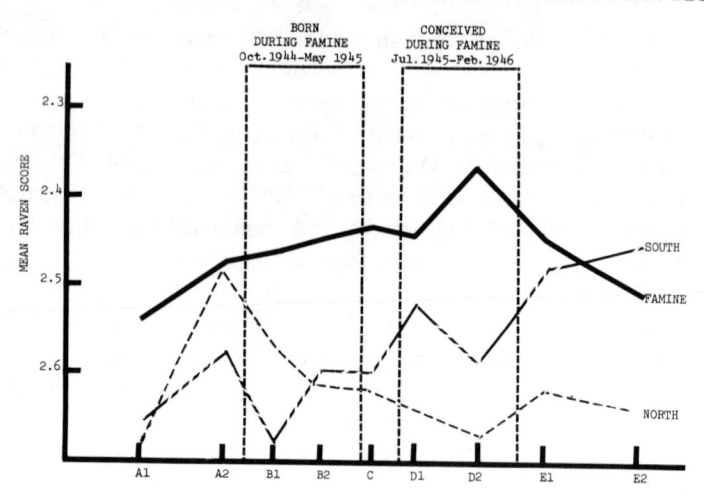

Figure 14.1. Raven scores by area (mean Raven scores by cohort in famine, Northern control, and Southern control areas)

ceded by no detectable organic impairment and is not always accompanied by the social role of mental handicap. If it is accompanied by handicap, the handicapped role may often be temporary, between the phases of pubescence and young adulthood. On the other hand, the social role of mental handicap is occasionally assigned to individuals who have neither impairment of the brain nor intellectual disability. Their social roles are inadvertently acquired by their admission to "treatment" because of a combination of behavior disorders and lack of social support. Thus a proportion of the inmates of many institutions for mental retardation have neither detectable clinical lesions nor IQs below the normal range (O'Connor and Tizard, 1956). In several countries during the past decade this proportion has been much reduced as a matter of policy.

With these clarifications in mind, we need not be dissuaded from the use of diagnoses of mild and severe mental retardation as clinical indices of mental performance, and we shall proceed to analyze them for what they can yield. Our analysis of mental retardation is based on prevalence among survivors at the military induction examination. Rejection for military service on account of any condition, including mental retardation, was the responsibility of the medical officer in charge of the induction center. He reviewed every record, and where necessary he obtained the previous clinical records of handicapped persons from the institutions and other places in which they resided.

The clinical levels of severe and mild retardation in the data of the military induction examination are consistent with usual standards—that is, a division around IQ 50 separates the two levels of severity.* The two conditions were

---

*The classification of the American Association of Mental Deficiency (Grossman, 1973) has three grades of retardation—moderate, severe, and profound—for those with IQ under

MENTAL PERFORMANCE AFTER PRENATAL EXPOSURE TO FAMINE

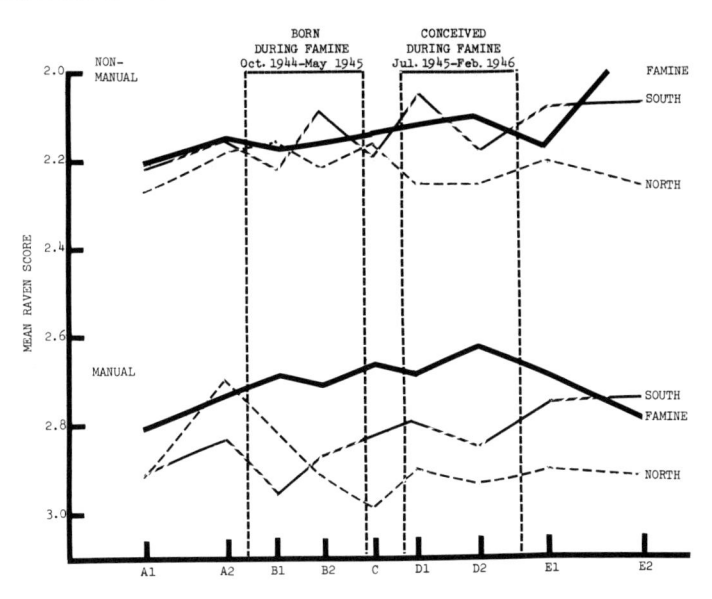

Figure 14.2. Raven scores by area and class (mean Raven scores by cohort in famine, Northern control, and Southern control areas, comparing manual and non-manual occupational classes)

defined in terms of the clinical diagnosis assigned at the induction examination. Diagnoses used were coded for the record according to the International Classification of Diseases (ICD) of the World Health Organization (1948). Severe mental retardation includes the codes for idiocy (3250), imbecility (3251), mongolism (3254), and all others (3255); mild mental retardation covers the codes moron (3252) and borderline intelligence (3253).** All those allocated these codes were included in the analysis, whether the diagnoses were given as a primary or as a secondary cause of rejection for military service.

Raven Progressive Matrices

A. Raven Scores Among Cohorts by Time and Place (Figures 14.1 and 14.2 and Appendix)

A numerically higher Raven score signifies a poorer performance. No variation in Raven scores in association with prenatal exposure to famine, either early or late in gestation, is detectable in Figure 14.1. The D2 cohort, conceived at the height

---

50. We consider that these grades are covered by the ICD codes 3250, 3251, 3254, and 3255.
 **The AAMD grade of mild mental retardation probably has a lower IQ ceiling than the ICD grades 3252 and 3253.

of the famine, actually bettered the performance of other cohorts on the Raven test (that is, the D2 numerical score was lower). This was a consequence of the effect of famine, not on mental performance, but on fertility.

By far the most striking variation is between the mean scores of the non-manual and manual classes (Figure 14.2). The influence of the social class variable is underlined by the sensitivity of Raven scores to differential fertility among the social classes. The D2 cohort owed its improved mean score to the altered proportions of the social classes in that cohort; in Chapter 9 we showed that in this cohort the fertility of the manual classes had fallen more than that of the non-manual social classes. The slight advantage maintained by the D2 cohort in each of the two classes analyzed in Figure 14.2 disappeared in an analysis of nine occupational classes.

B. Multiple Regression Analysis of Food Rations and Raven Scores

The quantitative relations of food rations in each trimester and Raven scores confirm the negative result of the graphic analysis. We have chosen for practical reasons to present only one form of analysis, that for individual scores. The scoring of the Raven in the military data is such that if food deprivation had depressed mental performance, the effect would be expressed in a negative correlation between caloric rations and test scores. As expected from the graphs, all correlations of Raven scores with caloric rations in any trimester are trivial and all but one were positive.*

A number of supporting analyses were made to detect confounding in the effects of food rations on mental performance. The correlations of social class, family size, and birth order with Raven scores were consistent across the famine area, the North and the South. (Table 14.1 shows the matrix for the three areas combined. The correlation with social class was strongest, r = .24.) Religion, social class, family size, and birth order were differently distributed across the three areas, but with the possible exception of family size their distributions were not related to those of food rations. Their bivariate correlations with food rations were small. Hence, although they are potential confounding variables, in that they could conceal an existing association through distortion if any should be related by opposite signs to caloric rations and mental performance, it is unlikely that they do so. The small size of the bivariate correlations with caloric rations made unnecessary futher exploration by partial correlations. The possible distorting effects of early mortality are dealt with later in this chapter. Meanwhile, we can be assured that the array of variables so far analyzed gives no hint that prenatal famine exposure influenced Raven Progressive Matrices scores.

Other Standardized Tests of Mental Performance

All the five tests given at induction were highly correlated with each other. The four tests besides the Raven were Language Comprehension, Arithmetic, Clerical

*The correlation in the South of C_3 with Raven scores was r = −.05.

Aptitude, and the Bennett Test of Mechanical Comprehension. The Test of Mechanical Comprehension had a lower range of intercorrelations with other tests, between .47 and .54, whereas the range of intercorrelations among other tests lay between .63 and .76 (Table 14.1).

Most of the additional tests had stronger associations than the Raven Progressive Matrices with such variables as social class, family size, and birth order (Marolla, 1973). In their relations with prenatal exposure to famine, however, there were no essential differences from the Raven. The same conclusions apply to the Global Psychometric Score, the combined score of all the tests together. To discuss these analyses further would be to impose redundancy on our readers. The analyses were extensive but merely replicated the negative findings of the Raven test.

Mild Mental Retardation

A. Mild Mental Retardation Among Cohorts by Time and Place

There is a huge disparity among social classes in the frequency of mild mental retardation. In Figure 14.3, therefore, we show prevalence among classes divided from the outset by manual and non-manual occupations. As expected, sons of fathers in manual work had far higher rates of mild mental retardation than sons of fathers in non-manual work. The over-all rates among social classes (shown in the Appendix) were much more dissimilar than those among areas.

Variation in the prevalence of mild mental retardation was related neither to conception nor to birth during the famine. In comparisons by place, prevalence in famine and control cities was similar among both social classes. In comparisons by time also, there is no consistent relation of prevalence of mild mental retardation with prenatal exposure to famine. Among the manual working class in the famine area, the rise in prevalence in the B2 cohort, born at the height of the famine, is matched in the North and exceeded by the rise in the E2 cohort conceived and born after the famine. The decline in the D2 cohort, conceived at the height of the famine, is analogous with that of the Raven Progressive Matrices in the same cohort and can be accounted for by the pattern of differential fertility among the social classes during the famine.

B. Multiple Regression Analysis of Food Rations and Mild Mental Retardation

The correlations of food rations in any trimester with the prevalence of mild mental retardation in the famine area are negligible. In the absence of meaningful relationships there was no need to pursue the analysis further.

Severe Mental Retardation

A. Severe Mental Retardation Among Cohorts by Time and Place

The frequency of severe mental retardation among survivors of the birth cohorts is related neither to conception nor to birth during the famine (Figure 14.4 and

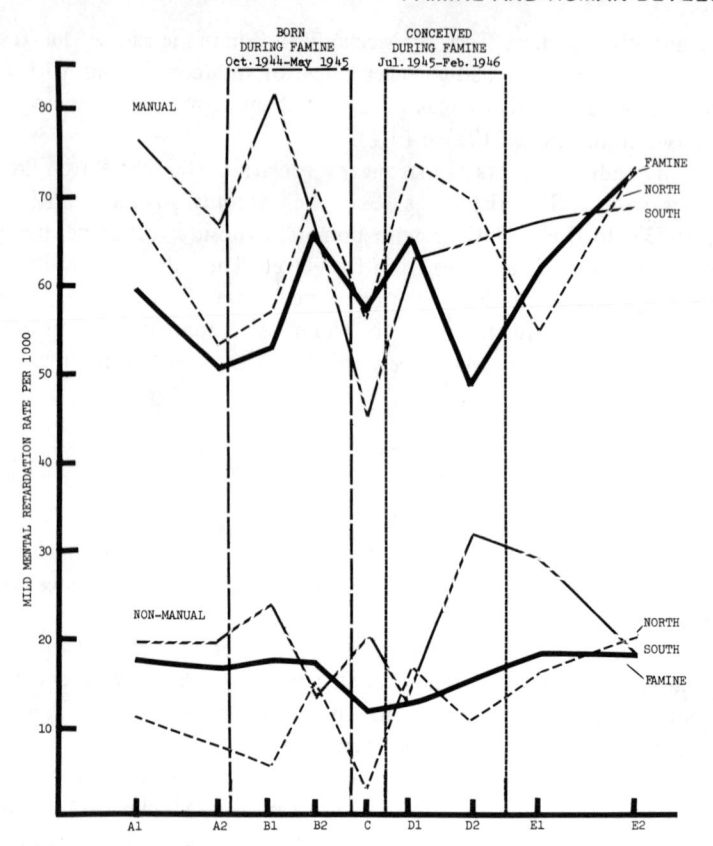

Figure 14.3. Mild mental retardation by area and social class (rates of mild mental retardation, per 1000 total births by cohort in famine, Northern control and Southern control areas, comparing manual and non-manual occupational classes)

Appendix). A slight rise in frequency in the famine cities is concurrent with the decline in birthweight in the most affected cohorts (B2), although the frequency rises further in the C cohort among whom birthweight had begun to recover. In any event, this rise among cohorts born during the famine must be discounted as an effect of famine because of a concurrent rise in the frequency of severe mental retardation in the control cities. The rise in the D1 cohort conceived during the famine is larger than among cohorts born during the famine. At the time of the D1 cohort conceptions, however, the famine was milder than at the time of the D2 cohort conceptions, and there was no real rise in the frequency of severe mental retardation in the D2 cohort. The numbers involved in the rise in the D1 cohort are small: 13 cases were expected and 18 observed. We conclude that the data on severe mental retardation may indicate a rising trend with time, but not a relation with prenatal exposure to famine.

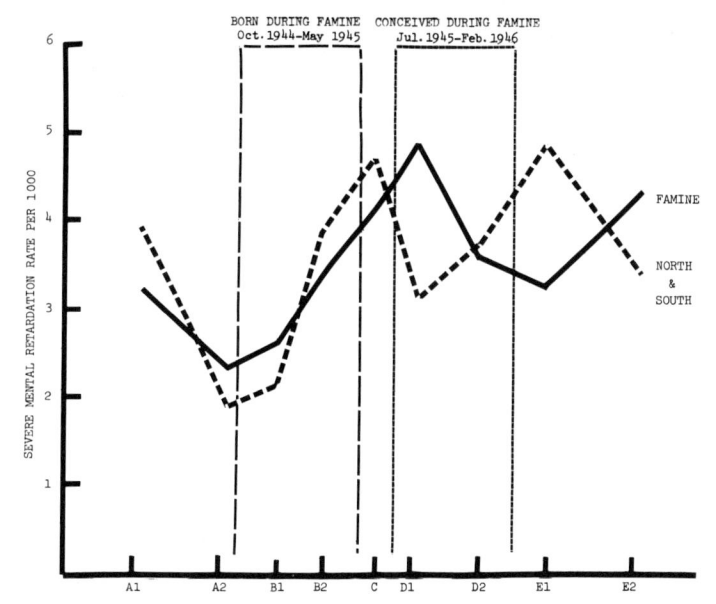

Figure 14.4. Severe mental retardation by area (rates of severe mental retardation per 1000 total births by cohort: famine area and combined Northern and Southern control areas)

Selective Survival and Mortality

The distribution of mental performance has given no indication of an effect of prenatal famine exposure. This negative result rests on intensive analysis of several measures of mental competence and refutes persuasive hypotheses that are strongly held by many scientists. The biological significance of the result is too great to leave the matter there. To contradict existing hypotheses is also to accept a mandate to explore contrary explanations. We are therefore obliged to examine such alternative explanations of our negative finding as our data will permit us to test. In this section we outline our efforts to make such tests.

The negative result rules out only one of several hypotheses broadly stated in the opening chapters—that the type and degree of impairment inflicted on the gestating individual varies in a continuum according to the severity of the prenatal insult. This hypothesis is tenable in relation to slowed fetal growth and early death. The hypothesis fails when mental competence is added as another among the hierarchy of effects. The logic of the hypothesis requires that an increase in mental impairment, a lesser effect, must accompany an increase in mortality, the maximum effect. The results cannot be made to conform with this model.

An alternative hypothesis is that those with potential mental impairment because of prenatal famine exposure were carried off by the concurrent excess mortality. In consequence the frequency of mental impairment among the survivors might have been left unchanged. The same hypothesis can be applied equally to other impairments of health. An hypothesis of this type would seem to require the operation of an all-or-none rule in which death was the consequence of any famine-induced impairment that could affect mental performance. This hypothesis is of limited interest to the study of mental competence in survivors; it is another way of stating that the pathogenesis of deaths induced by prenatal exposure to famine is through impairment of the brain.

The hypothesis takes on greater interest if it is construed as one extreme form, famine-induced, of a general process. In the general process nutritional impairment of the fetal brain would act, along with other factors, to lower resistance to the forces of mortality. The lowered resistance would be most evident where the forces of mortality were greatest. This process implies the selective survival of individuals whose brains have not been nutritionally impaired, and in consequence a relative reduction in the frequency of mental competence under harsh environmental conditions. In relation to the frequency of severe mental retardation in Europe that has prevailed since World War II, a corollary of a hypothesis of this kind could be sustained. Thus during this period of improving nutrition and social conditions, declining infant mortality with increased survival has been associated with a rising prevalence of severe mental retardation. At the same time there has been, in all probability, a declining incidence of brain impairment. The increase in prevalence of severe mental retardation can be attributed to the increase in the number of survivors among impaired individuals (Stein and Susser, 1971). In contrast the trend of mild mental retardation does not sustain such a hypothesis; the best estimates suggest that prevalence as well as incidence have been declining. The divergent trends of severe and mild mental retardation put us on notice to regard the distinctions between the two syndromes, particularly in terms of their relations with brain damage and social class (see Chapter 2). They also indicate that the trends to be predicted on a hypothesis of selective survival are not self-evident.

Whether the prevalence of subsequent mental impairment were to be raised or lowered by selective survival would depend on at least two unknown factors. One factor is the balance between the incidence of fetal brain impairment sufficient to cause mental retardation and the probable duration of subsequent survival among the impaired. Another factor is the degree to which the prenatal insult lowered resistance to mortality among those whose brains were impaired by other causes than nutritional deprivation. Severe mental retardation and congenital anomalies in themselves carry a heightened susceptibility to early death. If the famine exaggerated this susceptibility, then individuals with these conditions might have died instead of having contributed to the number among survivors of the famine.

Fortunately, in trying to explain our failure to find an association between famine exposure and mental competence by selective survival, we can place limits on the direction of the postulated effect on the prevalence of mental impairment. The limit follows from our results so far. If selective survival had masked a famine effect on mental competence and thereby led us to a falsely negative conclusion, we can infer that the effect must have been to reduce the prevalence of mental impairment or at the least to leave it unchanged. Given the absence of a detectable association between prenatal famine exposure and mental impairment and assuming that selective survival had obliterated or distorted an initially existing causal association between prenatal famine exposure and mental impairment, we must postulate a negative correlation between related mortality and mental impairment (Susser, 1973). These relationships are represented below.

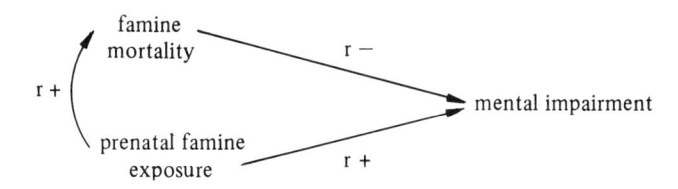

```
              famine
              mortality              r —
    r +                                    → mental impairment
              prenatal famine
              exposure               r +
```

The positive correlation of prenatal famine exposure with mortality has been established in Chapters 12 and 13. In order to detect any possible distortion of the postulated positive correlation of prenatal famine exposure with mental impairment, therefore, our first step will be to search for negative correlations between famine-related mortality and mental impairment. We shall consider in turn mean Raven scores, rates of mild mental retardation, and rates of severe mental retardation. The appropriate age-specific death rates are those for the first three months of life. Only among these deaths in the first three months was there a demonstrable effect of prenatal famine exposure; consequently, only they could have masked the differences in mental performance we sought and failed to find between famine-exposed and control cohorts. For each measure of mental performance, graphs are shown in relation to the mortality curves for the first three months of life. In addition, correlations have been made where relevant.

Figure 14.5 shows *mean Raven scores* for the famine and the two control areas. Analysis by social class is omitted, since the results do not alter. For both famine and control areas, the fluctuation in the mortality rates are sharper than in the mean test scores; the pairs of curves for mortality and Raven score have no evident relation to each other, and certainly no negative relation that is unique to famine exposure. Similar relations obtain in both famine and control areas. Correlations bear out this inspection; the coefficient in the famine area is only $r = -.05$. In the instance of Raven scores, then, we may dismiss the hypothesis of selective survival because the prerequisite correlation with famine mortality is absent.

In the instance of *mild mental retardation* the analysis is less definitive, partly because the rates are less stable than the mean Raven scores. Figure 14.6 shows

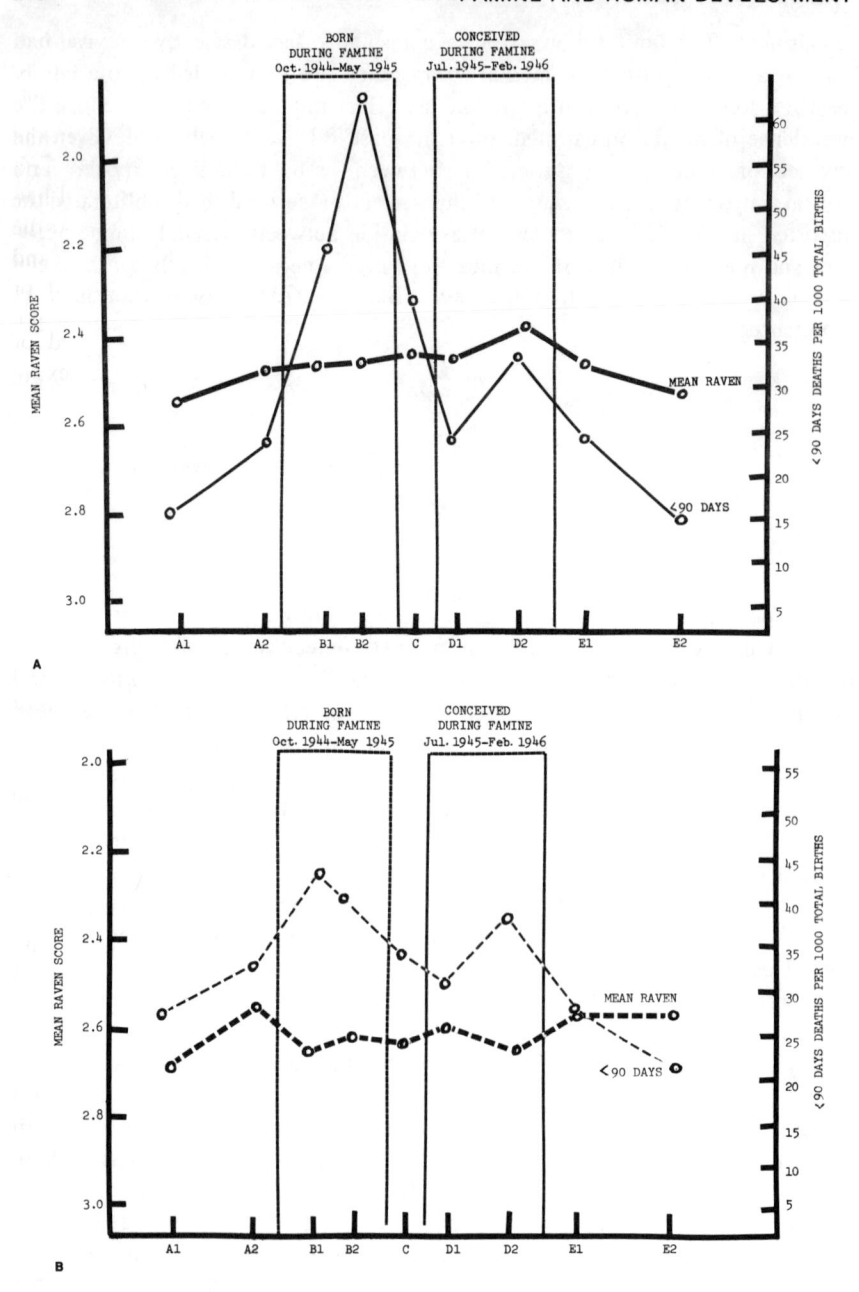

Figure 14.5. Raven scores and mortality by area (mean Raven scores and deaths occurring at ages less than 90 days, per 1000 total births by monthly cohort: **A.** famine cities and **B.** control cities)

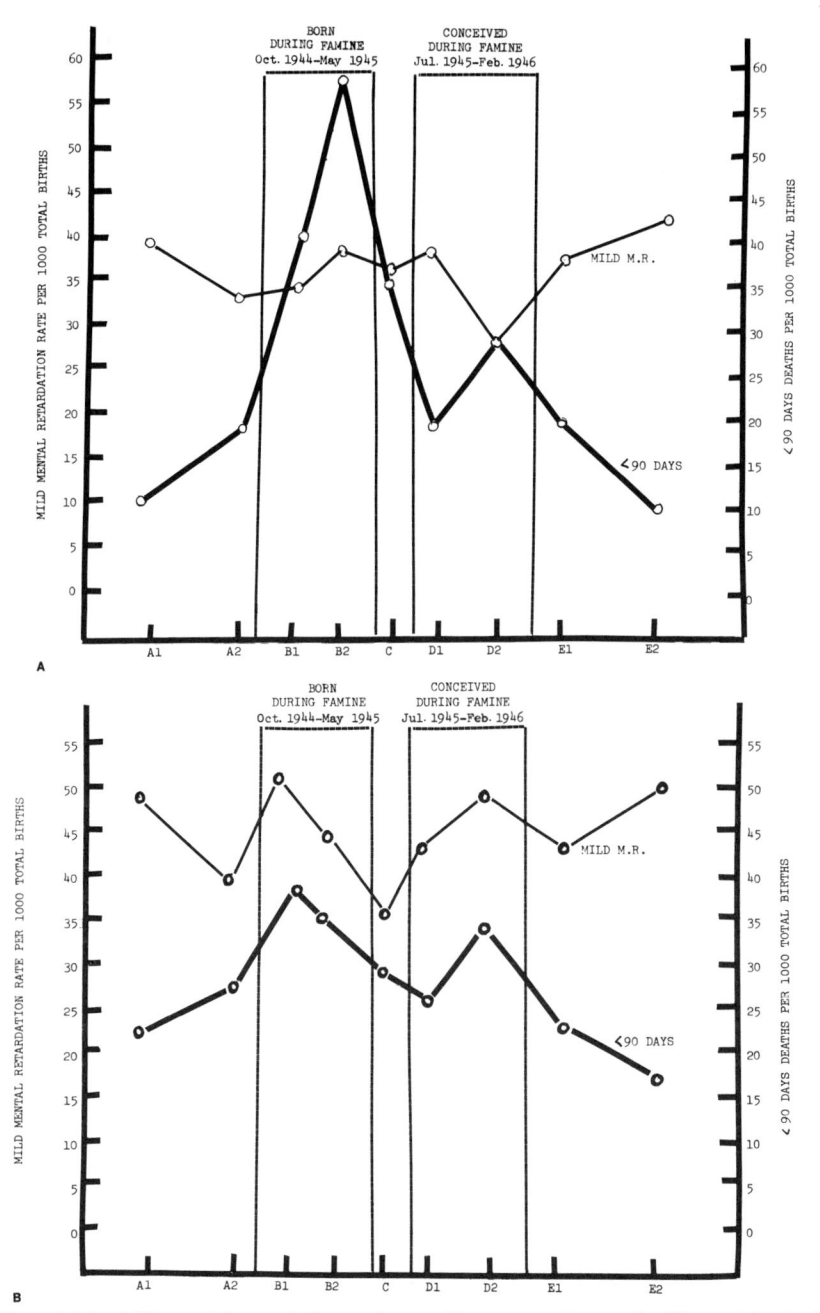

Figure 14.6. Mild mental retardation and mortality by area (rates of mild mental retardation and deaths occurring at ages less than 90 days by nine birth cohorts: **A.** famine cities and **B.** control cities)

rates for mild mental retardation and early mortality. The two control areas are combined in order to enhance numbers and the stability of rates in each cohort.

The graphs give no consistent support for the notion that selective survival during the famine produced our negative finding. It is true that in both famine and control areas, prevalence and mortality rates of cohorts born outside the famine period move in opposite directions. During the famine, which is the period of prime concern, the pattern among cohorts B1, B2, and C is for the prevalence and mortality rates to move in the same direction. This effect, if significant, was not caused by the famine; it appears more marked in control than in famine cohorts. Correlations of mortality in the first 3 months of life with the prevalence of mild mental retardation for 36 monthly birth cohorts in both the famine and control areas likewise provide no support; the coefficients are small and positive.

Birth cohort graphs for *severe mental retardation* and early mortality for famine and control areas are shown in Figure 14.7. The two curves for each area again bear no evident relation to each other, nor any negative relation unique to the famine. The sharp increase in mortality in the famine-born cohorts (B1, B2, C) is not matched by noticeable change in the prevalence curve for severe mental retardation. Correlations were calculated for grouped cohorts and not for monthly cohorts because of small numbers of cases. Among the nine cohorts, correlations were $r = .17$ in the famine area and $-.26$ in the control area; they do not approach statistical significance.

On the basis of these analyses, we dismiss selective mortality as an explanation for the failure of our analysis to detect an effect of prenatal famine exposure on mental competence.

Summary

Several measures of mental performance in a national population of young men at military induction show no effect of prenatal exposure to famine. The measures of mental performance analyzed include five tests (Raven Progressive Matrices; Language Comprehension; Arithmetic; Clerical Aptitude; Bennett Test of Mechanical Comprehension) and a score combining the results of all these tests. Only one test, the Raven Progressive Matrices, is presented and discussed in detail, but all tests are in agreement with regard to the absence of a famine effect. In addition, the prevalence of mild and of severe mental retardation was analyzed and similarly showed no famine effect. We also sought evidence of interaction of prenatal famine exposure with indices of social environment that might have influenced compensatory learning opportunities and subsequent mental performance. No such evidence was found in analyses of social class, religious affiliation, family size, and birth order. We explored the relation of measures of mental performance to famine-induced mortality in order to test the explanation that selective survival might have masked or distorted an association of prenatal famine exposure with mental competence. No distortion was apparent, and this alternative hypothesis can be dismissed.

MENTAL PERFORMANCE AFTER PRENATAL EXPOSURE TO FAMINE

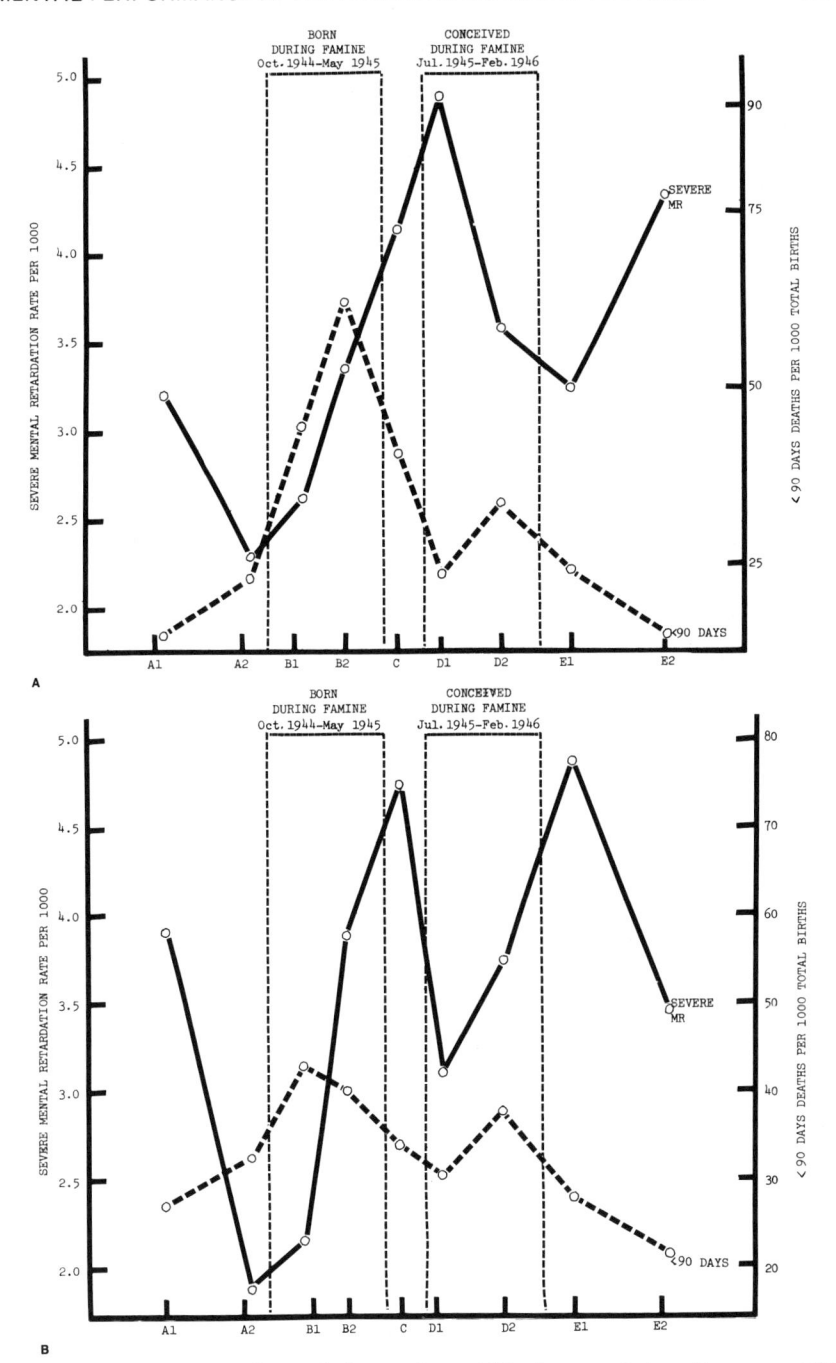

Figure 14.7. Severe mental retardation and mortality by area (rates of severe mental retardation and deaths occurring at ages less than 90 days by nine birth cohorts: A. famine cities and B. control cities)

Table 14.1. Food rations, social variables, mental performance, and height (correlation matrix of psychometric indices, caloric rations (C_1, C_2, C_3), and other attributes among individuals born from January 1, 1944, through December 31, 1946: in all cities combined)

	C_1	C_2	C_3	Social Class	Family Size	Birth Order	Height	Global Psychometric	Raven Progressive Matrices	Bennett Test of Mechanical Comprehension	Arithmetic Test	Language Test	Clerical Test
C_1	1.00	.87	.72	−.01	−.02	.00	.30	.04	.03	.05	.04	.04	.05
C_2		1.00	.89	−.00	−.03	−.00	.25	.03	.02	.04	.03	.02	.04
C_3			1.00	.01	−.03	.01	.23	.02	.01	.03	.03	.01	.03
Social Class				1.00	.09	.08	.08	.34	.24	.25	.32	.33	.30
Family Size					1.00	.64	.06	.14	.19	.09	.13	.15	.14
Birth Order						1.00	.02	.14	.10	.09	.12	.15	.14
Height							1.00	−.01	−.00	.03	.00	−.00	−.00
Global								1.00	.79	.70	.87	.84	.85
Raven									1.00	.52	.63	.59	.64
Bennett										1.00	.54	.47	.45
Arithmetic Test											1.00	.76	.74
Language Test												1.00	.76
Clerical Test													1.00

15 Prenatal Famine Effects on Body Size

Height

Adult height varies with the environment in which growth occurs. Japanese immigrants in California of two decades ago grew much taller than Japanese in Japan, for example, and within many Western societies there are trends toward a rise in height (Kiil, 1939; Tanner, 1962). In the Netherlands a similar trend has been observed in the post-World War II period (Wieringen, Wafelbakker, Verbrugge, and de Haas, 1971). These trends seem to be sensitive to the conditions in which children are reared (Markowitz, 1955). For instance, in Greece among army conscripts, a trend toward increasing stature was found among those born and reared in the period 1927 to 1935; among those born and reared in the subsequent decade, a decade affected by famine and high morbidity among children, this trend was halted (Valaoras, 1970).

Evidence on the causes of the observed variations in height with environment is not conclusive. Among possible causes, the evidence for nutrition in childhood is plausible (Adrianzen, Baertl, and Graham, 1973). Small stature is certainly associated with poverty, as indicated by social class differences, and by the trends that have accompanied rising standards of living. On the other hand, the search for the effects of early and severe malnutrition on growth in later childhood and pubescence has given conflicting results, as discussed in the opening chapters (Hiernaux, 1964; Garrow and Pike, 1967; Birch and Gussow, 1970; Hansen, Freeseman, and Moodie, 1971).

Infection early in childhood probably also retards growth. In a prospective study of young children in Britain, such retardation was inferred from the coincidence of recorded infections with changes in skeletal radiographs. The radiographic changes indicated that bone growth was affected (Hewitt, Westropp, and Acheson, 1955). In a longitudinal study of children in a village in Gambia, West Africa, growth in height related better to the prevalence of malaria than to food supply (McGregor, Billewicz, and Thomson, 1961).

Birthweight and length at birth have been found to relate to adult height (Tanner, Healy, Lockhart, Mackenzie, and Whitehouse 1956; Falkner, 1971; Miller, Billewicz, and Thomson, 1972). But these analyses were not controlled for factors like social class that could be the common cause of a non-causal association. Another analysis of a national sample of births in Britain, which was controlled for social class, found an association of birthweight with height at 7 years of age (Davie, Butler, and Goldstein, 1972). From height at 3 years of age, however, one can predict adult height much better than from either birthweight or length at birth (Tanner, Healy, Lockhart, Mackenzie, and Whitehouse, 1956).

In our study, we seek to show an effect of prenatal exposure to famine on adult height. We take height at 19 years of age to be a good approximation of full-grown stature.

A. Cohort Analysis of Height by Time and Place

Figure 15.1 sets out mean height for cohorts in famine and control areas among cohorts within two social classes, manual and non-manual; the classes are derived as before from the record of father's occupation at the time of induction. The pattern of change among cohorts bears no evident relation to prenatal famine experience. The disparities in mean height among the three areas and between the two social classes are notable. Another feature is the somewhat irregular secular trend toward increasing stature that begins in cohorts born after 1944.

The D2 cohort, conceived at the height of the famine, has an advantage in stature over its predecessors (Figure 15.2A), as it also had in IQ. The analysis of mean height by month within social class for each area (Appendix) shows that this advantage in stature of the D2 cohort has two elements. In part it is owed to the change in social class composition caused by the decline in fertility at the height of the famine (see Chapter 9); even crude analysis within only two social classes removes most of the advantage of the D2 cohort over its predecessors among the non-manual classes in the famine area (Figure 15.1). In part, the advantage of the D2 cohort is also owed to its position in relation to the rising trend in height with time. This trend was most marked in the manual classes of the cities of the famine area and the North, and in the non-manual classes of the South.

B. Quantitative Analysis of Food Rations and Adult Stature (Table 15.1)

In this quantitative analysis of food rations, the unit of analysis of the dependent variable presented throughout is individual height. The results are consistent with the conclusion that there is no specific effect of prenatal famine exposure on adult stature. We make this inference despite the positive and significant correlation, in several analyses, of food rations with height. While

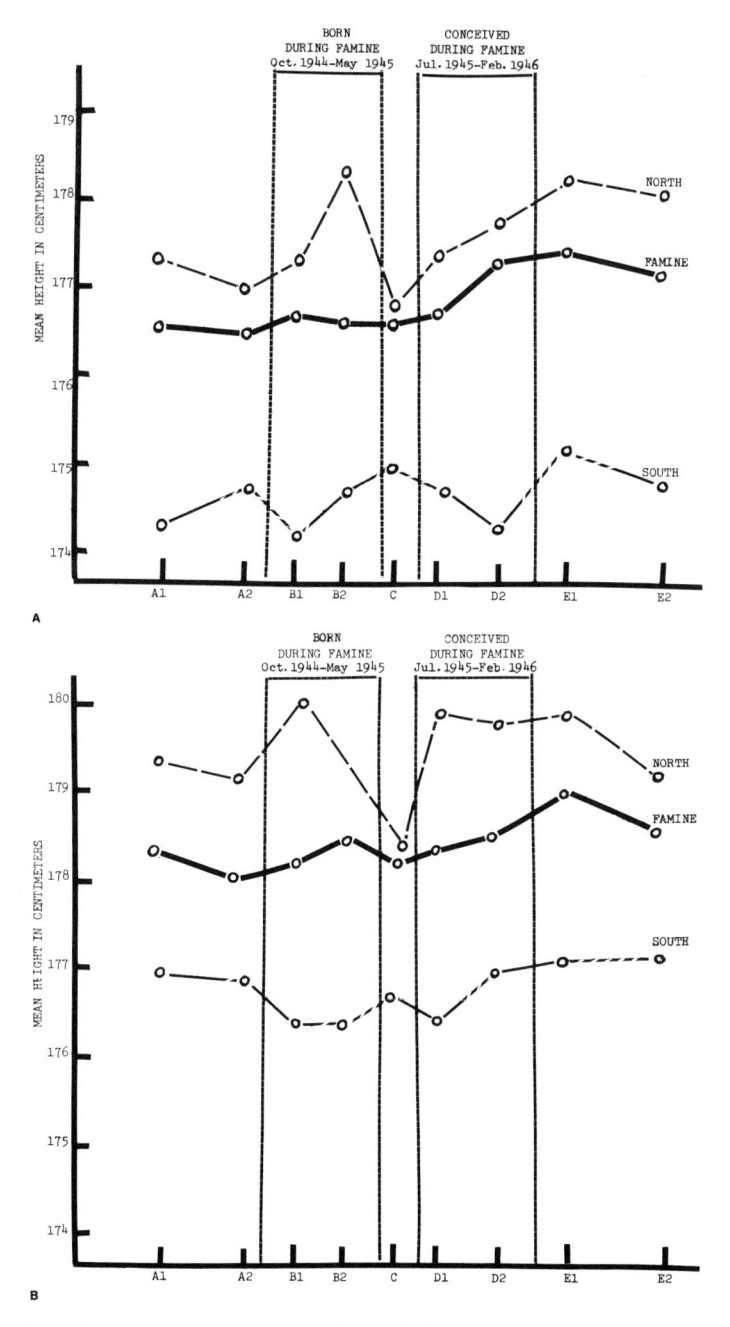

Figure 15.1. Height by area and class (mean height of survivors at military induction among nine birth cohorts in the famine, Northern control, and Southern control areas, in two social classes based on occupation of the father at time of birth: **A.** manual and **B.** non-manual)

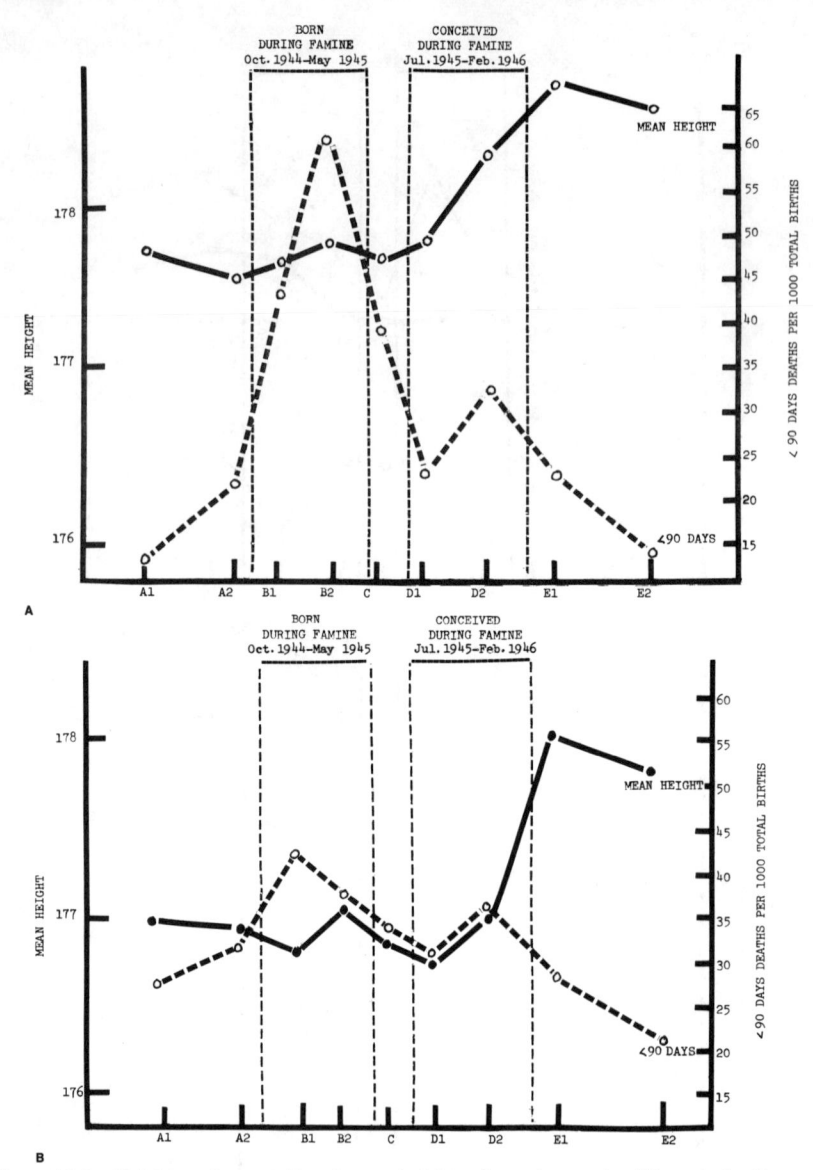

Figure 15.2. Height and mortality (mean height of survivors at military induction and death rates under 90 days of age per 1000 total births among nine birth cohorts: **A.** famine cities and **B.** control cities)

these correlations could reflect a nutritional effect, they cannot be attributed to a prenatal famine effect.

In the analysis by area, the correlation of height with caloric rations in the first trimester is strongest in the famine area ($r = .20$). In the two control areas, correlations of height with food ration measures are weak; none rise above $r = .1$.

On turning to the analysis of different nutritional conditions, however, we find that the correlation coefficients with food rations are weaker under the famine condition than under the non-famine condition. Indeed, under the famine condition the correlations show no relationship worth noting.

Height correlates with social class, family size, and birth order. The association between each of these variables and caloric rations was negligible. For this reason, as discussed in the preceding chapter, statistical control of these potentially confounding variables would make no practical difference to the strength of the initial associations between the two study variables.

To take account of the possibility that selective mortality distorted and masked the association of prenatal famine exposure and stature, we can be guided by the same set of inferences and procedures as in the analysis of mental competence (see pp. 207-12). Figure 15.2 is a cohort graph of adult stature and of mortality up to 3 months of age in famine and control cities. For famine-related mortality to cause distortion of a prenatal famine effect on height there must be (as we previously argued in relation to mental competence) a correlation between height and mortality that is opposite in sign to the correlation between height and prenatal famine exposure.

In the famine cities taken alone, the graphs do not put the possibility of distortion by selective survival out of court. The mortality curve among cohorts B1, B2, and C—among whom the famine-related excess occurred—moves in the same general direction as does the curve for height. Among the later cohorts born after the war, when there was no famine-related excess of deaths, the curves diverge. Nonetheless, the hypothesis does not hold in the face of the pattern for the control cities. Concomitant variation of mortality with height during the famine period is no less marked in the control than in the famine cities; hence any distortion of associations is not an effect only of famine-related mortality. The correlation coefficient between mortality and height among the nine birth cohorts was negligible in the famine cities and in the control cities.

We conclude that there was no effect of prenatal famine exposure on adult stature. The associations of food rations with height are not generated by the effects of famine; they follow from the rising trend of height in the postwar period. Improved nutrition is a likely cause of this rising trend, but in this research design nutrition in the postwar period cannot be isolated with certainty from other factors in the social environment that improved concurrently, including the control of acute infectious disease. About the postwar improvement in social environment there can be no doubt, and one visible index is the steady decline of early infant mortality among later cohorts to be seen in Figure 15.2. The failure of extremes of food deprivation in pregnant women to produce an effect in their offspring must count against the existence of a *prenatal* nutritional effect in milder circumstances. Hence any influence of nutrition on adult stature, highly probable in the light of all the published evidence taken together, can be expected to act in *postnatal* life.

Weight

Weight is highly dependent on height. In any consideration of weight in its own right, therefore, the confounding effects of height must be removed (Billewicz, Kemsley, and Thomson, 1962). Among various methods for controlling height in the analysis of variations in weight, we have chosen to use Quételet's index, $\frac{weight}{height^2}$ (Quételet, 1870). This index is widely used, and serves better than most others as a measure of obesity, for it is highly correlated with body weight and independent of height. (Khosla and Lowe, 1967). While the numbers in our data are sufficient to arrange weight within height categories—and we did so arrange them in preliminary work—for convenience of presentation and quicker comprehension, we present here only Quételet's index. The index is a summarizing statistic, and the results do not diverge in any way from our detailed analysis of weight by height. The results give no indication of an effect of prenatal exposure to famine on weight.

Cohort Analysis of Quételet's Index by Time and Place

In Figure 15.3 no famine effect can be seen in the pattern of mean values of Quételet's index among cohorts. The direction of change is consistent with a secular trend toward greater body weight in the period studied. This trend seemed to begin with a sharp rise in the B2 cohort born at the height of the famine, and thus began sooner than the trend toward taller stature.

A social class analysis (not presented here) shows that the secular trend toward greater weight resides mainly among the manual classes. It also confirms again the effect of the changed social class composition of the D2 cohort (Chapter 9). This effect appears in the slight decline in Quételet's index in the D2 cohort, conceived at the height of the famine, as compared with its predecessors C and D1. No other famine effects are apparent in these graphs.

The rising trend with time suggested by Quételet's index is confirmed by the diagnosis of obesity assigned at the military induction examination (see Figure 16.1C). In both famine and control cities, the rate of diagnosed obesity in the cohorts born after mid-1945 is three times higher than in those born in 1944. Even the cohort born at the height of the famine (B2) forms part of the rising trend.

No further analysis is needed to exclude an effect of prenatal famine exposure on weight. A quantified analysis of food rations and weight, while clearly of relevance to a study of nutrition in general, can contribute no more to the hypotheses under test in this study. At this point, we may safely conclude that prenatal exposure to famine had no direct effect on body size in terms of either height or weight.

Summary

The data from military induction examinations in the Netherlands have enabled us to test the effect of prenatal famine exposure on adult height. We take height

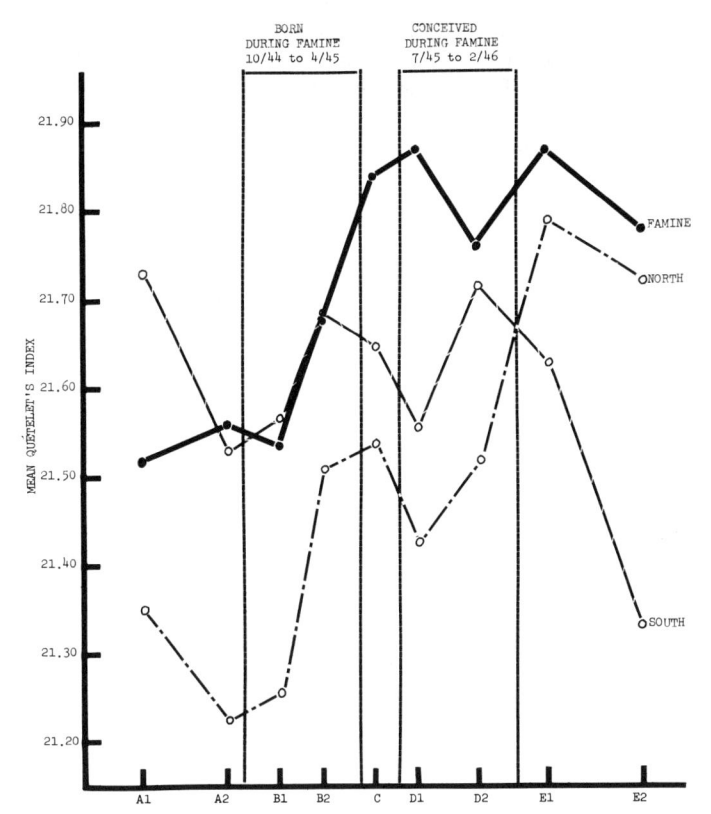

Figure 15.3. Mean Quételet's index in famine area and Northern and Southern control areas among nine birth cohorts.

at 19 years of age to be a good approximation of full adult height. No effect of prenatal famine exposure could be detected. The possibility that selective survival of infants removed those who would have grown into adults of small stature was not sustained in our examination of the data.

Associations between food rations and height were found; these were not related to prenatal famine exposure, and were attributed rather to a secular trend. In the short period under study, the trend was toward increasing height. This trend is consistent with nutritional trends, as our correlations with food rations show, but the absence of a prenatal famine effect indicates that if the trend has a nutritional cause, it is likely to be postnatal. Our research design cannot specifically isolate postnatal or non-famine effects.

Quételet's index was used as an index of weight that would control confounding by height. No effect of prenatal famine exposure on this index could be detected. The validity of the rising secular trend present in the postwar cohorts was strongly supported by an analysis of diagnosed obesity. This trend was concentrated in the manual working classes.

Table 15.1. Correlations of height and body size with food rations (correlation matrices of mean height and of Quételet's index with average caloric rations by trimester (C_1, C_2, C_3) in famine and control areas, and under famine and non-famine conditions)

	Data Set	C_1	C_2	C_3
Height	Famine	0.20	0.14	0.12
	South	0.09	0.06	0.06
	North	0.10	0.10	0.10
	Famine Condition	0.04	0.08	0.06
	Non-famine Condition	0.25	0.23	0.24
	All	0.30	0.25	0.23
Quételet's Index	Famine Condition	0.10	0.005	0.003
	Non-famine Condition	0.09	0.04	−0.002
	All	0.04	0.02	0.01

16 Prenatal Famine Effects on Health Status

ICD Categories

At the medical examination for military induction, each man filled in a questionnaire which covered his past medical history. A routine standardized physical examination was made by trained medical officers. Preliminary diagnosis was based on findings of the questionnaire and the physical examination. In the case of a pre-existing and previously recognized health disorder, supporting information was obtained from the previous medical attendants. Where necessary, further investigations were made and specialist opinion was obtained. All the evidence so collected was used to make a final diagnosis. This diagnosis was confirmed by the medical officer in charge of the induction center. Seven such centers served the whole country. The diagnosis was assigned, recorded, and coded in terms of the International Classification of Diseases (World Health Organization, 1948). Of the men in the cohorts studied 40% received one diagnosis, and 6% more than one. Where more than one diagnosis had been coded, the more serious condition was coded as primary; the other was coded as secondary. To obtain prevalence rates from these data, we included both primary and secondary diagnoses.

We have no means of evaluating the reliability of the coded diagnoses. Frequencies of coded diagnoses are more likely to underestimate than to overestimate the extent of morbidity. Thus a condition is likely to be overlooked where no symptoms appear on the questionnaire, where no physical signs accompany it, and where no note is supplied by a previous medical attendant. This could happen, for instance, with asthma or psychosis if not reported in the history. When a positive history of previous illness was given at the induction examination, it was always checked before acceptance. Other problems of reliability and validity could arise, in comparisons of data collected at different times and places, from the influence of opinion particular to time and place upon diagnostic judgments. Our data are well-protected from this source of unreliability by the standardized procedures, the small number of induction centers, and the short time span of the observation period.

The coded ICD data were analyzed in terms of prevalence rates for each month of birth in famine and control cities. These data were consolidated into rates for the same grouping of birth cohorts that were defined in relation to the famine period and used for analyzing the outcome measures throughout this book. To begin with, the over-all frequency of all coded diagnoses was examined. Conditions coded rarely or not at all were discarded; others that were etiologically or clinically related were grouped or separated to produce workable rates. At this stage, conditions with prevalence rates of less than one per thousand in any cohort were laid aside. The numbers of cases for the remaining 26 conditions in each cohort, in the famine area and in the control areas combined, are shown in the Appendix. Rates for selected conditions are shown in the Appendix.

With regard to the prevalence of health disorders among cohorts *exposed early in gestation,* there was a rise in the prevalence of *congenital anomalies of the central nervous system** in the D2 cohort conceived at the height of the famine. This peak in prevalence supports the supposition of a prenatal famine effect. The relative risk for the D2 cohort in the famine area was doubled, and although numbers were small the deviation from the norm for the famine area was statistically significant ($p < .025$).

Without regard to probability values, a number of manifestations of the D2 cohort cohere with this rise in congenital anomalies of the central nervous system to give it biological significance. Some of these findings appeared in the analysis of mortality (Chapter 13) and some in the analysis of maternities (Chapter 10). In the analysis of mortality both stillbirths and first-week death rates showed peaks in the D2 cohort of the famine area. Those peaks were not unique to the famine area, although higher than in the control areas. That the peaks were higher in the famine area than in the control areas pointed to the presence of interaction between famine exposure early in gestation, and some other factor common to all areas. This other factor behaved like an infective agent spreading across the country over several months. In addition, in the analysis of certified causes among perinatal deaths in the D2 cohort in the famine area, one stood out. This cause was prematurity (more precisely, birth-

---

*In Figure 16.1, the category includes spina bifida and hydrocephalus (ICD 751-753). Cerebral palsy (ICD 351) varies in the same manner as the other central nervous system anomalies combined. Thus in the D2 cohort, 2 cases were expected and 5 observed, and the pattern remains the same whether or not it is included with central nervous system congenital anomalies.

weight less than 2500 grams). The analysis of maternities pointed to short gestation as a likely intervening factor in a causal sequence.

When we turn to examine the prevalence of health disorders among cohorts born during the famine and *exposed late in gestation* (B1, B2, C), no prenatal famine effects are apparent. The frequency of the diagnosis of "immature personality" rose among cohorts born in the famine cities during the famine (i.e. B1, B2, C) and not among those born in control cities. But frequency in the famine city cohorts did not decline among cohorts born or conceived after the famine. Moreover, the rise in prevalence in the control cities beginning with the D1 or D2 cohort suggests the presence of a time trend rather than a famine effect. Three other assigned diagnoses—asthma, obesity, and psychoneurosis—showed trends clearly rising over time. These rising trends were found equally in famine and in control city cohorts.

Rates for congenital anomalies are of special interest because of their prenatal origin; most of these remained stable throughout the period of study. The apparent epidemic of clubfoot in the E1 cohort (born and conceived after the famine) in the control area is intriguing but in no way related to famine. Another exception was congenital heart disease. An epidemic with a rate two to three times as high as in earlier or later years occurred across the country among births during 1944; although the diagnosis was frequently assigned in the famine cities, the pattern was similar everywhere. We have been able to ascertain that this epidemic occurred in relation to a rubella epidemic.*

Annual Rubella notifications 1940-45 in the Netherlands:

1940	1941	1942	1943	1944	1945
8,837	7,197	12,694	28,566	22,487	4,813

ABOHZIS

In addition to the coding under the ICD of all diagnosed conditions, the examining doctors rated each man on each of seven scales. The scales, known by the acronym ABOHZIS, refer to the following assessments: (1) general build and state of health; (2) upper extremity; (3) lower extremity; (4) hearing; (5) vision; (6) mental state; and (7) stability (social and psychological). Assessments of individuals for each area were scored on a five-point scale. Unlike the ICD, the ABOHZIS rating allows for positive scoring of favorable states of health and not merely for the recognition of unfavorable states of ill-health. Men are assigned to one of five categories on each scale, ranging from totally fit to rejected.

The ABOHZIS assessments were analyzed in the same way as the ICD diagnoses by each month of birth in famine and in control cities. No associations were found between prenatal famine exposure and any of the seven scales, and

*Dr. J. W. H. Van den Berg, Head of the Department of Medical Statistics of the Netherlands Central Bureau of Statistics, kindly supplied these data.

CONGENITAL MALFORMATIONS

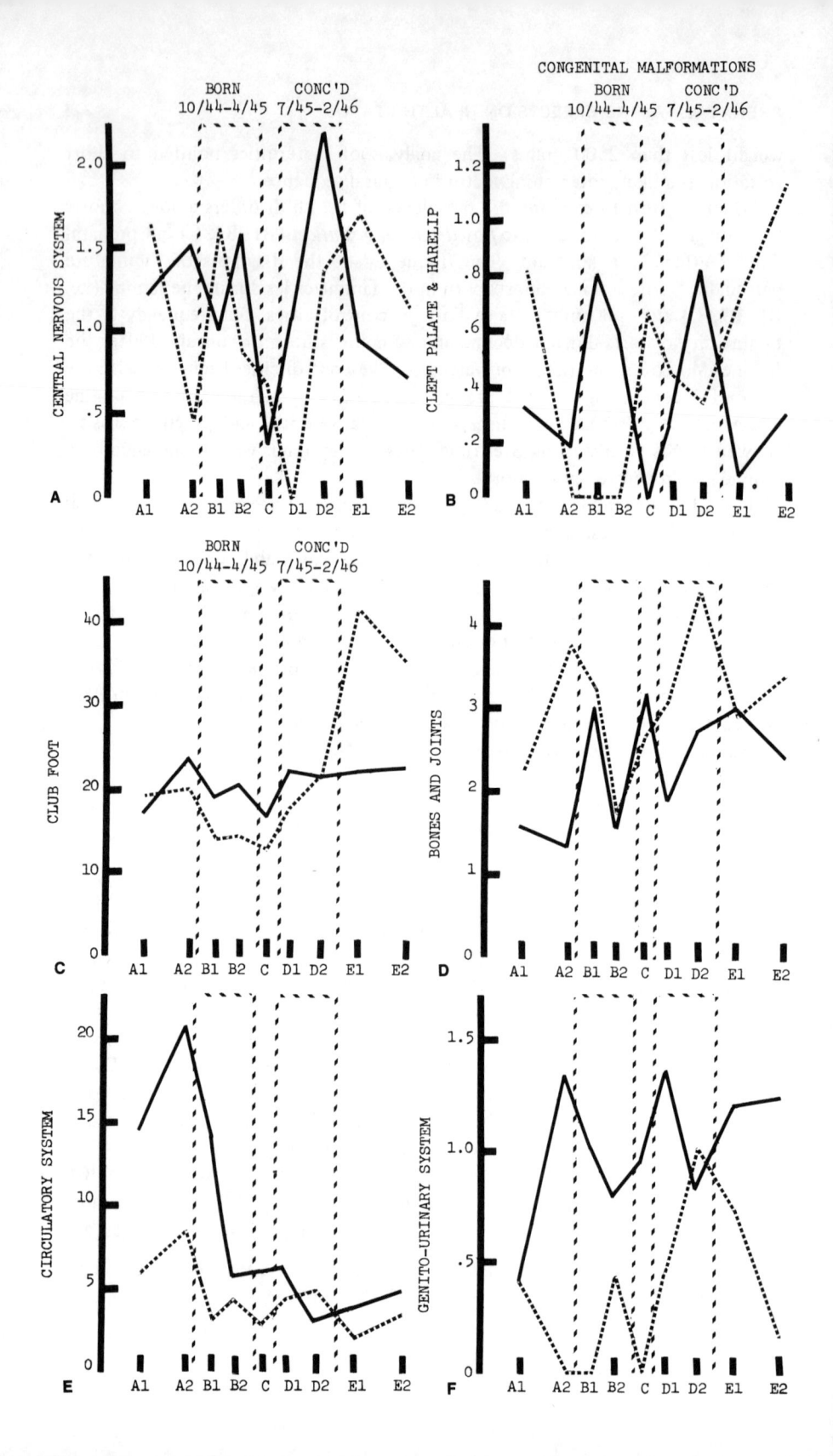

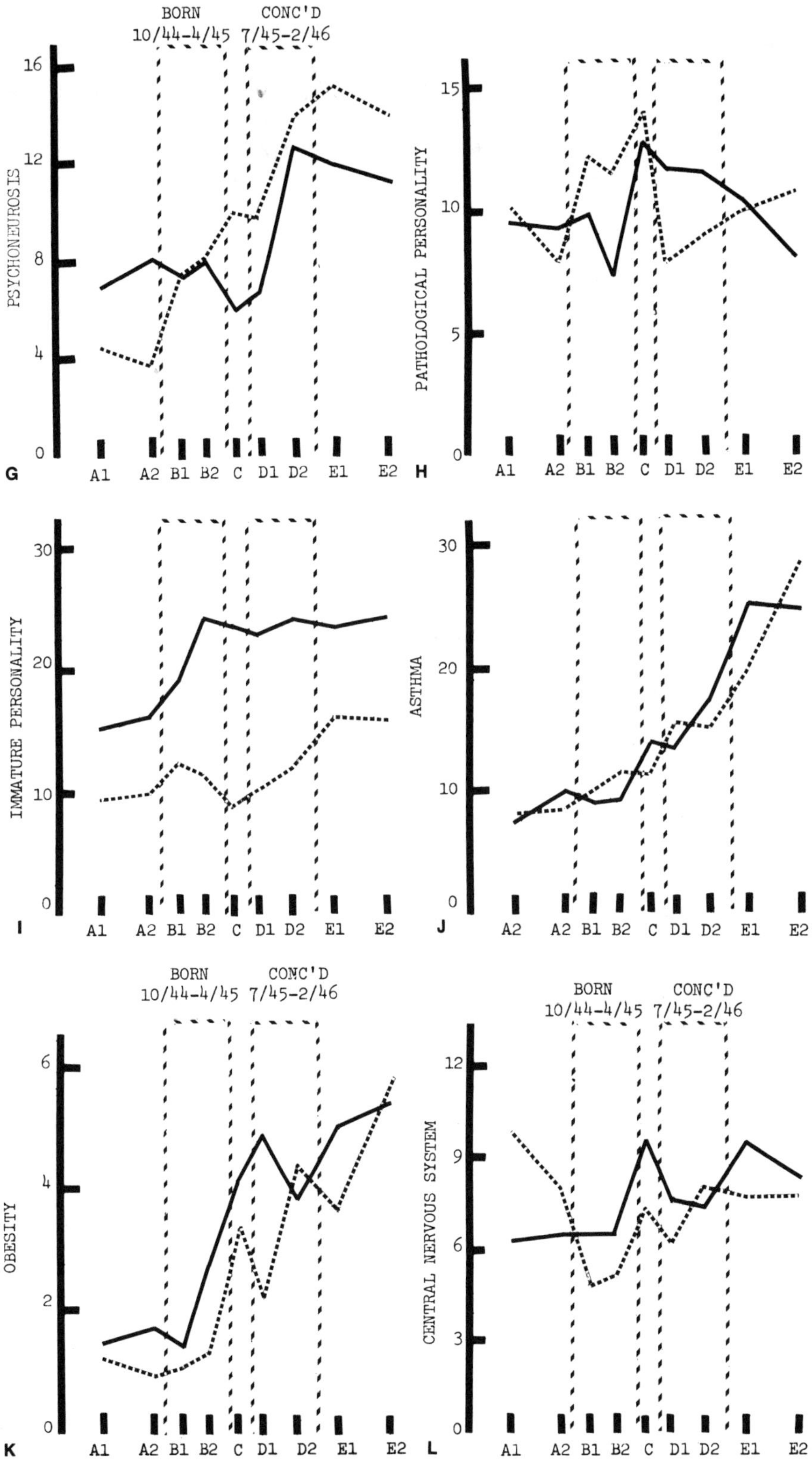

BORN
10/44-4/45
CONC'D
7/45-2/46
PSYCHONEUROSIS
16
12
8
4
0
A1 A2 B1 B2 C D1 D2 E1 E2
G
PATHOLOGICAL PERSONALITY
15
10
5
0
A1 A2 B1 B2 C D1 D2 E1 E2
H
IMMATURE PERSONALITY
30
20
10
0
A1 A2 B1 B2 C D1 D2 E1 E2
I
ASTHMA
30
20
10
0
A2 A2 B1 B2 C D1 D2 E1 E2
J
BORN
10/44-4/45
CONC'D
7/45-2/46
OBESITY
6
4
2
0
A1 A2 B1 B2 C D1 D2 E1 E2
K
BORN
10/44-4/45
CONC'D
7/45-2/46
CENTRAL NERVOUS SYSTEM
12
9
6
3
0
A1 A2 B1 B2 C D1 D2 E1 E2
L

the data are not presented. There is substantial overlap between the lower categories of ABOHZIS assessment and the ICD coding of diagnosis. For instance, scores on the mental status scale in ABOHZIS are influenced by the psychometric criteria analyzed and presented in Chapter 14.

Fitness Categories

A third mode of assessment at the medical examination was expressed in a "decision code." This code summarized the fitness for service of the examinee in five categories as follows: (1) fit; (2) temporarily unfit (subject to reclassification); (3) unfit; (4) deferred; and (5) exempted. The decision code was analyzed in the same manner as the other medical criteria. No associations were found between prenatal famine exposure and acceptance for any category of service. In these categories, redundancy with the prevalence of ICD code diagnoses is substantial and the data are not presented.

Summary

Only one clear association was found between prenatal exposure to famine and any of three different medical criteria. One medical criterion was the prevalence of health disorders recorded under the code of the International Classification of Diseases (World Health Organization, 1948) in the population at military induction. Twenty-six conditions had a frequency of more than one per 1000, a rate which was taken to be a minimum for the purpose of examining trends among cohorts. In only one, congenital anomalies of the central nervous system, was there evidence of a raised prevalence related to prenatal famine exposure. An epidemic of congenital heart disease occurred across the country during the first half of 1944, but this was related to rubella and not famine. Rising time trends for asthma, obesity, "immature personality," and psychoneurosis are also not famine-related. A second medical criterion was the rating of the health status of individuals in the population on seven scales, each relating to a particular area of examination. A third medical criterion was the category of fitness for military service to which individuals were assigned. No distributions were famine-related by the second and third criteria.

Figure 16.1. Selected diagnostic categories by ICD code assigned at induction examinations in rates per 1000 for nine successive cohorts in famine cities and in Northern and Southern control cities combined (scales vary from diagram to diagram).

Congenital Anomalies
  A. Central nervous system (ICD 751-753)
  B. Cleft palate and harelip (ICD 755)
  C. Club foot (ICD 748)
  D. Bone and joint (ICD 758)
  E. Circulatory System (ICD 754)
  F. Genito-urinary (ICD 757)

Psychiatric
  G. Psychoneurosis (ICD 310-318)
  H. Pathological personality (ICD 320)
  I. Immature personality (ICD 321)

Other
  J. Asthma (ICD 241)
  K. Obesity (ICD 287)
  L. Central nervous system (ICD 330-357)

17 Conclusions

The provenance of this study was the strong association between social conditions and the mental performance of mature adults. The broad question posed was how much of this association, if any, could be explained by the variation across society of prenatal nutrition. The more specific question tested was whether severe but balanced deficiency in the nutrients supplied to groups of mothers during any stage of pregnancy had detectable effects on the mental and physical states of the offspring in their maturity. To this question we can give an unequivocal answer: in a large population of young men there were, with one exception, no detectable effects of exposure to famine on various measures of mental performance, nor on physical stature, nor on disorders of health.

In this adult population, the single outcome of the many measured which varied in frequency with prenatal exposure to famine was the prevalence of anomalies of the central nervous system diagnosed at military induction, namely spina bifida and hydrocephalus, and also cerebral palsy. The time relations as well as the process of development require that this outcome was determined early in gestation. Co-incident effects in the same birth cohort suggest connections among them. Thus peaks in the D2 cohort of the famine area were evident for shortened periods of gestation, for very low birthweight,* for perinatal and neonatal mortality, for low birthweight as a cause of perinatal death, and for later deaths attributed to meningitis.

The numbers in the D2 cohort in the famine area were not large because of infertility at the height of the famine, and each specific outcome affected a small

---

*Note that mean birthweight was not reduced in spite of an excess of numbers in this extreme group.

number of individuals. Thus taken one at a time the effects were not remarkable in magnitude, and some were not statistically significant. Taken together, however, they form the elements of a plausible causal sequence. The sequence begins with nutritional deprivation, which interferes with organogenesis of the central nervous system during the first trimester of pregnancy, leads on to premature birth with low birthweight and ends either with perinatal or neonatal death, with later deaths caused by meningitis complicating spina bifida and hydrocephalus, or with survival into adulthood despite the presence of spinal bifida and hydrocephalus.

Nutritional deprivation did not seem to act alone to produce the whole of this sequence. Certain effects in the D2 cohort occurred in the control areas as well as in the famine area: although less striking, configurations for length of gestation and for perinatal mortality in the control areas were similar to those in the famine areas. These configurations did not relate to low food rations during early gestation, and a coherent explanation requires interaction between famine exposure in early gestation and an unknown co-determinant common to all areas of the country. The pattern of perinatal mortality by time and place in the affected cohorts was compatible with an infection spreading gradually across the country; hence maternal infection could be the postualted co-determinant. It is important to note that all our postulates about links between observations on the reproductive process and subsequent observations on deaths and survivors are subject to the ecological fallacy. With this caution in mind, at this point we can represent the postulated links as follows:

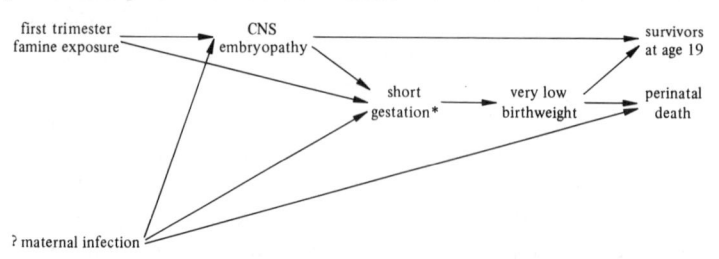

```
first trimester ─────▶ CNS ──────────────────────▶ survivors
famine exposure ─▶ embryopathy ─▶                    at age 19
                        ▶ short ──▶ very low ──▶ perinatal
                          gestation*   birthweight    death
? maternal infection ─ ─ ─▶
```

*Note that the path from maternal infection to short gestation is shown by a broken line. Although lengh of gestation in the D2 cohort was reduced outside the famine area, we could not demonistrate its relation to very low birthweight in those areas, nor to perinatal death caused by prematurity. We do not know whether the inconsistency between the famine and control areas in respect of the connection between shortened gestation and very low birthweight arises from unreliability of data on gestation, from lack of power to detect effects on fetal size, or from other causes.

The salient aspects of the starting hypotheses about the ultimate effects of prenatal nutritional deprivation, however, were negated by our results. Yet the absence of association between prenatal famine exposure and mental competence or health status should not be accepted without carefully considering the validity of our results and the elaboration of the starting hypotheses by our

CONCLUSIONS

many extensive analyses. The elaboration relates to intermediate stages of the life course, at conception, at birth, and at death.

The congruence of certain results with those of many other studies can be taken to support in some measure the validity of the results in this study. Social conditions, for which we use social class as a chief index, related in the expected manner to mental and physical adult development, that is, those at a social disadvantage were also at a developmental disadvantage. Social advantage also influenced nutritional deprivation; for this we have indirect evidence from the greater impact of the famine on fertility in the lower social classes. The variation of the effect of the famine on fertility among social classes was large enough to alter the level of adult mental performance among successive cohorts. It is reasonable to infer that this fertility pattern reflected the pattern of maternal nutrition among the social classes.

The effects of prenatal nutritional deprivation, although inapparent in those who reached adulthood in all but one respect, were apparent at birth in indices of fetal growth. It follows that under the famine condition the mother was an imperfect buffer between adverse environment and the fetus. The effects of prenatal nutrition on indices of fetal growth appeared only below threshold values of food deprivation; above the threshold values, prenatal caloric intake had little influence. The mother absorbed the first impact of food deprivation and did so presumably until her own nutrient stores were exhausted. This sequence was inferred from the time order of changes in maternal and fetal dimensions through the famine. The most affected indices of fetal growth were birthweight and placental weight; infant length and head circumference at birth were least affected. This rank order of effects we interpreted as a reflection of threshold values that were successively lower for each fetal dimension. The higher threshold for head circumference and the small effect on it is consistent with brain sparing mechanisms that have been postulated to explain the results of animal experiments and human observations.

Demonstrable and unequivocal effects of prenatal nutrition on fetal growth were confined to the third trimester of gestation, and these effects were not mediated by a shortened period of gestation.* Maternal weight was an intervening factor in the causal chain of third trimester effects. The interrelations between caloric intake, maternal weight, and fetal growth appeared to change below a famine threshold. Above the threshold, the minimal association of caloric intake with fetal growth seemed to be mediated entirely through maternal weight; below the threshold a direct path appeared between caloric intake and fetal growth. Path models were constructed and the assumption examined that in conditions of adequate nutrition the rate of placental growth was determined by fetal growth, and that the normal placenta did not limit fetal

---

*The single exception in which shortened gestation did mediate, and which is referred to above, was the contribution of prenatal nutrition in the first trimester to lowered birthweight.

growth. In conditions of severe nutritional deprivation, however, the contrary assumption was examined; namely, that the placenta mediated the supply of nutrients to the fetus and that it supplied its own metabolic needs before those of the fetus. These assumptions were founded on inferences made from intensive preliminary analysis of the time order and causal sequences among variables; they produced plausible results.

Prenatal nutritional deprivation in the third trimester increased the early mortality of the cohorts born during the famine as well as retarding fetal growth. This further emphasizes fetal vulnerability despite maternal buffering against nutritional deprivation. The gradient of excess mortality did not include still-births, but increased through the three affected age groups up to three months of age. There was a slight excess of deaths in the first week of life, a larger excess in the rest of the first month, and a substantial excess thereafter through the third month of life. The indices of fetal growth displayed the characteristics of intervening variables in the causal associations of prenatal food deprivation with early infant mortality, although they could not account for the entire association. From this analysis, we inferred that early infant mortality caused by prenatal nutritional deprivation was mediated in part by fetal growth retardation and in part was a direct effect.

Infant mortality after three months of age was extremely high among cohorts born during the famine period. Detailed analysis supported prenatal factors as predominant in this excess mortality, but the hypothesis of prenatal famine exposure as the cause could not be sustained. Fetal growth indices, too, were not related to mortality after three months of age. Mortality up to 18 years of age also was unrelated to famine exposure.

Our over-all negative result at once ruled out one of the hypotheses broadly stated in Chapter 1, namely, that the type and degree of impairment inflicted on the gestating individual varies in a continuum according to the severity of the prenatal insult. Retarded fetal growth and a raised risk of early death can readily be conceived as a hierarchy of effects. In our analysis these effects on growth and survival were consecutive and formed part of a single causal chain leading from prenatal nutritional deprivation to early death. The hypothesis of a continuum fails when we seek a place in the hierarchy for mental competence, a milder effect. The depression of mental competence required by the model as the logical accompaniment of excess mortality is entirely absent. The same applies to other indices of health status among survivors at age 19.

The general failure of this study to detect effects of prenatal exposure to famine on the mental competence and state of health of adult survivors obliged us to consider seriously other explanations than the simple absence of an effect, and to test those explanations where possible. One contention could be that food deprivation was insufficient in severity to breach a brainsparing mechanism that protected the integrity of the brain. Some animal experiments and human observations have suggested that when fetal growth is retarded the brain is affected less than other organs. In our own data, as noted, head circumference was the least affected of the fetal dimensions measured at birth, and head circumference has been taken as a crude index of brain growth. We could not test the hypothesis of insufficient deprivation further within the limits of our data. Should it hold, then it would have significance for the biology of development, but would do little to alter the social meaning of our findings in relation to prenatal nutrition. Nutritional deprivation more severe than in the Dutch hunger winter hardly occurs aside from famine, even in the harshest environments. Should it occur, then the total inhibition of reproduction by infertility and even heavier mortality are likely to be more conspicuous results than depressed mental competence.

Another and more plausible contention could be that prenatal famine exposure did in fact retard brain growth, but that the deficit did not become manifest in mental performance. As we outlined in the opening chapter, animal experiment and human observations both support the likelihood that prenatal nutritional deficiency impairs brain growth. If so, three possibilities suggest themselves.

A first possibility is that those in whom prenatal famine exposure induced brain impairment and potential mental impairment were removed by coincident excess mortality. This coincidence of famine effects could have left unchanged the distribution of measures of mental competence. (The same hypothesis can be applied equally well to other impairments of health.) Such a result requires the operation of an all-or-none rule in which death followed all or most brain impairments conducive to mental impairment. The explanation would shed no light on the causes of depressed mental competence in survivors; it is more cogent as a limited statement about the pathogenesis of deaths induced by famine through brain impairment.

This explanation of pathogenesis has broader implications, however, if it is not construed as an all-or-none effect, but in terms of the balance between the incidence of impairment and the survival of those impaired. The prevalence of mental impairment in an adult population, which is the measure available to us, is a function of the incidence of impairment and the duration of survival of the impaired individuals. In the Dutch population that survived prenatal exposure to famine up to the age of 19 years, both incidence and survival are unknown. Another unknown is the degree to which the prenatal insult also carried off infants with brains impaired by other causes. Nonetheless, our knowledge of the prevalence of mental impairment and of mortality in the affected cohorts places some limits on the direction in which a hypothesis of selective survival could have acted: the hypothesis was eliminated when we did not find the prerequisite negative associations of excess famine-induced early mortality with measures of mental impairment. Had the incidence of mental impairment been associated with prenatal famine exposure, and had that association been distorted by the early mortality produced by prenatal famine exposure, then early mortality must have correlated negatively with the prevalence of mental impairment.

A second possibility is that postnatal learning contributes so large a part of the variance in adult mental function that the organic loss of brain cells was completely overshadowed by functional acquisitions through subsequent learning. If learning compensates for depressed mental function that results from cell depletion, one might anticipate interaction between the famine effect and the quality of the postnatal learning experience afforded by the social environment. Social or occupational class is a measure of the macroculture that has many times been shown to affect learning. Family size and birth order are measures of the microculture of families, and they too have clear-cut effects on learning and mental performance (Scottish Council for Research in Education, 1953; Nisbet and Illsley, 1963; Belmont and Marolla, 1973). The effect of birth order in particular excludes confounding by genetic factors and is, therefore, a highly valid index of environment. In our data these three indices of the quality of the learning environment all related to mental performance, but no interaction with prenatal nutrition was evident. On this ground we incline to eliminate the hypothesis that prenatal brain impairment was compensated by postnatal learning.

A third possible circumstance that could prevent the expression of a brain deficit in mental dysfunction is the existence of a reserve of brain cells large enough to protect function in the face of cell depletion. This hypothesis is congruent with those animal experiments in which a degree of nutritional deprivation sufficient to produce organic effects on the brain has been insufficient to produce recognizable functional effects on learning. The hypothesis cannot be eliminated by the data from our study nor by argument from other studies. In our view, it stands as the most likely explanation of our negative result. Possibly, a prolongation of nutritional deprivation through infancy would be capable of producing functional effects. The view has recently been advanced that the human brain growth spurt, and the vulnerability associated with it, continues at least through the second postnatal year. If so, nutritional deprivation confined to the prenatal period may be too brief to produce much effect.

Therefore our results should not be lightly generalized to the effects of *chronic* malnutrition in *postnatal* life, either with adequate calories but unbalanced dietary combinations, or with sustained caloric deprivation. Both types and mixed types of dietary deficiency occur in preindustrial societies. Many relevant animal experiments fit the model of the Dutch famine rather than that of preindustrial peasant societies, however. Our study warns that such experiments may not be apt models of the circumstances of chronic malnutrition.

Moreover, postnatal learning undoubtedly contributes to the variability in adult mental function in all societies, and in peasant societies as elsewhere the relative size of its contribution and that of nutrition has still to be estimated. The place of postnatal learning in our results is suggested by the variation in

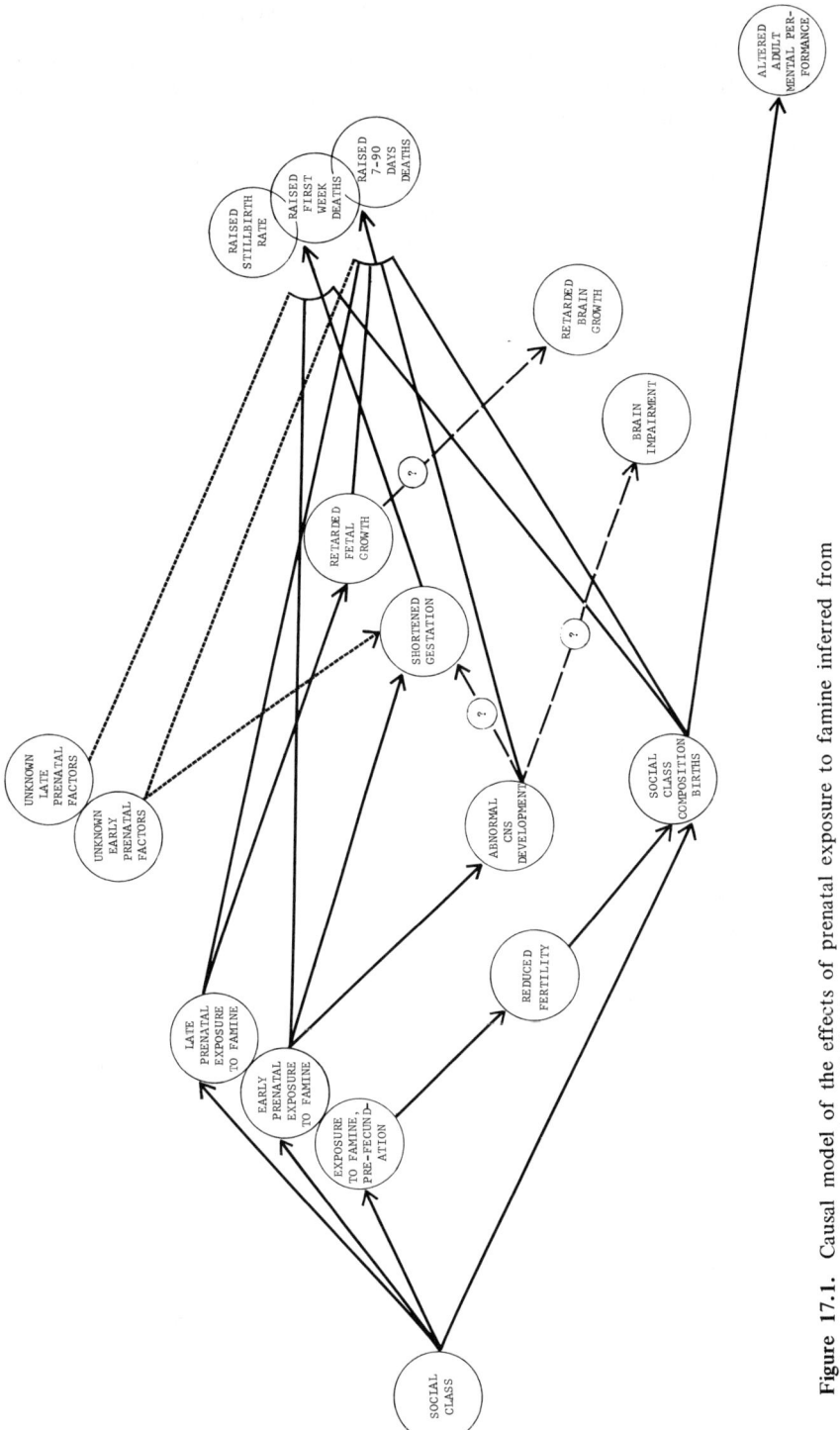

Figure 17.1. Causal model of the effects of prenatal exposure to famine inferred from study of the Dutch hunger winter 1944-45

mental performance among strata of the Dutch population defined by occupational class, education, urban or rural residence, family size, and birth order. The studies and arguments reviewed in the opening pages of this book make postnatal learning an attractive explanation for a great part of these differences among social strata. Significant intervening factors between social position and mental competence are likely to be found, we believe, in those intra-familial experiences of the child that are determined by the social position of the family. This view gains strength from the findings on birth order, from our own earlier studies of the association of mild mental retardation with particular family types, and from those of others on its familial distribution.

The findings of the present study, and some of the strong inferences that can be made from them, are set out in Figure 17.1.

We conclude as follows:

1. Below a threshold value of food rations, fertility in the population declined parallel with the availability of food. Infecundity, it is inferred, contributed to such infertility. There was an appreciable social class gradient in these effects, with the lowest classes affected most.

2. Above a threshold value of food intake, a mother afforded the fetus protection from nutritional deprivation.

3. Below the nutritional threshold, the fetus was vulnerable to some extent in the first trimester of gestation to abnormal development of the central nervous system, premature birth and very low birthweight, and perinatal death. These effects depended on the interaction of nutritional deprivation with some other cooperating cause, possibly infection. The numbers affected were small.

4. Below the nutritional threshold, the fetus was most vulnerable in the third trimester of gestation in terms of intrauterine growth and early postnatal mortality. Of the fetal dimensions measured, weight was most sensitive to nutritional effects, and length and head size least sensitive. Slowed fetal growth was a mediating factor between prenatal nutritional deprivation and raised death rates in the first three months of life. The numbers affected were substantial.

5. Prenatal brain cell depletion in fetuses exposed to the famine during the third trimester probably occurred. If it occurred, this outcome points to great resilience on the part of surviving fetuses, for the organic impairment did not become manifest in dysfunction.

6. Among adult survivors, we could find no evidence that prenatal nutrition impaired mental competence in some classes and not others. That is to say, if postnatal learning compensated for such adverse effects of prenatal nutrition as may have occurred, it did so equally well across the social classes.

7. Finally, we believe we must accept that poor *prenatal* nutrition cannot be considered a factor in the social distribution of mental competence among surviving adults in industrial societies. This is not to exclude it as a possible factor in combination with poor *postnatal* nutrition, especially in preindustrial societies.

Appendix

Table 1. Births and deaths (numbers of live births and numbers of deaths in successive age groups among male and female cohorts from January 1944 to December 1946: A. famine area, B. North control area, and C. South control area)

A. FAMINE AREA

Year and month of birth	Male Deaths					Female Deaths					Live Born		Still Born
	<6 Days	7–29	30–89	90–364	1–18 Yrs.	<6 Days	7–29	30–89	90–364	1–18 Yrs.	Male	Female	
1944,1	9	7	7	9	19	12	7	7	6	16	2061	1764	91
2	22	1	6	11	19	9	4	7	12	22	1934	1785	74
3	18	9	15	10	28	8	6	4	7	28	1973	1962	109
4	21	12	11	23	34	15	7	9	15	22	1971	1753	81
5	19	8	9	20	40	14	8	5	22	18	1975	1916	98
6	28	4	5	34	26	13	6	3	27	22	1924	1918	93
7	16	9	4	36	35	10	8	7	31	16	2027	1925	82
8	24	9	11	51	20	10	9	5	26	23	1988	1865	85
9	38	17	14	48	31	17	8	10	43	19	2132	2005	62
10	29	15	23	74	9	18	12	12	57	9	2047	1899	77
11	25	9	30	69	33	21	19	21	56	31	1982	1918	62
12	30	45	48	77	33	22	28	31	59	29	1942	1957	84
1945,1	39	36	51	68	42	26	19	42	53	33	2099	2007	76
2	48	55	47	62	29	31	30	44	60	19	1965	1943	88
3	32	43	62	72	31	30	33	37	47	34	2058	1946	100
4	34	57	67	77	24	22	50	46	56	24	2157	2032	66
5	38	19	51	55	34	26	15	27	48	21	2146	1929	93
6	28	17	29	39	24	12	11	35	26	27	1689	1688	66
7	10	9	24	38	25	17	13	7	21	16	1703	1623	72
8	22	7	19	34	20	11	3	8	18	21	1435	1366	62
9	11	7	11	23	19	11	5	6	18	9	1100	1011	41
10	15	6	8	3	9	12	4	5	5	11	917	835	61
11	18	7	15	11	15	8	9	8	7	13	861	780	47
12	26	2	7	7	15	21	3	10	4	16	1008	926	84
1946,1	32	6	10	11	19	19	15	8	5	14	1307	1258	99
2	44	14	16	10	22	29	14	17	10	21	2020	1880	119
3	61	23	11	37	56	49	18	16	16	25	3463	3267	159
4	59	28	18	30	39	38	9	11	18	29	3726	3491	186
5	56	14	13	35	49	39	21	11	18	31	3960	3610	160
6	40	17	13	28	38	26	8	7	16	23	3558	3342	129
7	31	12	7	27	56	44	7	9	22	23	3576	3205	134
8	30	14	10	27	44	17	10	9	23	21	3368	3133	130
9	23	14	17	19	35	23	7	16	16	16	3116	2895	147
10	33	8	8	13	29	22	4	3	7	13	2876	2792	143
11	24	9	13	16	17	9	8	11	18	24	2672	2455	151
12	28	12	19	15	31	13	8	16	19	19	2830	2709	141

B. NORTH CONTROL AREA

Year and Month of Birth	Male Deaths					Female Deaths					Live Born		
	<6 Days	7–29	30–89	90–364	1–18 Yrs.	<6 Days	7–29	30–89	90–364	1–18 Yrs.	Male	Female	Still Born
1944, 1	6	5	2	4	6	6	3	2	1	4	393	352	36
2	4	2	1	5	7	3	3	3	3	4	324	314	36
3	7	2	3	7	6	6	4	0	4	3	361	404	30
4	4	1	3	6	9	7	0	2	3	11	389	336	24
5	3	2	1	5	9	1	8	1	4	6	394	404	22
6	7	1	6	8	7	7	0	2	6	6	332	312	34
7	10	1	1	6	9	6	3	2	5	6	385	364	31
8	3	2	2	6	11	3	3	1	7	4	389	330	29
9	6	1	3	9	5	2	0	2	3	1	391	363	18
10	6	2	6	9	7	2	3	4	4	6	386	354	23
11	9	3	0	10	10	2	2	3	4	6	307	299	26
12	6	3	8	7	5	4	3	2	9	5	345	305	33
1945, 1	5	4	6	7	8	6	3	4	11	10	338	409	27
2	1	9	7	14	9	4	2	10	7	6	429	370	19
3	8	7	8	9	7	4	4	4	9	15	441	388	39
4	3	4	7	13	7	3	3	3	14	5	426	442	30
5	5	1	5	8	14	1	2	3	18	5	414	363	18
6	4	7	4	11	10	3	3	2	8	5	337	324	28
7	5	0	12	15	9	3	3	7	11	1	402	335	25
8	4	0	12	11	10	4	3	4	12	7	314	354	23
9	4	1	2	7	9	2	2	3	8	7	350	317	19
10	9	6	3	7	4	9	1	2	7	7	318	261	29
11	8	3	7	3	6	7	3	4	7	4	288	290	33
12	5	2	1	7	7	4	4	4	3	3	370	307	18
1946, 1	6	8	5	6	14	6	4	2	1	8	454	406	33
2	5	8	2	11	8	9	3	4	6	8	466	472	57
3	12	8	4	4	13	7	2	4	5	9	570	573	47
4	13	0	1	5	10	4	5	0	5	11	551	514	40
5	11	1	2	6	11	9	2	5	4	7	572	515	50
6	6	6	3	7	6	5	1	1	9	6	511	448	39
7	6	1	4	6	17	4	1	3	2	6	523	476	36
8	9	3	3	3	7	7	3	1	4	7	517	460	35
9	7	1	3	6	6	4	2	3	5	5	485	429	40
10	2	1	2	3	4	4	1	1	3	5	459	421	43
11	11	3	3	1	8	10	0	0	5	6	386	377	43
12	8	4	1	3	8	9	0	2	3	1	404	399	27

C. SOUTH CONTROL AREA

Year and Month of Birth	Male Deaths					Female Deaths					Live Born		Still Born
	<6 Days	7–29	30–89	90–364	1–18 Yrs.	<6 Days	7–29	30–89	90–364	1–18 Yrs.	Male	Female	
1944,1	5	2	8	5	2	10	0	7	5	3	461	408	34
2	10	2	5	6	2	8	2	2	2	5	472	441	27
3	9	5	12	9	7	4	1	3	6	5	530	479	30
4	7	3	3	7	4	5	2	3	5	3	468	458	28
5	5	5	9	14	7	5	2	3	17	1	496	493	39
6	8	4	2	7	6	4	1	2	8	7	469	463	31
7	5	1	8	8	7	3	3	2	19	2	513	444	30
8	5	4	7	10	9	9	5	3	15	6	523	502	32
9	12	2	9	17	10	10	4	8	8	7	476	447	31
10	11	3	10	16	3	12	1	2	12	2	481	430	36
11	8	4	6	14	5	8	2	7	9	6	393	402	34
12	13	13	12	11	7	6	6	4	16	11	441	440	47
1945,1	12	6	7	20	8	7	7	4	11	9	484	466	34
2	11	7	10	19	9	13	4	7	17	6	474	429	29
3	15	7	8	17	9	4	5	9	20	8	555	583	35
4	9	6	9	23	6	3	1	12	13	4	532	474	41
5	7	1	8	26	10	6	3	7	8	6	511	524	36
6	12	6	9	11	4	7	4	4	14	6	464	452	38
7	4	5	10	10	8	8	3	7	5	5	534	466	33
8	8	4	7	14	6	5	4	6	4	10	560	499	34
9	9	7	6	9	6	3	4	2	10	8	523	477	40
10	7	3	7	9	2	12	3	8	2	4	541	530	46
11	10	2	9	5	6	12	4	8	3	8	516	502	45
12	10	8	6	2	7	8	9	1	3	9	518	496	46
1946,1	9	4	4	4	8	3	3	4	3	7	553	480	53
2	11	9	4	7	10	11	3	2	2	4	562	494	43
3	17	7	5	13	7	4	0	3	5	6	719	593	47
4	14	1	3	8	12	9	3	1	2	6	649	561	50
5	15	6	4	8	17	9	1	5	4	6	681	633	53
6	12	4	4	6	9	4	4	2	2	10	620	550	41
7	5	2	3	6	9	5	0	2	8	9	550	585	35
8	7	3	2	4	7	7	2	1	2	6	550	506	40
9	9	0	2	6	11	5	1	2	4	2	545	498	34
10	14	3	11	8	6	3	2	0	3	1	559	503	45
11	6	4	2	5	6	10	0	4	0	6	497	445	41
12	8	1	6	8	3	3	1	2	4	7	529	532	46

Table 2. Food rations by trimester of gestation (nutrient constituents of the official food ration in the first (1), second (2), and third (3) trimester of pregnancy from January 1944 to December 1946: A. famine area, B. North control area, and C. South control area)

A. FAMINE AREA

Year and Month of Birth	Protein 1	Fat 1	Calories 1	Carbohy-drate 1	Protein 2	Fat 2	Calories 2	Carbohy-drate 2	Protein 3	Fat 3	Calories 3	Carbohy-drate 3
1944,1	49	21	1697	307	48	27	1717	307	46	28	1743	312
2	49	21	1670	307	48	27	1727	309	45	28	1747	308
3	48	27	1713	306	47	27	1713	308	44	27	1717	303
4	48	27	1717	307	46	28	1743	312	44	25	1633	292
5	48	27	1727	309	45	28	1747	308	44	26	1567	287
6	47	27	1713	308	44	27	1717	303	44	29	1563	285
7	46	28	1743	312	44	25	1633	292	44	32	1578	287
8	45	28	1747	308	44	26	1567	287	42	32	1512	275
9	44	27	1717	303	44	29	1563	285	41	32	1462	265
10	44	25	1633	292	44	32	1578	287	40	28	1405	256
11	44	26	1567	287	42	32	1512	275	40	25	1414	253
12	44	29	1563	285	41	32	1462	265	36	21	1277	227
1945,1	44	32	1578	287	40	28	1405	256	28	18	1011	175
2	42	32	1512	275	40	25	1414	253	21	15	740	127
3	41	32	1462	265	36	21	1277	227	16	12	590	105
4	40	28	1405	256	28	18	1011	175	16	10	618	111
5	40	25	1414	253	21	15	740	127	14	12	670	119
6	36	21	1277	227	16	12	590	105	23	21	868	144
7	28	18	1011	175	16	10	618	111	41	40	1361	212
8	21	15	740	127	14	12	670	119	55	54	1757	268
9	6	12	590	105	23	21	868	144	61	58	2045	313
10	6	10	618	111	41	40	1361	212	58	53	1995	310
11	14	12	670	119	55	54	1757	268	61	50	2083	333
12	23	21	868	144	61	58	2045	313	61	49	2127	345
1946,1	41	40	1361	212	58	53	1995	310	62	49	2171	358
2	55	54	1757	268	61	50	2083	333	73	65	2514	394
3	61	58	2045	313	61	49	2127	345	83	80	2857	429
4	58	53	1995	310	62	49	2171	358	94	96	3200	465
5	61	50	2083	333	73	65	2514	394	94	96	3200	465
6	61	49	2127	345	83	80	2857	429	94	96	3200	465
7	62	49	2171	358	94	96	3200	465	94	96	3200	465
8	73	65	2514	394	94	96	3200	465	94	96	3200	465
9	83	80	2857	429	94	96	3200	465	94	96	3200	465
10	94	96	3200	465	94	96	3200	465	94	96	3200	465
11	94	96	3200	465	94	96	3200	465	94	96	3200	465
12	94	96	3200	465	94	96	3200	465	94	96	3200	465

B. NORTH CONTROL AREA

Year and Month of Birth	Protein 1	Fat 1	Calories 1	Carbohydrate 1	Protein 2	Fat 2	Calories 2	Carbohydrate 2	Protein 3	Fat 3	Calories 3	Carbohydrate 3
1944,1	49	21	1697	307	48	27	1717	307	46	28	1743	312
2	49	21	1670	307	48	27	1727	309	45	28	1747	308
3	48	27	1713	306	47	27	1713	308	44	27	1717	303
4	48	27	1717	307	46	28	1743	312	44	25	1633	292
5	48	27	1727	309	45	28	1747	308	44	26	1567	287
6	47	27	1713	308	44	27	1717	303	44	29	1563	285
7	46	28	1743	312	44	25	1633	292	44	32	1578	287
8	45	28	1747	308	44	26	1567	287	42	32	1512	275
9	44	27	1717	303	44	29	1563	285	41	32	1462	265
10	44	25	1633	292	44	32	1578	287	41	29	1440	261
11	44	26	1567	287	42	32	1512	275	42	26	1450	259
12	44	29	1563	285	41	32	1462	265	41	23	1430	256
1945,1	44	32	1578	287	41	29	1440	261	39	23	1380	244
2	42	32	1512	275	42	26	1450	259	38	23	1345	237
3	41	32	1462	265	41	23	1430	256	37	22	1311	230
4	41	29	1440	261	39	23	1380	244	36	22	1276	223
5	42	26	1450	259	38	23	1345	237	43	26	1392	237
6	41	23	1430	256	37	22	1311	230	49	30	1507	250
7	39	23	1380	244	36	22	1276	223	56	34	1623	264
8	38	23	1345	237	43	26	1392	237	58	39	1755	283
9	37	22	1311	230	49	30	1507	250	60	44	1894	301
10	36	22	1276	223	56	34	1623	264	61	50	2033	320
11	43	26	1392	237	58	39	1755	283	61	50	2083	333
12	49	30	1507	250	60	44	1894	301	61	49	2127	345
1946,1	56	34	1623	264	61	50	2033	320	62	49	2171	358
2	58	39	1755	283	61	50	2083	333	73	65	2514	394
3	60	44	1894	301	61	49	2127	345	83	80	2857	429
4	61	50	2033	320	62	49	2171	358	94	96	3200	465
5	61	50	2083	333	73	65	2514	394	94	96	3200	465
6	61	49	2127	345	83	80	2857	429	94	96	3200	465
7	62	49	2171	358	94	96	3200	465	94	96	3200	465
8	73	65	2514	394	94	96	3200	465	94	96	3200	465
9	83	80	2857	429	94	96	3200	465	94	96	3200	465
10	94	96	3200	465	94	96	3200	465	94	96	3200	465
11	94	96	3200	465	94	96	3200	465	94	96	3200	465
12	94	96	3200	465	94	96	3200	465	94	96	3200	465

APPENDIX 243

C. SOUTH CONTROL AREA

Year and Month of Birth	Protein 1	Fat 1	Calories 1	Carbohydrate 1	Protein 2	Fat 2	Calories 2	Carbohydrate 2	Protein 3	Fat 3	Calories 3	Carbohydrate 3
1944, 1	49	21	1697	307	48	27	1717	307	46	28	1743	312
2	49	21	1670	307	48	27	1727	309	45	28	1747	308
3	48	27	1713	306	47	27	1713	308	44	27	1717	303
4	48	27	1717	307	46	28	1743	312	44	25	1633	292
5	48	27	1727	309	45	28	1747	308	44	26	1567	287
6	47	27	1713	308	44	27	1717	303	44	29	1563	285
7	46	28	1743	312	44	25	1633	292	44	32	1578	287
8	45	28	1747	308	44	26	1567	287	42	32	1512	275
9	44	27	1717	303	44	29	1563	285	41	32	1462	265
10	44	25	1633	292	44	32	1578	287	41	29	1440	261
11	44	26	1567	287	42	32	1512	275	42	25	1403	251
12	44	29	1563	285	41	32	1462	265	42	20	1337	240
1945, 1	44	32	1578	287	41	29	1440	261	41	19	1241	220
2	42	32	1512	275	42	25	1403	251	44	21	1375	245
3	41	32	1462	265	42	20	1337	240	47	23	1508	269
4	41	29	1440	261	41	19	1241	220	50	25	1642	294
5	42	25	1403	251	44	21	1375	245	50	28	1692	300
6	42	20	1337	240	47	23	1508	269	51	30	1743	306
7	41	19	1241	220	50	25	1642	294	51	33	1793	312
8	44	21	1375	245	50	28	1692	300	53	38	1864	317
9	47	23	1508	269	51	30	1743	306	56	43	1946	320
10	50	25	1642	294	51	33	1793	312	59	49	2028	323
11	50	28	1692	300	53	38	1864	317	61	50	2083	333
12	51	30	1743	306	56	43	1946	320	61	49	2127	345
1946, 1	51	33	1793	312	59	49	2028	323	62	49	2171	358
2	53	38	1864	317	61	50	2083	333	73	65	2514	394
3	56	43	1946	320	61	49	2127	345	83	80	2857	429
4	59	49	2028	323	62	49	2171	358	94	96	3200	465
5	61	50	2083	333	73	65	2514	394	94	96	3200	465
6	61	49	2127	345	83	80	2857	429	94	96	3200	465
7	62	49	2171	358	94	96	3200	465	94	96	3200	465
8	73	65	2514	394	94	96	3200	465	94	96	3200	465
9	83	80	2857	429	94	96	3200	465	94	96	3200	465
10	94	96	3200	465	94	96	3200	465	94	96	3200	465
11	94	96	3200	465	94	96	3200	465	94	96	3200	465
12	94	96	3200	465	94	96	3200	465	94	96	3200	465

Table 3. Indices of the reproductive process (mean, standard deviation and number of cases for indices of the reproductive process from August 1944 to March 1946: A. famine area, B. North control area, C. South control area, and D. Rotterdam)

A. FAMINE AREA

Year and Month of Birth	Birth Weight			Placental Weight			Duration of Gestation			Length at Birth			Head Circumference			Maternal Weight		
	Mean	SD	N	Mean	SD	N	Mean	SD	N	Mean	SD	N	Mean	SD	N	Mean	SD	N
1944,8	3290	667.4	99	576.2	130.9	41	39.4	2.22	99	50.0	3.61	98	34.4	2.3	31	58.1	5.89	37
9	3308	620.3	120	620.8	146.6	36	39.5	2.00	86	50.1	3.17	116	35.5	1.7	34	60.2	5.77	32
10	3408	590.6	124	607.7	135.5	39	39.5	1.61	86	50.6	2.69	119	35.9	1.6	34	58.8	7.99	33
11	3418	516.9	110	551.7	112.2	29	39.5	2.39	83	50.3	5.32	107	34.9	1.7	27	59.7	5.67	23
12	3157	629.0	110	536.7	117.4	30	39.4	2.05	77	49.5	2.97	108	35.1	1.6	26	56.4	5.59	31
1945,1	3095	562.2	112	546.7	114.5	34	39.3	2.16	83	49.5	2.68	110	34.6	1.9	33	56.5	8.01	32
2	2999	687.6	106	496.7	100.8	30	38.9	2.95	78	48.8	4.34	105	34.2	2.0	30	55.8	5.17	34
3	3027	539.3	102	532.4	94.5	34	39.2	1.75	78	49.0	3.59	97	34.0	1.8	32	56.1	7.85	35
4	3008	556.7	116	502.9	79.8	37	39.4	2.12	96	48.9	4.39	114	34.8	1.6	30	57.2	7.50	37
5	3036	511.9	106	525.8	125.7	31	39.5	2.09	84	49.3	2.71	95	35.1	1.8	28	55.9	7.06	34
6	3026	715.5	89	553.1	104.8	34	39.0	3.77	72	49.1	4.14	79	34.3	1.9	31	59.3	5.78	35
7	3289	546.0	118	569.8	114.5	43	39.7	1.45	91	49.8	3.19	106	34.9	1.7	40	60.5	6.51	41
8	3388	553.1	99	562.2	156.2	29	39.7	1.64	73	50.2	2.66	94	35.7	1.6	25	59.6	6.88	30
9	3467	584.2	75	610.9	111.8	23	39.3	3.66	58	50.7	2.60	75	35.9	1.1	17	63.2	9.69	23
10	3421	618.8	125	599.8	126.9	43	39.6	1.89	105	50.0	5.10	123	34.9	1.8	35	61.3	6.72	40
11	3284	835.0	106	567.6	117.9	37	38.9	3.45	93	49.2	5.36	96	35.2	2.2	26	62.2	7.38	38
12	3317	815.5	119	616.2	134.1	34	38.8	4.29	104	49.9	4.39	116	35.5	1.6	28	61.2	6.36	26
1946,1	3219	791.1	175	608.3	144.9	60	38.9	3.33	153	49.2	4.26	171	35.4	1.7	54	62.7	8.20	61
2	3264	699.2	160	566.8	146.6	56	39.4	2.64	133	49.6	3.90	127	35.2	2.3	41	61.2	7.07	58
3	3339	637.4	237	610.7	144.5	75	39.9	1.40	203	49.7	5.48	104	35.1	2.3	41	63.2	6.75	68

B. NORTH CONTROL AREA

Year and Month of Birth	Birth Weight			Placental Weight			Duration of Gestation			Length at Birth			Head Circumference		
	Mean	SD	N	Mean	SD	N	Mean	SD	N	Mean	SD	N	Mean	SD	N
1944,8	3542	756.1	45	696.2	194.3	45	39.9	1.11	37	50.3	3.32	45	33.6	1.6	44
9	3435	617.0	64	665.0	145.1	64	39.3	1.98	58	49.6	3.56	67	33.9	1.2	61
10	3186	703.1	51	637.6	169.8	49	39.3	2.77	41	48.9	3.65	51	33.1	1.3	47
11	3384	752.6	49	605.8	176.1	48	39.7	1.65	35	49.2	4.70	48	33.5	1.1	44
12	3349	627.4	58	643.9	192.2	57	39.5	2.31	46	49.4	2.48	59	33.4	1.2	56
1945,1	3273	662.9	65	611.8	108.3	59	39.7	1.36	60	48.9	4.16	66	33.1	0.9	62
2	3223	554.7	73	585.8	124.2	69	39.7	1.62	63	49.6	1.98	73	33.1	1.3	71
3	3264	732.7	70	598.3	152.3	69	39.6	2.66	55	49.4	2.60	68	33.3	0.9	61
4	3154	452.8	85	565.1	145.2	70	39.4	2.66	61	49.2	2.78	71	33.2	1.0	68
5	3096	609.8	53	532.8	89.9	50	39.4	1.63	41	48.8	3.19	53	33.6	1.2	49
6	3244	485.2	69	573.4	119.2	64	39.4	1.45	53	49.8	2.12	68	33.2	1.3	64
7	3470	582.2	52	646.0	139.3	52	40.0	1.96	38	50.5	2.18	51	34.6	1.8	46
8	3268	722.6	65	654.8	200.7	62	39.3	2.68	47	48.9	4.26	64	34.3	1.5	62
9	3343	740.7	64	678.3	173.9	63	39.2	2.40	50	49.4	3.70	64	34.5	1.6	57
10	3298	799.3	63	700.4	189.5	60	39.2	2.79	52	48.9	4.13	64	33.8	1.7	59
11	3389	901.3	63	665.6	181.3	60	39.0	3.23	49	47.7	4.59	62	34.7	2.2	54
12	3487	637.2	56	715.5	152.2	54	39.0	4.64	46	47.9	3.39	56	34.3	1.3	54
1946,1	3312	780.9	69	652.4	164.0	66	39.1	2.36	56	49.9	4.09	68	34.2	1.9	67
2	3367	821.0	85	695.5	194.7	84	39.6	3.05	57	49.9	4.58	84	34.0	2.0	68
3	3353	640.4	91	680.3	205.9	91	39.5	2.14	76	49.4	2.95	90	33.8	1.6	85

C. SOUTH CONTROL AREA

Year and Month of Birth	Birth Weight			Placental Weight			Duration of Gestation			Length at Birth			Head Circumference		
	Mean	SD	N	Mean	SD	N	Mean	SD	N	Mean	SD	N	Mean	SD	N
1944, 8	3353	629.3	42	55.0	125.4	40	39.9	1.54	42	49.8	2.81	42	35.4	1.5	40
9	3322	616.1	37	540.3	130.4	36	38.8	3.23	37	49.8	2.38	36	35.5	1.7	34
10	3401	406.4	54	567.8	119.7	53	39.7	1.17	53	50.0	1.90	54	35.6	1.7	52
11	3214	597.6	48	498.3	124.3	48	39.8	1.98	48	49.2	3.37	48	35.1	1.7	46
12	3257	622.5	38	608.1	432.8	36	39.3	2.93	38	49.6	3.56	36	35.1	1.6	36
1945, 1	3462	524.9	36	546.2	139.9	34	38.8	3.24	34	49.2	3.31	36	35.1	1.7	35
2	3351	575.9	45	600.0	195.4	45	39.2	1.53	44	50.2	2.53	45	35.3	1.8	42
3	3315	482.1	63	523.2	135.4	63	39.7	2.64	61	49.7	2.43	62	35.0	2.8	61
4	3218	647.4	57	525.9	126.1	56	39.5	3.60	53	49.3	3.49	54	34.8	1.8	50
5	3355	461.8	59	567.9	129.1	59	39.8	2.31	57	49.3	2.07	57	35.1	1.8	58
6	3275	439.7	52	594.8	128.1	51	39.9	1.42	48	49.8	2.06	52	34.7	1.5	52
7	3250	395.5	54	597.9	127.8	52	40.2	2.35	54	49.5	1.69	54	34.5	1.8	53
8	3317	536.0	94	560.3	140.0	87	39.6	2.64	92	49.7	2.35	92	34.7	1.9	89
9	3536	483.0	60	635.4	129.4	60	39.8	2.22	56	50.0	3.15	59	35.7	1.6	44
10	3277	576.8	78	620.1	136.4	76	39.6	2.18	75	49.5	3.05	77	34.6	1.6	32
11	3308	606.1	70	614.6	135.1	70	39.6	3.34	66	49.4	2.81	69	36.4	2.3	14
12	3421	499.0	70	597.2	121.6	50	39.3	3.07	50	49.3	2.75	56	34.5	0.6	4
1946, 1	3439	570.5	64	594.8	186.7	61	39.3	2.41	60	50.2	2.62	64	36.4	1.3	5
2	3436	582.2	58	572.1	139.8	53	39.1	2.76	51	49.8	2.38	56	34.0	0.0	1
3	3364	664.4	69	542.7	134.7	67	39.1	2.25	53	49.2	4.34	69	35.0	0.0	1

APPENDIX

D. ROTTERDAM*

Year and Month of Birth	Birth Weight			Duration of Gestation			Length		
	Mean	Std. Dev.	N	Mean	Std. Dev.	N	Mean	Std. Dev.	N
1944,8	3225.1	743.8	41	39.0	3.2	41	49.6	4.7	41
,9	3377.6	721.3	37	39.6	2.3	36	50.5	3.2	37
,10	3411.3	507.2	40	39.8	1.0	39	50.4	2.1	39
,11	3358.0	601.6	30	39.2	3.5	31	50.0	4.0	30
,12	3092.4	566.0	33	39.3	1.8	32	49.2	2.3	32
1945,1	3099.2	630.9	37	39.2	2.2	36	48.7	3.0	37
,2	2931.4	705.9	35	38.7	3.6	35	47.9	5.1	34
,3	3093.2	463.6	37	39.7	1.0	35	49.3	2.4	36
,4	3065.0	434.8	40	39.8	1.2	39	49.8	2.2	39
,5	3090.0	408.7	33	39.6	2.1	32	50.1	2.0	33
,6	3116.7	647.3	36	39.4	2.7	35	49.6	4.3	34
,7	3335.2	622.2	44	39.8	1.4	43	50.3	3.5	44
,8	3356.3	695.6	30	39.5	2.5	30	49.9	3.3	29
,9	3320.8	642.9	24	38.4	5.5	25	49.1	3.6	24
,10	3296.2	603.6	45	39.7	1.1	43	49.5	3.6	44
,11	3281.5	795.6	39	38.6	3.8	39	48.8	4.4	39
,12	3222.3	781.1	35	38.1	5.7	35	49.4	3.5	34
1946,1	3331.7	754.7	63	39.1	3.2	60	49.3	3.7	63
,2	3146.3	820.9	60	39.2	3.5	58	48.8	4.6	60
,3	3374.2	579.1	76	40.0	2.2	75	49.3	5.5	73

*The Rotterdam data for Maternal weight, Placental weight and Head Circumference are the same as shown in Table 3 A. They were omitted here to avoid repetition.

Table 4. 19-year-old men at induction (numbers of men at induction in monthly birth cohorts from January 1944 to December 1946 by father's occupational class in famine area and North and South control areas)

Year and Month of Birth	Manual			Non-manual			Farm			Others and Unknown			All		
	Famine	North	South	Famine	North	South	Famine	North	South	Famine	North	South	Famine	North	South
1944,1	853	198	187	804	130	106	32	15	11	158	19	28	1847	362	332
2	754	160	186	707	108	113	36	12	7	180	18	21	1677	298	327
3	827	172	208	756	149	147	35	11	10	157	12	30	1775	344	395
4	821	180	201	726	128	107	34	21	8	113	16	28	1694	345	344
5	744	185	188	793	151	151	29	15	9	152	22	28	1718	373	376
6	786	145	182	702	138	129	32	7	9	137	18	24	1657	308	344
7	786	182	189	822	154	125	28	18	20	157	20	28	1793	374	362
8	821	173	208	777	151	143	28	9	9	141	24	29	1767	357	389
9	799	174	183	787	160	136	26	12	5	134	13	18	1746	359	342
10	817	156	196	757	132	130	33	13	7	129	23	26	1736	324	359
11	778	145	180	700	96	110	26	4	4	128	18	18	1632	263	312
12	770	158	178	682	120	130	25	12	10	118	13	22	1595	303	340
1945,1	810	150	203	759	103	130	22	6	11	133	17	19	1724	276	363
2	694	161	200	749	149	133	26	13	19	126	22	33	1595	345	385
3	772	168	213	753	172	171	30	14	14	124	24	20	1679	378	418
4	758	192	232	858	142	146	27	15	14	141	25	27	1784	374	419
5	788	164	208	764	176	158	18	12	16	138	25	30	1708	377	412
6	652	143	196	650	150	131	24	10	14	105	23	24	1431	326	365
7	640	172	231	659	153	145	27	10	11	121	22	31	1447	357	418
8	535	157	230	564	120	175	25	15	5	99	12	39	1223	304	449
9	442	159	237	454	131	134	18	19	3	86	21	17	1000	330	391
10	304	148	217	396	121	148	18	14	10	85	21	27	803	304	402
11	294	108	228	380	119	128	17	17	4	56	25	38	747	269	398
12	319	162	213	484	143	151	21	16	11	69	22	29	893	343	404
1946,1	482	201	204	596	163	169	24	28	11	80	20	27	1182	412	411
2	721	214	214	901	193	162	29	20	14	159	18	27	1810	445	417
3	1355	266	258	1451	254	215	35	27	14	254	40	47	3095	587	534
4	1546	240	251	1438	263	182	43	16	11	257	35	42	3284	554	486
5	1601	284	242	1573	259	197	40	19	12	281	24	48	3495	586	499
6	1420	233	219	1451	204	200	48	27	14	248	34	36	3167	498	469
7	1377	241	209	1443	209	178	40	22	9	274	37	29	3134	509	425
8	1257	215	228	1354	233	150	41	22	7	263	39	34	2915	509	419
9	1170	225	203	1295	189	158	43	23	9	229	45	30	2737	482	400
10	1092	197	213	1177	206	172	35	18	6	222	31	30	2526	452	421
11	1034	188	203	1114	155	158	40	19	15	216	30	23	2404	392	399
12	1026	181	189	1227	146	166	32	20	8	226	38	32	2511	385	395

APPENDIX

Table 5. Raven Progressive Matrices (mean Raven scores for monthly birth cohorts from January 1944 to December, 1946 by occupational class of father and area: A. manual. B. non-manual, and C. all classes)

A. MANUAL

Year and Month of Birth	Famine Area		North		South	
	Mean	S.D.	Mean	S.D.	Mean	S.D.
1944,1	2.920	1.381	2.838	1.357	2.909	1.416
2	2.809	1.377	3.025	1.341	2.891	1.418
3	2.832	1.319	2.988	1.427	3.180	1.397
4	2.759	1.306	3.096	1.487	2.903	1.487
5	2.725	1.350	2.816	1.293	2.806	1.394
6	2.808	1.355	2.908	1.424	2.819	1.406
7	2.818	1.386	2.796	1.361	2.767	1.305
8	2.756	1.333	2.630	1.317	2.798	1.310
9	2.641	1.336	2.772	1.260	2.858	1.457
10	2.788	1.377	2.686	1.348	3.009	1.408
11	2.664	1.306	2.641	1.268	2.870	1.412
12	2.720	1.323	2.880	1.284	3.124	1.380
1945,1	2.681	1.351	2.940	1.382	2.921	1.422
2	2.730	1.352	2.881	1.393	2.818	1.362
3	2.668	1.352	2.798	1.408	2.977	1.369
4	2.732	1.405	3.057	1.473	2.778	1.320
5	2.707	1.345	2.890	1.329	2.851	1.396
6	2.616	1.313	3.112	1.410	2.774	1.299
7	2.728	1.323	2.952	1.330	2.898	1.377
8	2.654	1.291	2.795	1.318	2.807	1.346
9	2.682	1.346	2.949	1.436	2.621	1.313
10	2.676	1.261	2.858	1.375	2.848	1.392
11	2.599	1.278	3.019	1.434	2.891	1.405
12	2.603	1.325	2.907	1.355	2.859	1.392
1946,1	2.632	1.274	2.975	1.387	2.734	1.433
2	2.670	1.380	2.873	1.333	2.786	1.456
3	2.683	1.337	2.903	1.330	2.767	1.362
4	2.672	1.355	2.935	1.326	2.653	1.339
5	2.735	1.388	2.917	1.405	2.793	1.338
6	2.755	1.353	2.734	1.376	2.801	1.522
7	2.777	1.379	2.728	1.375	2.635	1.403
8	2.742	1.397	2.904	1.376	2.662	1.313
9	2.791	1.391	2.991	1.521	2.796	1.491
10	2.855	1.349	3.037	1.434	2.836	1.391
11	2.827	1.399	3.119	1.494	2.825	1.373
12	2.889	1.457	3.081	1.457	2.848	1.462

B. NON-MANUAL

Year and Month of Birth	Famine Area		North		South	
	Mean	S.D.	Mean	S.D.	Mean	S.D.
1944,1	2.134	1.092	2.488	1.257	2.307	1.234
2	2.243	1.193	2.306	1.089	2.288	1.150
3	2.223	1.196	2.295	1.276	2.270	1.278
4	2.204	1.172	2.165	1.125	2.053	1.128
5	2.199	1.171	2.351	1.229	2.273	1.262
6	2.175	1.163	2.212	1.134	2.217	1.105
7	2.232	1.182	2.138	1.004	2.191	1.106
8	2.146	1.132	2.193	1.054	2.104	1.219
9	2.133	1.176	2.181	1.063	2.172	1.230
10	2.193	1.169	2.136	0.947	2.205	1.142
11	2.199	1.176	2.042	1.071	2.101	0.975
12	2.140	1.157	2.242	1.167	2.353	1.342
1945,1	2.185	1.154	2.175	1.150	2.305	1.374
2	2.170	1.184	2.347	1.259	2.118	1.156
3	2.164	1.135	2.193	1.134	2.213	1.269
4	2.165	1.163	2.134	1.186	1.939	0.910
5	2.094	1.041	2.188	1.108	2.254	1.240
6	2.224	1.243	2.140	1.111	2.048	1.082
7	2.068	1.106	2.205	1.115	2.095	1.085
8	2.194	1.210	2.200	1.066	2.038	1.014
9	2.160	1.127	2.400	1.273	2.040	1.150
10	2.082	1.110	2.225	1.111	2.333	1.224
11	2.091	1.131	2.395	1.195	2.006	1.141
12	2.057	1.053	2.224	1.258	2.069	1.037
1946,1	2.210	1.181	2.218	1.209	2.271	1.330
2	2.211	1.168	2.237	1.157	2.157	1.143
3	2.153	1.152	2.145	1.261	2.129	1.208
4	2.249	1.222	2.241	1.247	1.950	1.157
5	2.110	1.129	2.222	1.176	2.054	1.048
6	2.160	1.177	2.113	1.132	2.030	1.125
7	2.175	1.162	2.268	1.251	2.103	1.134
8	2.184	1.210	2.374	1.315	1.958	1.124
9	2.228	1.251	2.162	1.102	2.109	1.191
10	2.241	1.212	2.319	1.264	2.081	1.075
11	2.347	1.262	2.262	1.229	2.109	1.111
12	2.227	1.217	2.419	1.256	2.213	1.230

C. ALL CLASSES

Year and Month of Birth	Famine Area		North		South	
	Mean	S.D.	Mean	S.D.	Mean	S.D.
1944,1	2.565	1.309	2.780	1.383	2.697	1.366
2	2.574	1.338	2.768	1.307	2.710	1.360
3	2.570	1.303	2.698	1.404	2.768	1.387
4	2.516	1.280	2.746	1.421	2.624	1.433
5	2.482	1.305	2.633	1.287	2.589	1.365
6	2.532	1.304	2.597	1.356	2.574	1.334
7	2.538	1.325	2.546	1.259	2.588	1.252
8	2.478	1.278	2.453	1.218	2.499	1.311
9	2.415	1.287	2.514	1.222	2.527	1.396
10	2.526	1.334	2.489	1.231	2.703	1.359
11	2.471	1.275	2.460	1.276	2.551	1.323
12	2.467	1.290	2.605	1.257	2.805	1.412
1945,1	2.453	1.296	2.657	1.361	2.669	1.407
2	2.459	1.307	2.672	1.370	2.629	1.379
3	2.441	1.280	2.550	1.327	2.665	1.357
4	2.450	1.319	2.637	1.426	2.481	1.262
5	2.427	1.259	2.593	1.308	2.609	1.367
6	2.437	1.303	2.648	1.346	2.584	1.270
7	2.437	1.279	2.625	1.301	2.636	1.317
8	2.452	1.292	2.571	1.264	2.463	1.297
9	2.442	1.276	2.702	1.384	2.464	1.309
10	2.366	1.222	2.580	1.303	2.662	1.384
11	2.354	1.239	2.789	1.379	2.601	1.385
12	2.307	1.209	2.652	1.408	2.558	1.316
1946,1	2.425	1.252	2.701	1.372	2.531	1.400
2	2.433	1.292	2.659	1.330	2.505	1.334
3	2.420	1.281	2.594	1.375	2.558	1.352
4	2.490	1.328	2.623	1.349	2.359	1.296
5	2.445	1.310	2.609	1.354	2.502	1.270
6	2.478	1.314	2.493	1.347	2.478	1.383
7	2.476	1.309	2.526	1.335	2.421	1.326
8	2.469	1.341	2.654	1.398	2.415	1.291
9	2.518	1.353	2.640	1.412	2.484	1.425
10	2.555	1.327	2.694	1.403	2.403	1.247
11	2.591	1.355	2.742	1.441	2.518	1.335
12	2.561	1.384	2.842	1.439	2.468	1.369

Table 6. Global psychometric score (mean global psychometric scores for monthly birth cohorts from January 1944 to December 1946 by area)

Year and Month of Birth	Famine Area		North		South	
	Mean	S.D.	Mean	S.D.	Mean	S.D.
1944,1	2.744	1.378	2.851	1.350	2.931	1.434
2	2.765	1.364	2.956	1.366	2.961	1.450
3	2.784	1.352	2.822	1.371	3.011	1.449
4	2.730	1.312	2.860	1.352	2.891	1.431
5	2.682	1.330	2.714	1.310	2.843	1.447
6	2.755	1.318	2.738	1.336	2.851	1.427
7	2.737	1.346	2.738	1.317	2.858	1.349
8	2.668	1.328	2.649	1.283	2.737	1.421
9	2.687	1.344	2.732	1.275	2.832	1.398
10	2.759	1.364	2.741	1.274	2.971	1.349
11	2.745	1.330	2.700	1.305	2.827	1.446
12	2.702	1.344	2.780	1.353	2.938	1.435
1945,1	2.683	1.355	2.914	1.381	2.949	1.489
2	2.687	1.368	2.860	1.328	2.957	1.451
3	2.694	1.324	2.677	1.256	2.944	1.393
4	2.670	1.367	2.710	1.388	2.881	1.384
5	2.689	1.344	2.773	1.349	2.938	1.417
6	2.723	1.363	2.773	1.412	2.895	1.365
7	2.766	1.371	2.869	1.403	3.032	1.385
8	2.756	1.377	2.782	1.354	2.819	1.379
9	2.697	1.310	2.820	1.374	2.793	1.392
10	2.614	1.263	2.725	1.345	2.925	1.399
11	2.601	1.305	2.882	1.408	2.895	1.436
12	2.524	1.278	2.804	1.428	2.942	1.417
1946,1	2.651	1.303	2.813	1.290	2.850	1.439
2	2.616	1.311	2.766	1.326	2.893	1.349
3	2.704	1.329	2.694	1.335	2.869	1.433
4	2.793	1.362	2.742	1.340	2.779	1.436
5	2.738	1.352	2.796	1.347	2.793	1.349
6	2.736	1.339	2.713	1.408	2.815	1.426
7	2.792	1.369	2.700	1.308	2.683	1.318
8	2.719	1.349	2.832	1.335	2.803	1.379
9	2.793	1.379	2.801	1.366	2.803	1.465
10	2.842	1.341	2.931	1.358	2.778	1.347
11	2.882	1.386	2.977	1.375	2.897	1.346
12	2.813	1.359	3.065	1.450	2.766	1.400

APPENDIX

Table 7. Mental retardation (numbers of cases of mental retardation for monthly birth cohorts from January 1944 to December 1946 by I. C. D. category* and area)

Year and Month of Birth	FAMINE					NORTH			SOUTH		
	Severe			Mild		Severe	Mild		Severe	Mild	
	325.0	325.1	324.4.5	325.2	325.3		325.2	325.3		325.2	325.3
1944,1	2	3	0	71	20	1	20	0	4	18	0
2	0	5	1	68	16	0	16	0	0	19	0
3	5	3	1	52	21	2	14	0	3	23	0
4	1	0	1	46	19	0	23	1	2	21	0
5	1	3	1	59	13	1	15	0	1	27	0
6	2	2	1	55	15	1	16	0	2	16	0
7	0	6	1	68	25	0	12	2	2	19	0
8	2	2	0	59	17	0	10	1	2	19	0
9	1	1	1	48	14	0	13	1	1	20	0
10	1	4	0	58	10	1	12	1	0	18	0
11	1	5	0	44	10	0	12	0	1	16	0
12	0	3	0	53	16	0	10	0	1	25	0
1945,1	1	3	0	59	15	2	14	1	0	26	0
2	2	4	3	57	9	1	14	1	3	22	2
3	2	4	1	65	8	2	14	2	0	19	0
4	0	1	0	69	14	1	17	2	2	22	0
5	3	4	1	71	8	1	13	1	1	15	0
6	2	3	0	43	9	3	14	1	2	16	0
7	2	6	1	51	9	3	15	5	1	21	0
8	2	2	1	42	11	0	9	5	2	19	1
9	2	1	1	40	9	1	13	4	0	16	0
10	2	1	1	25	2	1	11	3	2	19	0
11	1	0	0	27	2	0	12	1	1	22	0
12	2	2	1	23	4	1	21	3	1	20	0
1946,1	0	3	0	32	5	1	16	5	4	28	0
2	4	3	1	69	8	1	12	1	4	25	0
3	6	2	1	113	17	4	30	2	4	34	1
4	2	5	1	126	21	3	18	2	2	30	0
5	5	6	2	129	26	2	19	3	0	21	0
6	4	3	2	122	21	0	23	2	2	22	0
7	4	4	6	118	25	0	20	7	2	20	1
8	4	10	5	119	28	1	19	5	1	23	0
9	3	4	1	106	22	0	26	4	3	28	0
10	3	5	6	95	23	3	12	5	2	20	0
11	4	6	3	106	16	3	19	6	1	18	0
12	1	6	0	110	28	1	27	6	2	25	0

*Severe Mental Retardation: 325.0, Idiocy; 325.1, Imbecility; 325.4, Mongolism. Mild Mental Retardation: 325.2, Moron; 325.3, Borderline Intelligence.

Table 8. Medical diagnosis (numbers of selected diagnoses coded at induction examinations for 9 birth cohorts by area)

Diagnosis (I. C. D. code)	Famine Area								
	A1	A2	B1	B2	C	D1	D2	E1	E2
Poliomyelitis (081)	15	12	4	5	6	4	7	15	23
Neoplasms (140–205, 210–229)	10	6	4	5	3	6	8	20	21
Asthma (241)	91	52	44	47	44	50	64	298	487
Obesity (287)	18	9	7	14	13	18	14	59	105
Neurosis (310–318)	86	43	37	40	19	25	46	140	220
Pathological Personality (320)	115	49	49	37	40	43	42	122	158
Immature Personality (321)	186	86	96	123	74	84	88	274	473
CNS (330–357)	77	34	56	33	30	28	27	112	165
Deaf (398)	97	42	43	50	26	36	39	119	172
Refraction error (380)	1653	807	718	714	451	542	499	1592	2783
Rheumatic Heart Disease (400–402, 410–416)	28	11	13	9	5	8	6	24	37
Other Heart Disease (420–422, 433, 434, 430–432, 440–443)	34	19	21	22	7	11	18	35	51
Hypertension (440–447)	56	28	25	20	14	19	9	38	69
Bronchitis (500–502)	35	11	10	6	7	11	9	33	56
Stomach and Duodenum (540–545)	35	20	18	11	12	13	12	61	75
Hernia (560–561)	13	8	12	14	10	9	3	17	22
Skin (701–706)	13	7	5	4	4	3	3	10	26
Joints (730–738)	191	80	94	107	66	81	89	262	395
Clubfoot (748)	214	125	95	104	53	81	78	259	443
Congenital CNS (751–753)	15	8	5	8	1	4	8	11	14
Cleft Palate (755)	4	1	4	3	0	1	3	1	6
Congenital Genito-urinary (757)	5	7	5	4	3	5	3	14	24
Congenital Bone and Joint (748)	19	7	15	8	10	7	10	35	47
Other Congenital (759)	175	56	66	70	46	51	44	172	262
Tuberculosis (001–008, 010–019)	172	71	62	46	35	52	40	124	184
Congenital Circulatory (754)	177	109	70	29	19	23	11	45	93

				North and South				
1	A2	B1	B2	C	D1	D2	E1	E2
7	4	2	2	5	1	5	11	7
8	3	1	4	6	1	0	6	10
40	18	19	27	17	35	45	83	179
6	2	2	3	5	5	13	15	36
22	8	14	19	15	22	41	63	86
50	17	23	27	21	18	27	42	67
47	21	23	27	13	23	36	67	99
48	17	9	12	11	14	24	32	48
40	23	10	18	12	19	20	38	51
28	286	212	272	185	283	353	506	716
11	3	4	3	5	5	3	5	15
27	9	9	8	8	5	10	23	32
28	22	22	14	8	26	23	22	37
5	2	3	3	2	9	10	11	21
12	3	10	9	6	11	12	19	19
6	2	4	4	3	5	2	2	6
3	1	2	1	0	0	0	3	6
77	45	30	46	19	36	48	95	144
93	43	26	34	19	40	64	171	217
8	1	3	2	1	0	4	7	7
4	0	0	0	1	1	1	3	7
2	0	0	1	0	1	3	3	1
11	8	6	4	4	7	13	12	21
47	32	22	17	18	29	40	65	86
60	21	15	21	14	28	16	27	35
29	18	6	10	4	10	13	8	22

Table 9. Stature (mean height in centimeters for monthly birth cohorts from January 1944 to December 1946 by occupational class of father and area: A. manual, B. non-manual)

A. MANUAL

Month of Birth	Famine Area		North		South	
	Mean	S.D.	Mean	S.D.	Mean	S.D.
1944,1	176.38	5.96	177.30	7.21	174.32	5.83
2	176.52	6.65	177.79	6.27	174.05	6.44
3	176.91	6.40	177.79	6.98	174.59	6.11
4	176.49	6.29	176.39	6.91	174.81	6.63
5	176.59	6.31	177.45	6.49	174.23	6.56
6	176.47	6.23	177.60	6.89	174.98	5.76
7	176.76	6.09	177.26	6.75	173.57	6.04
8	176.54	6.33	176.31	5.99	175.13	6.10
9	176.57	6.21	177.31	6.81	174.79	7.09
10	176.49	6.33	177.76	6.51	174.35	6.09
11	176.53	6.22	177.60	6.03	174.71	6.73
12	176.41	6.89	177.57	6.37	173.53	6.16
1945,1	177.23	6.27	176.88	6.21	174.44	5.59
2	176.95	6.59	178.35	6.65	174.08	6.42
3	176.57	5.89	178.97	6.29	174.57	6.23
4	176.41	6.48	178.07	6.83	175.43	6.25
5	176.86	6.13	176.73	6.51	174.99	7.02
6	176.31	5.99	176.93	5.93	175.01	6.68
7	176.64	6.37	177.45	6.30	174.25	5.47
8	176.80	6.33	177.37	6.81	175.10	6.26
9	176.51	6.63	176.97	6.87	174.84	6.10
10	176.92	6.93	176.81	6.93	174.06	5.69
11	177.09	6.71	177.95	6.17	174.32	6.31
12	177.48	6.73	177.38	5.89	174.00	5.93
1946,1	177.53	6.45	177.40	6.31	174.79	6.80
2	177.06	6.20	178.01	7.05	175.47	6.56
3	177.77	6.21	179.05	6.60	174.90	6.00
4	177.23	6.25	178.09	6.35	175.00	6.74
5	177.41	6.49	177.85	6.06	175.47	6.92
6	177.25	6.19	178.31	6.88	175.07	6.25
7	176.91	6.38	178.44	6.67	175.12	6.39
8	177.51	6.59	177.99	5.87	174.82	6.62
9	177.01	6.19	178.23	5.85	174.69	5.79
10	176.97	6.28	178.13	6.49	174.45	6.67
11	176.59	6.39	177.28	5.98	174.75	5.98
12	177.21	6.18	178.07	5.99	174.48	6.19

B. NON-MANUAL

Month of Birth	Famine Area		North		South	
	Mean	S.D.	Mean	S.D.	Mean	S.D.
1944,1	178.54	6.41	179.53	5.84	177.95	6.49
2	178.14	6.57	179.74	6.23	176.67	5.79
3	178.23	6.73	179.57	6.39	177.01	6.43
4	178.44	6.79	179.31	7.03	176.91	5.95
5	178.41	6.45	179.31	6.51	176.42	6.20
6	178.35	6.39	179.30	6.73	176.58	6.51
7	178.39	5.89	179.00	6.73	176.95	6.68
8	178.12	6.23	179.13	6.71	176.15	6.64
9	178.15	6.21	178.83	5.97	177.43	5.66
10	177.93	6.19	179.57	6.51	177.31	6.47
11	178.32	6.09	179.97	5.93	177.24	6.53
12	177.91	6.21	180.00	6.29	176.51	6.11
1945,1	178.55	6.39	180.30	6.29	175.63	5.50
2	178.61	6.33	179.25	6.47	176.86	5.92
3	178.57	6.11	179.12	5.81	176.08	6.19
4	177.95	6.26	179.47	5.98	176.34	6.14
5	178.23	6.15	178.32	6.29	177.40	6.10
6	178.11	6.31	178.43	6.45	175.91	5.92
7	178.93	6.35	179.85	6.45	176.39	6.12
8	177.98	6.45	179.57	6.01	176.18	6.24
9	178.47	6.33	180.31	6.08	176.78	5.48
10	178.17	5.96	180.91	6.63	176.44	6.04
11	178.97	6.65	178.75	6.66	176.66	6.06
12	178.25	6.41	179.71	6.01	177.35	6.37
1946,1	178.56	6.28	179.65	6.17	177.29	6.01
2	178.85	6.43	179.17	6.63	176.83	6.63
3	178.97	6.17	179.69	6.41	177.07	5.69
4	179.05	6.17	179.79	5.76	178.12	6.83
5	178.65	6.19	179.89	6.45	176.50	6.08
6	178.63	6.25	179.98	6.64	176.58	6.57
7	178.47	6.31	179.46	5.97	176.84	6.12
8	178.77	6.23	179.17	6.06	177.62	5.98
9	178.49	6.29	178.58	6.48	177.02	6.09
10	178.38	6.15	178.97	5.90	177.49	6.36
11	178.43	6.46	179.23	6.65	176.99	6.26
12	178.45	6.19	178.95	5.53	176.52	5.94

Table 10. Quételet's index (mean Quételet's index scores for monthly birth cohorts from January 1944 to December 1946 by area)

Year and Month of Birth	FAMINE		NORTH		SOUTH	
	Mean	S.D.	Mean	S.D.	Mean	S.D.
1944,1	215.1	26.7	214.6	24.1	219.5	26.6
2	215.0	24.8	210.5	20.4	217.5	27.2
3	214.5	26.9	213.7	21.1	217.6	26.1
4	214.5	24.2	214.7	28.9	216.9	29.8
5	215.6	27.2	211.3	21.2	216.6	26.6
6	214.1	22.1	212.4	23.1	215.8	25.6
7	215.8	26.2	213.7	26.0	213.7	24.6
8	215.7	25.0	213.8	22.5	216.5	28.3
9	215.6	23.5	210.5	22.0	214.2	24.1
10	214.4	23.1	210.9	21.5	217.2	29.4
11	213.9	25.6	210.0	19.3	215.7	29.2
12	214.8	23.1	209.6	19.7	214.2	22.7
1945,1	216.3	23.3	216.8	27.9	217.3	24.2
2	216.0	25.1	214.0	21.6	216.7	22.7
3	216.2	25.5	215.3	20.2	216.0	25.0
4	217.1	24.5	214.4	21.9	214.6	26.9
5	218.2	24.8	215.0	22.1	215.8	26.4
6	217.6	24.7	214.8	23.5	216.0	27.8
7	217.9	26.1	213.6	20.1	213.4	24.4
8	218.6	26.8	213.6	25.1	217.1	26.3
9	218.5	25.9	214.2	20.6	215.9	23.3
10	217.5	26.7	215.0	23.3	217.6	30.0
11	216.3	25.1	215.9	24.5	217.1	28.4
12	215.4	23.6	211.8	20.2	215.8	29.1
1946,1	218.8	26.6	216.1	22.9	218.2	28.3
2	219.1	25.0	217.2	22.5	216.4	23.3
3	219.2	27.2	217.4	23.1	217.5	23.2
4	218.3	26.7	217.4	23.5	215.2	22.9
5	217.6	25.3	217.5	22.3	215.6	25.5
6	217.4	26.4	218.5	25.4	213.0	25.4
7	218.1	26.2	216.0	26.5	213.5	25.3
8	217.8	25.5	216.4	23.4	215.3	26.9
9	217.9	25.9	217.3	24.9	212.7	24.4
10	218.4	25.5	217.1	24.7	216.1	31.4
11	216.6	24.5	216.6	23.1	212.5	24.0
12	216.4	24.6	215.0	26.0	211.6	22.5

References

Acheson, R. M., and D. Hewitt. 1954. Oxford Child Health Survey: Stature and skeletal maturation in the pre-school child. *Brit. J. Prev. Soc. Med.* 8:59-65.

Adlard, B. P., and J. L. Smart. 1971. Plasma 11-hydroxy corticosteroid concentrations in stressed adult rats after undernutrition in early life. *Biochem. J.* 125:12P-13P.

Adrianzen T. B., J. M. Baertl, and G. G. Graham. 1973. Growth of children from extremely poor families. *Am. J. Clin. Nutr.* 26:926-930.

Aherne, W. 1966. A weight relationship between the foetus and placenta. *Biol. Neonat.* 10:113-118.

Altman, J., K. Sudarshan, G. D. Das, N. McCormick, and D. Barnes. 1971. The influence of nutrition on neural and behavioral development III Development of some motor, particularly locomotor patterns during infancy. *Develop. Psychobiol.* 4:97-114.

Antonov, A. N. 1947. Children born during siege of Leningrad in 1942. *J. Pediat.* 30:250-259.

Armitage, P., J. D. Boyd, W. J. Hamilton, and B. C. Rowe. 1967. A statistical analysis of a series of birthweights and placental weights. *Hum. Biol.* 39:430-444.

Banning, C. 1946. Food shortage and public health, first half of 1945. *Ann. Am. Acad. Pol. Soc. Sc.* 245:93-100.

Barker, D. J. P. 1966. Low intelligence: Its relation to length of gestation and rate of foetal growth. *Brit. J. Prev. Soc. Med.* 20:58-66.

Barnes, R. H., A. U. Moore, I. M. Reid, and W. G. Pond. 1968. Effect of food deprivation on behavioral patterns. In N. S. Scrimshaw and J. E. Gordon, eds., *Malnutrition, Learning, and Behavior.* Cambridge, Mass., MIT Press, pp. 203-217.

REFERENCES

Barnes, R. H., A. U. Moore, and W. G. Pond. 1970. Behavioral abnormalities in young adult pigs caused by malnutrition in early life. *J. Nutr.* 100:149-155.

Barnes, R. H., I. M. Reid, W. G. Pond, and A. U. Moore. 1968. The use of experimental animals in studying behavioral abnormalities following recovery from early malnutrition in R. A. McCance and E. M. Widdowson, eds., *Calorie Deficiencies and Protein Deficiencies.* London, J. and A. Churchill, pp. 203-217.

Baum, J. D., and D. Searls. 1971. Head shape and size of pre-term low-birth-weight infants. *Develop. Med. Child. Neurol.* 13:576-581.

Bell, R. W. 1973. *Early Nutritional Deficits and Crowding Stress.* Paper presented at the Kittay Scientific Foundation First International Symposium: Nutrition and its contribution to mental functions. March 29-30, 1973.

Belmont, L. and F. A. Marolla. 1973. Birth order, family size, and intelligence. *Science* 182:1096-1101.

Benton, A. L. 1940. Mental development of prematurely born children: A critical review of the literature. *Amer. J. Orthopsychiat.* 10:719.

Bergner, L., and M. W. Susser. 1970. Low birthweight and prenatal nutrition: An interpretative review. *Pediatrics* 46:946-966.

Bernard, C. 1859. Sur une nouvelle fonction du placenta. *J. Physiol. Paris.* II:31-41.

Billewicz, W. Z., W. F. Kemsley, and A. M. Thomson. 1962. Indices of adiposity. *Brit. J. Prev. Soc. Med.* 16: 183-188.

Binet, A. 1911. Nouvelles recherchés sur la mesure du niveau intellectual chez les enfants d'école. *Ann. Psych.* 17:145-201.

Birch, H. G. 1972a. Issues of design and method in studying the effects of malnutrition on mental development. *Nutrition, the Nervous System and Behavior.* Pan American Health Organization Scientific Publication No. 251, pp. 115-128.

Birch, H. G. 1972b. Malnutrition, learning and intelligence. *AJPH* 62:773-784.

Birch, H. G., and J. D. Gussow. 1970. *Disadvantaged Children: Health, Nutrition and School Failure.* New York, Harcourt, Brace & World, and Grune & Stratton.

Birch, H. G., S. A. Richardson, D. Baird, G. Horobin, and R. Illsley. 1970. *Mental Subnormality in the Community: A Clinical and Epidemiologic Study.* Baltimore, The Williams and Wilkins Company.

Blalock, H. M. 1964. *Causal Inference in Non-experimental Research.* Chapel Hill, University of North Carolina Press.

Blix, G., Y. Hofvander, and B. Vahlquist. 1971. *Famine Symposium Dealing with Nutrition and Relief Operations in Times of Disaster.* Published for the Swedish Nutritional Foundation, Uppsala, Almqvist & Wiksells.

Boerema, I., ed. 1947. *Medische Ervaringen in Nederland Tijdens de Bezetting, 1940-1945.* Groningen, J. B. Wolters.

Bojlen, K., and M. W. Bentzon. 1968. The influence of climate and nutrition on age at menarche: A historical review and a modern hypothesis. *Hum. Biol.* 40:69-85.

REFERENCES

Bourne, G. H. 1943. *Starvation in Europe.* London, George Allen & Unwin, pp. 20, 23, 77-84.

Bowlby, J., M. Ainsworth, M. Boston, and D. Rosenbluth. 1956. The effects of mother-child separation: A follow-up study. *Brit. J. Med. Psychol.* 29:211-247.

Boyd, J. D., and W. J. Hamilton. 1967. Development and structure of the human placenta from the end of the 3rd month of gestation. *J. Obstet. Gynaec. Brit. Cwlth.* 74:161-226.

Breunis, J. 1946. The food supply. *Ann. Am. Acad. Pol. Soc. Sc.* 245:87-92.

Brock, J. F., and M. Autret. 1952. *Kwashiorkor in Africa.* Geneva, World Health Organization.

Broom, L., and F. L. Jones. 1969. Career mobility in three societies: Australia, Italy and the United States. *Amer. Soc. Rev.*

Brown, R. E. 1965. Decreased brain weight in malnutrition and its implications. *E. Afr. Med. J.* 42:584-595.

Bulmer, M. G. 1970. *The Biology of Twinning in Man.* London, Oxford University Press.

Burger, G. C. E., J. C. Drummond, and H. R. Sandstead, eds. 1948. *Malnutrition and Starvation in Western Netherlands: September 1944-July 1945.* The Hague, General State Printing Office.

Burrell, R. J. W., M. J. R. Healy, and J. M. Tanner. 1961. Age at menarche in South African Bantu schoolgirls living in the Transkei Reserve. *Hum. Biol.* 33:250-261.

Burt, C. 1912. The inheritance of mental characteristics. *Eugen. Rev.* 4:168-204.

Burt, C. 1943. Ability and income. *Brit. J. Educ. Psychol.* 13:83-98.

Burt, C. 1966. The genetic determination of differences in intelligence. *Brit. J. Psychol.* 57:137-153.

Burt, C. and M. Howard, 1956. The multifactorial theory of inheritance and its application to intelligence. *Brit. J. Statist. Psychol.* 9:95-131.

Burt, C., and M. Howard. 1957. Heredity and intelligence: A reply to a criticism. *Brit. J. Statist. Psychol.* 10:33-63.

Butler, N. R., and D. G. Bonham. 1963. *Perinatal Mortality: The First Report of the 1958 British Perinatal Mortality Survey under the Auspices of the National Birthday Trust Fund.* Edinburgh, E. and S. Livingstone.

Cabak, V., and R. Najdanvic. 1965. Effect of undernutrition in early life on physical and mental development. *Arch. Dis. Child.* 40:532-534.

Carr, D. H. 1965. Chromosome studies in spontaneous abortions. *Obstet. Gynec.* 26:308-326.

Cattell, R. B. 1950. The state of national intelligence: Test of a thirteen-year prediction. *Eugen. Rev.* 42:136-148.

Cattell, R. B. 1963. Theory of fluid and crystallized intelligence: A critical experiment. *J. Educ. Psychol.* 54:1-22.

Champakam, S., S. Scrikartia, and S. Gopalon. 1968. Kwashiorkor and mental development. *Amer. J. Clin. Nutr.* 21:844-852.

Chase, H. P., and H. P. Martin. 1970. Undernutrition and child development. *New Eng. J. Med.* 282:933-939.

Churchill, J. A. 1965. The relationship between intelligence and birthweight in twins. *Neurology* 15:341-347.

Clarke, A. D. B., A. M. Clarke, and S. Reiman. 1958. Cognitive and social changes in the feebleminded: Three further studies. *Brit. J. Psychol.* 49:144-157.

Cohen, J. 1968. Multiple regression as a general data-analytic system. *Psych. Bull.* 70:426-443.

Conway, J. 1958. The inheritance of intelligence and its social implications. *Brit. J. Statist. Psychol.* 11:171-190.

Cowley, J. J. and R. D. Griesel. 1959. Some effects of a low protein diet on a first filial generation of white rats. *J. Genet. Psychol.* 95:187-201.

Crome, L. 1972. Non-specific developmental abnormalities and unclassified mental retardation in J. B. Cavanagh, ed., *The Brain in Unclassified Mental Retardation*. Baltimore, The Williams and Wilkins Company, pp. 283-289.

Davie, R., N. R. Butler, and H. Goldstein. 1972. *From Birth to Seven: The Second Report to the National Child Development Survey* (Studies in Child Development). New York, Humanities Press.

Davies, P. A. and J. P. Davies. 1970. Very low birth weight and subsequent head growth. *Lancet* ii:1216-1219.

Dawes, G. S. 1968. *Foetal and Neonatal Physiology: A Comparative Study of the Changes at Birth.* Chicago, Year Book Medical Publishers.

de Groot, J. 1947. Over den invloed welke de laatste oorlogsmaanden gehad hebben op de ontwikkeling der kinderen, geboren in en na deze periode, mede in verband met het toenemen van het aantal aangeboren misvormingen. *Tijdschr, voor Soc. Geneesk.* XXV:117-123.

de Haas-Postuma, J. H., and J. H. de Haas. 1968. *Infant Loss in the Netherlands.* Vital and Health Statistics, Series 3, No. 11.

Dobbing, J. 1964. The influence of early nutrition on the development and myelination of the brain. *Proc. Roy. Soc. (Biol.)* 159:503-509.

Dobbing, J. 1973. The later development of the central nervous system and its vulnerability. In J. A. Davis and J. Dobbing, eds., *Scientific Foundations of Pediatrics*. London, William Heinemann Medical Books.

Dobbing, J. 1974. The later growth of the brain and its vulnerability. *Pediatrics* 53:2-6.

Dobbing, J., and J. Sands. 1973. Quantitative growth and development of human brain. *Arch. Dis. Childh.* 48:757-767.

Dobbing, J., and J. L. Smart. 1973. Early undernutrition, brain development and behavior. In S. A. Barnett, ed., *Clinics in Developmental Medicine, No. 47: Ethology and Development*. London, William Heinemann Medical Books.

Dols, M. J. L., and D. J. A. M. van Arcken. 1946. Food supply and nutrition in the Netherlands during and immediately after World War II. *Mil. Mem. Fund. Quart.* 24:319-355.

REFERENCES

Douglas, J. W. B. 1960. "Premature" children at primary schools. *Brit. Med. J.* i:1008-1013.

Drillien, C. M. 1964. *The Growth and Development of the Prematurely Born Infant.* Baltimore, The Williams and Wilkins Company.

Drillien, C. M. 1970. The small-for-date infant: Etiology and prognosis. *Pediatric Clinics of North America.* 17:9-24.

Eaves, L. J., and J. L. Jinks. 1972. Insignifcance of evidence for differences in heritability of IQ between races and social classes. *Nature* 240:84-88.

Edwards, J. H. 1969. Familial predisposition in man. *Brit. Med. Bull.* 25:58-64.

Eells, K., A. Davis, R. J. Havighurst, V. E. Herrick, and R. Tyler. 1951. *Intelligence and Cultural Differences: A Study of Cultural Learning and Problem Solving.* Chicago, University of Chicago Press.

Eichmann, E., and H. Gesenius. 1952. Die Missgeburtenzunahme in Berlin und Umgebung in den Nachkriegsjahren. *Arch. Gynak.* 181:168-184.

Emmett, W. G. 1950. The trend of intelligence in certain districts of England. *Population Studies* 3:324-337.

Erhardt, C. L., G. B. Joshi, F. G. Nelson, B. H. Kroll, and L. Wiener. 1964. Influence of weight and gestation on perinatal and neonatal mortality by ethnic group. *AJPH* 54:1841-1855.

Erlenmeyer-Kimling, L., and L. F. Jarvik. 1963. Genetics and intelligence: A review. *Science* 142:1477-1479.

Evans, D. E., A. D. Moodie, and J. D. L. Hansen. 1971. Kwashiorkor and intellectual development. *S. Afr. Med. J.* 45:1413-1426.

Fairweather, D. V. I., and R. Illsley. 1960. Obstetric and social origins of mentally handicapped children. *Brit. J. Prev. Soc. Med.* 14:149-159.

Falconer, D. S. 1967. The inheritance of liability to certain diseases estimated from the incidence among relatives. *Ann. Hum .Genet.* 31:1-20.

Falkner, F. 1971. Skeletal maturity indicators in infancy. *Am. J. Phys. Anthro.* 35:393-394.

Fish, I., and M. Winick. 1969. Effect of malnutrition on regional growth of the developing rat brain. *Exp. Neurol.* 25:534-540.

Fowler, R. E., and R. G. Edwards. 1973. The genetics of early human development. In A. G. Steinberg and A. G. Bearn, eds., *Progress in Medical Genetics,* Vol. IX. New York, Grune & Stratton, pp. 49-112.

Fox, J. P., F. L. Black, and A. Kogon. 1968. Measles and readiness for reading and learning, V: Evaluative comparison of the studies and overall conclusions. *Amer. J. Epidem* 88:359-367.

Frankova, S. 1971. Relationship between nutrition during lactation and maternal behavior of rats. *Act. Nerv. Super. (Praha).* 13:1-8.

Frankova, S., and R. H. Barnes. 1968. Influence of malnutrition in early life on exploratory behavior of rats. *J. Nutr.* 96:477-484.

Garrow, J., and M. C. Pike. 1967. The long-term prognosis of severe infantile malnutrition. *Lancet* i:1-4.

Gerlach, H. 1962. *Statistische Untersuchungen über das Gewicht der Placenta und ihrer Anhänge sowie über das Verhältnis von Placentagewicht und Fruchtmasszahlen.* Thesis, University of Halle, cited in Armitage, Boyd, Hamilton & Rowe (1967).

Gibson, J. R., and T. McKeown. 1950. Observations on all births (23,970), in Birmingham, 1947, I: Duration of gestation. *Brit. J. Soc. Med.* 4:221-233.

Gibson, J. R. and T. McKeown. 1951. Observations on all births (23,970), in Birmingham, 1947, III: Survival. *Brit. J. Soc. Med.* 5:177-183.

Gordon, H. 1923. *Mental and Scholastic Tests Among Retarded Children.* Educational Pamphlet No. 44. London, Board of Education.

Gordon, J. E. 1966. Social contributions to infectious disease: Causality, behavior, after effects. In H. F. Eichenwald, ed., *The Prevention of Mental Retardation Through Control of Infectious Diseases. Proceedings of the Conference on Mental Retardation through Control of Infectious Diseases,* June 9-11, 1966, Cherry Hill, N.J. Bethesda, National Institute of Child Health and Human Development, pp. 249-261.

Grossman, H. J., ed. 1973. *Manual on Terminology and Classification in Mental Retardation.* American Association on Mental Deficiency, Special Publication Series No. 2.

Gruenwald, P. 1963. Chronic fetal distress and placental insufficiency. *Biol. Neonat.* 5:215-265.

Gruenwald, P. 1966. Growth of the human fetus, I: Normal growth and its variation. *Amer. J. Obstet. Gynec.* 94:1112-1119.

Gruenwald, P., and H. N. Minh. 1961. Evaluation of body and organ weights in perinatal pathology, II: Weight of body and placenta of surviving and autopsied infants. *Amer. J. Obstet. Gynec.* 82:312-319.

Guilford, J. P. 1959. Three faces of intellect. *Am. Psychol.* 14:469-479.

Guthrie, H. A., and M. L. Brown. 1968. Effect of severe undernutrition in early life on growth, brain size and composition in adult rats. *J. Nutr.* 94:419-426.

Hammes, L. M., and A. E. Treloar. 1970. Gestational interval from vital records. *AJPH* 60:1496-1505.

Hansen, J. D., C. Freesemann, and A. D. Moodie. 1971. What does nutritional growth retardation imply? *Pediatrics* 47:299-313.

Harrison, G. A., J. S. Weiner, J. M. Tanner, and N. A. Barnicot. 1964. *Human Biology: An Introduction to Human Evolution, Variation and Growth.* London, Oxford University Press.

Heber, R., H. Garber, S. Harrington, C. Hoffman, and C. Falender. 1972. *Rehabilitation of Families at Risk for Mental Retardation.* Rehabilitation Research and Training Center in Mental Retardation, Madison, Wisconsin, University of Wisconsin.

Heise, D. R. 1969. Problems in path analysis and causal inference. In E. Borgatta, ed., *Sociological Methodology.* San Francisco, Jossey Bass, pp. 38-73.

Henderson, M. 1967. Differences in duration of pregnancy. *Arch. Environ. Hlth.* 14:904-911.

REFERENCES

Hertzig, M. E., H. G. Birch, S. A. Richardson, and J. Tizard. 1972. Intellectual levels of school children severely malnourished during the first two years of life. *Pediatrics* 49:814-823.

Hewitt, D., C. K. Westropp, and R. M. Acheson. 1955. Oxford Child Health Survey: Effects of childish ailments on skeletal development. *Brit. J. Prev. Soc. Med.* 9:179-186.

Hiernaux, J. 1964. Weight-height relationship during growth in Africans and Europeans. *Hum Biol.* 36:273-293.

Higgins, J. V., E. W. Reed, and S. C. Reed. 1962. Intelligence and family size: A paradox resolved. *Eugen. Quart.* 9:84-90.

Hill, R. H. 1969. *Occupations and the Social Structure.* Englewood Cliffs, N.J., Prentice-Hall.

Holmer, A. J. M. 1947. Verloskunde en Vrouwenziekten. In I. Boerema, ed., *Medische Ervaringen in Nederland tijdens de Bezetting, 1940-1945.* Groningen, J. B. Wolters, pp. 131-157.

Hoorweg, J., and P. Stanfield. 1972. The influence of malnutrition on psychologic and neurologic development: Preliminary communications. In *Nutrition, the Nervous System, and Behavior.* Pan American Health Organization Scientific Publication No. 251, pp. 55-63.

Hosemann, K. 1949. Schwangerschaftsdauer und Neugeborenengewicht. *Archiv Gynäk.* 176: 109-123.

Howard, E., and D. M. Granoff. 1968. Increased voluntary running and decreased motor coordination in mice after neonatal corticosterone implantation. *Exp. Neurol.* 22:661-673.

Hytten, F. E., and I. Leitch. 1971a. *The Physiology of Human Pregnancy.* Oxford, Blackwell Scientific Publications.

Hytten, F. E. and I. Leitch. 1971b. *The Physiology of Human pregnancy.* Oxford, Blackwell Scientific Publications, pp. 440-460.

James, D. A. 1967. Some effects of immunological factors on gestation in mice. *J. Reprod. Fert.* 14:265-275.

Jelliffe, D. B. 1968a. *Infant Nutrition in the Tropics and Subtropics,* 2nd ed. World Health Organization Monograph Series No. 29.

Jelliffe, D. B. 1968b. *Child Health in the Tropics,* 3rd ed. Baltimore, The Williams and Wilkins Company.

Jensen, A. R. 1969. How much can we boost IQ and scholastic achievement? *Harvard Educ. Rev.* 39:1-123.

Jinks, J. L., and D. W. Fulker. 1970. Comparison of the biometrical, genetical, MAVA, and classical approaches to the analysis of human behavior. *Psychol. Bull.* 73:311-349.

Kaelber, C. T., and T. F. Pugh. 1969. Influence of intrauterine relations on the intelligence of twins. *New Eng. J. Med.* 280:1030-1034.

Kahn, E. 1952. *The Etiology of Summer Diarrhoea.* M. D. thesis, Witwatersrand University.

Kahn, E. 1954. A neurological syndrome in infants recovering from malnutrition. *Arch. Dis. Childh.* 29:256-261.

Kark, E. 1943. Menarche in South African Bantu girls. *S. Afr. J. Med. Sc.* 8:35-40.

Karn, M. N., and L. S. Penrose. 1951. Birth weight and gestation time in relation to maternal age, parity and infant survival. *Ann. Eugen.* 16:147-164.

Keys, A. B., J. Brožek, A. Henschel, O. Mickelson, and H. L. Taylor. 1950. *The Biology of Human Starvation.* Minneapolis, University of Minneapolis Press, pp. 745-763.

Khosla, T. and C. R. Lowe. 1967. Indices of obesity derived from body weight and height. *Brit. J. Prev. Soc. Med.* 21:122-128.

Kiil, V. 1939. Stature and growth of Norwegian men during the past 200 years. *Skr. norske VidenskAkad* No. 6.

Klatskin, G., W. T. Salter, and F. D. Humm. 1947. Gynecomastia due to malnutrition, I: Clinical studies. *Am. J. Med. Sci.* 21:19-30.

Kloosterman, G. J. 1966. Prevention of prematurity. *Ned. T. Verlosk.* 66:361-380.

Knack, A. V., and J. Neumann, 1917. Beiträge zur Oedemfrage. *Deut. Med. Ws.* 43:901-906.

Knobloch, H., and B. Pasamanick. 1962. Mental subnormality: Medical progress. *New Eng. J. Med.* 266:1045-1051, 1092-1096, 1155-1161.

Laga, E. M., S. G. Driscoll, and H. N. Munro. 1972a. Comparison of placentas from two socio-economic groups, I: Morphometry. *Pediatrics* 50:24-32.

Laga, E. M., S. G. Driscoll, and H. N. Munro. 1972b. Comparison of placentas from two socio-economic groups, II: Biochemical characteristics. *Pediatrics* 50:33-39.

Land, K. C. 1969. Principles in path analysis. In E. Borgatta, ed., *Sociological Methodology.* San Francisco, Jossey Bass, pp. 3-37.

Lazarsfeld, P. F., and P. L. Kendall. 1950. Problems of survey analysis. In R. K. Merton and P. F. Lazarsfeld, eds., *Continuities in Social Research.* Glencoe, Free Press, pp. 133-196.

Lesser, G., G. Fifer, and D. H. Clarke. 1965. Mental abilities of children from different social-class and cultural groups. *Monogr. Soc. Res. Child Dev.* 30, No. 4.

Levitsky, D. A. 1973. *Malnutrition and Cognitive Development in Animals.* Paper presented at the Kittay Scientific Foundation First International Symposium: Nutrition and its contribution to mental functions, March 29-30, 1973.

Levitsky, D. A., and R. H. Barnes. 1970. Effects of early malnutrition on the reaction of adult rats to aversive stimuli. *Nature* 225:468-469.

Lewis, E. O. 1929. *The Report of the Mental Deficiency Committee,* Part 4. London, His Majesty's Stationery Office.

Lewis, E. O. 1933. Types of mental deficiency and their social significance. *J. Ment. Sc.* 79:298-304.

Lewis, O. 1966. *La Vida: A Puerto Rican Family in the Culture of Poverty.* New York, Random House.

REFERENCES

Lilienfeld, A. M., and B. Pasamanick. 1956. The association of maternal and fetal factors with the development of mental deficiency, 2: Relation to maternal age, birth order, previous reproductive loss and degree of mental deficiency. *Amer. J. Ment. Def.* 60:557-569.

Lin, C. C. and I. Emanuel. 1972. A comparison of American and Chinese intrauterine growth standards. *Amer. J. Epidem.* 95:418-430.

Lipset, S. M., and R. Bendix. 1958. *Social Mobility in Industrial Society.* New York, John Wiley.

Lopreato, J. 1970. *Theories and Studies in Social Stratification.* San Francisco, Chandler Publishing Company.

Maas, W. B. 1970. *The Netherlands at War: 1940-1945.* London, Abelard-Schuman, pp. 116-126.

McCance, R. A. 1962. Food, growth and time. *Lancet* ii:621-626; 671-675.

McCance, R. A., and E. M. Widdowson. 1940. *The Chemical Composition of Foods.* Medical Research Council Special Report Series No. 235. London, His Majesty's Stationery Office.

McCance, R. A., and E. M. Widdowson. 1974. Review lecture: The determinants of growth and form. *Proc. Roy. Soc. Lond. (Biol.)* 185:1-17.

McCance, R. A., E. M. Widdowson, R. F. A. Dean, and L. A. Thrussell. 1951. *Studies of Undernutrition, Wuppertal 1946-9.* Medical Research Council Special Report Series No. 275, London, His Majesty's Stationery Office.

McDonald, A. 1964. Intelligence in children of very low birth weight. *Brit. J. Prev. Soc. Med.* 18:59-74.

McGregor, I. A., W. Z. Billewicz, and A. M. Thomson. 1961. Growth and mortality in children in an African village. *Brit. Med. J.* ii:1661-1671.

McKeown, T. and J. R. Gibson. 1951. Observations on all births (23,970) in Birmingham, 1947, II: Birth weight. *Brit. J. Soc. Med.* 5:98-112.

McKeown, T., and R. G. Record. 1953. The influence of placental size on foetal growth in man, with special reference to multiple pregnancy. *J. Endocrin.* 9:418-426.

McLaren, A. 1965. Genetic and environmental effects on foetal and placental growth in mice. *J. Reprod. Fertil.* 9:79-98.

McLaren, A., and D. Michie. 1963. Nature of the systemic effect of litter size on gestation period in mice. *J. Reprod. Fertil.* 6:139-141.

McLaren, D. S. 1966. A fresh look at protein-calorie malnutrition. *Lancet* ii:485-488.

McMahon, B., and J. M. Sowa. 1961. Physical damage to the fetus. *Milbank Mem. Fund. Quart.* 39:14-73.

McNemar, Q. 1940. A critical examination of the University of Iowa studies of environmental influences upon the IQ. *Psych. Bull.* 37:63-92.

Markowitz, S. D. 1955. Retardation in growth of children in Europe and Asia during World War II. *Hum. Biol.* 27:258-273.

Marolla, F. A. 1973. Intelligence and Demographic Variables in a 19-Year-Old Cohort in the Netherlands: An Analysis of Their Relationship from the

Perspective of the Two-Component Theories of Intelligence. Ph.D. dissertation, New School for Social Research.

Martin, H. P. 1970. Microcephaly and mental retardation. *Amer. J. Dis. Childh.* 119:128-131.

Miller, F. J. W., W. Z. Billewicz, and A. M. Thomson. 1972. Growth from birth to adult life of 442 Newcastle-Upon-Tyne children. *Brit. J. Prev. Soc. Med.* 26:224-230.

Miller, R. W. 1956. Delayed effects occurring within the first decade after exposure of young individuals to the Hiroshima atom bomb. *Pediatrics* 18:1-18.

Miller, R. W., and W. J. Blot. 1972. Small head size after in-utero exposure to atomic radiation. *Lancet* ii:784-787.

Monckeberg, F. 1968. Effect of early marasmic malnutrition on subsequent physical and psychological development. In N. S. Scrimshaw and J. E. Gordon, eds., *Malnutrition, Learning, and Behavior.* Cambridge, Mass., MIT Press, pp. 269-277.

Morley, D. 1969. Medicine in the tropics, I: Severe measles in the tropics. *Brit. Med. J.* 1:297-300.

Naeye, R. L. 1970. Structural correlates of fetal undernutrition. In H. W. Waisman and G. R. Kerr, eds., *Fetal Growth and Development.* New York, McGraw-Hill, pp. 241-252.

Naggan, L. 1969. The recent decline in the prevalence of anencephaly and spina bifida. *Am. J. Epidem.* 89:154-160.

Nelson, K. B., and J. Deutschberger. 1970. Head size at one year as a predictor of four-year IQ. *Develop. Med. Child Neurol.* 12:487-495.

Newman, H. H., F. N. Freeman, and K. J. Holzinger. 1937. *Twins: A Study of Heredity and Environment.* Chicago, University of Chicago Press.

Nilsson, A. 1920. Über sog. Kriegsamenorrhoe. *Zbl. Gynäk.* 44:876.

Nisbet, J. D., and R. Illsley. 1963. The influence of early puberty on test performance at age eleven. *Brit. J. Educ. Psychol.* 33:169.

O'Connor, N., and J. Tizard. 1956. *The Social Problem of Mental Deficiency.* London, Pergamon Press.

Pasamanick, B., and H. Knobloch. 1966. Retrospective studies of the epidemiology of reproductive casualty, old and new. *Merrill-Palmer Quart.* 12:7-26.

Pasamanick, B., and A. M. Lilienfeld. 1955. Association of maternal and fetal factors with the development of mental deficiency, I: Abnormalities in the prenatal and paranatal periods. *JAMA* 159:155-160.

Pasma, F. 1947. Aangeboren gebreken als gevolg van voedingstekorten. *Tijdschr. voor Soc. Geneesk.* XXV:177-178.

Payne, P. R., and E. F. Wheeler. 1967a. Growth of the foetus. *Nature* 215:849-850.

Payne, P. R., and E. F. Wheeler. 1967b. Comparative nutrition in pregnancy. *Nature* 215:1134-1136.

REFERENCES

Pearson, K. 1909. *The Scope and Importance to the State of the Science of National Eugenics,* 2nd ed., University of London, Galton Laboratory for National Eugenics, Eugenics Laboratory Lecture Series 1. London, Dulau & Company.

Penrose, L. S. 1939. Eugenic prognosis with respect to mental deficiency. *Eugen. Rev.* 31:35-39.

Penrose, L. S. 1962. *Biology of Mental Defect,* 2nd ed. New York, Grune & Stratton.

Peraita, M. 1946. Deficiency neuropathies observed in Madrid during the Civil War (1936-39). *Brit. Med. J.* 2:784.

Peterson, J. 1925. *Early Conceptions and Tests of Intelligence.* Yonkers-on-Hudson, N.Y., World.

Platt, B. S., and R. J. C. Stewart. 1968. Effect of protein-calorie deficiency on dogs, I: Reproduction, growth, and behavior. *Develop. Med. Child. Neurol.* 10:3-24.

Platt, B. S., and R. J. C. Stewart. 1969. Effect of protein-calorie deficiency on dogs, II: Morphological changes in the nervous system. *Develop. Med. Child. Neurol.* 11:174-192.

Platt, B. S., and R. J. C. Stewart. 1971. Reversible and irreversible effects of protein-calorie deficiency on the central nervous system of animals and man. *Wld. Rev. Nutr. Diet* 13:43-85.

Pollitt, E. 1969. Ecology, malnutrition, and mental development. *Psychosom. Med.* 31:193-200.

Polman, A. 1947. Monstruositeit en andere Vormgebreken als oorzaak van doodgeboorte. *Tijdschr. voor Soc. Geneesk.* XXV:69-72.

Quételet, L. A. J. 1870. *Anthropométrie ou Mesure des Différentes Facultés de l'Homme.* Brussells, C. Marquardt.

Rayner, S. 1964. An investigation of the changes in prevalence of mental deficiency in Sweden. *Hereditas* 51:297-314.

Record, R. G., T. McKeown, and J. H. Edwards. 1969. The relation of measured intelligence to birth weight and duration of gestation. *Ann. Hum. Genet. Lond.* 33:71-79.

Record, R. G., T. McKeown, and J. H. Edwards. 1970. An investigation of the difference in measured intelligence between twins and single births. *Ann. Hum Genet. Lond.* 34:11-20.

Richardson, A. H., and G. R. Leslie. 1970. Residential mobility, life-cycle and career pattern in T. R. Ford, and F. D. Gordon, eds., *Social Demography.* Englewood Cliffs, N.J., Prentice-Hall.

Richardson, S. A. 1972. Ecology of malnutrition: Nonnutritional factors influencing intellectual development. In *Nutrition, the Nervous System, and Behavior.* Pan American Health Organization Scientific Publication No. 251, pp. 101-110.

Richardson, S. A., H. G. Birch, E. Grabie, and K. Yoder. 1972. The behavior of children in school who were severely malnourished in the first two years of life. *J. of Hlth. Soc. Behav.* 13:276-284.

Richardson, S. A., H. G. Birch, and M. E. Hertzig. 1973. School performance of children who were severely malnourished in infancy. *Amer. J. Ment. Def.* 77:623-632.

Riley, M. W., and A. Foner. 1968. *Aging and Society,* Vol. I: *An Inventory of Research Findings.* New York, Russell Sage Foundation.

Roberts, J. A. F. 1952. The genetics of mental deficiency. *Eugen. Rev.* 44:71-83.

Roberts, J. 1971. *Intellectual Development of Children by Demographic and Socioeconomic Factors.* Vital and Health Statistics Series 11 No. 110.

Robinson, W. S. 1950. Ecological correlates and the behavior of individuals. *Amer. Soc. Rev.* 15:351-357.

Rosado, A., A. Bernal, A. Sosa, M. Morales, J. Urrusti, P. Yoshida, S. Frenk, L. Velasco, T. Yoshida, and J. Metcoff. 1972. Human growth retardation, III: Protein, DNA, RNA, adenine nucleotides and activities of the enzymes pyruvic and adenylate kinase in placenta. *Pediatrics* 50:568-577.

Rush, D., H. Davis, and M. Susser. 1972. Antecedents of low birthweight in Harlem, New York City. *Interntl. J. Epidem.* I:393-405.

Rush, D., Z. Stein, G. Christakis, and M. Susser. 1974. The Prenatal Project: The first twenty months of operation. In M. Winick, ed., *Proceedings of the Symposium on Nutrition and Fetal Development.* New York, John Wiley, pp. 95-125.

Rush, D., Z. Stein, and M. Susser. 1973. The rationale for, and design of, a randomized controlled trial of nutritional supplementation in pregnancy. *Nutr. Rep. Internat.* 7:547-553.

Rutter, M., P. Graham, and W. Yule. 1970. *A Neuro-psychiatric Study in Childhood* (*Clinics in Developmental Medicine* Nos. 35/36). London, William Heinemann Medical Books.

Rutter, M., J. Tizard, and K. Whitmore. 1970. *Education, Health and Behavior.* London, Longman Group.

Ryder, N. B. 1965. The measurement of fertility patterns. In M. C. Sheps and J. C. Ridley, eds., *Public Health and Population Change: Current Research Issues.* Pittsburgh, The University of Pittsburgh, pp. 287-306.

Sachs, S. B. 1952. The social aetiology of malignant malnutrition. *S. Afr. Med. J.* 26:430-432.

Sanders, B. S. 1934. *Environment and Growth.* Baltimore, Warwick & York.

Savage, F. M. A. 1967. A year of measles. *Med. J. of Zambia* 1:67-72.

Scarr-Salapatek, S. 1971 a. Unknowns in the IQ equation. *Science* 174:1223-1228.

Scarr-Salapatek, S. 1971 b. Race, social class, and IQ. *Science* 174:1285-1295.

Schaie, K. W., and J. Roberts. 1971. *School Achievement of Children by Demographic and Socioeconomic Factors.* Vital and Health Statistics Series 11 No. 109.

REFERENCES

Scottish Council for Research in Education. 1949. *The Trend of Scottish Intelligence: A Comparison of the 1947 and 1932 Surveys of Intelligence of Eleven-Year-Old Pupils.* London, University of London Press.

Scottish Council for Research in Education. 1953. *Social Implications of the 1947 Scottish Mental Survey.* London, University of London Press.

Scrimshaw, N. S., C. E. Taylor, and J. E. Gordon. 1968. *Interactions of Nutrition and Infection.* World Health Organization Monograph No. 57.

Searle, L. V. 1949. The organization of hereditary maze-brightness and maze-dullness. *Genet. Psychol. Mon.* 39:279.

Shields, J. 1962. *Monozygotic Twins Brought Up Apart and Brought Up Together.* London, Oxford University Press.

Simonson, M., and B. F. Chow. 1970. Maze studies on progeny of underfed mother rats. *J. Nutr.* 100:685-690.

Simonson, M., R. W. Sherwin, J. K. Anilane, W. Y. Yu, and B. F. Chow. 1969. Neuromotor development in progeny of underfed mother rats. *J. Nutr.* 98:18-24.

Sindram, I. S. 1945. De invloed van ondervoeding op de groei van de vrucht. *Ned. T. Verlosk.* 45:30-48.

Skeels, H. M. 1966. Adult status of children with contrasting early life experiences. *Mon. Soc. Res. Child Dev.* 51, No. 3.

Skodak, M., and H. M. Skeels. 1945. A follow-up study of children in adoptive homes *J. Genet. Psych.* 66:21-58.

Smart, J. L., and J. Dobbing. 1971a. Vulnerability of developing brain, II: Effects of early nutritional deprivation on reflex ontogeny and development of behavior in the rat. *Brain Res.* 28:85-95.

Smart, J. L., and J. Dobbing. 1971b. Vulnerability of developing brain, VI: Relative effects of fetal and early postnatal undernutrition on reflex ontogeny and development of behavior in the rat. *Brain Res.* 33:303-314.

Smith, C. A. 1947. Effects of wartime starvation in Holland on pregnancy and its products. *Amer. J. Obstet, Gynec.* 53:599-608.

Solth, K. 1961. Das Wachstum der Placenta in zusammenhang mit Kindsgewicht und Tragzeitlange. *Zbl. Gynak.* 83:1558-1559.

Spearman, C. 1927. *The Abilities of Man.* New York, The Macmillan Company.

Stein, Z. A., and H. Kassab. 1970. Nutrition. In J. Wortis, ed., *Mental Retardation.* II New York, Grune & Stratton, pp. 92-116.

Stein, Z. A., and M. W. Susser. 1960a. Families of dull children, II: Identifying family types and subcultures. *J. Ment. Sc.* 106:1296-1303.

Stein, Z. A., and M. W. Susser. 1960b. Families of dull children, III: Social selection by family type. *J. Ment. Sc.* 106:1304-1310.

Stein, Z. A., and M. W. Susser. 1960c. Families of dull children, IV: Increments in intelligence. *J. Ment. Sc.* 106:1311-1319.

Stein, Z. A., and M. W. Susser. 1963. The social distribution of mental retardation. *Amer. J. Ment. Def.* 67:811-821.

Stein, Z. A., and M. W. Susser. 1969. Mild mental subnormality: Social and epidemiological studies. *Social Psychiatry* XLVII:62-85.

Stein, Z. A., and M. W. Susser. 1970. Mutability of intelligence and epidemiology of mild mental retardation. *Review of Educational Research* 40:29-67.

Stein, Z. A., and M. W. Susser. 1971. Changes over time in the incidence and prevalence of mental retardation. In J. Hellmuth, ed., *Exceptional Infant.* Vol. 2: *Studies in Abnormalities.* New York, Brunner Mazel, Inc., pp. 305-340.

Stein, Z., M. Susser, G. Saenger, and F. Marolla. 1973a. Nutrition and mental performance *Science* 178:708-713.

Stein, Z., M. Susser, G. Saenger, and F. Marolla. 1973b. Intelligence test results of individuals exposed during gestation to World War II famine in the Netherlands. *T. soc. Geneesk.* 50:766-774.

Stevenson, A. C. 1962. Discussion of paper by H. A. Heinz and P. Stoll: Sex determinations in intra-uterine death by means of sex chromatin. *Acta Cytol.* Phila. 6:116.

Stoch, M. B., and P. M. Smythe. 1963. Does undernutrition during infancy inhibit growth and subsequent intellectual development? *Arch. Dis. Child.* 38:546-552.

Stockard, C. R. 1921. Developmental rate and structural expression: An experimental study of twins, "double monsters," and single deformities and the interaction among embryonic organs during their origin and development. *Am. J. Anat.* 28:115-277.

Stroink, J. 1947. De duur der zwangerschap en het gewicht der neonati in de hongerperiode, 1944-1945. *Ned. T. Verlosk.* 47:101-105.

Susser, M. W. 1957. African township: A socio-medical study. *Medical World* 86:385-400.

Susser, M. W. 1968. *Community Psychiatry: Epidemiologic and Social Themes.* New York, Random House.

Susser, M. W. 1973. *Causal Thinking in the Health Sciences: Concepts and Strategies in Epidemiology.* New York, Oxford University Press.

Susser, M. W., F. A. Marolla, and J. Fleiss. 1972. Birthweight, fetal age and perinatal mortality. *Amer. J. Epidem.* 96:197-204.

Susser, M. W., and W. Watson. 1971. *Sociology in Medicine,* 2nd ed. New York, Oxford University Press.

Tanner, J. M. 1962. *Growth at Adolescence,* 2nd ed. London, Blackwell Scientific Publications.

Tanner, J. M., M. J. R. Healy, R. D. Lockhart, J. D. Mackenzie, and R. H. Whitehouse. 1956. Aberdeen growth study, I: The prediction of adult body measurements from measurements taken each year from birth to 5 years. *Arch Dis. Child.* 31:372-381.

Teitelbaum, M. S., and N. Mantel. 1971. Socio-economic factors and the sex ratio at birth. *J. Biosoc. Sci.* 3:23-41.

Thomson, A. M. 1959. 3 Diet in relation to the course and outcome of pregnancy. *Brit. J. Nutr.* 13:509-525.

Thomson, A. M., and W. Z. Billewicz. 1961. Height, weight and food intake in man. *Brit. J. Nutr.* 15:241-252.

Thomson, A. M., W. Z. Billewicz, and F. E. Hytten. 1969. The weight of the placenta in relation to birthweight. *J. Obstet. Gynaec. Brit. Cwlth.* 76:865-872.

Thurstone, L. L. 1935. *Vectors of Mind: Multiple Factor Analysis for the Isolation of Primary Traits.* Chicago, University of Chicago Press.

Trowell, H. C., J. N. P. Davies, and R. F. A. Dean. 1954. *Kwashiorkor.* London, Arnold.

Turkewitz, G. 1973. Paper presented at the Kittay Scientific Foundation First International Symposium: Nutrition and its Contribution to mental functions, March 29-30, 1973.

Valaoras, V. G. 1946. Some effects of famine on the population of Greece. *Milbank Mem. Fund. Quart.* 24:215-234.

Valaoras, V. G. 1970. Biometric studies of army conscripts in Greece. *Hum. Biol.* 42:184-201.

Vernon, P. E. 1968. Measurements of learning. In N. S. Scrimshaw and J. E. Gordon, eds., *Malnutrition, Learning, and Behavior.* Cambridge, Mass., MIT Press, pp. 486-496.

Warmbrunn, W. 1963. *The Dutch Under German Occupation.* Stanford, Stanford University Press.

Warburton, D., and F. C. Fraser. 1964. Spontaneous abortion risks in man: Data from reproductive histories collected in a medical genetics unit. *Am. J. Hum. Genet.* 16:1-25.

Weiss, W., and E. C. Jackson. 1969. Maternal factors affecting birthweight. In *Perinatal Factors Affecting Human Development.* Pan American Health Organization Scientific Publication No. 185, pp. 54-59.

Wheeler, L. R. A. 1942. A comparative study of the intelligence of East Tennessee Mountain children. *J. of Ed. Psych.* 33:321-334.

Wiener, G. 1970. The relationship of birthweight and length of gestation to intellectual development at ages 8 to 10 years. *J. of Ped.* 76:694-699.

Wieringen, J. C., F. Wafelbakker, H. P. Verbrugge, and J. H. de Haas. 1971. *Growth Diagrams, 1965, Netherlands. Second National Survey on 0-24-Year-Olds.* Groningen, Wolters-Noordhoff.

Williams, C. D. 1933. A nutritional disease of childhood associated with a maize diet. *Arch. Dis. Childh.* 8:423-433.

Winick, M. 1967. Cellular growth of human placenta, III: Intrauterine growth failure. *J. of Ped.* 71:390-395.

Winick, M. 1971. Cellular changes during placental and fetal growth. *Amer. J. Obstet. Gynec.* 109:166-176.

Winick, M., J. A. Brasel, and P. Rosso. 1972. Nutrition and cell growth. In M. Winick, ed., *Nutrition and Development.* New York, John Wiley & Sons, pp. 49-97.

Winick, M., A. Coscia, and A. Noble. 1967. Cellular growth in human placenta, I: Normal placental growth. *Pediatrics* 39:248-251.

Winick, M. and A. Noble. 1966. Cellular response in rats during malnutrition at various ages. *J. Nutr.* 89:300-306.

Winick, M., and P. Rosso. 1969. Head circumference and cell growth of the brain in normal and marasmic children. *J. of Ped.* 74:774-778.

World Health Organization. 1938. *Manual of the International Statistical Classification of Diseases, Injuries, and Causes of Death*, Geneva. *Groote Internationale Lijst van Doodsoorzaken 1938* 's Gravenhage, Centraal Bureau voor de Statistiek.

World Health Organization. 1948. *Manual of the International Statistical Classification of Diseases, Injuries, and Causes of Death.* Geneva.

World Health Organization. 1969. *Biological Components of Human Reproduction: Studies of their Variation in Population Groups.* Technical Report Series No. 435, Geneva.

Yamazaki, J. N., S. W. Wright, and P. M. Wright. 1954. Outcome of pregnancy in women exposed to the atomic bomb in Nagasaki. *Amer. J. Dis. Childh.* 87:448-463.

Zamenhof, S., E. van Marthens. and F. L. Margolis. 1968. DNA (cell number) and protein in neonatal brain: Alteration by maternal dietary protein restriction. *Science* 160:322-323.

Zimmermann, R. R., D. A. Strobel, P. Steere, and C. R. Geist. 1973. Behavior and malnutrition in the Rhesus monkey. In L. Rosenblum, ed., *Primate Behavior.* New York, Academic Press.

Zschiesche, W., and H. Gerlach. 1963. Biometrische Untersuchungen über die Placenta und die Beziehungen zwischen Placenta und Frucht. *Arch. Gynäk.* 199:199-208.

Author Index

Acheson, R. M., 29, 216
Adlard, B. P., 20
Adrianzen, T. B., 215
Aherne, W., 127–28
Ainsworth, M., 31
Altman, J., 20
Anilane, J. K., 20
Antonov, A. N., 24, 72, 75, 99
Armitage, P., 96, 126–29, 131
Autret, M., 34

Baertl, J. M., 215
Baird, D., 8, 10, 14, 26
Banning, C., 40, 51, 53
Barker, D. J. P., 26
Barnes, D., 20
Barnes, R. H., 20–21, 33–34
Barnicot, N. A., 72
Baum, J. D., 101
Bell, R. W., 20
Belmont, L., 234
Bendix, R., 41
Benton, A. L., 24
Bentzon, M. W., 72
Bergner, L., 18, 24, 27, 35, 92–93, 125, 153
Bernal, A., 127
Bernard, C., 87
Billewicz, W. Z., 29, 96, 98, 106, 126, 129, 131, 216, 220
Binet, A., 8
Birch, H. G., 8, 10, 14, 26–27, 29–32, 215
Black, F. L., 29
Blalock, H. M., 12, 134

Blix, G., 4
Blot, W. J., 102
Boerema, I., 72
Bojlen, K., 72
Bonham, D. G., 104, 138
Boston, M., 31
Bourne, G. H., 43
Bowlby, J., 31
Boyd, J. D., 96, 126–29, 131
Brasel, J. A., 18
Breunis, J., 40
Brock, J. F., 34
Broom, L., 67
Brown, M. L., 20
Brown, R. E., 101
Brožek, J., 72–73
Bulmer, M. G., 77
Burger, G. C. E., 43, 46, 48–52, 82
Burrell, R. J. W., 72
Burt, C., 8, 11–12
Butler, N. R., 104, 138, 216

Cabak, V., 30
Carr, D. H., 82
Cattell, R. B., 11, 199
Champakam, S., 30
Chase, H. P., 101
Chow, B. F., 20–21
Christakis, G., 4
Churchill, J. A., 24
Clarke, A. D. B., 13
Clarke, A. M., 13
Clarke, D. H., 9

Cohen, J., 110
Conway, J., 11
Coscia, A., 96
Cowley, J. J., 20
Crome, L., 201

Das, G. D., 20
Davie, R., 216
Davies, J. N. P., 34
Davies, J. P., 101
Davies, P. A., 101
Davis, A., 9
Davis, H., 24, 125
Davison, A. N., 16
Dawes, G. S., 122, 127
de Groot, J., 149
de Haas, J. H., 149, 215
de Haas-Postuma, J. H., 149
Dean, R. F. A., 24, 34
Deutschberger, J., 101–2
Dobbing, J., 15–17, 19–21
Dols, M. J. L., 40, 43
Douglas, J. W. B., 26
Drillien, C. M., 24, 26–27
Driscoll, S. G., 96, 127–28
Drummond, J. C., 43, 46, 48–52, 82

Eaves, L. J., 12
Edwards, J. H., 11, 26
Edwards, R. G., 71
Eells, K., 9
Eichmann, E., 24
Emanuel, I., 89
Emmett, W. G., 11
Erhardt, C. L., 89, 150
Erlenmeyer-Kimling, L., 12
Evans, D. E., 30

Fairweather, D. V. I., 9
Falconer, D. S., 11
Falender, C., 13
Falkner, F., 216
Fifer, G., 9
Fish, I., 17
Fleiss, J., 153
Foner, A., 77
Fowler, R. E., 71
Fox, J. P., 29
Frankova, S., 20
Fraser, F. C., 84
Freeman, F. N., 12
Freesemann, C., 30, 215
Frenk, S., 127
Fulker, D. W., 12

Garber, H., 13
Garrow, J., 30, 215

Geist, C. R., 20–21, 33–34
Gerlach, H., 96, 131
Gesenius, H., 24
Gibson, J. R., 24, 96
Goldstein, H., 216
Gopalon, S., 30
Gordon, H., 9
Gordon, J. E., 29
Grabie, E., 30
Graham, G. G., 215
Graham, P., 201
Granoff, D. M., 21
Griesel, R. D., 20
Grossman, H. J., 202
Gruenwald, P., 98–99, 101, 122–23, 129
Guilford, J. P., 199
Gussow, J. D., 26–27, 215
Guthrie, H. A., 20

Hamilton, W. J., 96, 126–29, 131
Hammes, L. M., 89
Hansen, J. D. L., 30, 32, 215
Harrington, S., 13
Harrison, G. A., 72
Havighurst, R. J., 9
Healy, M. J. R., 72, 216
Heber, R., 13
Heise, D. R., 134
Henderson, M., 104
Henschel, A., 72–73
Herrick, V. E., 9
Hertzig, M. E., 30–31
Hewitt, D., 29, 216
Hiernaux, J., 215
Higgins, J. V., 81
Hill, R. H., 67
Hoffman, C., 13
Hofvander, Y., 4
Holmer, A. J. M., 72
Holzinger, K. J., 12
Hoorweg, J., 30
Horobin, G., 8, 10, 14, 26
Hosemann, K., 129
Howard, E., 21
Howard, M., 11
Humm, F. D., 72
Hytten, F. E., 77, 90, 96, 98, 126, 129, 131

Illsley, R., 8–10, 14, 26, 234

Jackson, E. C., 24
James, D. A., 127
Jarvik, L. F., 12
Jelliffe, D. B., 28
Jensen, A. R., 9, 11, 199
Jinks, J. L., 12

AUTHOR INDEX

Jones, F. L., 67
Joshi, G. B., 89

Kaelber, C. T., 24
Kahn, E., 29
Kark, E., 72
Karn, M. N., 129
Kassab, H., 25, 29
Kemsley, W. F., 220
Kendall, P. L., 125
Keys, A. B., 72–73
Khosla, T., 220
Kiil, V., 215
Klatskin, G., 72
Kloosterman, G. J., 35, 92
Knack, A. V., 72
Knobloch, H., 5
Kogon, A., 29
Kroll, B. H., 89

Laga, E. M., 96, 127–28
Land, K. C., 134
Lazarsfeld, P. F., 124
Leitch, I., 77, 90
Leslie, G. R., 67
Lesser, G., 9
Levitsky, D. A., 20–21
Lewis, E. O., 9–11
Lewis, O., 11
Lilienfeld, A. M., 5, 83
Lin, C. C., 89
Lipset, S. M., 41
Lockhart, R. D., 216
Lopreato, J., 67
Lowe, C. R., 220

Maas, W. B., 44
McCance, R. A., 16–17, 24, 29, 48
McCormick, N., 20
McDonald, A., 26–27
McGregor, I. A., 29, 216
Mackenzie, J. D., 216
McKeown, T., 24, 26, 96, 126–27, 129
McLaren, A., 24, 127, 129
McLaren, D. S., 127
McMahon, B., 5
McNemar, Q., 13
Mantel, N., 82
Margolis, F. L., 15, 33
Markowitz, S. D., 215
Marolla, F. A., 153, 205, 234
Martin, H. P., 101–2
Metcoff, J., 127
Michie, D., 24, 127
Mickelson, O., 72–73
Miller, F. J. W., 216
Miller, R. W., 83, 102

Minh, H. N., 101, 123, 129
Monckeberg, F., 23, 101
Moodie, A. D., 30, 215
Moore, A. U., 20–21, 33–34
Morales, M., 127
Morley, D., 29
Munro, H. N., 96, 127–28

Naeye, R. L., 101, 123
Naggan, L., 24
Najdanvic, R., 30
Nelson, F. G., 89
Nelson, K. B., 101–102
Neumann, J., 72
Newman, H. H., 12
Nilsson, A., 77
Nisbet, J. D., 234
Noble, A., 15, 96

O'Connor, N., 202

Pasamanick, B., 5, 83
Pasma, F., 149
Payne, P. R., 24, 34, 127–28
Pearson, K., 11
Penrose, L. S., 81, 102, 129
Peraita, M., 72
Peterson, J., 8
Pike, M. C., 30, 215
Platt, B. S., 15–16, 33
Pollitt, E., 30
Polman, A., 269
Pond, W. G., 20–21, 33–34
Pugh, T. F., 24

Quételet, L. A. J., 220

Rayner, S., 11
Record, R. G., 26, 126–27, 129
Reed, E. W., 81
Reed, S. C., 81
Reid, I. M., 20–21, 33–34
Reiman, S., 13
Richardson, A. H., 67
Richardson, S. A., 8, 10, 14, 26, 30, 32
Riley, M. W., 77
Roberts, J., 9
Roberts, J. A. F., 10
Robinson, W. S., 12, 64
Rosado, A., 127
Rosenbluth, D., 31
Rosso, P., 18, 101
Rowe, B. C., 96, 126–29, 131
Rush, D., 4, 24, 125
Rutter, M., 8, 10, 201
Ryder, N. B., 71

AUTHOR INDEX

Sachs, S. B., 31
Saenger, G., 272
Salter, W. T., 72
Sanders, B. S., 77
Sands, J., 17
Sandstead, H. R., 43, 46, 48–52, 82
Savage, F. M. A., 29
Scarr-Salapatek, S., 12
Schaie, K. W., 9
Scottish Council for Research in Education, 8–9, 11, 234
Scrikartia, S., 30
Scrimshaw, N. S., 29
Searle, L. V., 21
Searls, D., 101
Sherwin, R. W., 20
Shields, J., 12
Simonson, M., 20–21
Sindram, I. S., 35, 92, 104
Skeels, H. M., 13
Skodak, M., 13
Smart, J. L., 20–21
Smith, C. A., 24, 27, 35, 63, 92, 99, 120
Smythe, P. M., 23, 29, 101
Solth, K., 96, 129, 131
Sosa, A., 127
Sowa, J. M., 5
Spearman, C., 199
Stanfield, P., 30
Steere, P., 20–21, 33–34
Stein, Z. A., 4, 8, 10–11, 13, 25, 29, 200, 208
Stevenson, A. C., 82
Stewart, R. J. C., 15–16, 33
Stoch, M. B., 23, 29, 101
Stockard, C. R., 6
Strobel, D. A., 20–21, 33–34
Stroink, J., 35, 92
Sudarshan, K., 20
Susser, M. W., 4, 8, 10–11, 13–14, 18, 24, 27, 31, 35, 72, 81, 92–93, 95, 125, 153, 200, 208–9

Tanner, J. M., 72, 215–16
Taylor, C. E., 29
Taylor, H. L., 72–73
Teitelbaum, M. S., 82
Thomson, A. M., 29, 96, 98, 106, 124, 126, 129, 131, 216, 220
Thrussell, L. A., 24

Thurstone, L. L., 199
Tizard, J., 8, 10, 30, 202
Treloar, A. E., 89
Trowell, H. C., 34
Turkewitz, G., 21
Tyler, R., 9

Urrusti, J., 127

Vahlquist, B., 4
Valaoras, V. G., 72, 215
van Arcken, D. J. A. M., 40, 43
van Marthens, E., 15, 33
Velasco, L., 127
Verbrugge, H. P., 215
Vernon, P. E., 199

Wafelbakker, F., 215
Warburton, D., 84
Warmbrunn, W., 43–44
Watson, W., 72, 81
Weiner, J. S., 72
Weiss, W., 24
Westropp, C. K., 216
Wheeler, E. F., 24, 34, 127–28
Wheeler, L. R. A., 11
Whitehouse, R. H., 216
Whitmore, K., 8, 10
Widdowson, E. M., 16–17, 24, 48
Wiener, G., 24, 89
Wiener, L., 89
Wieringen, J. C., 215
Williams, C. D., 34
Winick, M., 15, 17–18, 96, 101, 127
World Health Organization, 60, 72, 165, 202, 223, 228
Wright, P. M., 83
Wright, S. W., 83

Yamazaki, J. N., 83
Yoder, K., 30
Yoshida, P., 127
Yoshida, T., 127
Yu, W. Y., 20
Yule, W., 201

Zamenhof, S., 15, 33
Zimmermann, R. R., 20–21, 33–34
Zschiesche, W., 131

Subject Index

Aberdeen, Scotland, 106
Abohzis, 60, 225
Abortions, 82
Achievement tests, 198
Agriculture, in Netherlands, 1939–1945, 43
All-or-none effect, 5, 83, 208, 233
Amenorrhea, 71, 76–77
Amsterdam, 60, 79, 87, 91
   maternal age, 77, 85
   parity, 77, 85
Analyses of groups, 111
Analyses of individuals, 111, 123
Analysis of differences, 91, 112
Arithmetic ability test, 67, 200, 204
Arnhem, 44
Aspirant families, 10
Asthma, 225, 228
Atrophy, infant death rates, 180

Behavior, and protein lack in animals, 33
Bennett Test of Mechanical Comprehension, 200, 205
Birth cohorts, see Cohorts
Birth order, 197
   in famine area, 86
   in North control area, 86
   in South control area, 86
Births
   in famine area, 238
   in North control area, 239
   in South control area, 240
Birthweight
   and congenital defects, 26
   and famine, 92 ff
   in famine area, 244
   and height, 216
   and infant length, 122
   and maternal nutrition, 24, 87
   and maternal weight, 124
   and maternal weight gain, 125
   moderately low, 26
   in North control area, 245
   and placental weight, 126
   in Rotterdam, 247
   in South control area, 246
   very low, 26
   Z scores, 142
Black market, 50
Brain cells
   hyperplasia, 17
   hypertrophy, 17
Brain growth
   critical period, 15
   duration of maximum, 18
   East Africa, 101
   protein lack in animals, 33
   spurt, 234
Brain sparing, 6, 232

Caloric intake
   and birthweight, 124
   and maternal weight, 124
Cape Town, 31–32
   kwashiorkor, 29
   sib-comparison study, 30
Case-control design, 55

Causes of death, 165, 179 ff
Central Bureau of Statistics, 62, 67
  deaths, 165
Central kitchens, 49–50
Cerebral palsy, 201, 224
Chronic malnutrition, 234
Classification of occupations, 67
Clerical aptitude test, 200, 204
Clubfoot, 225
Cohort analysis, 167
  by place, 89
  by time, 89
Cohort death rates, 167
  and periodic rates, 158
Cohort studies, 55
  prospective, 61
  retrospective, 61
Cohorts, 5, 56, 57
  definition of, 57
Congenital anomalies, 225
  and birthweight, 26
  of the central nervous system, 224, 228
  death rates, 182
  and prenatal nutrition, 23
Congenital defects, see Congenital anomalies
Congenital heart disease, 225, 228
Congenital malformations, see Congenital anomalies
Critical period, 6
  and brain growth, 15
  lack of evidence for, 32
Cultural-familial syndrome, 10, 26
  changes with age, 14

Death rates
  acute infections, 179
  atrophy, 180
  by cohort, 158, 167
  congenital malformations, 182
  gastrointestinal, 179
  meningitis, 182
  mental retardation, 182
  obstetric causes, 180
  prematurity, 180, 182
  respiratory disease, 179
  sclerema, 180
  and social class, 183
  and starvation, 179
Death record, 64
Deaths, 64
  at 0 to 6 days, 153 ff
  at 7 to 29 days, 155 ff
  at 30 to 89 days, 158 ff
  at 90 to 364 days, 161 ff
  at 1 to 18 years, 163 ff
  Central Bureau of Statistics, 165
  and famine, 149
  in famine area, 238
  local registry offices, 165
  from malnutrition, 52
  in North control area, 239
  in South control area, 240
Demotic families, 10
Denver, Colorado, 32
Disability, 201
Down's syndrome, 201

East Africa, brain weight, 201
Educational indices, 198
Europe, World War II, 208

Family size, 197, 204
  in famine area, 86
  and fecundability, 78
  in North control area, 86
  in South control area, 86
Famine, 4, 43
  and adult weight, 220
  and age of mothers, 77
  and amenorrhea, 72
  and birthweight, 92 ff
  and clinical signs of malnutrition, 45
  and deaths, 149
  and deaths at 0 to 6 days, 153 ff
  and deaths at 7 to 29 days, 155 ff
  and deaths at 30 to 89 days, 158 ff
  and deaths at 90 to 364 days, 161 ff
  and deaths at 1 to 18 years, 163 ff
  and deaths from malnutrition, 52
  and fecundity, 72, 76
  and fertility, 72, 231
  and first-week deaths, 153 ff
  and fitness categories, 228
  and food supplies, 49
  and gestation, duration of, 104 ff
  and head size, 101 ff
  and height, 215
  and hospital care, 46
  and ICD categories, 223 ff
  and infant diet, 50
  and infant length, 99 ff
  in Leningrad, 75
  and maternal weight, 106 ff
  and mortality rates, 52
  onset of, 44
  and parity, 77
  and placental weight, 96 ff
  and rations for pregnant women, 51
  and Raven Progressive Matrices, 202 ff
  regions affected, 45
  severity of, 47
  and social class, 231
  social class and fertility, 79
  social class differences, 51

SUBJECT INDEX

and stillbirths, 151 ff
typical diets, 45
weight loss, 52
Famine area
   birth order, 86
   family size, 86
   food rations, 241
Famine threshold, 90
Fecundability, 71, 78
   and age, 77
   and family size, 78
   and parity, 77
Fecundity, 71
   and famine, 72, 76
Fertility, 62, 71
   and nutrition, 71
   and famine, 72, 231
   famine and social class, 79
   and social class, 231
Fetal growth
   and gestation, duration of, 123
   and placental growth, 122, 127
First-week deaths, 224
   and famine, 153 ff
Fitness categories, 228
Food rations, 64–65
   in famine area, 241
   in North control area, 242
   in South control area, 243
Forced sequences, 110

Genetic factors, and IQ, 11, 199
Germany
   World War I, 77, 87
   World War II, 87
Gestation, duration of
   in famine, 104 ff
   in famine area, 244
   and fetal growth, 123
   and maternal nutrition, 87
   in North control area, 245
   in Rotterdam, 247
   in South control area, 246
Gestation, length of
   Z scores, 143
Glia, 17
Global Psychometric Score, 200, 252
Gonadotrophin, 71
Greece, stature in, 215
Groningen, 87, 91
   maternal age, 77, 85
   parity, 77, 85
Group means, 111

Hammersmith Hospital, head size, 101
Handicap, 201
Harlem Hospital, births, 125

Head circumference
   in famine area, 244
   in North control area, 245
   in South control area, 246
   Z scores, 142
Head size
   and famine, 101 ff
   at Hammersmith Hospital, 101
   and infant length, 122
   and IQ, 102
   and irradiation, 102
   and malnutrition, 101
   and maternal nutrition, 87
   and mental function, 101
   in premature infants, 101
Heerlen, 87, 91
   maternal age, 77, 85
   parity, 77, 85
Height, 215
   and birthweight, 216
   and famine, 215
   in Gambia, 216
   and Japanese immigrants, 215
   and length at birth, 216
   and malaria, 216
   and nutrition, 30, 215
Hengelo, 62
Hiroshima, 83, 102
Hongertochten, 47
Hunger oedema, 45

ICD, *see* International Classification of Diseases
Immature personality, 225, 228
Impairment, 200
Infant diet, during famine, 51
Infant length
   and birthweight, 122
   and famine, 99 ff
   and head size, 122
   and maternal nutrition, 87
Infection, and nutrition, 29
Intellectual stimulation, index of, 32
Intelligence, 199
   see also Mental competence; Mental performance
Intelligence Quotient, 199
   and changes with age, 13
   and head size, 101, 102
Intelligence tests, 198–99
Interchurch Bureau (IKB), 46
International Classification of Diseases, 60, 165, 202, 223 ff
   and causes of death, 180 ff
   and military induction, 254
Intervention studies, effects on mental performance, 13

IQ, *see* Intelligence Quotient
Irradiation, and head size, 102

Jamaica, 31
  sib-comparison study, 30
Jews, deportation of, 44

Kwashiorkor, 29, 31, 34
  in Cape Town, 29

Lactation, 72
Language comprehension test, 67, 200, 204
Leiden, 87, 91
  maternal age, 77, 85
  parity, 77, 85
Length at birth
  in famine area, 244
  and height, 216
  in North control area, 245
  in Rotterdam, 247
  in South control area, 246
Leningrad, 87
  famine, 75
  World War II, 99
Local registry offices, and deaths, 165

Malnutrition
  and head size, 101
  and mental retardation, 30
  and poverty, 30
  and height, 30
Malnutrition syndromes, and mental competence, 28
Marasmus, 34
Maternal age
  in Amsterdam, 77, 85
  and fecundability, 77
  in Groningen, 77, 85
  in Heerlen, 77, 85
  in Leiden, 77, 85
  in Rotterdam, 77, 85
Maternal buffer, 5
Maternal height, and maternal weight, 106
Maternal nutrition
  and behavioral change, 20
  and birthweight, 24, 87
  and gestation, duration of, 87
  and head size, 87
  and infant length, 87
  and maternal weight, 87
  and placental weight, 87
  threshold value, 120
Maternal weight
  and birthweight, 124
  and caloric intake, 124
  in famine, 106 ff
  in famine area, 244
  and maternal height, 106
  and maternal nutrition, 87
  in Rotterdam, 107
  Z scores, 141
Maternal weight gain, and birthweight, 125
Maternities, 63
Maternity hospitals, reliability of data, 88
Measles, and mental performance, 29
Measured intelligence, *see* Intelligence Quotient
Mechanical comprehension, Bennett test of, 67
Medical diagnosis, 254
Medical examination
  at military induction, 59
  and psychological tests, 59
  record of, 59
Menarche, 72
Menopause, 72
Mental competence
  and malnutrition syndromes, 28
  and postnatal nutrition, 28
  and prenatal nutrition, 22
  see also Intelligence; Intelligence Quotient; Mental performance
Mental development, and nutritional deficiency, 23
Mental function, head size, 101
Mental impairment, and selective survival, 208
Mental performance
  and changes over time, 11
  and ethnic group, 8
  genetic explanations, 11
  and intervention studies, 13
  and measles, 29
  measures of, 198
  and nutrition, 197
  and place of residence, 9
  and postnatal nutrition, 28
  and protein lack in animals, 33
  and skin color, 9
  and social class, 8
  and social deprivation, 8
  in twins, 12
  see also Intelligence; Intelligence Quotient; Mental competence
Mental retardation, 198, 253
  and changes with age, 13
  and low birthweight, 26
  and malnutrition, 30
  pathological types, 10
  and protein deficiency, 34
  and radiation, 83
  in rural areas, 9

SUBJECT INDEX

and social class, 26
subcultural type, 10
in urban areas, 9
Microcephaly, 101
and radiation, 83
Mild mental retardation, 10
and mortality, 210
Military induction, 59, 198
and ICD, 254
medical examination, 59
in Netherlands, 56
and occupational class, 248
Mortality
cohort rates, 172
and famine, 52
and food rations, 165
and mild mental retardation, 210
periodic rates, 175
and Raven scores, 210
and selective survival, 207
and severe mental retardation, 212
Multiple Regression Analysis, 90, 109

Nagasaki, 83
Nazi occupation, 4
Netherlands
educational system, 41
food consumption, 40
food supply, 40
military induction, 56
mortality rates, 40
occupational structure, 41
population of, 39
provinces of, 39
public health, 40
religious affiliations, 40
schools for the mentally retarded, 42
social class, 40
World War II, 42
Neurones, 17
Nidation, 82
Nijmegen, 44
North control area
birth order, 86
family size, 86
Nutrient intake, 4
Nutrition
and birthweight, 24
and fertility, 71
and infection, 29
and mental performance, 197
and social class, 24
Nutritional deficiency, and mental development, 23
Nutritional deprivation, animal experiments, 19

Obesity, 220, 225, 228
Obstetric causes of death, 180
Occupation, classifications, 67
Occupational class
and fertility, 231
at military induction, 248
and Raven Progressive Matrices, 249
and stature, 256
Oligospermia, 73
Ovulation, 71

Parity
in Amsterdam, 77, 85
and fecundability, 77
in Groningen, 77, 85
in Heerlen, 77, 85
in Leiden, 77, 85
in Rotterdam, 77, 85
Path analysis, 119, 123
Path models, 135 ff
Model A, 136, 140
Model B, 136, 140
Periodic analysis, 167
Periodic death rates, 167, 175
and cohort rates, 158
Placenta
and birthweight, 126
and famine, 96 ff
in famine area, 244
and fetal growth, 122
and infant length, 122
and maternal nutrition, 87
mediating organ, 127
in North control area, 245
in Rotterdam, 96
in South control area, 246
weight, 96, 126
Z scores, 141
Postnatal learning, 26, 34, 233
Postnatal nutrition, and mental competence, 28
Poverty
and malnutrition, 30
and stature, 215
Pregnancy
food rations for, 51
metabolic rate in, 90
Premature infants, 224
deaths, 180, 182
head size, 101
Prenatal insult, compensated, 6
Prenatal nutrition
congenital defects, see Congenital anomalies
hypothesis, 3
and mental competence, see Mental com-

petence; Mental performance; Intelligence tests
Prevalence, of severe mental retardation, 208
Primates, protein deficiencies in, 34
Protein deficiencies
  and mental retardation, 34
  in primates, 34
Protein lack
  and behavior, 33
  and brain growth, 33
  and mental performance, 33
Psychological tests, at military induction, 59
Psychometric indices, 198
Psychoneurosis, 228

Quételet's index, 220, 258

Radiation
  and mental retardation, 83
  and microcephaly, 83
Rations
  calories in, 49
  history of, 43
  and mortality, 165
  official food, 88
  for pregnant women, 51
  regional differences, 48
  supplements in pregnancy, 50
  Western region, 48
Raven Progressive Matrices, 67, 199
  and famine, 202 ff
  and mortality, 210
  and occupational class, 249
Regression coefficients, 110
Religion, 197, 204
Reproductive casualty continuum, 5, 83, 207, 232
Research design, 5, 57
  geographic control, 58
  summary of, 66
  time control, 56
Reserve of brain cells, 234
Rotterdam, 62, 87, 91
  maternal age, 77, 85
  maternal weight, 106
  parity, 77, 85

Sclerema
  death rates, 180
Selective mortality, 197, 207
  and mental impairment, 208
  and stature, 219

Severe mental retardation
  and mortality, 212
  prevalence, 208
Sex ratio, 82
SHAEF, 47
Sib-comparison study
  in Cape Town, 30
  in Jamaica, 30
Social class, 204
  death rates, 182
  differences in famine, 51
  and famine, 231
  famine and fertility, 79, 231
  nutrition and birthweight, 24
South control area
  and birth order, 86
  and family size, 86
Starvation, and death rates, 179
Stature, 215
  and occupational class, 256
  and poverty, 215
  and selective mortality, 219
Stillbirths, 224
  and famine, 151 ff
Strike of Dutch rail workers, 44
Study design, see Research design
Supplements in pregnancy, 50
Sweden, World War I, 77

Tests
  arithmetic ability, 67, 200, 204
  clerical aptitude, 67, 200, 204
  language comprehension, 67, 200, 204
  mechanical comprehension, Bennett, 67, 200, 205
  Raven Progressive Matrices, 59, 67, 199
Threshold value, maternal nutrition, 120
Tilburg, 60, 79
Twin studies, birthweight and intelligence, 24

Validation study, 60

Weight, and famine, 220
Weight loss, in famine, 52
Winter, Netherlands, 1944–1945, 44
World War I
  Germany, 77, 87
  Sweden, 77
World War II, 4
  Europe, 208
  Germany, 87
  Leningrad, 99
  Netherlands, 42 ff